HOW PUBLIC LIBRARIES BUILD SUSTAINABLE COMMUNITIES IN THE 21ST CENTURY

ADVANCES IN LIBRARIANSHIP

Advances in Librarianship Editor

Bharat Mehra, The University of Alabama, Series Editor

Advances in Librarianship Editorial Board

Denise E. Agosto, Drexel University, USA
Wade Bishop, University of Tennessee Knoxville, USA
John Buschman, Seton Hall University, USA
Michelle Caswell, University of California Los Angeles, USA
Sandra Hughes-Hassell, University of North Carolina at Chapel Hill, USA
Paul T. Jaeger, University of Maryland, USA
Don Latham, Florida State University, USA
Jerome Offord, Harvard University, USA

ADVANCES IN LIBRARIANSHIP   VOLUME 53

HOW PUBLIC LIBRARIES BUILD SUSTAINABLE COMMUNITIES IN THE 21ST CENTURY

EDITED BY

KAURRI C. WILLIAMS-COCKFIELD
University of Tennessee, USA

AND

BHARAT MEHRA
University of Alabama, USA

United Kingdom – North America – Japan
India – Malaysia – China

Emerald Publishing Limited
Howard House, Wagon Lane, Bingley BD16 1WA, UK

First edition 2023

Editorial matter and selection © 2023 Kaurri C. Williams-Cockfield and Bharat Mehra.
Individual chapters © 2023 The authors.
Published under exclusive licence by Emerald Publishing Limited.

Reprints and permissions service
Contact: www.copyright.com

No part of this book may be reproduced, stored in a retrieval system, transmitted in any form or by any means electronic, mechanical, photocopying, recording or otherwise without either the prior written permission of the publisher or a licence permitting restricted copying issued in the UK by The Copyright Licensing Agency and in the USA by The Copyright Clearance Center. Any opinions expressed in the chapters are those of the authors. Whilst Emerald makes every effort to ensure the quality and accuracy of its content, Emerald makes no representation implied or otherwise, as to the chapters' suitability and application and disclaims any warranties, express or implied, to their use.

British Library Cataloguing in Publication Data
A catalogue record for this book is available from the British Library

ISBN: 978-1-80382-436-9 (Print)
ISBN: 978-1-80382-435-2 (Online)
ISBN: 978-1-80382-437-6 (Epub)

ISSN: 0065-2830 (Series)

Printed and bound by CPI Group (UK) Ltd, Croydon, CR0 4YY

INVESTOR IN PEOPLE

This book is dedicated to the steadfast and brave librarians of the Ukraine and to Ms Larysa Luhova, Director of the Lviv Regional Library for Children and Vice President of the Ukrainian Library Association at the time work on this publication began. Ms Luhova was selected to submit a chapter about public library ecological projects for children that were in development prior to the start of the Ukrainian War. Once the war began, Ms Luhova had to stop working on her chapter for this publication and devote her time to preserving Ukrainian culture. Our hope is that she will share this story with the library profession at some time in the future.

CONTENTS

List of Figures and Tables	*xi*
About the Contributors	*xiii*
Series Editor's Introduction Bharat Mehra	*xxi*

Introduction
Kaurri C. Williams-Cockfield and Bharat Mehra *1*

SECTION ONE
THEORETICAL FOUNDATIONS AND RESEARCH

**Introduction to Section One: Sustainable Communities
and the Role of the Public Library**
Kaurri C. Williams-Cockfield and Bharat Mehra *13*

**Chapter 1 "The Library Serves as an Amplifier and Connector
in the Community it Serves": Building Bridges to Legal
Assistance**
Brooke Doyle, Lynn Silipigni Connaway and Lesley A. Langa *17*

**Chapter 2 Sustaining Ourselves, Sustaining Relationships,
Sustaining Communities**
Noah Lenstra and Christine D'Arpa *27*

**Chapter 3 Collective Praxis: Leveraging Local and
Heritage-based Values for Public Librarian Professional
Development**
Vanessa Irvin *37*

**Chapter 4 Community Engagement Through Public
Library Social Inclusion: The View and Practice of
Librarians in Gunungkidul County, Yogyakarta, Indonesia**
Ida Fajar Priyanto, Agung Wibawa and Siti Indarwati *57*

vii

viii CONTENTS

**Chapter 5 Applying ESG to Modern Librarianship:
Lessons from the Business World**
Samantha Connell and Micaela Porta 73

SECTION TWO
LIBRARIES ADVOCATING FOR SOCIAL JUSTICE

**Introduction to Section Two: Sustainable Communities and the
Role of the Public Library**
Kaurri C. Williams-Cockfield and Bharat Mehra 87

**Chapter 6 Anti-racism in Practice: The Development of a Black
Community Public Library in Canada**
Amber Matthews and Sandie Thomas 91

**Chapter 7 Public Library Pride: A Journey of Small Steps
Toward Inclusivity**
Debra Trogdon-Livingston 105

**Chapter 8 A Call to Action: Libraries Leaning in for Unhoused
LGBTGEQ + Youth**
Julie Ann Winkelstein 113

**Chapter 9 Let's Learn Together Outside: Families Playing,
Building Relationships, and Connecting with Their Community
in Nature**
Emily Sedgwick and Wendee Mullikin 125

Chapter 10 Sustainability, Outdoor Life, and Libraries
Hilde Ljødal and Tordis Holm Kverndokk 137

**Chapter 11 Older Adults, Public Libraries, and Sustainable
Development Goals**
Nicole K. Dalmer and Meridith Griffin 153

SECTION THREE
LIBRARIES MOBILIZING CLIMATE CHANGE

**Introduction to Section Three: Sustainable Communities and
the Role of the Public Library**
Kaurri C. Williams-Cockfield and Bharat Mehra 163

**Chapter 12 Inspiring Climate Action:
A Collaborative Effort and a Perfect Partnership**
Lynn Blair, Andrea Bugbee and John Meiklejohn 165

Contents

Chapter 13   How Repair Events in Libraries Can Create Socially and Ecologically Compassionate Culture and Resilient Communities
Gabrielle Griffis   175

Chapter 14   A Small Library Making Big Changes: A Case Study of the Baramsup Library
Yong Ju Jung   185

SECTION FOUR
LIBRARIES PROMOTING ECONOMIC DEVELOPMENT

Introduction to Section Four: Sustainable Communities and the Role of the Public Library
Kaurri C. Williams-Cockfield and Bharat Mehra   199

Chapter 15   Public Libraries as Key Knowledge Infrastructure Needed to Empower Communities, Promote Economic Development, and Foster Social Justice
Sarah E. Ryan, Sarah A. Evans and Suliman Hawamdeh   203

Chapter 16   Libraries as Public Health Partners in the Opioid Crisis
Kendra Morgan   219

Chapter 17   Partnering for Social Infrastructure: Investigating the Co-location of a Public Library in an Affordable Housing Building
Kaitlin Wynia Baluk, Ali Solhi and James Gillett   229

SECTION FIVE
LIBRARIES NURTURING POSITIVE PEACE

Introduction to Section Five: Sustainable Communities and the Role of the Public Library
Kaurri C. Williams-Cockfield and Bharat Mehra   245

Chapter 18   Libraries Are Sustainability Leaders
Rebekkah Smith Aldrich and Lisa Gangemi Kropp   249

Chapter 19   Reflecting on Public Library–Social Work Collaboration: Current Approaches and Future Possibilities
Rachel D. Williams and Lydia P. Ogden   263

Chapter 20   The Intersection of US Public Libraries and Public Health
Suzanne Grossman   *273*

Chapter 21   Public Libraries' Contribution to Sustainable Dementia-Friendly Communities
Timothy J. Dickey   *283*

Chapter 22   With Literacy and Justice for All: Library Programs for Refugees and Newcomers
Claire Dannenbaum   *293*

Index   *305*

LIST OF FIGURES AND TABLES

Introduction
Fig. 1.   The PLSC Framework That Connects Collective Impact and
             Public Libraries to Center Equity and Build Sustainable
             Communities.   8

Chapter 1
Fig. 1.   Average Ranking of Responses for Libraries' Potential to
             Impact SDGs.   20

Chapter 2
Fig. 1.   A Model of Supporting Sustainable Communities by
             Supporting Library Workers.   33

Chapter 3
Fig. 1.   State of Hawaii.   41
Fig. 2.   Participant Communication on Slack, November 2018.   46
Fig. 3.   Principal Investigator Field Notes from Hui 'Ekolu Site
             Visit, January 2019.   48
Fig. 4.   Reflective Memo January 2020.   49
Fig. 5.   Collective Praxis Model by Vanessa Irvin.   50

Chapter 4
Fig. 1.   Number of Libraries in Indonesia.   60
Fig. 2.   Batik Clothes Made by the Community After Attending
             Batik-Making Training.   65
Fig. 3.   Gardu Pintar Public Library for Social Inclusion Program.   68
Fig. 4.   Another Side of Gardu Pintar Public Library.   69
Fig. 5.   Library Backyard.   69
Fig. 6.   Herbal Products Sold at the Library.   70
Fig. 7.   Cassava Crackers Sold in the Library.   70
Fig. 8.   Tortilla Made by the Community.   71
Table 1.   Rural Public Libraries and Their Activities in 2021.   67

Chapter 5
Fig. 1.   ESG is a rapidly increasing topic in corporate earnings calls
             since 2019.   75
Fig. 2.   Triple Bottom Line.   76

xii   LIST OF FIGURES AND TABLES

Chapter 7

Fig. 1.	Debra Trogdon-Livingston at Charlotte Pride (2019).	106

Chapter 9

Fig. 1.	Sample agenda for Let's Learn Together Outside.	128
Fig. 2.	Outdoor Resources Web activity template from Let's Learn Together Outside.	132
Table 1.	Population Demographics by Library Location.	133

Chapter 10

Fig. 1.	The Cottage "Klettenhytta" at Kinn in Deknedalen in Møre og Romsdal County.	147
Fig. 2.	The Cottage «Sjøbua» in Alver in Vestland County with the Theater Company "Eventyr I parken" (Fairytale in the Park in English).	148
Fig. 3.	The Cottage "Vardetangen" in Austrheim, Norway's Most Western Point in Vestland County.	148
Fig. 4.	The Cottage "Larsbulia" in Øygarden, Vestland County.	149
Fig. 5.	From the Opening of the Cottage "Orrebu" in Leikanger in Vestland County.	149

Chapter 12

Table 1.	PVLC's Programming for 2021 Climate Preparedness Week.	170

Chapter 14

Fig. 1.	The Baramsup Picturebook Library (New Building).	187
Fig. 2.	Inside of the Baramsup Picturebook Library Showing How Picture Books Are Displayed.	189
Fig. 3.	Wind Forest Library Built in a School in Laos.	192
Fig. 4.	Picture Books Made by Children in Laos.	193

Chapter 17

Fig. 1.	Photograph of McQuesten Lofts and HPL's Parkdale Branch.	230

ABOUT THE CONTRIBUTORS

Rebekkah Smith Aldrich (MLS, LEED AP) is currently the Executive Director of the Mid-Hudson Library System (NY). Rebekkah is the Co-founder and Board President of the Sustainable Libraries Initiative and Principal Author of the award-winning Sustainable Library Certification Program. Rebekkah is the author of *Sustainable Thinking: Ensuring Your Library's Future in an Uncertain World* and *Resilience*, part of the American Library Association's Futures Series; and co-editor of *Libraries & Sustainability: Programs and Practices for Community Impact.*

Kaitlin Wynia Baluk, PhD, is a Postdoctoral Fellow in the DeGroote School of Business at McMaster University. At McMaster, Kaitlin likewise received her PhD in Health and Society in 2021. Her current research explores digital literacy training solutions for older adults living in affordable social housing.

Lynn Blair is a Public Librarian in Western Massachusetts. She has a Bachelor's in English with a minor in Biology, and a Master's in Library Science. In libraries, she has worked in children's services, teen services, and has worked as a Library Director for seven years.

Andrea Bugbee holds a BA in English and an MAT in Secondary English. During her 10 years as a teacher and 22 years as a freelance feature writer, Ms Bugbee has remained a staunch supporter of local libraries. She has twice served on the Southwick Public Library Strategic Planning Committee, she is a Founding Member of the Pioneer Valley Library Collaborative, and she remains an active patron volunteer for the PVLC.

Lynn Silipigni Connaway, PhD, Executive Director, Research, has authored numerous journal publications, is an international speaker, and is co-author of the 4th and 5th editions of *Basic Research Methods for Librarians* and the 6th and 7th editions of *Research Methods in Library and Information Science.* She is Past President of the Association for Information Science and Technology, Past Chair of the Association of College and Research Libraries Value of Academic Libraries Committee, the recipient of the ASIS&T 2019 Watson Davis Award, and the 2020 Distinguished Alumna at the University of Wisconsin–Madison Information School. She held the Chair of Excellence, Departmento de Biblioteconomía y Documentación, Universidad Carlos III de Madrid, was a Visiting Researcher in the Department of Information Studies, University of Sheffield, and Visiting Scholar at the Royal School of Library and Information Science, Denmark.

xiv ABOUT THE CONTRIBUTORS

Samantha Connell is a Librarian at New Canaan Library, Connecticut, USA. She earned her Bachelor's degree from the University of Pennsylvania and her Master of Library and Information Sciences at Rutgers University. She is currently the Chair of the Connecticut Library Association' Equity, Diversity, and Inclusion Section and has a passion for amplifying marginalized and absent voices.

Christine D'Arpa, PhD, is an Assistant Professor in the School of Information Sciences at Wayne State University in Detroit. Her research focuses on the history of libraries; the role of the federal government in information provision; and public libraries and community engagement. Her educational training includes an MS and PhD in Library and Information Science from the University of Illinois at Urbana–Champaign.

Nicole K. Dalmer, MLIS, PhD, is an Assistant Professor in the Department of Health, Aging and Society at McMaster University. She is also an Associate Director of the Gilbrea Centre for Studies in Aging. With a background in Library and Information Sciences, Nicole's work is centered at the intersection of information and care, working with and learning from family care providers, older library patrons, and older adults who use (and/or refuse!) technologies.

Claire Dannenbaum is a Reference and Instruction Librarian at Lane Community College in Eugene, Oregon, USA. She received a BA in Visual Arts from Antioch College, an MA in Visual Ethnography from San Francisco State University, and an MLIS from the University of British Columbia. Claire's professional work focuses on information literacy, feminist pedagogy, and the possibilities for civic engagement in undergraduate education. Her enduring personal interests in visual art and anthropology inform her teaching, learning, and research.

Timothy J. Dickey, winner of the 2022 ALA-RUSA Margaret E. Monroe Award for Library Adult Services and a 2021 ASIS&T Distinguished Member, is an Adult Services Librarian with the Columbus (OH) Metropolitan Library. He teaches on the graduate LIS faculties of Kent State University and San Jose State University, and prior to that assisted Dr Lynn Silipigni Connaway at the OCLC Office of Research. Dr Dickey's book *Library Dementia Services: How to Meet the Needs of the Alzheimer Community* was published by Emerald in 2020.

Brooke Doyle, M.Ed., is a Senior Project Coordinator with OCLC. Brooke's expertise in curriculum development and grant management serve her well at OCLC where her work includes being a co-author on the OCLC briefing, *New Model Library: Pandemic Effects and Library Directions* and assisting in the Building a National Finding Aid Network project.

Sarah A. Evans is Assistant Professor in the College of Information at University of North Texas. She serves as the Director for the Children's and Young Adult Librarianship Program and as Co-Director of the Multiple Literacies Lab. Her research examines the literacies and identities taken up in voluntary learning experiences.

About the Contributors

James Gillett, PhD, is an Associate Professor in McMaster University's Department of Health, Aging, and Society and the Associate Dean of Graduate Studies and Research in the Faculty of Social Sciences. Dr Gillett's key areas of research include human–animal relationships; sport, leisure, and recreation; mental health and well-being; media and communications; perspectives on living with health and illness across the life course; and inquiry as an approach to education and learning.

Meridith Griffin, PhD, is an Associate Professor in the Department of Health, Aging, and Society at McMaster University and she is also an Associate Director of the Gilbrea Centre for Studies in Aging. Her research is focused upon lived experiences, spaces and places, and critical exploration of inequalities therein. Her work explores the topics of physical culture(s) and inclusivity, and she also looks broadly at leisure: engagement, accessibility, and the ways in which it is integrated into identity/selfhood and meaning-making across the life course. She is interested in the intersections between public libraries and community well-being.

Gabrielle Griffis is the Assistant Youth Services Librarian for Brewster Ladies' Library, Repair Event Coordinator, Advocate, and a leading member of the Blue Marble Librarians. She is a contributor to *Libraries and Sustainability: Programs and Practices for Community Impact* as well as *25 Ready-to-Use Sustainable Living Library Programs* from ALA Editions, and *Repair Revolution: How Fixers are Transforming Our Throwaway Culture* from New World Library.

Suzanne Grossman is an Assistant Professor in Health Sciences at James Madison University. Her research focuses on the role of public libraries in promoting the health of historically underrepresented populations and communities. She earned her DrPH in Community Health and Prevention with a minor in immigrant and Latinx populations from Drexel University, an MSc in Cultural Studies from the University of Edinburgh, and a BA in Anthropology and Theatre from Smith College.

Suliman Hawamdeh is a Regents Professor in the Department of Information Science, College of Information, University of North Texas. He founded and directed several academic programs. He is the Editor-in-Chief of the *Journal of Information and Knowledge Management (JIKM)* and the editor of the book series on Innovation of Knowledge Management published by World Scientific.

Siti Indarwati is a Librarian at the Public Library of Gunungkidul, Yogyakarta, Indonesia. She was awarded the Best Librarian of the Year by the National Library of Indonesia in 2015. Currently, she is Vice Chair of Gunungkidul Library Association, Secretary of Gunungkidul Reading Development, and Coordinator of Yogyakarta Reading Development.

Vanessa Irvin is an Associate Professor with the Master of Library Science Program at East Carolina University, Greenville, North Carolina. Her research

xvi ABOUT THE CONTRIBUTORS

has centered on public libraries and librarian professional development. Dr Irvin's work has been published in *Public Library Quarterly, Journal of Education in Library and Information Science (JELIS)* and *Education for Information: An Interdisciplinary Journal of Information Studies.*

Yong Ju Jung is an Assistant Professor in the School of Library and Information Studies at the University of Oklahoma. She received her PhD in Learning, Design, and Technology from the Pennsylvania State University. Her research focuses on embodied interactions and interest-driven learning of children and families in libraries, museums, and makerspaces.

Lisa Gangemi Kropp is the Director of the Lindenhurst Memorial Library, which was the third public library to achieve Sustainable Libraries Certification from the Sustainable Libraries Initiative. She is the past Coordinator of the ALA's sustainability roundtable, SustainRT, and serves as the Chair of the Sustainability Committee for her state library association. She is a member-at-large advisory board member of the Sustainable Libraries Initiative.

Tordis Holm Kverndokk is currently the chief librarian at Vestby Public Library in Norway. Between 2013 and 2022, Kverndokk was the Senior Advisor first at Akershus County Library. Prior experience includes service as a children's librarian for two public libraries in the Oslo area from 1984 to 2013.

Lesley A. Langa, PhD, is an Associate Research Scientist with OCLC. Lesley's research interests include information access and availability, preservation, and metadata.

Noah Lenstra is an Associate Professor of Library and Information Science and an Affiliated Faculty Member in the Gerontology Program at the University of North Carolina at Greensboro, where he founded Let's Move in Libraries in 2016. Lenstra is a Principal Investigator of multiple federal and state government funded programs focused on understanding and supporting public library workers as critical community health partners. Lenstra's educational training includes an MS and PhD in Library and Information Science from the University of Illinois at Urbana–Champaign.

Hilde Ljødal is currently the Senior Advisor at the Department for Library Development at the National Library of Norway, Oslo. From 2007 to 2010, Ljødal served as the Senior Advisor at the Department for Libraries at the Center for Archives, Museum and Library in Norway. Prior experience includes 24 years working as a librarian in both public library and special libraries.

Amber Matthews is a Library and Information Science (LIS) Doctoral candidate at Western University and holds a Master of LIS degree. She was the recipient of the prestigious Canada Graduate Scholarship (Doctoral) from the Social Sciences and Humanities Research Council in 2021. Through a variety of professional and

About the Contributors xvii

scholarly mediums, she challenges institutional and systemic barriers to engagement and aims to create anti-oppressive spaces and practices that support all youth.

Bharat Mehra is EBSCO Endowed Chair in Social Justice and Professor in the School of Library and Information Studies at the University of Alabama, USA. His research focuses on diversity and social justice in library and information science and community informatics including the use of information and communication technologies to empower minority and underserved populations to make meaningful changes in their everyday lives. He has applied action research to further engaged scholarship and community engagement while collaborating with racial/ethnic groups, international diaspora, sexual minorities, rural communities, low-income families, small businesses, and others, to represent their experiences and perspectives in the design of community-based information systems and services.

John Meiklejohn, MSW, LICSW, is a Member of the Voices for Climate [V4C] Committee, a grassroots community partner with the Pioneer Valley Library Collaborative. V4C supports the Collaborative in being a hub for climate conversation and public education. Mr Meiklejohn is retired from a career of psychotherapy for children, youth, and adults.

Kendra Morgan is a Senior Program Manager at OCLC and is particularly interested in the role libraries play in supporting healthy communities, and has managed a number of grant-funded programs that address these issues. Kendra received her MLIS from the University of Hawai'i; and prior to joining OCLC in 2007, she provided training and technology support in hundreds of libraries as part of the Bill & Melinda Gates Foundation's US Libraries Program, and served as a Technology Consultant at The Library of Virginia.

Wendee Mullikin uses her 26 years' experience as an educator; editing certification; and diversity, equity, and inclusion in the workplace certification to provide comprehensive editorial review of professional development and training, publications, and Wonders of the Day® on NCFL's award-winning website, Wonderopolis®. Before joining the team at NCFL, Wendee taught K–12 music, 6–12 English/language arts, collegiate-level composition (developmental, Comp I, and rhetoric), provided K–12 special education services, and worked with adjudicated youth. She holds Bachelor's degrees in Music and English as well as a Master's degree in Special Education with supervisor coursework completed.

Lydia P. Ogden, PhD, MSW, is an Associate Professor at the Simmons University School of Social Work and a Licensed Psychotherapist. Her scholarship is informed by her social work practice experience with persons living with serious mental illnesses in housing and other social service and psychotherapy settings. Dr Ogden's scholarship is centered on the aim of improving the mental health and wellbeing of all persons, including those who seek services and those who provide them.

xviii ABOUT THE CONTRIBUTORS

Micaela Porta is the Environmental, Social, and Governance (ESG) Coordinator at New Canaan Library in Connecticut, where she is Project Lead on its Design for Freedom pilot partnership toward eliminating forced labor from the global construction supply chain. As a freelance writer, editor, and curator, she has worked on community nonprofit initiatives in the arts, ecology, and civics.

Ida Fajar Priyanto is a Senior Lecturer at Gadjah Mada University in Yogyakarta, Indonesia. He was formerly Director of Gadjah Mada (2002–2012) and Chair of Yogyakarta Library Council (2011–2015). He has been active in various library associations especially the Indonesian academic and school library associations and he is also active in promoting rural libraries and their activities.

Sarah E. Ryan is an Associate Professor of Information Science and Director of the Law Librarianship Program at the University of North Texas. She was the nation's first empirical legal research librarian, at Yale Law School. Sarah researches in the areas of A.I. solutions for legal research and open government challenges, criminal justice reform, and iSchool curriculum.

Emily Sedgwick serves as a Content Specialist – Family Engagement for NCFL, where she provides support for several initiatives. As NCFL's staff librarian, she also works to develop family literacy relationships with libraries and library organizations across the country. Before joining NCFL in 2014, she served as the Federal Government Documents and reference librarian for the Kentucky Department for Libraries and Archives (KDLA). Emily earned her Master of Science in Library and Information Science from the University of Kentucky. She earned her Post Baccalaureate Certification in Family Literacy from Penn State University.

Ali Solhi, MA, is a PhD student in the Department of Health, Aging, and Society at McMaster University. Ali's doctoral research focuses on social inequality, psychological well-being, and health equity among immigrants and marginalized groups. He has work experience in both academic and public libraries, as well as a background and interest in film production.

Pastor **Sandie Thomas** is the Director and CEO of the Where We Are Now Black Community Centre and Public Library. She also sits on the Board of Directors for several local initiatives including Internet Sense First, the Community, Diversity and Inclusion Strategy – Anti-Black Racism and Anti-Oppression Working Group for the City of London, the Anti-Black Racism Citizen Advisory Panel for the London Police Service, and the Anti-Racism Panel for the London Middlesex Health Unit. She is also an Advisor and mentor for Black businesses in the Canadian Black Chambers of Commerce.

Debra Trogdon-Livingston is the User Experience and Education Strategist for Region 2 of the Network of the National Library of Medicine in Charleston, SC, USA. She has more than 18 years of library experience and has presented at local,

About the Contributors xix

regional, and national conferences. Debra's current research interest is library equity with a focus on LGBTQIA+ equity.

Agung Wibawa is a Librarian at Public Library of Gunungkidul, Yogyakarta, Indonesia. He was awarded the Best Librarian of the Year by the National Library of Indonesia in 2016. He is currently Chair of Gunungkidul Library Association and Master Trainer for library social inclusion programs.

Rachel D. Williams is an Assistant Professor at the Simmons University School of Library and Information Science. Her research examines public library services for people in crisis. Dr Williams' scholarship is centered on considering the role of interprofessional collaboration between social workers and public librarians and boundary management in supporting people in crisis in public libraries.

Kaurri C. Williams-Cockfield, MLIS, has 30+ years of progressively responsible work experience in both US and international library settings including public, academic, school, and corporate institutions. Between 2003 and 2021, Ms Williams-Cockfield served as a Public Library Director in Tennessee and in the Cayman Islands. She retired as a Public Library Director in May 2021 and currently teaches, writes, and presents on public libraries, community social justice issues, and how public libraries impact the development of sustainable communities. Ms Williams-Cockfield has been teaching at the University of Tennessee Knoxville School of Information Science, USA, since the spring of 2010.

Julie Ann Winkelstein, MLIS, PhD, is an Activist Librarian, Writer, and Teacher. Her writings include *Libraries and Homelessness: An Action Guide*, as well as several book chapters and articles. She has presented internationally on the topic of libraries and homelessness, including LGBTGEQ+ youth homelessness, and teaches a library school class on this topic.

SERIES EDITOR'S INTRODUCTION

I am delighted to take this opportunity and introduce myself as the new Series Editor of *Advances in Librarianship* since January 2021. In this capacity, I plan to extend the series' impact via integrating a critical perspective that spotlights social justice and inclusive praxis from the shadows to become an emerging canon at the very core of who we are and what we value as legit in Library and Information Science (LIS) scholarship and practice. This strategic vision requires destabilizing of entrenched hegemonies within our privileged ranks and external communities to alleviate intersecting political, economic, social, and cultural anxieties, and power imbalances we witness today. As we move toward the quarter-century mark, we also need to effectively document such paradigmatic shifts in LIS, serving as a foundation of inspiration upon which, together in our multiple identities and diversities, we can proudly contribute to the building of a meaningful society toward a brighter future for our children to inherit.

New stimulating models reimagining (or extending) the roles for cultural memory institutions (e.g., libraries, museums, archives, schools, etc.) and the field of information are much required to develop symbolic and real infrastructures for moving us forward. We also need to better tell our stories of information activism and community mobilization in the face of overwhelming challenges to human existence, from forces of neoliberal corporatization, political ransacking, media irresponsibility, climate change, environmental degradation, pandemic dis/misinformation, etc. What do the contemporary threats of human extinction and cultural decay mean for LIS professionals, be it scholars, researchers, educators, practitioners, students, and others embedded in a variety of information settings? Not only does it require actions in the "doing" of resistance via information to decenter dysfunctional powerbrokers and their oppressions and entitled privileges. However, disseminating a forward-thinking agenda and narrative beyond our internally focused bastardized institutional bastions is equally important, as we adopt an active stance to promote fairness, justice, equity/equality, change agency, empowerment, community building, and community development.

Advances in Librarianship holds a special place in the hands, hearts, and minds of readers as a key platform to support creative ideas and practices that change and better articulate the vital contributions of libraries and the impact of information on diverse multicultural communities in a global network information society. Moving forward, my aim for the series is to engage our diverse professional communities in critical discourse that enable real transformations to occur. It is important to propel progress in shifting entrenched positionalities in LIS, while making visible content related to the "margins." Decentering canons and practices toward equity of representation, inclusivity, and progressive change will

SERIES EDITOR'S INTRODUCTION

naturally occur. Intersecting social, cultural, political, and economic upheavals in recent times demand an urgent response from the LIS professions in this regard.

I am truly honored and privileged to build on the legacy of Paul T. Jaeger, who served as Series Editor of *Advances in Librarianship* since 2013. His research helped to mobilize LIS in addressing concerns surrounding equity, diversity, and inclusion more substantially beyond past lip service, also shaping the focus of the book series. I plan to operationalize new directions for single- or multi-authored book-length explorations and edited collections by shifting focus on understudied spaces, invisible populations from the margins, and knowledge domains that have been under-researched or under-published in what we consider as high impactful venues in LIS and beyond. Examples might involve a reflective journey that established, or newly emerging LIS scholars, researchers, practitioners, and students critically reflect, assess, evaluate, and propose solutions or actions to change entrenched practices and systemic imbalanced inequities in different library and information-related settings. It might also involve decolonizing LIS publication industries in their biased Euro/Anglo-centricities with inclusion of content from geographical diversities around the world.

I am reaching out to our multiple audiences for their support toward these goals in spreading the word for proposals to new volumes in the series. Let us find our "collective voice" in the LIS professions to make us all uncomfortable as we continue to "push the buttons," thereby, becoming stronger in our quest to further social justice and develop our humanity, human dignity, respect, and potential to the fullest.

Bharat Mehra
EBSCO Endowed Chair in Social Justice and Professor
School of Library and Information Studies
University of Alabama

INTRODUCTION

Kaurri C. Williams-Cockfield and Bharat Mehra

How Public Libraries Build Sustainable Communities in the 21st Century posits that public libraries are key local institutions for developing and sustaining community partnerships that bring about social change (Mehra & Srinivasan, 2007). Kania and Kramer (2011) discuss the importance of using collective impact initiatives to bring about "large-scale social change in a community" (p. 38). In their research, the authors identify five conditions of success:

- Participants have a common understanding of the problem;
- Participants develop and engage in a shared data collection agreement;
- Participants are diverse and work together in an ongoing manner;
- A trust relationship between participants across the spectrum (nonprofit, corporations, government agencies, etc.) is developed through ongoing interactions and a recognition of the common motivation of participating entities;
- A separate entity is needed to serve as the backbone support organization to coordinate the collective aspects of the collaboration between the participating members.

Since 2011, Kania and Kramer, in partnership with other institutions, have published eight principles of practice for implementing collective impact and five strategies for centering equity within the collective impact framework. The Collective Impact Forum (2016), in partnership with the Aspen Institute Forum for Community Solutions, the Forum for Youth Investment, FSG, Grantmakers for Effective Organizations, Living Cities, PolicyLink, the Tamarack Institute, and United Way Worldwide, published the following eight principles of practice for collective impact:

- Design and implement the initiative with a priority placed on equity;
- Include community members in the collaborative;

How Public Libraries Build Sustainable Communities in the 21st Century
Advances in Librarianship, Volume 53, 1–10
Copyright © 2023 by Kaurri C. Williams-Cockfield and Bharat Mehra
Published under exclusive licence by Emerald Publishing Limited
ISSN: 0065-2830/doi:10.1108/S0065-283020230000053035

- Recruit and co-create with cross-sector partners;
- Use data to continuously learn, adapt, and improve;
- Cultivate leaders with unique system leadership skills;
- Focus on program and system strategies;
- Build a culture that fosters relationships, trust, and respect across participants;
- Customize for local context.

Since 2011, Kania et al. (2021) have conducted research on the implementations of collective impact to assess the effectiveness of and the different ways that groups have adapted the model. The key finding from their analysis centers on equity and the importance of making it the central focus of collective impact efforts.

- Ground the work in data and context, and target solutions;
- Focus on systems change, in addition to programs and services;
- Shift power within the collaborative;
- Listen to and act with community;
- Build equity leadership and accountability.

Public libraries, through their mission, vision, and position in the community, play a significant part in developing community sustainability and are already strategically positioned to serve as a "backbone support organization" for collective impact initiatives (Kania & Kramer, 2011, p. 40; Mehra & Davis, 2015). However, their efforts are often unrecognized by local governments and other social justice organizations. This publication, through research, case studies, and personal narratives representing both national and international perspectives, examines the capacity of public libraries to impact social change at the community level (Mehra & Rioux, 2016). The overarching goal is to change the narrative with community stakeholders by presenting illustrative examples of how public libraries are driving community change and how these efforts align with the United Nations' Sustainable Development Goals (UN SDGs) outlined in the *2030 Agenda for Sustainable Development* (United Nations, 2015).

The 17 UN SDGs are:

SDG 1: To end poverty in all its forms everywhere.

SDG 2: To end hunger, achieve food security and improved nutrition, and promote sustainable agriculture.

SDG 3: To ensure healthy lives and promote well-being for all ages.

SDG 4: To ensure inclusive and equitable quality education and promote life-long learning opportunities for all.

SDG 5: To achieve gender equality and empower all women and girls.

SDG 6: To ensure availability and sustainable management of water and sanitation for all.

SDG 7: To ensure access to affordable, reliable, sustainable, and modern energy for all.

SDG 8: To promote sustained, inclusive, and sustainable economic growth, full and productive employment, and decent work for all.

Introduction 3

SDG 9: To build resilient infrastructure, promote inclusive and sustainable industrialization, and foster innovation.

SDG 10: To reduce inequality within and among countries.

SDG 11: To make cities and human settlements inclusive, safe, resilient, and sustainable.

SDG 12: To ensure sustainable consumption and production patterns.

SDG 13: To take urgent action to combat climate change and its impacts.

SDG 14: To conserve and sustainably use the oceans, seas and marine resources for sustainable development.

SDG 15: To protect, restore, and promote sustainable use of terrestrial ecosystems, sustainably manage forests, combat desertification, and halt and reverse land degradation and halt biodiversity loss.

SDG 16: To promote peaceful and inclusive societies for sustainable development, provide access to justice for all and build effective, accountable and inclusive institutions at all levels.

SDG 17: To strengthen the means of implementation and revitalize the global partnership for sustainable development (United Nations, 2015).

This book is organized into five sections. The first section focuses on theoretical foundations and research related to community sustainability, global models and frameworks, challenges and opportunities, and historical and contemporary scholarship related to public libraries and social change. It also includes discussion on how public libraries, through resources, programs, and services, support and/or build community sustainability applying the principles of "collective impact" (Kania & Kramer, 2011, p. 38). Section One ["Theoretical Foundations & Research"] includes case studies and narratives that advance SDG 17.

The remaining four sections (two to five) focus on libraries advocating for social justice, libraries mobilizing climate change, libraries promoting economic development, and libraries nurturing positive peace respectively. Section Two ["Libraries Advocating for Social Justice"] includes case studies and narratives that advance SDG 1 through SDG 5 and SDG 10 as these SDGs focus on social justice topics such as poverty, hunger, health, education, equity, and inequity. Section Three ["Libraries Mobilizing Climate Change"] includes case studies and narratives that advance SDG 6, SDG 7, SDG 12, and SDG 13 as these SDGs focus on the planet's resources (water, energy, consumption and production, climate change). Section Four ["Libraries Promoting Economic Development"] includes case studies and narratives that advance SDG 8, SDG 9, and SDG 11 as these SDGs focus on economic growth and development, infrastructure, innovation, and safe cities. Section Five ["Libraries Nurturing Positive Peace"] includes case studies and narratives that advance SDG 16 which focuses on building peaceful, inclusive societies that are sustainable through the building of strong institutions.

Each section includes: (1) a framing of the subject content, the strategic collective actions, key concepts and terms relevant in that section, and resources and relevant organizations; (2) public library case studies where the program goals align with the chapter's subject content; (3) reflective narratives that share individual perspectives on public libraries and the section's subject content. The

4   INTRODUCTION

strategic collective actions can be used to reinforce the role of public libraries as "social infrastructure" and to aid libraries in the development and/or expansion of library programs strong enough to address the "individual structural inequalities" that impact community members' ability to reach their full potential (Mehra, 2022; Wilcox & Monobe, 2021, p. 5). The section content areas map the book chapters in relation to the UN SDGs. The 17th goal, which focuses on key partnerships, will be discussed in the narrative under the "strategic collective actions" section for Chapters 2–4. For further details about the chapters in each section, see the introductory framing brief of the five sections.

The chapters in this book were subjected to a rigorous review process consisting of analysis by the editors along with a review from professionals working in the information science field with experience in the different program content areas. The editors appreciate the generous gift of time and effort provided by the peer reviewers and extend their thanks to (alphabetically listed by last name): Brittany Baum, Florida State University; Eric Ely-Ledesma, PhD Candidate in the Information School at the University of Wisconsin – Madison; Rachel Fenningsdorf, Community Engagement Coordinator for Jackson District Library in Jackson, MI, MSIS Candidate at University of Tennessee-Knoxville; Allison Ferguson, University of Alberta; Suzanne Grossman, PhD, James Madison University; Amanda Harrison, PhD, Assistant Professor, University of Central Missouri, Department of Educational Technology and Library Science; Megan Janicki, American Library Association; Eva Hourihan Jansen, Independent Researcher/Sessional Instructor at the University of Toronto; Sarah Johnson, Cincinnati State Technical & Community College; Christopher Knapp, Youth Community Engagement Librarian with the Prince George Public Library, Prince George, BC, Canada; David Leonard, President; BPL, LIS Doctoral Candidate, Simmons University; Alicia K. Long, University of Missouri; Valerie Lookingbill, University of South Carolina; Brady Lund, PhD, Assistant Professor at University of North Texas Department of Information Science; Karen O'Leary, PhD, CEO of One Bookshelf (non-profit); Leighann Pennington, PhD, Sweet Briar College, Visiting Assistant Professor of Education; Alexander Vera, PhD Candidate, University of South Carolina iSchool; Elizabeth A Wahler, Director of UNC Charlotte School of Social Work and Founder/Owner of Beth Wahler Consulting; Joseph Winberry, PhD Candidate, the University of Tennessee; Xiaohua Awa Zhu, Associate Professor, University of Tennessee, Knoxville. Some of the reviewers agreed to be identified regarding the chapter they reviewed and have provided statements made available in the introduction to each of the five sections.

HISTORY OF THE UN SDGs AND LIBRARY AND INFORMATION PROFESSIONALS

The process to reflect, discuss, operationalize, and implement the UN SDGs began in 2021 at the RIO+20 Conference (United Nations *Conference on Sustainable Development*) in Rio de Janeiro, Brazil, to expand on the nine

Millennium Goals adopted in 2000 to address poverty, hunger, disease, and education (United Nations, n.d.). The final 17 goals, which were created through an inclusive two-year data gathering process (panels, consultations, the *My World* survey), represented input from international organizations, educational institutions, businesses, and citizens. In 2014, the UN General Assembly Open Working Group proposed these goals in *Transforming Our World: The 2030 Agenda for Sustainable Development* which was adopted in 2015 and represents a plan of action for "people, planet and prosperity" that outlines 17 goals for sustainability along with 169 implementation targets to be met globally by 2030 (United Nations, 2015).

The correlation between public libraries and the UN SDGs is clearly given that "information is a central component of sustainable development goals" (Kosciejew, 2020, p. 330). The International Federation of Library Associations and Institutions' (IFLA) direct involvement in the data gathering and planning processes for the SDGs ensured that information access was part of every goal and identified as the common connector between the goals (Kosciejew, 2020, p. 332). IFLA (2014) developed the *Lyon Declaration on Access to Information and Development*. This declaration, which was signed by 600 global institutions and associations, made

> an international commitment to the use of the United Nations post-2015 development agenda to ensure that everyone has access to, and is able to understand, use and share information that is necessary to promote sustainable development and democratic societies. (para. 3)

In *Access and Opportunity for All: How libraries contribute to the United Nations 2030 Agenda*, the IFLA (2019) outlines how libraries support all the SDGs by promoting literacy, providing access to information, serving as a network hub, supporting digital inclusion, encouraging research and academics, and by preserving culture and heritage.

In 2019, at the annual meeting for the Association for Information Science and Technology (ASIS&T), the conference advisory committee consisting of Kendra S. Albright, Jia Tina Du, Bharat Mehra and led by President Clara Chu, invited participants to join in advancing diversity, inclusion, collective impact, ethics of care, and sustainability by connecting through a keen sense of identity, thriving, and connecting to each other and the local and global society (Mehra et al., 2019). The following 2020 ASIS&T conference focused on information professionals connecting their work (information practice, research, education, and professional development) to the UN (2015) SDGs. The conference advisory committee developed an information action brief form (IAB) to gather input on actions the information services (IS) community could undertake with respect to the implementation of the SDGs. The IAB comprises seven core elements that are key to connecting the IS community to the SDGs and to the five conditions required for "collective impact" (Albright et al., 2019).

In 2020, the OCLC Global Council began a year-long focus on the SDGs and libraries. The council, while supporting all the SDGs, narrowed their focus for this project to five of the SDGs: Quality education (SDG #4); Decent work and economic growth (SDG #8); Reduced inequalities (SDG #10); Peace, justice, and strong institutions (SDG #16); and Partnerships for the goals (SDG #17). The council produced a series of webinars, through their *Transformative Leaders* series, designed to guide information professionals on how libraries align with the SDGs and what collective actions can be used to support community change (OCLC Global Council, 2020).

Additionally, the council conducted a survey to assess how library staff were thinking about and using the SDGs in their planning processes. The survey results were published in September 2021 (OCLC Global Council, 2021). There were 1,722 survey respondents representing 99 countries who provided input on a series of questions designed to determine their knowledge on the SDGs (54%–78%), the incorporation of the SDGs in their strategic planning processes (20%–43%), and where respondents believed libraries could have the greatest impact (SDG #4 Quality Education Activities). The top activities for public libraries for the remaining SDGs included:

> job preparedness and participation in community strategic planning (SDG #8); offering services, programs, and collections to promote awareness and education around diversity, and provide employee training around equity, diversity, and inclusion (SDG #10); serve as a welcoming space in the community and promote active involvement in civic activities (SDG #16); develop strong partnerships with other libraries and librarians through associations, consortia, and collaborate with other community agencies to provide classes for the community (SDG #17). (OCLC Global Council, 2021)

Mansour (2020), in his research on how rural public libraries in Egypt "can contribute to the achieving of the SDGs," suggests libraries can support the SDGs in the following ways:

- "Raising awareness of developmental issues covered in SDGs;
- Making an appropriate space for discussion on various developmental issues, particularly with regard to rural community development;
- Creating and designing powerful and effective library programmes to contribute to the implementation of SDGs. These include literacy programmes, especially for older persons, as well as programmes that help increase the demand to visit the library;
- Selecting suitable resources based on the development indicators raised in SDGs;
- Enhancing and providing rural libraries with appropriate collections to meet the needs of the library community, as well as understand its various issues and problems to help solve them;
- The need for the use of ICT tools for sustainability in rural public libraries is imperative to advance their services. The evolution of ICT tools and growth of electronic resources have made it possible for libraries to embrace green collections, as well as green technologies;
- Hosting local forums to enable the discussion of the challenges faced by rural communities and institutions, such as infectious diseases, which are wide-spread in the rural areas, community health, education, human rights, etc.;
- Strengthening community partnership between rural libraries and other relevant state agencies for easy understanding, exchange, and joint coordination to meet SDGs" (p. 128).

Introduction 7

As public awareness and advocacy for the SDGs increases, the work of public libraries in community building is receiving greater attention by the community-at-large. The next step in advocating for the role of public libraries is as a "backbone support organization" for achieving local social change and for inclusion in community initiatives that address inequalities thereby changing the narrative with stakeholders (Kania & Kramer, 2011, p. 40). This connection is best illustrated by correlating the voices, programs, and research of the IS community to the SDGs, and by examining the collective strategic actions needed to achieve "collective impact" (Albright et al., 2022; Collective Impact Forum, 2016; Kania et al., 2021; Library of the Future, n.d.; Lynn et al., 2018; Paschalville Partnership, n.d.; Vecchiarelli, 2018; Williams-Cockfield, 2021; Wojceichowska, 2021).

IMPORTANCE AND APPLICATION

Public libraries are already "implicitly recognized" in the US 2030 agenda as openly accessible providers of information in all formats, technology and Internet access, information literacy skills, and as a community center for cultural exchange (Kosciejew, 2020). There are three prevalent themes in the historical and contemporary positionality of the profession. Given this recognition, the inclusion of the local public library in community level strategic planning is vital, yet public libraries are often overlooked when these planning teams are assembled given the inclusive nature of the profession and the reluctance of information professionals to engage with the community at large (Mehra, 2021). This work provides concrete examples of how public libraries, through strategic planning, community partnerships and collaboration, local and regional networking, and program development and implementation, are already impacting social change in their communities and illustrates that their efforts directly support the global goals for sustainability (United Nations, 2015).

This publication is structured around internationally recognized sustainability goals, presents public library research, narratives and initiatives using a framework that is widely recognized, and clearly illustrates the correlation between public libraries and community sustainability. It builds on the work done by IFLA (2019), the 2019 ASIS&T conference advisory committee (Mehra et al., 2019), the OCLC Global Council (2020), and Mansour (2020) by taking their research from theory and best practices to actual application. These offer a holistic perspective on how public libraries support the totality of the 17 SDGs in their own unique ways in varied settings across local communities.

The topics covered in this work include:

- How public libraries support/build community sustainability;
- Social justice issues (poverty, hunger, health and well-being, education, reduced inequalities, and gender equality);
- Climate change issues (clean water, sanitation, responsible consumption and production, and affordable and clean energy);
- Economic issues (decent work, economic growth, innovation, and infrastructure);

- Peace issues (justice, safety, strong government institutions);
- Community partnerships;
- Communicating the value of the public library;
- Changing the dialog and perspective of local government and community partners;
- Collective strategic actions that can be taken by public libraries to impact local social change.

Fig. 1 provides a visual representation of the public library – sustainable communities (PLSC) framework which brings together the following three main elements that form the foundation and spirit underlying this book: (1) select theoretical attributes of collective impact in past scholarship that are listed as "collective impact actions"; (2) relating these to the five sections (integrating the SDGs) used to organize the book; and (3) the specific keywords associated with the included chapters that illustrate case studies and perspectives of how public libraries can center the concept or equity to build sustainable communities. Future research initiatives and assessment of case study public libraries will test the applicability and relevance of the various intertwining elements of the PLSC framework.

Additionally, this publication provides context for framing future public library programs, services, resources, and research on how public libraries build sustainable communities. It also presents concrete examples of the work of public libraries in building sustainable communities, highlights both national and international perspectives, and examines the connection between public library work, local social justice issues, social change, and collective impact. The collection applies a qualitative, humanistic, constructivist, and comparative research focus, but also includes analytical and critical analysis substantiated by quantitative statistical data in the case studies.

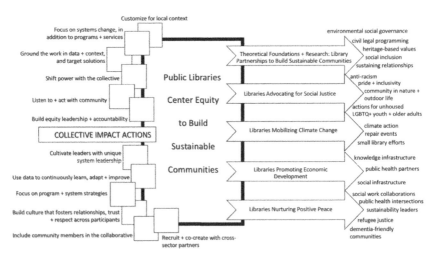

Fig. 1. The PLSC Framework That Connects Collective Impact and Public Libraries to Center Equity and Build Sustainable Communities.

Introduction 9

The book's intended market includes national and international public library staff, academic library staff and researchers, information science students, community planners, local and regional government employees, members of national and international organizations that promote sustainability, and the members of national and international information science organizations.

This work presents research, case studies, and narratives solicited from the 27 geographical subregions identified by the UN Statistics Division (September 30, 2021) in an effort to provide the broadest range possible for library work examples. The call for participation was distributed across international information science networks. This research solicited international input based on the 6 regional, 17 subregional, and 9 sub-sub regional groups identified in the United Nations geoscheme (Wikipedia, 2021).

REFERENCES

Albright, K. S., Chu, C. M., & Du, J. T. (2022). Inspiring information communities to advance the UN Sustainable Development Goals: Information action briefs for social transformation. In B. Mehra (Ed.), *Social justice design and implementation in library and information science* (pp. 270–282). Routledge.

Collective Impact Forum. (2016, April 20). *Collective Impact Principles of Practice*. Collective Impact Forum [Online forum post]. https://collectiveimpactforum.org/resource/collective-impact-principles-of-practice/

International Federation of Library Associations and Institutions (IFLA). (2014). *The Lyon Declaration on Access to Information and Development*. The Lyon Declaration. Retrieved October 3, 2021, from https://www.lyondeclaration.org/

International Federation of Library Associations and Institutions (IFLA). (2019). *Access and Opportunity for All: How libraries contribute to the United Nations 2030 Agenda*. Retrieved September 30, 2021, from https://www.ifla.org/wp-content/uploads/2019/05/assets/hq/topics/libraries-development/documents/access-and-opportunity-for-all.pdf

Kania, J., & Kramer, M. (2011, Winter). Collective impact. *Stanford Social Innovation Review*, 36–41. https://ssir.org/articles/entry/collective_impact

Kania, J., Williams, J., Schmitz, P., Brady, S., Kramer, M., & Juster, J. (2021). Centering equity in collective impact. *Stanford Social Innovation Review*, 38 35. https://ssir.org/articles/entry/centering_equity_in_collective_impact#

Kosciejew, M. (2020). Public libraries and the UN 2010 Agenda for Sustainable Development. *International Federation of Library Associations and Institutions*, 46(4), 328–346. https://doi.org/10.1177/0340035219898708

Library of the Future. (n.d.). *Collective impact*. American Library Association. https://www.ala.org/tools/future/trends/collectiveimpact

Lynn, J., Gase, L., Roos, J., Oppenheimer, S., & Dane, A. (2018). *When collective impact has an impact: A cross-site study of 25 collective impact initiatives*. ORISIMPACT & Spark Policy Institute. https://www.orsimpact.com/blog/When-Collective-Impact-Has-Impact-A-Cross-Site-Study-of-25-Collective-Impact-Initiatives.htm

Mansour, E. (2020). Libraries as agents for development: The potential role of Egyptian rural public libraries towards the attainment of Sustainable Development Goals based on the UN 2030 Agenda. *Journal of Librarianship and Information Science*, 52(1), 121–136. https://doi.org/10.1177/0961000619872064

Mehra, B. (2021). Elfreda Annmary Chatman in the 21st Century: At the intersection of critical theory and social justice imperatives. *Journal of Critical Library and Information Studies*, 3 (Special Issue theme – Chatman Revisited: Re-examining and resituating social theories of identity, access, and marginalization in LIS. Edited by N. A. Cooke and A. N. Gibson). https://journals.litwinbooks.com/index.php/jclis/article/view/142

Mehra, B. (2022). Toward an impact-driven framework to operationalize social justice and implement ICT4D in the field of information. *Journal of the Association for Information Science and Technology*. https://doi.org/10.1002/asi.24693

Mehra, B., Albright, K., & Du, J. T. (2019). President-Elect's International Incubator: Transformational Actions Using Information to Advance the UN Sustainable Development Goals [Paper]. *Program of the Association for Information Science and Technology ASIS&T 82nd Annual Meeting*, Melbourne, Australia, October 19–23, 2019.

Mehra, B., & Davis, R. (2015). A strategic diversity manifesto for public libraries in the 21st century. *New Library World*, 116(1/2), 15–36.

Mehra, B., & Rioux, K. (Eds.). (2016). *Progressive community action: Critical theory and social justice in library and information science*. Library Juice Press.

Mehra, B., & Srinivasan, R. (2007). The library-community convergence framework for community action: Libraries as catalysts of social change. *Libri: International Journal of Libraries and Information Services*, 57(3), 123–139.

OCLC Global Council. (2020). *Sustainable development and libraries: Global goals and collective action*. OCLC. Retrieved October 1, 2021, from https://www.oclc.org/go/en/sustainable-development-goals.html

OCLC Global Council. (2021, September). *United Nations Sustainable Development Goals Study 2021*. OCLC Research. Retrieved October 1, 2021, from https://www.oclc.org/research/publications/2021/sustainable-development-goals-study-2021.html

Paschalville Partnership. (n.d.). *A toolbox for library-led collective impact and neighborhood-based collaboration*. Free Library of Philadelphia and the Institute of Museum and Library Services. https://libwww.freelibrary.org/assets/pdf/programs/paschalville-partnership/paschalville-partnership-toolbox.pdf

United Nations. (2015). *Transforming Our World: The 2030 Agenda for Sustainable Development*. United Nations Department of Economic and Social Affairs. Retrieved September 12, 2021, from https://sdgs.un.org/publications/transforming-our-world-2030-agenda-sustainable-development-17981; https://sdgs.un.org/goals

United Nations. (n.d.). *Who We Are: From MDGs to SDGs*. Sustainable Goals Development Fund. Retrieved September 12, 2021, from https://www.sdgfund.org/mdgs-sdgs

Vecchiarelli, J. (2018, February 28). A library and its community make a collective impact. *ProLiteracy Blog* [Online Forum]. https://www.proliteracy.org/Blogs/Article/320/A-Library-and-Its-Community-Make-a-Collective-Impact

Wikipedia. (2021, October 4). *United Nations Geoscheme*. Wikipedia: The Free Encyclopedia. Retrieved October 10, 2021, from https://en.wikipedia.org/wiki/United_Nations_geoscheme

Wilcox, P., & Monobe, D. (2021, April 29). Matrix of humanistic lifelong learning for public libraries. *Public Library Quarterly*, 40(5), 379–405. https://doi.org/10.1080/01616846.2020.1254056

Williams-Cockfield, K. (2021). Blount County Recovery Court Life Skills Program: A public library's response to addiction recovery. In B. Mehra (Ed.), *Social justice design and implementation in library and information science*. Routledge. https://www.routledge.com/Social-Justice-Design-and-Implementation-in-Library-and-Information-Science/Mehra/p/book/9780367653828

Wojceichowska, M. D. (2021, February 2). The role of public libraries in the development of social capital in local communities: A theoretical study. *Library Management*, 42(3), 198–196. Emerald Insight. http://doi.org/10.1108/LM-10-2020-0139

SECTION ONE

THEORETICAL FOUNDATIONS AND RESEARCH

INTRODUCTION TO SECTION ONE: SUSTAINABLE COMMUNITIES AND THE ROLE OF THE PUBLIC LIBRARY

Kaurri C. Williams-Cockfield and Bharat Mehra

FRAMING OF SECTION ONE ["THEORETICAL FOUNDATIONS & RESEARCH"]

In the development of SDG 17, the United Nations (2015) identifies partnerships as a key role in building sustainable communities: Target Goal 17.17 states (on a macro level) that countries should "encourage and promote effective public, public–private and civil society partnerships, building on the experience and resourcing strategies of partnerships." Applying this focus on a micro level, public libraries have experiences and resources needed for building local partnerships that are both sustainable and provide community-wide impact (Mehra et al., 2020). This section includes five chapters that establish theoretical foundations and illustrate research activities centered in partnerships. Chapters 1, 3–5 each present case studies of successful partnerships between public libraries and other community organizations where the library serves as the backbone organization. Chapter 2 discusses the importance of supporting library staff and their relationships to form partnerships for building sustainable communities. These chapters operationalize significant elements of the public library – sustainable communities (PLSC) framework visualized in the introduction to the book.

In Chapter 1 ["The library serves as an amplifier and connector in the community it serves: Building Bridges to Legal Assistance"], Brooke Doyle, Lynn Silipigni Connaway, and Lesley A. Langa discuss a series of programs featuring community partners that are designed to close the legal justice gap. Programs include partnerships with: (1) a trust company to help with estate planning;

How Public Libraries Build Sustainable Communities in the 21st Century
Advances in Librarianship, Volume 53, 13–16
Copyright © 2023 by Kaurri C. Williams-Cockfield and Bharat Mehra
Published under exclusive licence by Emerald Publishing Limited
ISSN: 0065-2830/doi:10.1108/S0065-283020230000053001

(2) legal aid groups to provide legal clinics; and (3) a volunteer lawyers' service to provide cyber clinics to rural areas. These three case studies in Chapter 1 demonstrate how public libraries are community connectors and lessons are all easily adaptable for use in other libraries.

In Chapter 2 ["Sustaining Ourselves, Sustaining Relationships, Sustaining Communities"], Noah Lenstra and Christine D'Arpa propose a sustainable communities model, based on four separate research projects that centralize the contributions of public library staff workers at the core of community building given their complex relationships within service communities.

In Chapter 3 ["Collective Praxis: Leveraging Local and Heritage-Based Values for Public Librarian Professional Development"], Vanessa Irvin discusses a research project funded by the Institute of Museum and Library Services entitled "Hui 'Ekolu" that spotlights a partnership between the Hawaii State Library for the Blind and Print Disabled, the Native Hawaiian Library, and the University of Hawai'i at Mānoa LIS Program. This chapter describes the grant-funded project that developed a community of practice between library and information science students, practitioners, Hawaiian cultural practitioners, and university professors ensuring the inclusion of native Hawaiian culture and values in the training of librarians.

In Chapter 4 ["Community Engagement Through Public Library Social Inclusion: The View and Practice of Librarians in Gunungkidul County, Yogyakarta, Indonesia"], Ida Fajar Priyanto, Agung Wibawa, and Siti Indarwati discuss the Perpuseru program based on the work of local librarians that focuses on local, cultural, and social inclusion programs provided through public libraries in Yogyakarta, Indonesia. Reviewer Brady Lund, Assistant Professor at the University of North Texas, Department of Information Science writes:

> In light of recent destabilizing events around the world, our public libraries serve an increasingly vital role as sources of community and information access to patrons of all generational, social, cultural, and economic backgrounds. This resource demonstrates how libraries globally are fulfilling this crucial obligation.

In Chapter 5 ["Applying ESG to Modern Librarianship: Lessons from the Business World"], Samantha Connell and Micaela Porta focus on a case study located in New Canaan, Connecticut, USA that examines the application of ESG to New Canaan Public Library policies, strategic plans, and operational culture to create sustainability within their library organization. Reviewer Allison Ferguson, University of Alberta, states:

> As the modern public library continues to focus on serving its communities in a rapidly evolving world, sustainability is a key issue, and a complex one. It can be difficult to decide on a way forward, and this work provides exactly the kind of real-world example necessary to both inspire change and offer practical ideas on how to do it.

STRATEGIC COLLECTIVE ACTIONS

The thematic threads flowing through the five chapters in this section highlight how different library case studies operationalize the following significant strategic collective actions:

Introduction to Section One 15

- Use global models and action-oriented frameworks (ESG) to improve library systems and operations;
- Demonstrate public libraries serving as connectors within their local communities;
- Preserve local culture and history through staff development/training and cultural program development and implementation;
- Recognize the importance of diverse local community networks established by library staff.

These case studies demonstrate effective public library–community partnerships between libraries and local organizations as well as between federal, state, and local library organizations. Additionally, the narratives provided in this section provide a foundation for future opportunities for implementing the UN SDGs in local initiatives.

KEY CONCEPTS AND TERMS

Community of Praxis – Group of people who come together to share and exchange knowledge to learn from one another to improve professional practice and heighten cultural competency.

ESG – Environmental, social, and governance practices in the corporate world that support sustainability and social equity.

Legal Aid Clinic – In person or virtual event designed to provide free civil legal advice for individuals.

Library Social Inclusion – The involvement of community in the practical training and similar activities organized by librarians with the aim of helping individuals in the community to do activities such as traditional dancing, traditional music, yoga, and so on for cultural preservation or for making a product from local resources.

Triple Bottom Line Framework – Institutional policies and procedures which are environmentally sound, economically feasible, and socially equitable.

REFERENCES

United Nations. (2015). *Transforming Our World: The 2030 Agenda for Sustainable Development*. United Nations Department of Economic and Social Affairs. Retrieved September 12, 2021, from https://sdgs.un.org/publications/transforming-our-world-2030-agenda-sustainable-development-17981; https://sdgs.un.org/goals.

RESOURCES AND RELEVANT ORGANIZATIONS

ALU Like/Native Hawaiian Library, Hawaii, US. https://www.alulike.org/services/ka-waihona-puke-oiwi/
Asset Management Working Group, UN Environment Programme. https://www.unepfi.org/industries/investment/the-asset-management-working-group-what-why-who/
Bill and Melinda Gates Foundation, Seattle, WA, US. https://www.gatesfoundation.org/
Hawaii State Library for the Blind and Print Disabled, Hawaii, US. https://www.librarieshawaii.org/branch/library-for-the-blind-and-print-disabled/

Hawaii State Public Library System, Hawaii, US. https://www.librarieshawaii.org/
Hui 'Ekolu Professional and Cultural Development Program, Hawaii, US. http://huiekolu.weebly.com/
Improving Access to Civil Legal Justice through Libraries project, WebJunction, US. https://www.web-junction.org/news/webjunction/improving-access-to-civil-legal-justice.html
International Federation of Library Associations and Institutions (IFLA). https://www.ifla.org/
Justice Gap Report, Legal Services Corporation, Washington, D.C., US. https://justicegap.lsc.gov/
Mehra, B., Sikes, E. S., & Singh, V. (2020, May). Scenarios of Technology Use to Promote Community Engagement: Overcoming Marginalization and Bridging Digital Divides in the Southern and Central Appalachian Rural Libraries. *Information Processing & Management* (Special Issue: Marginalized Communities, Emerging Technologies, and Social Innovation in the Digital Age. Edited by Jia Tina Du, Iris Xie, and Jenny Waycott), 57(3). Article 102129. https://doi.org/10.1016/j.ipm.2019.102129
PerpuSeru Program, Coca-Cola Indonesia. https://www.cocacola.co.id/news/perpuseru-ciptakan-dampak-perubahan-kemandirian-ekonomi-hingga-1
The University of Hawai'i at Mānoa, Honolulu, Hawaii, US. https://manoa.hawaii.edu/

CHAPTER 1

"THE LIBRARY SERVES AS AN AMPLIFIER AND CONNECTOR IN THE COMMUNITY IT SERVES"[1]: BUILDING BRIDGES TO LEGAL ASSISTANCE

Brooke Doyle, Lynn Silipigni Connaway and
Lesley A. Langa

OCLC Research

ABSTRACT

OCLC Research conducted a global survey focusing on libraries' strategic goals that incorporate five of the United Nations Sustainable Development Goals (SDGs) where libraries could have the greatest impact. More than 1,700 library staff completed the survey and identified how they were integrating these five SDGs [Quality Education (SDG 4), Decent Work and Economic Growth (SDG 8), Reduced Inequality (SDG 10), Peace, Justice and Strong Institutions (SDG 16), and Working in Partnership to Achieve the Goals (SDG 17)] in their strategic framework and the activities that staff undertook as part of their overall mission.

Results from the survey combined with other projects provide examples of how the SDGs inform library strategic planning and how the library staff's activities impact sustainable development in their communities. Quality education

How Public Libraries Build Sustainable Communities in the 21st Century
Advances in Librarianship, Volume 53, 17–26
Copyright © 2023 by Brooke Doyle, Lynn Silipigni Connaway and Lesley A. Langa
Published under exclusive licence by Emerald Publishing Limited
ISSN: 0065-2830/doi:10.1108/S0065-283020230000053002

(SDG 4) was the top goal that respondents believe libraries can impact through community training and classes. Public libraries also often are the main source of credible information and facts in a community.

This commitment to quality education and credible information is demonstrated in the role libraries play in helping community members to access legal information. This chapter describes several different partnerships where libraries are important connectors to legal information which often can be life changing to the community, such as providing information on how to expunge a criminal record to obtain employment.

Keywords: Quality education; civil legal justice; sustainable development goals; partnerships; public libraries; community engagement

INTRODUCTION

In 2015, during the protests in response to Freddie Gray's death in Baltimore, the Pennsylvania Avenue branch of the Enoch Pratt Free Library stayed open even as violence erupted around it. Gray, 25, was arrested and transported in the back of a police van with his hands cuffed behind his back and his legs shackled. In transit, Gray suffered a severe neck injury and died a week later in the hospital. Protests followed and violence spread in downtown Baltimore (Hermann, 2020). As Dr Carla Hayden, then Pratt Library CEO and current Librarian of Congress said in Megan Cottrell's interview,

> The library has been the community's anchor. It's the heart of the community at good times and bad times…If we close, we're sending a signal that we're afraid or that we aren't going to be available when times are tough. We should be open especially when times are tough. (2015, May 1)

Libraries have built the trust of the community and need to be there when the community is in crisis.

Similarly, when a natural disaster strikes, libraries are there to help. In 2019 in California, when many were forced from their homes due to forest fires and power outages, libraries like Folsom Public Library became a refuge for people who needed to charge devices, use WiFi, or just have a place to go (Folsom Library, 2019, October 9). Libraries were able to provide practical assistance in a crisis.

Why did people turn to libraries during these crises? In many cases, libraries had suffered the same catastrophic losses as their neighbors; in the fires, staff had perished or been injured, buildings completely destroyed or unusable, resources gutted. People turn to libraries after a disaster because of social capital – those networks of relationships among people who live and work in a particular society, enabling that society to function effectively.

While we do not understand all the mechanics of how social capital is built within a community, we do know that social capital is one reason why communities value public libraries. Libraries are one of the most tangible manifestations of local, civic engagement, a place that represents a public community investment in learning and shared space. As libraries create social capital through bridging (when people in different subgroups within a community are brought together) and bonding (when people within different subgroups come together), libraries are solidifying their role as community anchors and building trust. Therefore, when a crisis happens as in the Baltimore and California examples, people often automatically turn to the library, which has been engaged with and responsive to its community (Cyr, 2019).

Data from a global survey of library leaders about how libraries impact the SDGs help frame the chapter. This chapter then outlines several different approaches library staff have taken to offer civil legal programming. These programs demonstrate the interconnectedness of the SDGs and the role libraries can play in furthering and supporting quality education, decent work and economic growth, reduced inequality, peace, justice and strong institutions, and working in partnership. There is little evidence identifying if and how SDGs influence library strategic planning, and this chapter begins to outline directions for future research.

LIBRARIES AND THE SDGs

The community-engaged library is a natural fit with the United Nations SDGs, a group of 17 goals for the year 2030 addressing "poverty, inequality, climate change, environmental degradation, peace and justice" (United Nations, 2020). The Baltimore and California stories are very local examples that demonstrate how libraries sustain communities to ensure a global future. In other words, the SDGs are a shared blueprint to achieve peace and prosperity for all on a healthy planet. In fact, library staff played a vital role in the creation of the SDGs, and particularly, in leading the charge to include access to information in SDG 16 – Peace, Justice, and Strong Institutions as a tier one target – "Ensure public access to information and protect fundamental freedoms, in accordance with national legislation and international agreements" (target 16.10). Since their adoption, libraries have helped to further progress toward meeting the SDGs in their communities through related initiatives, programs, and activities.

The OCLC Global Council, a global library organization, selected libraries and the SDGs as its focus area for research and advocacy in 2020. As part of this focus, OCLC Research conducted a global survey on how the SDGs were informing libraries' strategic directions. A total of 1,722 library professionals completed the survey, including 1,125 respondents from 16 regions in the Americas, 448 respondents from 63 regions in EMEA (Europe, Middle East, and Africa), and 148 respondents from 20 regions in Asia Pacific. OCLC Global Council delegates identified the following five SDGs as those where libraries could have the greatest impact:

- Quality Education (SDG 4)
- Decent Work and Economic Growth (SDG 8)
- Reduced Inequality (SDG 10)
- Peace, Justice, and Strong Institutions (SDG 16)
- Working in Partnership to Achieve the Goals (SDG 17).

Fig. 1. Average Ranking of Responses for Libraries' Potential to Impact SDGs.

Fig. 1 represents the average ranking of the five SDGs where libraries could have the greatest impact according to the survey respondents.

The selected SDGs address economic and social inequalities, and this chapter provides insight into activities library staff are doing in support of these SDGs as well as the interconnectedness of the goals.

Strongest Impact on Quality Education

Quality Education (SDG 4) was the top goal that respondents believe libraries impact. This is demonstrated by the training and classes offered to the community, in addition to the resources and facilities libraries provide for remote learning. Some of the top examples of educational activities are outreach and programming, English language classes, computer literacy, and book clubs. The range of responses to this question was vast, including career certifications, CPR, food preservation, and life skills. For many libraries, quality education is a key part of their mission. Cleveland Public Library even made their tagline "The People's University" (Cleveland Public Library, 2022). As this Canadian public library respondent describes, "Ongoing lifelong learning is a theme with [the library's] programs, which aim to inform in many different areas..." including digital literacy, early literacy, and foreign language learning. For some libraries, educational outreach is a priority. As this American library respondent states,

> We have a solo Outreach Librarian who works full time in the community, partnering with local schools, daycares, faith-based and charitable organizations, teen and children's shelters, providing support for curricular education and singular extra-curricular educational activities.

In addition, public libraries often are the main sources of credible information and facts in communities. This respondent from a library in the Netherlands describes this role,

> Public libraries have always been a safe and reliable source for truthful information, thought development, debate. For communities to be safe, resilient, sustainable and above all inclusive we need to foster places where fake news and loud voices don't bludgeon us into submission of silence. Open to all, a stimulating environment is where you can enrich your ideas without prejudice or control.

In all of these different ways, libraries are impacting Quality Education (SDG 4).

Libraries and Access to Justice

This commitment to quality education and credible information is demonstrated in libraries' roles in helping the community access legal information. This can include individuals' need for acquiring information on how to expunge a criminal record to obtain employment or for identifying accurate information about the eviction process to access assistance.

The recent Justice Gap Report indicates that 71% of low-income US households experienced at least one civil legal problem in 2021, and that 86% of those problems went unresolved (Legal Services Corporation, 2022). Low-income Americans received no or inadequate legal help for a staggering 92% of all the civil legal problems that substantially impacted them. There are not enough legal aid attorneys to help everyone. The significant gap between people seeking fair legal treatment and the resources available in the United States means that public libraries have an important role to play in providing access to legal information when those questions are asked (Legal Services Corporation, 2022).

As a community anchor where people feel safe and comfortable asking questions, public libraries can serve as the first point of access by helping to identify when a legal issue is present and answer basic legal information questions. Depending on the complexity of the question, public library staff may be able to refer individuals to a law library or to an Ask-A-Lawyer program at the library. OCLC's *Improving Access to Civil Legal Justice* project helps library staff be that connector to legal information by offering a free four-course series that helps staff build foundational legal reference skills (OCLC, 2020). As library staff increase their understanding of legal issues and build relationships with the legal community such as legal aid, law librarians, and court staff, the community is better served and informed.

Community Partnerships Crucial in Access to Justice Work

So much of public libraries' role in assisting with civil legal information needs is about partnerships (SDG 17 – Working in Partnership to Achieve the Goals). Library partnerships support SDG 17.17, which says, "Encouraging and promoting effective public, public-private and civil society partnerships, building on the experience and resourcing strategies of partnerships." Libraries are connectors who are finding the relevant players in different issues and seeing if the library can facilitate engagement. This role could include offering space, technology, accessibility, or leadership. For example, libraries frequently invite tenants' rights groups to hold an educational event so that the community – both landlords and tenants – know their rights, can read a lease, and understand what reasonable accommodation means. Participants are equipped with the information needed to begin to negotiate a landlord-tenant issue. Another example is Kansas City Public Library's partnership with a trust company to deliver a webinar about Estate Planning in their End-of-Life series. Attendees learned about wills, trusts, beneficiary deeds, powers of attorney, and advance directives to avoid legal issues later (Jenny Garmon, email message to author, July 7, 2021). By offering free programming to the public about significant and common legal issues, public libraries are ensuring equal access to justice for all (SDG 16.3), facilitating public access to information and protecting fundamental freedoms (SDG 16.10) in pursuit of the overall goal of Peace, Justice, and Strong Institutions (SDG 16). Activities like these demonstrate how the public library can amplify an issue like access to justice and connect key players to find a solution.

Partnership: Library and Legal Aid. As reported by Yvonne Wenger, Gusty Taler, Maryland Legal Aid's (MLA) chief operating officer, was watching the protests, riots, arson, and looting after Freddie Gray died in police custody from Legal Aid's office near City Hall, which was surrounded by protesters and National Guard troops. Her lawyers felt restless. Then, she saw Dr Hayden, Pratt Library CEO, on television discussing her decision to keep the library located in the heart of the unrest open.

> All around her was crazy chaos, and she said she was keeping the library open because it was a safe haven and people had come to rely on it. I came up with the idea: Let's put lawyers in the library, said Taler. (2017, November 16)

The Pratt Library is an ideal partner for such a program. The library branches have great public transportation access, and they are trusted providers of information and services. Patrons know they can come to the library for internet and printer access and assistance with job searches as well as navigating social service benefits. The first clinics began in September 2015 with the moderate turnout, but during the Martin Luther King Jr long weekend in January 2016, 650 people showed up on a Saturday. Overflow crowds were directed to a clinic the next day at a nearby church and more than 700 people attended.

Amy Petkovsek, Deputy Chief Counsel for Maryland Legal Aid, guesses that the record numbers came because they had heard about the results from those first clinics in September. Those patrons expunged their criminal records and were able to secure employment, rent an apartment, and see their children, often for the first time. Expungement is a legal process that erases or seals a job seeker's prior criminal records, meaning that they no longer need to disclose this information. Filing for expungement can be expensive and confusing without legal guidance. Many people cannot afford the fee per expungement – particularly if they need to remove multiple items from their record. Petkovsek said clients leave the clinics free of problems that only a lawyer could fix. Some were in tears.

> An attorney can spend five to 20 minutes with one person here and literally change a life. They can get a job. They can have access to housing or access to their children just with 20 minutes of an attorney's time. That is a really big deal. (Wenger, 2017)

"The library serves as an amplifier and connector in the community it serves" 23

Partnership: Legal Aid on Wheels. The Lawyer in the Library program that began after Freddie Gray's death has continued to expand, and in August 2021 Baltimore County Public Library debuted its Mobile Library Law Center. "We are proud to be the first library system in the country to own and operate a mobile legal vehicle, servicing those who don't have access to legal help," said Baltimore County Public Library Director, Sonia Alcántara-Antoine (Patti, 2021). The unit travels twice a week to underserved areas on the east and west sides of Baltimore County, serving as a mobile legal office. Lawyers from Maryland Legal Aid provide free civil legal advice for those who are financially eligible in areas such as bankruptcy, child custody and support, debt collection, expungements, government benefits, housing, landlord/tenant, veterans' benefits, and unemployment benefits. Using census data and figures on assets, income and employment, the program targets individuals with disabilities, seniors, veterans, and those who are economically disadvantaged. A librarian also provides research resources and assists with intake. As reported by Sameer Rao, Executive Director Deb Seltzer of Maryland Legal Services Corporation noted,

> With the library as a trusted partner and recognized institution, a client may say, "Even if I don't go to the library often, I know what the library is, I know that that's a community resource, so even if I haven't heard of Maryland Legal Aid or I don't recognize that I need a lawyer, I'm going to check this out because I trust the resources the library has to offer." (2021, August 22)

By parking the mobile unit outside a public housing complex, the library has removed the stress of seeking out or finding assistance. Maryland Legal Aid Deputy Chief Counsel Amy Petkovsek said,

> The removal of stress is the goal here – to make people feel legally well, to make them feel healthy, to allow them to feel like they can make their own choices going forward. (Rao, 2021)

Several years ago, Maryland Legal Aid and its library partners met to talk about how the library served its most vulnerable patrons, and how lawyers could complement these services. In an OCLC article, Petkovsek explained how the partnership evolved,

> Libraries are connectors, resource providers, and they've been here forever. Libraries are experts at delivering services. We are experts at moving things through the legal system. In general – let's take our legal skills and just listen. That's our approach. How can we fit in? This collaboration works because we are cognizant of what each other is good at. (2021)

As they discussed how to maximize service delivery, the city mentioned that they had success with a mobile workforce unit that included library staff to help with resume writing and a lawyer to help with expungements. Unfortunately, the vehicles would break down, and maintenance became a headache. Maryland Legal Aid did not want responsibility for a vehicle, but the library was already in the business of owning and maintaining vehicles. Baltimore County suggested they could build a unit specifically for a mobile law library. This experiment with a mobile library center is groundbreaking and a great testament to authentic collaboration – each partner bringing its expertise to respond to a community need. Sonia Alcántara-Antoine, library director at Baltimore County, shared,

> Libraries are democratic institutions, giving everyone equal access to resources that will truly create an inclusive society. Initiatives such as this ensure that those most in need have equal access to justice. (OCLC, 2021)

Partnership: Cyber Clinics in Rural Areas. Workforce development staff at Wicomico Public Library in rural Maryland were also hearing frustration from patrons who were not finding employment due to prior criminal histories. Library staff knew their rural location limited access to legal aid attorneys so they partnered with Maryland Volunteer Lawyers Service (MVLS) to create a cyber-legal clinic. Participants attend clinics in person at Wicomico Public Libraries (WPL) Downtown Branch and connected with Baltimore lawyers remotely using Google Hangouts to receive full civil legal representation free of charge. Library staff connected with Baltimore-based MVLS – a nonprofit organization that connects low-income Marylanders with volunteer lawyers to deliver free civil legal assistance. Twice a month in the library's computer lab, WPL hosts a virtual legal clinic. Lawyers two hours away in Baltimore provide the legal advice, and WPL offers the outreach, space, technology, and digital navigation to make this partnership happen. "There are so many barriers that can prevent low-income individuals from moving forward," says Susan Francis, Executive Director of MVLS, "and the more we can do to remove those barriers, the better odds they have to stabilize their lives." Scott Mahler, WPL Adult Services Manager, adds that holding these clinics in a library helps participants feel more comfortable: "An experience like this feels more personal through the library. At the end of a session, you can see the relief on people's faces," Mahler reflects.

> They've been needing to do this for a long time but needed help overcoming those initial financial barriers. At the end of the clinic people hug us, and they cry, we cry. The day of the clinic is great, which is telling us that we're doing something right for our community. (Melko, 2019)

These clinics in their different forms are great examples of the library educating its community about legal issues and connecting those in need to legal assistance, which can pave the way to economic progress. The library has established relationships with its users and with key community partners, while also having the technology and the space to make this happen.

SDGs Represented in Library Legal Aid Programming

The libraries' programming with legal aid organizations demonstrates many of the SDGs. By removing barriers for patrons seeking employment, the clinics further SDG 8 Decent Work and Economic Growth with a particular focus on target 8.5, "By 2030, achieve full and productive employment and decent work for all women and men, including for young people and persons with disabilities, and equal pay for work of equal value."

As doors to employment open, the clinics address SDG 10 Reduced Inequality – with focus on 10.2, "By 2030, empower and promote the social, economic and political inclusion of all, irrespective of age, sex, disability, race, ethnicity, origin, religion or economic or other status as people's economic opportunities expand."

"The library serves as an amplifier and connector in the community it serves" 25

Making lawyers more accessible to all helps protect fundamental freedoms as described in SDG 16 Peace, Justice, and Strong Institutions – with a focus on 16.10, "Ensure public access to information and protect fundamental freedoms, in accordance with national legislation and international agreements" and 16.3 "Promote the rule of law at the national and international levels and ensure equal access to justice for all." A common thread in these examples is Quality Education (SDG 4) – whether it is learning about expungements or how to apply for a job. The goals of the SDGs are mutually reinforcing. As legal aid clinics create opportunities for decent work and economic growth, inequalities are reduced. These partnerships help strengthen peace, justice, and strong institutions. And a final common denominator in these examples is Working in Partnership to Achieve the Goals (SDG 17). To create a collective impact, library staff seek partners to deepen the library's mission, and the partners gain access to library expertise, space, and resources. Both organizations are amplifying each other's missions. Activities such as these demonstrate how the public library can leverage its social capital and community connections for environmental, economic, and social change.

CONCLUSION

The justice gap in the United States is significant, and libraries can fill part of that gap by providing legal information and by partnering with legal aid agencies. These examples described in the chapter provide a range of possibilities of what that programming might look like. Library leaders should be strategic about identifying their community's unmet legal needs and finding partners in the legal community to assist. Connecting this legal programming to the SDGs helps elevate its significance. The implication of this discussion is a need for new research to measure the impact of these programs particularly in identifying how public libraries support the SDGs within their communities. One way to measure this impact would be to identify how public libraries integrate the SDGs into their strategic planning. This type of study would provide data that could be measured and compared between libraries over time to discern impact.

NOTE

1. This quote came from a survey response from a US public librarian in OCLC's survey about the SDGs.

REFERENCES

Cleveland Public Library. (2022). *Cleveland Public Library*. Retrieved September 2022, from https://cpl.org/

Cottrell, M. (2015, May 1). Baltimore's library stays open during unrest. *American Libraries*. https://americanlibrariesmagazine.org/blogs/the-scoop/qa-carla-hayden-baltimore/

Cyr, C. (2019). Public libraries generate social capital that can save lives. *Programming Librarian*. Retrieved September 2022, from https://programminglibrarian.org/programs/dear-friend-quarantine-pen-pal-campaign

Folsom Library [@FolsomLibrary]. (2019, October 9). *For those in nearby communities affected by the power outages* [Tweet]. Twitter.com. https://twitter.com/FolsomLibrary/status/1182007950623285249

Hermann, M. (2020, April 25). Five years after Freddie Gray, Baltimore continues to struggle. *Washington Post.* https://www.washingtonpost.com/local/public-safety/five-years-after-freddie-gray-baltimore-continues-to-struggle/2020/04/25/918e53ac-8636-11ea-ae26-989cfce1c7c7_story.html

Legal Services Corporation. (2022). The justice gap: The unmet civil legal needs of low-income Americans. https://justicegap.lsc.gov/resource/executive-summary/

Melko, E. (2019). *Cyber legal clinics create access to employment at Wicomico Public Libraries.* WebJunction. https://www.webjunction.org/news/webjunction/cyber-legal-clinics-create-access.html

OCLC. (2020). *Improving access to civil legal justice through libraries.* WebJunction. https://www.webjunction.org/news/webjunction/improving-access-to-civil-legal-justice.html

OCLC. (2021). *Mobile library law center launches.* WebJunction. https://www.webjunction.org/news/webjunction/mobile-library-law-center-launches.html

Patti, J. (2021, September 13). *New mobile library law center on the road in Baltimore County.* [Radio broadcast transcript]. WBAL. https://www.wbal.com/article/532572/180/new-mobile-library-law-center-on-the-road-in-baltimore-county

Rao, S. (2021, August 22). Pioneering Md. center takes legal aid on the road. Law 360. https://www.law360.com/articles/1412253/pioneering-md-center-takes-legal-aid-on-the-road

United Nations. (2020). *Sustainable Development Goals.* https://www.un.org/sustainabledevelopment/sustainable-development-goals/

Wenger, Y. (2017, November 16). Working out of the library, Maryland Legal Aid helps people grapple with issues only a lawyer can fix. *Baltimore Sun.* https://www.baltimoresun.com/maryland/baltimore-city/bs-md-ci-lawyer-in-the-library-20171102-story.html

CHAPTER 2

SUSTAINING OURSELVES, SUSTAINING RELATIONSHIPS, SUSTAINING COMMUNITIES

Noah Lenstra and Christine D'Arpa

ABSTRACT

This chapter presents a preliminary model that frames public library workers as the foundations of how public libraries help build and support sustainable communities in the twenty-first century, particularly in the United States, specifically in rural America. For public libraries to continue to be key partners in sustaining their communities, and in supporting the United Nations' (UN) Sustainable Development Goals (SDGs), it is essential that public library work be valued, visible, and sustained over time. The UN defines sustainability as "meeting the needs of the present without compromising the ability of future generations to meet their own needs." Four studies of public library work during the COVID-19 pandemic found that public library workers are facing challenges in both meeting their own needs and meeting the needs of their communities. That finding led to a consideration of what is needed to place public library work at the center of sustainable thinking. Sustaining library workers will strengthen the library as a community hub, and help those workers in turn sustain community relationships necessary for the work of the library. These, in turn, will contribute to more sustainable communities.

Keywords: Public libraries; library labor; community development; staff development; public library worker; job satisfaction; social connectedness

---

How Public Libraries Build Sustainable Communities in the 21st Century
Advances in Librarianship, Volume 53, 27–35
Copyright © 2023 by Noah Lenstra and Christine D'Arpa
Published under exclusive licence by Emerald Publishing Limited
ISSN: 0065-2830/doi:10.1108/S0065-283020230000053003

INTRODUCTION

This chapter presents a preliminary model, based on four research projects, that frames public library workers as the foundations of how public libraries help build and support sustainable communities in the twenty-first century, particularly in the United States, specifically in rural America. For public libraries to continue to be key partners in sustaining their communities, and in supporting the UN SDGs, it is essential, we argue, that we think strategically and politically about how to ensure public library work is valued, visible, and sustained over time. Sustaining library workers will strengthen the library as a community hub, and help those workers in turn sustain community relationships necessary for the work of the library. These, in turn, will contribute to more sustainable communities.

FRAMING SDG CONTENT

The UN defines sustainability as "meeting the needs of the present without compromising the ability of future generations to meet their own needs" (United Nations, n.d.). Across four studies of public library work during the COVID-19 pandemic, we found public library workers facing challenges both meeting their own needs, and meeting the needs of their communities.

To advance the UN's sustainability goals, in 2015 the UN developed 17 SDGs. The research discussed in this chapter connects most explicitly to the following four goals, with the language below coming directly from the SDGs (United Nations, 2022, n.d.):

1. Good health and wellbeing – Ensure healthy lives and promote well-being for all ages.
2. Reduced inequalities – Reduce inequality within and among countries.
3. Sustainable cities and communities – Make cities and human settlements inclusive, safe, resilient, and sustainable.
4. Partnerships for the goals – Strengthen the means of implementation and revitalize the Global Partnership for Sustainable Development.

The idea of partnerships is seen as critical both to UN SDGs and to the work of librarianship. However, it is important to recognize/acknowledge/understand the nuances to library work as a form of community work. These are too often poorly understood in existing frameworks that position libraries in relation to the SDGs. This chapter sets out to address, fill, and close that gap.

LIMITATIONS OF EXISTING FRAMEWORKS FOR SUPPORTING LIBRARY WORK AS COMMUNITY WORK

This theoretical intervention is necessary because existing frameworks focus largely on plugging libraries into the UN SDGs, rather than asking more

Sustaining Ourselves, Sustaining Relationships, Sustaining Communities 29

fundamental questions about the relationship between the UN SDGs and the work of public librarianship. For instance, the International Federation of Library Association's (IFLA) *Libraries and the Sustainable Development Goals: A Storytelling Manual* (IFLA, 2018) helpfully explains how "librarians and library advocates" can communicate about the impacts libraries have on the SDGs. But, critically, the handbook focuses on what libraries offer communities, not on the unique roles of library workers as community partners in meeting community needs. In the section "What Story to Tell" the IFLA handbook states:

> How do libraries support the SDGs? Libraries around the world offer a wide range of products and services that promote the achievement of each and every one of the SDGs. From promoting literacy, to offering free access to information, libraries are safe, welcoming spaces, at the heart of communities. They come with the indispensable support of a dedicated staff with a deep understanding of local needs. They advance digital inclusion through access to Information and Communication Technology (ICT), internet connection and skills. They promote innovation, creativity and access to the world's knowledge for current and future generations. (p. 4)

Buried in the middle of this paragraph is the sentence "They [libraries] come with the indispensable support of a dedicated staff with a deep understanding of local needs" (p. 4). The implication of this framing is that library workers are an appendage to libraries. Libraries "come with" staff, rather than staff (library workers) being the engine that enables libraries to operate. This IFLA handbook, and its messaging, thus inadvertently perpetuates the invisibility of library work and workers. We instead argue that the stories important to gather and hear need to center on and critically engage library work and workers.

Similar blind spots can be found in resources created by the American Library Association (ALA), with the ALA's Fact Sheet on the SDGs stating, "What can you do? Libraries play a big part in helping to provide knowledge, understanding, and resources to our communities" (ALA, n.d.). Here again the focus is on what libraries do, and not on what library workers do in collaboration with communities.

FOUR RESEARCH STUDIES

Understanding Library Work in Relation to Sustainable Communities

In our work, we have sought to center library work and workers. These research projects included four studies: study one, national in scope, was a job satisfaction survey taken by public library workers during the first year of the COVID-19 pandemic; study two was a national survey on the social connectedness of older adults during the pandemic; study three was an interview-based study of rural library workers in four states – Michigan, North Carolina, Oklahoma, and Vermont – to determine levels of collaboration with their communities to support community health and wellness; and study four was an interview-based study of both how urban and rural library workers in 18 communities across 14 states lead and participate in community partnerships focused on increasing access to healthy eating and active living.

The last goal (Goal #17 of the SDGs): "Partnerships for the goals – Strengthen the means of implementation and revitalize the Global Partnership for Sustainable Development" (United Nations, 2022) and is further defined as focused on: "All sources of finance – public and private; domestic and international – need to be mobilized to advance sustainable development and ensure that no one is left behind" (United Nations, 2018). We see this goal as directly dovetailing with the model of collective impact developed by Americans John Kania and Mark Kramer (2011). Collective impact focuses on the fact that "Large-scale social change requires broad cross-sector coordination, yet the social sector remains focused on the isolated intervention of individual organizations" (p. 36).

However, both UN SDG Goal #17 and the framework of collective impact focus primarily on action at the macro level. In a widely cited critique of the framework of collective impact, Tom Wolff argues that there are at least "10 places where collective impact got it wrong," and his critique boils down to the fact that the framework of collective impact "promotes top-down decision making over grassroots voice" (Wolff, 2016, p. 49). A similar favoring of top-down decision making can be seen in UN SDG #17, where targets focus almost exclusively on the country-level (United Nations, 2022), with little explicit attention on localized efforts. As a result of this framing, the UN SDG, as currently written, does not provide an adequate framework to help us understand and support library workers as community partners working in and with communities in complex, and not fully supported ways.

FINDINGS

Our research instead found that the ways libraries contribute to the development of sustainable communities are fundamentally grounded in the work of librarians and other library staff. These workers must be seen as part of an engaged populace engaged in organic relationships with a multitude of community sectors, agents, and partners if we are to fully appreciate the function of the institution of the library as an agent of community change.

The following list conveys some of the key findings from these four projects, with a focus on how they enrich our understanding of public library workers as essential players in how public libraries help build sustainable communities.

Findings from Research Study One

Job satisfaction among public library workers during the first year of the COVID-19 pandemic. *Key findings*: The survey had more than 1,200 responses from across the United States. The open-ended responses were varied but many library workers noted a sense of isolation, loss of connection to each other and to their communities/patrons; they expressed concern about not being able to meet the needs of patrons and concern about the loss of the library as a vibrant community center. Some of the challenges library workers faced included a lack

Sustaining Ourselves, Sustaining Relationships, Sustaining Communities 31

of transparency about operating policies under COVID and, more generally, fear and uncertainty about their personal health and well-being. Qualitative data submitted in open-ended responses to survey prompts show that library workers felt a sense of responsibility to their patrons and communities, and they also experienced frustration at not being able to adequately meet those needs, as well as their own. *Implications*: Library workers experienced the impact of the pandemic on their own lives including their work lives but too often felt little power to affect change. Even with that frustration and uncertainty, library workers expressed interest in and concern for their patrons and communities and, especially, vulnerable populations.

Findings from Research Study Two

How rural library workers support the social connectedness of older adults during the pandemic. *Key findings*: Across America, a statistically significant random sample of rural library workers reported in survey responses offering a range of library services to ensure older adults remained connected to the library, and to each other, during the COVID-19 pandemic, including services that enabled older adults to stay connected across a range of modalities, including socially distant face-to-face at the library, telephone, homebound and off-site library services, mail, and virtual. However, the most reported way that rural library workers supported social connectedness among older adults during the COVID-19 pandemic was by cross-promoting others' efforts. In other words, the most common library service was not a service developed by a library working by itself. It instead emerged from the deep integration of library workers into communities. Nonetheless, library workers also reported feeling uncertain about how to continue this important work most effectively during the pandemic. *Implications*: Rural public library workers are essential in the social lives of older adults, and need to be framed as such in advocacy work (Lenstra et al., 2021).

Findings from Research Study Three

How rural library workers collaborate with their communities to support community health. *Key findings*: During the COVID-19 pandemic, rural library workers in four US States (Vermont, Michigan, Oklahoma, and North Carolina) reported in interviews and on social media posts a range of techniques focused on ensuring the communities they served continued to have access to vital primary, public, and preventative health services, including access to greenspace, up-to-date health information, and much more. Interviews revealed that library workers, and the agency of those workers, was a crucial ingredient in these library services. *Implications*: Rural library workers, at least in the United States, need to be seen, understood, and supported as crucial community partners and collaborators in sustainable health systems, rather than having this work be seen as an unfunded mandate for library workers (Rubenstein et al., 2021).

Findings from Research Study Four

How library workers – urban and rural – increase access to healthy eating and active living (HEAL) through engagement in community partnerships and coalitions. *Key findings*: During the COVID-19 pandemic, over 60 library workers and 60 library partners engaged in interviews focused on understanding the roles of libraries in community health partnerships and coalitions. This research found that library partners typically learn more about library work through their ongoing engagement with library workers. A typical evolution of thought is as follows:

- Stage 1 – no relationship – library seen as book repository.
- Stage 2 – some relationship – library seen as safe space for delivery of health services, distribution of health resources, or discussion of health issues.
- Stage 3 – strong relationship – library workers seen as critical partners in community health planning, policy, and service development.

Implications: The fact that library partners typically went through an ideological transformation while working with library workers suggests that crucial work is needed related to communicating the essential roles of library workers as active agents in sustainable community development (Lenstra, 2022).

Based on these four studies and their findings, we developed a model to re-frame public library workers as essential players in how public libraries help build sustainable communities in the twenty-first century.

As this empirical work proceeded, we sought to critically integrate existing frameworks, including both the UN's SDGs and the model of Collective Impact. The former's focus on developing and developed countries needs to be modified to grapple with the inequities that exist with a developed country like the United States. The latter's focus on top-down decision making (see Wolff, 2016, and below) needs to be modified to grapple with the more complicated and organic ways in which library workers collaborate with communities to support sustainable communities.

DISCUSSION

Collective impact as discussed by Kania and Kramer (2011) argues,

> successful collective impact initiatives typically have five conditions that together produce true alignment and lead to powerful results: a common agenda, shared measurement systems, mutually reinforcing activities, continuous communication, and backbone support organizations. (p. 39)

Our research finds that the partnerships library workers create and participate in are more subtle and complex. While the process is not as neat as that discussed by Kania and Kramer, the collective impact is significant.

The model introduced here (Fig. 1) and discussed in more detail below, schematically communicates some of the support library workers need to be able to continue working toward fostering and nurturing sustainable communities.

Sustaining Ourselves, Sustaining Relationships, Sustaining Communities 33

Fig. 1. A Model of Supporting Sustainable Communities by Supporting Library Workers. *Source*: Image created by Noah Lenstra and Christine D'Arpa.

The impetus for this model came from detailed studies of library work in the United States, especially in rural America, during the COVID-19 pandemic.

We have identified a commonality across these four studies, public library workers have complex relationships with the communities they serve. Their success, and that of the library, rests on the ability of public library workers to be supported in ways that allow them to sustain and nurture themselves, both their livelihood and their professional autonomy. That autonomy enables public library workers to form relationships with a diverse set of community partners, both individuals and institutions. Those partnerships and the broad representation of the communities of which they are a part are essential and form a solid foundation that enables public libraries to build sustainable communities through collaboratively developed programs, services, and initiatives.

Collective impact emerges from the complicated ways in which library workers both cultivate new and draw on existing relationships in communities – both institutional and individual. In our research on library work during the COVID-19 pandemic, we found library workers mobilizing, leveraging, and in some cases extending existing relationships to continue supporting communities. A critical aspect of what we saw and what we heard was that library workers marshaled what they knew and what resources they had to respond to the changing needs of their communities given exceptional and uncertain times. Unfortunately, too often they did that in ways that frontline workers across industries did (Kinder, 2020) – sacrificing their own needs and health. Given these findings, one important question is how we as Library & Information Science (LIS) educators can help prepare librarians to be creative and flexible and confident in both exceptional and mundane times, without compromising their own health and needs. Additionally, as LIS faculty we see ourselves as having the responsibility to use our platform to advocate for the value of understanding library work as community-engaged practice.

The COVID-19 pandemic is an important frame for this chapter as it caused existing relationships and practices to come under significant stress. Library workers whose pre-pandemic work was public facing found themselves with little or no face-to-face contact with patrons. Many worked remotely and had time to think and rethink their work and personal lives, as well as that of their workplace, the public library. The pandemic and shelter-in-place orders dramatically changed our daily lives and heightened the importance of social connections to the health of individuals and their communities. We also found evidence of concern among library workers about how to sustain the relationships between libraries and communities given the changes and challenges resulting from the pandemic. In this context, it is worth revisiting the multi-faceted roles of public libraries and communities, and the fundamental centrality of public library work to those roles.

CONCLUSIONS

This theoretical intervention of this chapter was needed for two reasons. First, as we have found (and others have as well – de la Peña McCook, 2000), public library workers are typically *not* seen as critical agents in community development. Ensuring that public libraries continue to help build sustainable communities in the twenty-first century requires starting from a foundation that values its workers and provides the support library workers need to be successful without compromising their own health. This begins with making library workers visible. Second, we have found (and, again, as others have as well – see Daurio, 2010), public library partnerships that result in broad community impacts are grounded in diverse communities, and as such these library partnerships are as complex and multifaceted as the communities themselves. They do not easily fit into existing models that are hierarchical or center on the institution. Foregrounding the complex ways in which library workers engage with and support communities. Its success as a community partner rests firmly with the people who work there. As we think about resources/resourcing public libraries in the twenty-first century, it behooves us to consider these workers and ask them what they need to succeed.

The model presented in this chapter is a start; a framework to help us think more carefully about what is needed to support public libraries as critical parts of sustainable communities in the twenty-first century. Additional research is needed to better understand both how local library workers collaborate with communities, and on how that work is supported and made visible at both local and macro levels. Given our positions in LIS programs located within universities, we also would like to see additional research and effort toward improving relationships between library workers and library scholars/educators, that could help public library workers sustain themselves, sustain their relationships, and sustain their communities. During the COVID-19 pandemic, with library buildings often closed, library work continued. This fact alone should alert us to the fact that library work and libraries are not synonymous. This research demonstrates the value of documentation and analysis of the voices of library workers and their critical contributions to nurture and sustain communities through their work.

REFERENCES

American Library Association (ALA). (n.d.). *What are the SDGs? What is the role of libraries? What can you do? Fact sheet*. https://www.ala.org/aboutala/ala-task-force-united-nations-2030-sustainable-development-goals

Daurio, P. V. (2010). *A library and its community: Exploring perceptions of collaboration* [PhD Dissertation]. Portland State University. https://www.proquest.com/docview/612689922

de la Peña McCook, K. (2000). *A place at the table: Participating in community building*. American Library Association. https://digitalcommons.usf.edu/si_facpub/116/

IFLA. (2018). *Libraries and the sustainable development goals: A storytelling manual*. https://www.ifla.org/wp-content/uploads/2019/05/assets/hq/topics/libraries-development/documents/sdg-story-telling-manual.pdf

Kania, J., & Kramer, M. (2011). Collective impact. *Stanford Social Innovation Review*, 9(1), 36–41. https://doi.org/10.48558/5900-KN19

Kinder, M. (2020). *Meet the COVID-19 frontline heroes*. Brookings Institute. https://www.brookings.edu/interactives/meet-the-covid-19-frontline-heroes/

Lenstra, N. (2022). *HEAL (Healthy Eating and Active Living) at the Library*. https://letsmovelibraries.org/about-us/heal/

Lenstra, N., Oguz, F., Winberry, J., & Wilson, L. S. (2021). Supporting social connectedness of older adults during the COVID-19 pandemic: The role of small and rural public libraries. *Public Library Quarterly*, 41(6), 596–616.

Rubenstein, E. L., Burke, S. K., D'Arpa, C., & Lenstra, N. (2021). Health equity and small and rural public libraries during COVID-19. *Proceedings of the Association for Information Science and Technology*, 58(1), 827–829.

United Nations. (2018). *High-level political forum on sustainable development*. https://sustainabledevelopment.un.org/content/documents/19853SDG17_Highlights.updated_format.pdf

United Nations. (2022). *Do you know all 17 SDGs?* https://sdgs.un.org/goals

United Nations. (n.d.). *Sustainability*. https://www.un.org/en/academic-impact/sustainability

Wolff, T. (2016). 10 places where collective impact gets it wrong. *Nonprofit Quarterly*, 23(2), 49–56.

CHAPTER 3

COLLECTIVE PRAXIS: LEVERAGING LOCAL AND HERITAGE-BASED VALUES FOR PUBLIC LIBRARIAN PROFESSIONAL DEVELOPMENT

Vanessa Irvin

ABSTRACT

In Hawaiʻi, two public library systems exist – a traditional municipal branch system and a Native Hawaiian rural community-based library network. The Hawaii State Public Library System (HSPLS) is the traditional municipal library system that services the state's diverse communities with 51 branch locations, plus its federal repository, the Hawaii State Library for the Blind and Print Disabled. The HSPLS primarily serves the local urban communities of Hawaiʻi, diverse in its citizenry. The Native Hawaiian Library, a unit of ALU LIKE, Inc. (a Hawaiian non-profit social services organization), boasts multiple locations across six inhabited Hawaiian Islands, primarily serving rural Hawaiian communities. The HSPLS focuses on traditional public library services offered by MLS-degreed librarians. In contrast, the Native Hawaiian Library (ALU LIKE) focuses on culturally oriented literacy services offered by Hawaiian cultural practitioners. As the state's only library and information sciences (LISs) educational venue, the University of Hawaiʻi at Mānoa's LIS program (UHM LIS) is a nexus point between these two library systems where LIS students learn the value of community-based library services while

How Public Libraries Build Sustainable Communities in the 21st Century
Advances in Librarianship, Volume 53, 37–55
Copyright © 2023 by Vanessa Irvin
Published under exclusive licence by Emerald Publishing Limited
ISSN: 0065-2830/doi:10.1108/S0065-283020230000053004

gaining the traditional technical skills of librarianship concerning Hawai'i as a place of learning and praxis.

This book chapter focuses on outcomes from the IMLS-funded research project called "Hui 'Ekolu," which means "three groups" in the Hawaiian language. From 2018 to 2021, the HSPLS, the Native Hawaiian Library (ALU LIKE), and the UHM LIS Program gathered as "Hui 'Ekolu" to create a community of praxis to share and exchange knowledge to learn from one another to improve professional practice and heighten cultural competency within a Hawaiian context. Native Hawaiian values were leveraged as a nexus point for the three groups to connect and build relationships for sustainable mentorship and culturally competent connections as a model for librarian professional development. The result is a model for collective praxis that leverages local and endemic cultural values for sustainable collaborative professional development for public librarianship.

Keywords: Community of practice; Hawaii; place-based learning; praxis; professional development; public librarians

Public libraries are community-based educational spaces where local cultural norms are the central lens through which librarians most competently provide information services. Within a North American context, contact zones like Chinatowns in large American cities, American Indian reservations contained within rural expanses, and island cultures in urban enclaves resonate with a social discourse of language, behavioral signifiers, and identity constructs that are specific and unique to the cultural group living in a specific area. However, in most North American LIS graduate programs where the terminal master's degree for librarianship is obtained, an Anglo-centric model of librarianship is taught to pre-service librarians, with little integration of diverse frameworks from multiple cultural information paradigms and practices.

It has been lamented that worldwide, LIS programs teach a linear, western, colonized approach to cultivating the professional librarian and archivist identity, hubris, and praxis (Ngoepe et al., 2021; Tumuhairwe, 2013). The western/colonist model of LIS education has been cited as the reason why librarians lack knowledge and appreciation of inclusivity in cataloging materials of various languages and contexts (Diao & Cao, 2016; Farnel et al., 2018a; Guo, 2020; Howard & Knowlton, 2018; Shunqing & Wei, 2018), why librarians non-critically conduct database searches in systems that lack honoring the authentic linguistic expressions of native and world languages (Farnel et al., 2018b; Soto et al., 2021), and why librarians too often inculcate a product-oriented (capitalistic) approach to information services and community-based literacy events that focuses on providing "the book" rather than effectively building and sustaining relationships within the community (Chang, 2000; LeMoine, 2012; Pawley, 1998, 2017).

Collective Praxis

SYNTHESIZING PUBLIC LIBRARIES IN HAWAIʻI

To investigate how the Anglo-centric LIS framework operates in a native land where (de)colonization marks the epistemological makeup of society, I conducted a two-year pilot study (2015–2017) working with 17 public librarians of the HSPLS. Called *The Librarians' Inquiry Forum* (LINQ), this two-year endeavor sought to explore ways to leverage librarians' personal and heritage-based knowledge while engaging technology to decrease or eliminate the geographic gap of miles between the Hawaiian Islands. From LINQ, it was learned that even though many public librarians in Hawaiʻi self-identify as Asian or of mixed Polynesian heritage, serving predominantly Asian or Hawaiian communities, the librarians admitted that their professional practice was to mete out the "traditional" linear, Anglo-centric style of information services that they learned in library school (Irvin et al., 2019; Irvin & Reile, 2018). Additionally, the local knowledge shared in LINQ revealed that while the HSPLS boasts a 51-branch public library system statewide, there also exists a statewide heritage-based public library system in Hawaiʻi called ALU LIKE/The Native Hawaiian Library.

From 1985 to 2005, ALU LIKE/The Native Hawaiian Library operated 10 locations across the islands with full staffing of MLS-degreed Hawaiian librarians, operating solely on federally awarded grant funds for three decades. In recent years, however, funding has decreased to the point that as a unit of the non-profit Hawaiian social services organization, ALU LIKE, Inc. (pronounced "AL-loo LEE-kay"), the Native Hawaiian Library is currently operated across six locations by paraprofessional Hawaiian cultural practitioners, not terminally degreed professional librarians.[1] Thus, ALU LIKE/Native Hawaiian Library needs support with traditional library skills to manage and sustain long-neglected collections and enhance staffing to ignite their communities with access to information and communication technology (ICT) and other community-oriented information services.

On the other hand, the HSPLS, while staffed by MLS-degreed professional librarians, needed support in promoting authentic, culturally appropriate collections, conferring culturally competent public services, and executing culturally authentic programming events because as HSPLS librarians themselves have identified, "they [HSPLS] are lacking authentic Indigenous representation in the branches which keeps Hawaiian people from coming to us" (Hui ʻEkolu participant, "Tia[2]," HSPLS librarian, informal interview, January 17, 2019). In turn, an ALU LIKE participant said: "We [the Native Hawaiian Library] need[s] help with these collections. How do we do the inventory? We need help with doing the library stuff" (Hui ʻEkolu participant, "Kelly," Native Hawaiian Library, informal interview, January 17, 2019).

From LINQ to Hui ʻEkolu

Considering these intersecting factors between HSPLS and ALU LIKE, the question arose: Why aren't these two public library systems working together to share and exchange cultural knowledge, professional practices, and socio-cultural resources? From the LINQ study with HSPLS librarians (Irvin & Reile, 2018, 2020) and early informal interviews during 2017–2018 with the founders of the Native Hawaiian Library, the answer was quick and precise: HSPLS librarians didn't have "the time" (per pilot study outcomes), and ALU LIKE – The Native Hawaiian Library had lost federal funding. Thus, they didn't have the money.

Moreso, through various informal interviews with ALU LIKE and HSPLS administrators, it was mutually realized that ALU LIKE needed staffing support for organizing their library catalogs and collections. In contrast, HSPLS needed staffing support for enacting culturally competent interactions and culturally authentic literacy programs and events. As a faculty member of the UHM LIS Program, I quickly recognized that students at the only American Library Association (ALA)-accredited LIS Program in Hawai'i, would greatly benefit from mentorship working with collaborative teams comprised of Hawaiian cultural practitioners and Hawai'i-based professional librarians interested and invested in providing community-based educational services to the local and native Hawaiian communities. It then became imperative to gather these "three groups" (or "hui 'ekolu" in Hawaiian – pronounced "hooey AYE-koh-loo") for the opportunity to learn, explore, and discover how Hawaiian ways of being and knowing can be synthesized with traditional LIS practices so that library workers across the career lifespan (preservice, paraprofessional, and professional) can enact culturally relevant and competent information services in local and Native Hawaiian communities. The federal entity, the Institute of Museum and Library Services (IMLS),[3] approved a grant application to fund a three-year professional development program (2018–2021) to devise a model to achieve these goals. We called that program Hui 'Ekolu to denote the three groups, HSPLS, ALU LIKE, and UHM LIS.

LOCAL CULTURE AS PRAXIS

Place-based ways of seeing, being, and knowing are vital tenets for respecting diverse communities' unique and specific embedded inclusivities worldwide (Borén & Schmitt, 2021). Reminiscent of the hip hop anthem, "*This is how we do it*" by Montell Jordan (1995), each community has its unique and specific way of reading and inscribing its local world, which connects and intersects with the broader world in unpredictable, organic ways. Literacy practices are diverse from person to person, home to home, community to community, and country to country. Thus, collective information needs and practices are custom to geographic- and heritage-based ontologies. At the same time, within American librarianship, local and native information practices are framed and therefore contained within the Anglo-centric American model of librarianship that was conceptualized and codified by the 1876 librarian convention (i.e., the birth of the American Library Association) and the 1876 report on public libraries (Miksa, 1973). Miksa clarifies:

> The 1876 Special Report has had a unique place in the history of the modern library movement in the United States. Together with the 1876 Philadelphia convention of librarians it marked the emergence of the profession. Standing as the magnum opus of American Library economy, it covered enough of the essentials of librarianship to become "must" reading for the aspiring librarian. (p. 30)

This original paradigm for American librarianship focused on "where the books go": Anglo-centric LIS has a tradition of being centered on "the things" of libraries for people, whereas, on a local level, library services have necessarily revolved around "the needs" of the people who visited the library (Osborne, 2004). These local information needs have been highlighted throughout LIS discourse, with more recent discussions about inclusivity in library services. In this early part of the twenty-first century, the public library service model has become more concerned about ensuring patrons are considered, respected, and heard. Yet, how those services are meted out in rural Appalachia compared to urban Honolulu, for example, will be specific and unique to those geographies and cultures.

Hawai'i is an exciting geography because the population is separated across six inhabited islands of the 137-island chain (Fig. 1).

The inhabited islands' county system is as follows:

Honolulu County	the entire island of O'ahu
Maui County	the islands of Maui, Moloka'i, and Lana'i (and the uninhabited island of Kaho'olawe)
Hawai'i County	the entire "Big Island" also named Hawai'i
Kaua'i County	the entire island of Kaua'i

Like counties within the "lower 48" states of the continental USA, the four counties of the state of Hawai'i are comprised of an intricate network of large

Fig. 1. State of Hawaii. *Source*: Map used with licensed permission via © www.gograph.com/Peterhermesfurian

and small cities, towns, and approximately 35 unincorporated communities (e.g., Miloli'i, the last fishing village of Hawai'i, located on the Big Island). With this zoomed lens into a geographical ontology of Hawai'i, the ideas and actions of the "local" reveal themselves as complex and nuanced. *Local* becomes even more kaleidoscopic when local culture is embedded within a heritage-based native Hawaiian culture. Thus, many questions arise from this consideration, especially in Hawai'i, where a traditional Anglo-centric public library system (HSPLS) and a native Hawaiian public library system (ALU LIKE) coexist.

RESEARCH QUESTIONS

Consequently, the salient questions for exploring the sustainability of librarian practice within a local context like Hawai'i include:

1. How do public library services occur in Hawaii within a native Hawaiian context?
2. What are the differences between the definition and function of "library" for Native Hawaiian libraries versus mainstream American public libraries (e.g., Hawai'i-based libraries)?
3. Is there a collective praxis for public librarianship that is specific and unique to geography and local culture? Is "this is how we do it here" a sustainable aspect of public library service?

Instead of "practice," I intentionally employ the concept of praxis to signify that librarians are embedded information professionals within diverse place-based, knowledge-based communities. Praxis indicates that librarian professional practices occur within contextualized, nuanced spaces where ways of seeing, being and knowing are locally and culturally specific. Once working in a library that lives within a community, a librarian's schooled knowledge from the Anglo-centric model can be profoundly informed by local and heritage-based praxis, especially if librarians collectively gather to engage in inquiry-based mutual support and professional development to synthesize practice with theory. Hence, the research questions and the contextual factors considered were the impetus for why the three Hawai'i-based LIS groups ("Hui 'Ekolu") gathered as a collective community of praxis to discover mutual values of librarianship within a native context.

LITERATURE REVIEW: A CONCEPTUAL FRAMEWORK FOR ANALYSIS

An analysis of Hui 'Ekolu is informed by three concepts that guide conceptual thinking and understanding of the data collected, the data interpreted, and the way to tell that data's story. Based on a theoretical framework synthesizing the ideals of "research is ceremony" (Wilson, 2008), affective knowledge (Schiele, 2002), and "triangulation as meaning" (Aluli-Meyer, 2006), Hui 'Ekolu was enacted with a methodology involving interwoven interactions across groups. While the initial conceptualization for the program focused on "three groups," from those three groups, it became clear that there were *seven groups* within the project, totaling 35 participants [i.e., 20 participants comprising LIS students, ALU LIKE library workers, and HSPLS librarians divided into five hui ("groups" in Hawaiian), plus the Native Hawaiian library association hui, Nā Hawai'i 'Imi Loa (NHIL), who served as the training facilitators, and the Hui 'Ekolu advisory council as a hui of LIS administrators, practitioners, students, and scholars].

Indigenous scholar Shawn Wilson (2008) identifies that "research is ceremony" because research is automatically qualitative and ethnographic from a heritage-based, native point of view. After all, for Wilson, learning often happens within the nuances of honoring protocols as a framework for building and sustaining relationships. Wilson posits that ethnographic research is ceremonial because action-based reflective inquiry is based on a collectivity where multiple realities exist simultaneously and are all valid. Wilson (2008) also asserts that research as the ceremony is relational because "bringing people, places, and things together so that they share the same space is what ceremony is all about" (p. 87). With Hui 'Ekolu, gathering people from various cultural locations (i.e., LIS students, cultural practitioners, paraprofessional library workers, and professional librarians) is action-based with multiple, interwoven layers of socio-cultural styles and norms. Thus, relationship building is reflective for all involved. In two years of training and online communications (interrupted by the COVID-19 pandemic), communal norms were established based on mainstream American cultural protocols. But also, a deeper look into Hui 'Ekolu's various modes of activity exposed nuanced practices that were inherently local, cultural, unique, and specific to Hawaiian values.

Thus, the work of Hui 'Ekolu privileged "the stuff" of localized social interactions as valid sources of knowledge. Jerome Schiele (2002) posits that "life experiences are essential for furthering knowledge" (p. 190). The Hui 'Ekolu community organically applied a holistic logic to the process of working with multiple parts of formed groups where feeling and thought within the spiritual oneness of human beings were honored. The dynamics of how various intersecting relationships expanded with fluidity (i.e., things are going well) and contracted with tension (i.e., things are not going well), served as a template to organize meaningful research into a triangulation of meaning where we use our body to see, our mind to know, and our spirit to reveal (re)newed questions, reflections, and considerations for working with others as a community of praxis (Aluli-Meyer, 2006).

METHODOLOGY: DESIGNING COLLECTIVE PRAXIS

Hui 'Ekolu was designed to focus on "three groups" coming together as a collaborative community of praxis to represent the career lifespan of public librarianship: master's degree students of the UHM LIS Program (pre-service), Hawaiian cultural practitioners working and managing heritage-based libraries (paraprofessional), and master's degree librarians working with the HSPLS (professional).

To sustain the organizational integrity of the project, 15 nationally and locally renowned LIS administrators and professionals were invited to represent theory, practice, and research in native and public librarianship, management of Hawai'i-based libraries, and LIS education in Hawai'i and beyond.

The primary program activity involved gathering the Hui 'Ekolu community biannually for two-day training sessions: one held at the beginning of each "new year" in August for the beginning of the academic year and January at the beginning of the societal year. Training sessions were facilitated by the Native Hawaiian Library Association, Nā Hawai'i 'Imi Loa (NHIL).[4]

NHIL facilitated biannual training to the Hui 'Ekolu community to teach traditional library skills (e.g., collection development, language specification for database searching, and community engagement) with a Hawaiian lens. The trainings were organized to anticipate that program participants would take knowledge exchanged at the trainings and independently work together in their location-specific hui (groups) via online communications on *Slack*, email, virtual meetups, or face-to-face collaboration. In addition to the biannual NHIL trainings, Hui 'Ekolu activities included the local work of Hui 'Ekolu participants in their location-specific teams/groups, feedback from the Hui 'Ekolu advisory council, feedback and communication from a project evaluator representing the funding agency, the IMLS, and ongoing NHIL planning and communications. The advisory council met twice a year to discuss and advise on the project's progress. Hui 'Ekolu ran from May 1, 2018 – June 30, 2021.[5]

Hui 'Ekolu employed a "practice-based professional development model" (Yukawa & Harada, 2009) to guide the discovery, collection, and analysis of a variety of qualitative data coming from the activities of the project. This qualitative approach to creating a collective community of praxis with UHM LIS, ALU LIKE, and HSPLS created a context through which the social intercourse of multiple participants across multiple library organizations in Hawai'i allowed for questions about professional praxis to be presented, asked, and explored (Brown, 2012). Indeed, the research questions can only be authentically answered by Hawaiian library workers and librarians; thus, responses to the research questions would be based on a triangulation of various data sources from the intense, multi-layered, interwoven interactions and relationship-building that happened with Hui 'Ekolu. Thus, I defer to the methodological approach of inquiry-based learning (Brown, 2012) and inquiry-based leadership to guide my actions and reflections in collaboratively facilitating Hui 'Ekolu and collecting necessary data from various sources (Brown, 2012).

DATA AND ANALYSIS: THE IMPACTS OF HUI 'EKOLU COLLECTIVE PRAXIS

Hui 'Ekolu collected data in the following ways: participant interviews (formal and informal), reflective memos (from the principal investigator and research assistant), field notes from library site visits and training sessions, meeting notes from advisory council meetings, knowledge-based artifacts created during

Collective Praxis 45

training session activities, images, participant surveys from trainings, and online communications via email and the online collaboration platform, *Slack*.[6]

For this presentation, three data types are highlighted to make sense of how cultural knowledge is centered (or not) in Hui 'Ekolu activities as a community of collective praxis. To that end, *communication from Slack is* reviewed to learn how participants connected with inquiry questions posed online beyond the Hui 'Ekolu trainings. Additionally, we composed *field notes* from library site visits to ensure that our lens was not overly critical and not glazed in terms of missing valuable relevancies. Reflective memos have been meaningful for analyzing ways in which Hui 'Ekolu is a sustainable method for librarian professional development.

Hui 'Ekolu is a sustainable method for librarian professional development. Triangulating the three data samples uncovers how Hawaiian ontology is organically centered within the Hawai'i-based LIS professional community.

Slack Communications: Sharing Knowledge Online

Slack participant communications were helpful because they gave Hui 'Ekolu community members a space to further reflect and respond to inquiry questions posed during the weekend workshop sessions and check in between training sessions. Fig. 2 shows a data sample of participant communication on *Slack* where Hui 'Ekolu members reflect on a question that emerged from a training session. The question that emerged from Hui 'Ekolu's collective praxis was: "What is a Native Hawaiian Library?" *Slack* communications captured indicators of cultural nuance and relevancy within the participant interactions and responses.

Throughout Hui 'Ekolu, participants communicated via various platforms: email, phone calls, face-to-face at trainings, at work, and *Slack's* online collaboration workspace. Fig. 2 shows that 3 of the 20 active participants responded to the question, "What is a Native Hawaiian library?" Two respondents were Hawaiian cultural practitioners and library workers with the Native Hawaiian Library/ALU LIKE, Inc. The third respondent was an HSPLS librarian of Hawaiian heritage.

In Fig. 2, the participants' responses to the question, "What is a Native Hawaiian Library?" convey an embodiment and identity of Hawaiian cultural knowledge that the participants connected to the idea of "library." For example, the first respondent, "Dana," a Hawaiian cultural practitioner with ALU LIKE, connects "library" with hula dancing as a form of embodied knowledge. Dana immediately sees the library as beyond a building and posits that the library "is our environment, as a whole." The second respondent, "Gisa," a Hawaiian librarian with the HSPLS, picks up on Dana's analogy and progresses that vision with the insight:

> The hula dancer is the connection between nature and humanity, just as librarians are the connection between information/knowledge and humanity. The hula dancer observes protocols in the exchange with nature, just as librarians must observe protocols in the exchange of information/knowledge. There are all kinds of information that exist in this world, and all of it must be treated with care: we cannot offer freely what is not meant to be offered freely. We have to be aware of what to share, how it is to be shared, and with whom it can be shared with. In observing protocols of the transfer of information and knowledge, we honor the sources that they come from. And honoring our sources enables us to give the information/knowledge the protection and power it needs to last throughout time. ("Gisa," HSPLS librarian, Hui 'Ekolu on *Slack*, November 2018)

46   VANESSA IRVIN

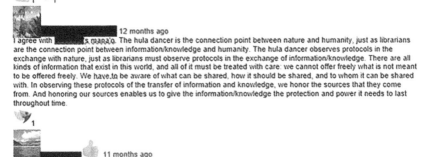

Fig. 2. Participant Communication on Slack, November 2018.

The third participant, "Alma," who is a Hawaiian cultural practitioner as well as a library worker with ALU LIKE's Native Hawaiian Library, encapsulates the discussion by sharing her wisdom about the connection between hula and knowledge as ceremony:

> Anciently ... the record keepers of events and history ... presented this knowledge [as hula] (author insertion), whether for ceremony, protocol, blessings, religious practices, and as entertainment. Hula, and ʻoli [Hawaiian chant] (author insertion) were the formal presentation of a library of oral history. ("Alma," Hui ʻEkolu on *Slack*, November 2018)

Collectively, these *Slack* responses present a rich discussion and demonstration of Aluli-Meyer's (2006) concept of "triangulation of meaning," where the Hawaiian worldview is wholistic in incorporating the energies of the body, mind, and soul as one presentation and understanding of the concept of "library." The discussion between Dana, Gisa, and Alma illustrates the beauty of the Hawaiian worldview as applied to the idea of what a library is, how a library functions, and how librarian practice is enacted and contributes to a knowledge-based society.

Alma's, Dana's, and Gisa's contributions are essential demonstrations of conversations where we recognize ways in which cultural knowledge and values, when expressed, discussed, and exchanged, informs LIS theory and librarian professional identity and practice in their specific geographies. This shared knowledge helps everyone in the community of praxis to broaden their ideas and understanding of "library" within a specific cultural context. This approach to LIS practitioner inquiry appropriately situates local and native/endemic knowledge in the context in which that knowledge lives. Regardless of heritage or background, all members of the Hui ʻEkolu collective praxis take the wisdom of their Hawaiian librarian colleagues and apply that information to their socio-cultural approach to LIS professional practice in Hawaiʻi. In this data sample from *Slack*, we appreciate how collective learning happens with Hawaiian participants sharing their information/knowledge and understanding of their worldview about what a library means within a Hawaiian ontology. The collective community retrieves this knowledge, learns from it, and adds it to their understanding of the geography of where they live and work.

Field Notes: Visualizing Place-Based Knowledge

Field notes were another data source that helped visualize the place-based knowledge of ALU LIKE and HSPLS libraries (see Fig. 3). For the author as principal investigator, it was crucial to compose detailed field notes to record a re-creation of the library spaces as best as possible as follows.

Questions from this site visit included: How does learning cultural knowledge impact LIS professional practice in diverse service communities? What is the catalyst for locally sustaining cross-cultural LIS relationships built in a collective community of praxis like Hui ʻEkolu? How will the knowledge learned via the Hui ʻEkolu model be sustainable for Zara, Alma, Gisa, and all the participants? In other words, what will stay with the participants as new knowledge for LIS praxis? Will this new knowledge impact the librarians' professional identity? Does a collective praxis fuse the personal and professional toward a holistic LIS identity?

The field notes show that collective praxis helps librarians gain a holistic LIS identity. We see that goal actualized with Zara's (who is not Hawaiian) enthusiasm to incorporate what she learned in the Hui ʻEkolu training into her everyday professional practice. Zara's willingness and excitement to learn Hawaiian phrases for the library attests to how local and native culture enact culturally appropriate and competent library service.

48 VANESSA IRVIN

Field notes - HSPLS and ALU LIKE Library Visit – January 2019

We left the house around 9:40 a.m. and arrived at the HSPLS Library at about 10:50 a.m. This HSPLS library is located in a predominantly Native Hawaiian community. The library building is traditionally built with a lobby that leads into a circulation/reference desk area where the library staff workspace is located directly behind. The beautifully decorated children's area is to the right of the circ/ref desk and the young adult/adult area is to the left of the circ/ref desk with eight computer charging stations and lounge area.

Going into the library - for this time of day, mid-week - the library was well attended. I counted about 25 people in the teen/adult area .... young to old, male/female about equal in ratio. In the children's room there was a family there - a mom and dad, and 2 boys between 3-5 years of age.

I then saw our librarian Hui 'Ekolu HSPLS participant, "Zara," at the reference desk and was warmly greeted by her. I could tell that the experiences she's having at training are positively affecting her ... she greeted us in the Hawaiian way with the side hug/cheek kiss.

After about 20 minutes of independently touring the library, Zara escorted us into her office in the back. She offered us tea and water. Once settled in our seating, it was clear that Zara was enthusiastic about talking with us. Zara said that from Hui 'Ekolu training2, she loved the flashcards activity. In fact, she is adapting that tool for her own personal professional development in learning Hawaiian words for library signage. She showed us a HSPLS handout of library sign phrases translated into Hawaiian. She had 3 sets of index cards on rings - like the flashcard idea from training2. She's going to transpose the handout onto those cards so that she can learn Hawaiian words.

Zara is enthusiastic about learning things that are directly related to her work - and that she understands to improve her work. Zara is incorporating new knowledge that she believes connects with what she's already doing in her professional practice in the name of doing her work "better". Another part of the training Zara liked was the group discussion on weeding. She appreciated learning the different contexts in which even her HSPLS colleagues are working.

After we left HSPLS Library, we did lunch, then headed to the neighboring ALU LIKE library location. This library is a ground level ranch home with a front lanai and grass yard, fenced all around, located in a residential neighborhood just a few short blocks from the HSPLS library. At this Native Hawaiian Library branch, there is a guardian shrine seated at the entrance of the yard and building.

This ALU LIKE library is clean and modest. I would guesstimate that the collection is about 500 books total - children's and adult collections. Their office area looked busy with a lot of files, folders, papers, and miscellaneous artifacts piled and collected. There is a large table for discussion with an ALU LIKE tablecloth: it is large, rectangular, seating 8 around. Hui 'Ekolu participants, Ms. Alma and Paul invited us to sit at the table with them. We began to have a conversation about the collection there. The collection is primarily children's books in Hawaiian, plus a reference collection that Ms. Alma suspects may be a bit out of date. Ms. Alma and Paul shared that they mostly use the space for kupuna (senior citizen) community activities and events. The space is not primarily used for traditional (Anglo-centric) library services anymore.

Fig. 3.   Principal Investigator Field Notes from Hui 'Ekolu Site Visit, January 2019.

Reflective Memos: Learning Local Intersectionalities

Another indicator of the sustainability of the Hui 'Ekolu model is that Zara, Alma, and Gisa became well-acquainted with one another due to the Hui 'Ekolu trainings. This relationship-building resulted in ALU LIKE conducting library programming at Zara's HSPLS location on a few occasions. However, reciprocity seemed challenging due to conflicting schedules and concerns about the impacts of librarian outreach based on HSPLS policies. Case in point, we recall Tia's concern from earlier in this chapter where during an informal interview, she reflected that the HSPLS was "lacking authentic Indigenous representation in the branches which keeps Hawaiian people from coming to us" (Hui 'Ekolu participant, "Tia," HSPLS librarian, informal interview, January 17, 2019). The collective praxis of the Hui 'Ekolu community revealed a compelling model for sustainable public librarian professional development based on socio-cultural local and native/endemic knowledge as the geography upon which wholistic professional relationships, therefore professional practices, are built.

The following *reflective memo* (Fig. 4), composed by the principal investigator for Hui 'Ekolu, reveals the holistic intersectionality of cultural values for Hawai'i-based LIS students, library workers, librarians, and native cultural practitioners of the Hui 'Ekolu community of praxis as follows.

At the time of this reflective memo, Hui 'Ekolu had been a community of collective praxis for two years. After two years of mutual learning and relationship-building, Hawaiian values were identifiable as a framework for Hui 'Ekolu. In harmony with Wilson's (2008) concept of "research is ceremony," Hui 'Ekolu was framed around ceremony. Collective work began and ended with a ceremony to honor the gathering of people. Information was transparent, and the project administration was held accountable for sharing funding clarifications, publications, and research intentionalities and practices. Local and Hawaiian culture honors everyone's knowledge; trust is built by recognizing that everyone is a leader and has something to bring to the group. Listening, responding, and following through were vital aspects of mutual respect within the Hui 'Ekolu community. Leadership was circular, not linear; everyone's questions, comments, and concerns were as valid as anyone else's, including LIS student participants. For example, LIS students were integral members of small group activities where

---

Reflective Memo – January 2020

Ways in which Hui 'Ekolu demonstrates Indigenous approach to practitioner inquiry:

- ceremonial opening and closing of community activities and events (honoring the spaces we gather brings in the attention and guidance of elders seen and unseen)
- transparency with information to the collective community (funding clarifications, sharing publications, sharing
- practices - like ethnographic data collection (site visits)), yet: honoring sacred information with sensitivity and wisdom within mini-communities within the collective community (nothing is secret, but some information is sacred, as in: emotional sharing, personal revelations, unpacking frustration) - this is the crux of where trust is built - people have to trust what is said and what is not said and honor only what is heard by their own ears
- honoring the knowledge everyone brings to the table; everyone is a leader - another area where trust is built
- respecting the needs of others - requires listening/responding to what people want and need and following through to meet those needs
- including everyone in the process of learning (this is vital for successful hālāwai - people are not engaged when talked to constantly - asking for people's expertise is very important)
- realizing that everyone carries their cultural knowledge with them even if it's not obvious (like "Kia" doing hula!)
- "I AM THE BOOK"

Fig. 4. Reflective Memo January 2020.

their pre-service questions about community-based information practices were leveraged with LIS professionalism and Hawaiian cultural knowledge. Inclusivity was a profound part of the learning process.

Envisioning the Collective Praxis Model

Intersectionality of socio-cultural knowledge and identity became evident with community discourse because gifts and talents were shared across cultures and identities, as trust was built, over time, amongst participants. Collaborative activities during the biannual trainings brought forth the wholistic identity of "I AM THE BOOK" by Hui 'Ekolu participants. The expression "I am the book" arose from a group-wide reflective activity centered once again on the question, "What is a Hawaiian library?" The culminating answer of "I am the book" conveys how local and native knowledge (of any geography) renders a wholistic idea, perception, and agency toward what a library is, what a library does, and how we, as local to our unique and specific geographies, carry that understanding in a myriad of ways. The Hui 'Ekolu model confirms that as public library practitioners, we exercise an intersectional holistic knowledge of the communities we serve. When we actively connect collectively to share this knowledge, our collective praxis becomes a tremendous power for the public good. The collective praxis framework for Hui 'Ekolu when expressed visually, reveals intricate interconnectivity (see Fig. 5).

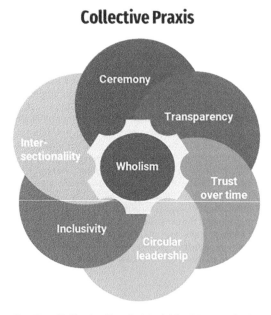

Fig. 5. Collective Praxis Model by Vanessa Irvin.

DISCUSSION: THE GEOGRAPHY OF LIS PRACTITIONER INQUIRY

This chapter shares ways in which cultural knowledge is specific and unique to a community's geography and, thus, to a community of praxis' relationship- and knowledge-building endeavors. As such knowledge is unique and sacred to space and place, it renders itself as a sustainable way to create, nurture, and maintain knowledge-bearing work in the form of LIS practice in public libraries. The qualitative data from the Hawai'i-based Hui 'Ekolu project encourages us to consider the Hui 'Ekolu professional development model as a sustainable approach for collective praxis for public librarians in various socio-cultural geographies worldwide. Hui 'Ekolu demonstrates that a sustainable way to learn from one another as a community of praxis involves centering local and native values and practices within traditional LIS work across locations and within organizations, ongoing and collectively over time.

Researcher Identity and Limitations

Admittedly, homing in on the local and endemic ("native" or "indigenous") ontologies of a geography and people raise complex concerns, especially if you are not a member of the local community. For example, as an African American woman from the Eastern Seaboard of the United States, 5,000 miles from Hawai'i, one could ask,

> Um, author? Besides you being at those trainings, on *Slack* reading those posts, and documenting your library visits, who are you to share the outcomes of Hui 'Ekolu given that you are not Native Hawaiian nor Hawai'i-born and raised?

These questions are fair and essential for every qualitative researcher who finds themselves in socio-cultural contexts away from their own to consider.

A plethora of research has been published that delves into the researcher's identity. In recent years, there's been ongoing discourse about privilege and allyship: how to discard privilege and do allyship "right." I am here to say that one never discards their privilege because we are all privileged in various contexts at various times. I am here to say that we may never do allyship "right" because there is always something that will be missed: misunderstood, misaligned, misconstrued, and mismanaged. Also, allyship is never guaranteed because outsiders are not always welcomed.

I refer back to Brown's (2012) article, "Seeking Questions, Not Answers," as a guide to my intentionality and agency during my work with Hui 'Ekolu. I intended to focus on what it means to ask questions to learn from colleagues and cultural practitioners; to the best of my ability, I respectfully considered elders in the LIS profession and the Hawaiian culture. As an African American woman, I felt my agency would be an understandable and reasonable correlation between Hawaiian librarians and their worldviews coupled with my worldview based on my culture and heritage. Alas, I learned that cultural groups often have thick walls forged by history, trauma, and grief that, while similar, are encoded differently. Thus, building trust often involves funambulating a delicate journey between kindred groups, culturally, socially, and geographically. Relationships tread a shifting ocean floor where rules, protocols, and kindnesses unpredictably shift from one conversation to another, moment to moment.

I don't want to say that LIS inquiry scholars and practitioners do best when they only approach their work within their own cultural or social groups. That exclusivity would keep LIS as westernized, colonized, and Anglo-centric as it is now in its theoretical foundations, conceptual frameworks, and professional practices. Therefore, xenophobic limitations become opportunities for LIS scholars and practitioners, particularly those of us in the 13% minoritized avenue of LIS demographics, to reach out to one another, and face the risks, challenges, and hardships to come to the other side of reflective inquiry which makes our work as information professionals pivotal and consequential to humanity's ever-evolving information needs. This kind of work takes commitment, time, and a thick skin.

Limitations of Inquiry-Based Practitioner Research

Another limitation of inquiry-based practitioner research is that to arrive at an idea about the sustainability of practice or theory, we make choices that privilege data while simultaneously silencing data. As a scholar, I am constantly (re)learning that the telling of a story precisely as it happened is an improbability because even though we all agree and consent to participate in research that will be disseminated, none of us ever read the fine print. We rarely subscribe to the adage, "I said what I said," especially when it comes to ways our culture may be represented beyond our control due to the unpredictable ways readers respond to text. In qualitative ethnographic research, we scholars have a responsibility and accountability to be extraordinarily sensitive to the words, actions, and experiences entrusted to us by others while telling a meaningful story that sheds light on an idea, concept, method, or practice. We must be tender in our storytelling because it might not be our story to tell even with the greatest of intentions. I hope and pray that the presentation I have shared in this chapter is understood and received with the intention and sincerity of heart I have written, interpreted, and discussed.

CONCLUSION

That said, the collective praxis model, as revealed by Hui 'Ekolu, behooves us to consider the sustainability of professional librarian practice as a collective, collaborative requisite because Hawai'i's specific and unique geography centers all the challenges we often face for librarian professional development: distance, local culture, and native/endemic values. Hui 'Ekolu examined how public librarians could sustain a collective praxis for professional development over time. The program sought to figure out: What "thing" would make such a program sustainable? The answer was about privileging and honoring the local values that are native and endemic to a place's geography. In Hawai'i, Hawaiian ways of thinking, seeing, and being must be included in how information is created and identified with knowledge for librarians providing information services in Hawai'i.

Collective Praxis 53

For another geography, the ontology will be similar in centering on socio-cultural local and endemic ontologies and traditions, but the "how we do it" part will be specific and unique to every community's history, culture, and social point of view. Therefore, a sustainable way to engage in librarian professional development is for librarians to gather consistently across communication platforms (i.e., face to face, online, etc.) to collectively learn how local and native culture in the space and place (geography) where they work is specific, unique, and shared.

The professional development model presented in this research intersects with a collective impact for LIS primarily by dissolving the silo-oriented approach that tends to occur in isolated library locations in rural communities and urban enclaves. The community that was built with Hui 'Ekolu confirms for LIS that meaningful, sustainable ideas, connections, and renewed practices emerge when librarians practice as a community, intentionally building relationships over time. An inquiry-based, collective praxis approach to communal professional development requires patience, resilience, and grace to center what we do as librarians, and the ways in which we ask hard questions to learn from one another iteratively. When we strategically work in partnership to learn about our work experiences and how they impact our ongoing practice and professional identity, the goal of alleviating librarian apathy and burnout toward a long-term enjoyable career is achieved.

ACKNOWLEDGMENTS

This work is the outcome of a workshop presented at the 41st Ethnography in Education Research Forum held at the University of Pennsylvania in February 2020 as part of the dissemination efforts for the Hui 'Ekolu grant program sponsored by the Institute for Museum and Library Services (IMLS), 2018–2021. The Hui 'Ekolu program was cleared by the Internal Review Board (IRB) of the University of Hawai'i at Mānoa; thus, all participant locations, quotes, and contributions are presented anonymously with permission. The author gratefully acknowledges Valerie Crabbe, Stacey Aldrich, Rich Gazan, Violet Harada, Sarah Nakashima, and Rae Montague for assistance and support with this research and appreciates the contributions of the 35 participants of Hui 'Ekolu, its stakeholders, and advisory board members.

NOTES

1. We use ALU LIKE and Native Hawaiian Library interchangeably throughout this chapter. ALU LIKE is the parent organization of The Native Hawaiian Library. However, the Native Hawaiian Library director and staff also perform work in other aspects of the ALU LIKE organization. Thus, they self-identify as "ALU LIKE."
2. All participant names are pseudonyms.
3. For more information about the IMLS, visit: http://www.imls.gov.
4. For more information about Nā Hawai'i 'Imi Loa, visit: https://www.nahawaiiimiloa.com/.
5. Hui 'Ekolu went virtual from April 2020 until the close of the project due to the COVID-19 pandemic.
6. For more information about *Slack*, visit: http://www.slack.com.

REFERENCES

Aluli-Meyer, M. (2006). Changing the culture of research: An introduction to the triangulation of meaning. *Hulili, 3*(1), 263–279.

Borén, T., & Schmitt, P. (2021). Knowledge and place-based development – Towards networks of deep learning. *European Planning Studies, 30*(5), 1–18. https://doi.org/10.1080/09654313.2021.1928042

Brown, K. (2012). Seeking questions, not answers: The potential of inquiry-based approaches to teaching library and information science. *Journal of Education for Library and Information Science, 53*(3), 189–199.

Chang, D. (2000). *Knowledge, culture, and identity: American influence on the development of library and information science in South Korea since 1945.* University of Austin-Texas.

Diao, J., & Cao, H. (2016). Chronology in Cataloging Chinese archaeological reports: An investigation of cultural bias in the library of congress classification. *Cataloging & Classification Quarterly, 54*(4), 244–262. https://doi.org/10.1080/01639374.2016.1150931

Farnel, S., Koufogiannakis, D., Bigelow, I., Carr-Wiggin, A., Feisst, D., Lar-Son, K., & Laroque, S. (2018a). Unsettling our practices: Decolonizing description at the University of Alberta Libraries. *The International Journal of Information, Diversity, & Inclusion (IJIDI), 2*(1/2), Special Section – Visual Presentations. https://jps.library.utoronto.ca/index.php/ijidi/article/view/32218

Farnel, S., Koufogiannakis, D., Bigelow, I., Carr-Wiggin, A., Feisst, D., Lar-Son, K., & Laroque, S. (2018b). Rethinking representation: Indigenous peoples and contexts at the University of Alberta Libraries. *The International Journal of Information, Diversity, & Inclusion (IJIDI), 2*(3), 9–23. https://doi.org/10.33137/ijidi.v2i3.32190

Guo, W. (2020). From a political order to a knowledge structure: The influence of western library science on Chinese classical literary system. *Neohelicon, 47,* 131–145. https://doi.org/10.1007/s11059-019-00511-3

Howard, S. A., & Knowlton, S. A. (2018). Browsing through bias: The Library of Congress classification and subject headings for African American studies and LGBTQIA studies. *Library Trends, 67*(1), 74–88. https://doi.org/10.1353/lib.2018.0026

Irvin, V., Cho, N., & Nakashima, S. (2019). Seeking an intentional crossroads: Working towards an understanding of community building in Hawai'i Public Libraries. *Collaborative Librarianship, 11*(3), Article 8. https://digitalcommons.du.edu/collaborativelibrarianship/vol11/iss3/8

Irvin, V., & Reile, W. (2018). LINQing librarians for better practice: Using *Slack* to facilitate professional learning and development. *Public Library Quarterly, 37*(2), 166–179. https://doi.org/10.1080/01616846.2017.1396198

Irvin, V., & Reile, W. (2020). Linking inquiry and practice with online librarian learning and development. In M. H. Moen & S. A. Buchanan (Eds.), *Leading professional development: Growing librarians for the Digital Age* (pp. 20–28). Libraries Unlimited.

Jordan, M. (1995). This is how we do it [Song.] Def Jam Recordings. Office music video. https://www.youtube.com/watch?v=0hiUuL5uTKc

LeMoine, B. (2012). Nailing jelly to the wall: Understanding postmodernism's influence on library information science. *Library Philosophy and Practice.* https://digitalcommons.unl.edu/libphilprac/701/

Miksa, F. (1973). The making of the 1876 special report on public libraries. *Journal of Library History, Philosophy, and Comparative Librarianship, 8*(1), 30–40. http://www.jstor.org/stable/25540392

Ngoepe, M., Saurombe, N., Lowry, J., & Sutherland, T. (2021). Africanisation of the South African archival curriculum: A preliminary study of undergraduate courses in an open distance e-learning environment. *Education for Information, 37*(1), 53–68.

Osborne, R. (2004). *From outreach to equity: Innovative models of library policy and practice.* American Library Association.

Pawley, C. (1998). Hegemony's handmaid? The library and information studies curriculum from a class perspective. *The Library Quarterly, 68*(2), 123–144.

Pawley, C. (2017). "Missionaries of the book" or "Central Intelligence" agents: Gender and ideology in the contest for library education in twentieth-century America. *Libraries: Culture, History, and Society, 1*(1), 72–96.

Schiele, J. (2002). Afrocentricity: An emerging paradigm in social work practice. In A. Mazama (Ed.), *The Afrocentric paradigm* (pp. 185–199). Africa World Press.

Shunqing, C., & Wei, G. (2018). From the imperial catalogue to western library science: The loss of meaning for classical Chinese literature. *Orbis Litterarum*, *73*(4), 328–340.

Soto, A., Heart Sanchez, A. B., Mueller-Alexander, J. M., & Martin, J. (2021). Researching Native Americans: Reflections on vocabulary, search strategies, and technology. *Online Searcher*, *45*(5), 10–19.

Tumuhairwe, G. K. (2013). Analysis of Library and Information Science/Studies (LIS) education today: The inclusion of indigenous knowledge and multicultural issues in LIS Curriculum. IFLA WLIC 2013 – Singapore – Future Libraries: Infinite Possibilities in Session 125 – Education and Training with Library Services to Multicultural Populations and Indigenous Matters Special Interest Group. http://library.ifla.org/id/eprint/276/1/125-tumhuwaire-en.pdf

Wilson, S. (2008). *Research is ceremony: Indigenous research methods*. Fernwood.

Yukawa, J., & Harada, V. (2009). Librarian-Teacher partnerships for inquiry learning: Measures of effectiveness for a practice-based model of professional development. *Evidence Based Library and Information Practice*, *4*(2), 97–119.

CHAPTER 4

COMMUNITY ENGAGEMENT THROUGH PUBLIC LIBRARY SOCIAL INCLUSION: THE VIEW AND PRACTICE OF LIBRARIANS IN GUNUNGKIDUL COUNTY, YOGYAKARTA, INDONESIA

Ida Fajar Priyanto, Agung Wibawa and Siti Indarwati

ABSTRACT

Gunungkidul Public Library in Yogyakarta, Indonesia, provides not only reading materials, but also a place to develop the community to produce various products to sell. The librarians in Gunungkidul have been holding various training sessions for the community – from how to make food and beverages to online marketing and preserving and reviving tradition and culture in their community. The librarians train the community to practice making various local products in the library and then the community and the librarians make and sell the products in the library and other places, including online markets. The products they make vary from cassava crackers to herbal medicine and from batik clothes to t-shirts. They also revived traditional choirs that had never been conducted for years. The librarians sometimes also invite experts or any skillful persons to train the community. Within the last two years, due to the COVID-19 pandemic, the training programs were moved to some rural libraries. The librarians hold the training in rural libraries instead of the county library in order to avoid the crowd during the pandemic. Luckily the moving

How Public Libraries Build Sustainable Communities in the 21st Century
Advances in Librarianship, Volume 53, 57–72
Copyright © 2023 by Ida Fajar Priyanto, Agung Wibawa and Siti Indarwati
Published under exclusive licence by Emerald Publishing Limited
ISSN: 0065-2830/doi:10.1108/S0065-283020230000053005

from the county public library to rural libraries has made more people engage in the library activities. The communities are enthusiastic to take part as they do not need to go too far away from their homes and they feel excited to learn and practice making products in the library as they can have more income.

Keywords: Rural public library; community engagement; social inclusion; Indonesia; cultural training program; PerpuSeru Program; community training

INTRODUCTION

Libraries are viewed as places for learning and self-development. People visit a library to learn and develop their knowledge and interests. Public libraries welcome anyone from any community for various activities, from looking for information resources; reading books and other media; studying their own subjects; to practicing their talents with friends. Due to patrons' differences in learning styles and interests, libraries provide various learning spaces and resources in order to best support them. Rural public libraries not only provide reading materials, but they also host a variety of activities for their communities. This purpose has been adopted in rural public libraries in Indonesia, especially in the last one decade. This chapter discusses the role of rural and public libraries to support the communities in developing various skills, preserving traditional performing arts, and coping with social and financial problems.

Indonesia is a country of over 17,000 islands. The big islands include Borneo, Java, and Sumatra in the western part and Sulawesi and Papua in the eastern part. The Indonesian population is nearly 300 million, which places it as the fourth biggest population in the world after China, India, and the United States and is one third of the total population of the ASEAN countries. Most of the big islands of Indonesia such as Sumatra, Borneo, Sulawesi, and Papua are not as densely populated as that of Java. Borneo, Papua, Sulawesi, and Sumatra have about 6.13%, 2.02%, 7.43%, and 21.73% of the population, respectively. Java, on the other hand, is a smaller island but it has 55.94% of the population.

Another interesting phenomenon is seen in the Indonesian population in which the number of people aged 40 years old or below accounts for 64.69%, while those aged above 40 years are 33.44%. In addition, the number of people living in the cities is also increasing. According to the 2019 data, the number of people living in cities is 55.8% of the total population and it is projected that by 2025, the number will reach 59.3% (Jayani, 2019). According to Kameke (2022), the population of Indonesia is similar to that of Brunei and Malaysia in which the number of Brunei's, Indonesian, and Malaysian population whose age range is between 20 and 54 years old is 57.3%, 52.4%, and 52.8% consecutively. With regard to libraries, this means that public libraries in Indonesia have started to consider their millennial and digital native users. The above reality is also reflected in the libraries' effort to change the design of activities and services. So far, the libraries in Indonesia have taken into consideration the changing landscape of users and their interests as a basis for redesign of the libraries' activities. These activities include helping people with social exclusion and with economic viability. These libraries invite talented young people from the community to provide training for the public.

Data from the National Library of the Republic of Indonesia show that the total number of libraries is 164,610 (see Fig. 1). This number comprises 34 provincial libraries; 496 city and county libraries; 1,685 sub-district public libraries; 33,929 rural libraries, 113,561 school libraries; 2,057 academic libraries; and 3,074 special libraries (Suharyanto, 2022). Furthermore, Suharyanto (2022) also states that there are 6,316 community libraries. School libraries are the biggest in number (68.98%); however, the condition of most school libraries depends on the capability of the local authorities to support them as public schools are under the management of the local authorities. Meanwhile the condition of private school libraries depends on the capability of each school or the association or organization that manages the schools. Many private schools are organized by religious organizations such as Bopkri (Christian schools), Nahdlatul Ulama (Islamic schools), Muhammadiyah (Islamic schools), and Tarakanita (Catholic schools). A religious organization such as Muhammadiyah, for example, has 1,094 basic schools, 1,128 middle schools, and 558 high schools, 554 vocational schools, besides 172 higher education institutions and 67 religious schools (Majlis Dikdasmen PP Muhammadiyah, 2022).

A similar condition exists in academic libraries, where public higher education institutions have libraries; while the condition of private higher education libraries depends on their own management or the organizations to which they belong. Similar to school libraries, academic libraries also have associations with other academic libraries that support collaboration and mutual development. The associations for academic libraries include Forum Perpustakaan Perguruan Tinggi Negeri (Forum of Public Higher Education Libraries), Forum Perpustakaan Perguruan Tinggi Indonesia (Forum of Indonesian Higher Education Libraries), Forum Perpustakaan Perguruan Tinggi Muhammadiyah dan Aisyiyah (Forum of Higher Education Libraries of Muhammadiyah and Aisyiyah), Forum Perpustakaan Perguruan Tinggi Nahdlatul Ulama (Forum of Nahdlatul Ulama Higher Education Libraries), Asosiasi Perpustakaan Perguruan Tinggi Katolik (Association of Catholic Higher Education Libraries), and Jaringan Perpustakaan Perguruan Tinggi Kristen (Indonesian Christian University Virtual Libraries). Public libraries consist of provincial, regency, city, and rural public libraries. The public libraries fall under the management of local authorities and include city libraries, provincial public libraries, and regency libraries.

Public libraries in all levels are more active now than those in the past, especially after PerpuSeru began a training program for librarians that supports social inclusion. PerpuSeru is a social inclusion program built on a train-the-trainer model. The trainers, who are librarians, then conduct activities in the public libraries and invite the community to participate. PerpuSeru's training for trainers emphasizes the importance of librarians in inviting community engagement and in collaborating with the community. Librarians are enthusiastic about

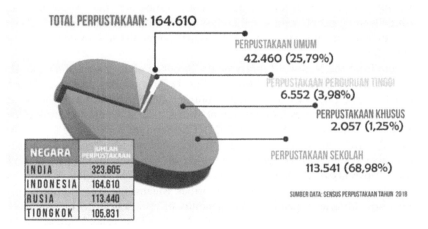

Fig. 1. Number of Libraries in Indonesia. https://www.pustakawanjogja.blogspot.com/2019/07/berapa-jumlah-perpustakaan-di-indonesia.html

collaborating with the community they serve. Supported by PerpuSeru, public libraries and librarians create and provide access to programming that builds community engagement while continuing to provide information and practical knowledge that library users may utilize at home.

Interesting and challenging activities exist in public libraries because the librarians transform the libraries not only for reading activities but also as a place where the communities learn by practice. One of these libraries is in Gunungkidul Regency, Yogyakarta, where the regency public library regularly organizes a variety of activities for the community to develop their cultural skills and knowledge. The activities include reading and practicing cloth dying using the batik method, traditional Javanese choir, tea-making, and online marketing. However, during the COVID-19 pandemic, the librarians scaled down the activities in the rural public libraries to limit the number of people attending the activities. The Public Library of Gunungkidul is a very active library in the promotion of the traditional arts. These training programs include dying cloth, food making, and other local cultural arts for the benefit of the community. The Public Library of Gunungkidul won an award for this social inclusion program and two librarians from this public library won an achievement award from the National Library of the Republic of Indonesia for their activities for the communities and for sharing their experience with other librarians in Indonesia.

Based on these achievements, this chapter discusses these cultural arts activities and how the activities are shared with the community. This chapter is the result of observation, site-visits to Gunungkidul Regency Public Library and to rural public libraries within the regency of Gunungkidul, as well as in-depth interviews with the librarians of the rural public library in Gunungkidul Yogyakarta. This chapter focuses on the development and implementation of social inclusion programs in the public libraries, the historical aspect of PerpuSeru Program, and how public library in Indonesia, in this case, the regency public library and rural public libraries in Gunungkidul regency, in Java island, help their communities to develop their skills and interests so that they are able to support themselves afterwards.

LIBRARY SOCIAL INCLUSION PROGRAM: THE INDONESIAN PERSPECTIVE

Social exclusion is a well discussed topic across professional literature. According to European Union (2004), social exclusion occurs when any individual cannot fully participate in the society due to poverty, joblessness, incompetence, lack of education, or suffers from any other form of discrimination. The problem of social exclusion causes the individuals to feel inferior, unacceptable, or unwanted. To cope with this exclusion, these individuals must be aware of the problems they face and work to find a solution to their situations. Public institutions or organizations including public libraries help these individuals identify solutions.

Social inclusion is a process that enables socially excluded people to successfully participate in everyday life. State and/or social Institutions often have programs to help an individual get a job, learn new skills and acquire new knowledge. A library is one of the institutions that helps individuals accomplish these actions and increase their feelings of social inclusion. This idea has resulted in Indonesian public libraries developing what is called Perpustakaan Berbasis Inklusi Sosial or social-inclusion-based libraries.

In Indonesia, the term social inclusion has been used in library activities for more than a decade. In this case, library social inclusion is defined as the involvement of community in the practical training and similar activities organized by librarians with the aim to help individuals in the community to do any practical activities such as traditional dancing, traditional music, yoga, and so on for cultural preservation or making products from local resources, learning how to make batik, or designing web for marketing products. The librarians provide training for the community that later they practice by themselves at home either for social or economic purposes. Some public libraries even help the community to market their products for their economic or social benefits by providing space for the products that the community makes. The library social inclusion programs are indeed aimed at helping the community to gain knowledge and skills from the library resources, librarians, and experts invited by the library.

A BRIEF HISTORY OF LIBRARY SOCIAL INCLUSION IN INDONESIA

Library social inclusion program has been held since 2011 when Indonesian Coca-Cola Foundation was appointed by the Bill & Melinda Gates Foundation to manage PerpuSeru or perpustakaan seru. Perpustakaan means a library; Seru means exciting. So, PerpuSeru means an exciting library or a library that makes everyone excited. The PerpuSeru program was actually initiated with a brief discussion when Bill and Melinda Gates invited librarians from Indonesia during the conference of International Federation of Library Association (IFLA) in Seoul, South Korea, in 2006. After several years of preparation, the program was finally started with training for trainers in 2011. In the beginning, PerpuSeru was aimed at helping librarians to become trainers before they developed their communities and designed their public libraries as community learning centers that provide training for the community and support the community to enable them to practice what they have learned from the training.

During the 11 years of the PerpuSeru program, PerpuSeru has provided training for 586 rural public libraries and 104 county libraries in 18 provinces. Currently more than 1,000 rural libraries have joined the program and both the regency and rural public libraries have carried out activities for the communities since 2011 until 2017. The director of National Library of the Republic of Indonesia stated that the PerpuSeru program has given a social impact on making a better quality of life for the community (Mahatma, 2017).

The implementation of the PerpuSeru program in both rural public libraries and county libraries is in the form of providing guidance, training, and practice; while the provincial libraries usually support the program by organizing or holding sharing sessions among rural and county libraries at the provincial level. The training that PerpuSeru has held for the librarians during the training for trainers includes theoretical and best practice activities for the community which cover job planning, excellent service, community empowerment, and information-technology promotion, and so forth. The training that PerpuSeru held for librarians has been carried out directly by PerpuSeru team and the training assistance from rural and county libraries. Meanwhile the program implementation for the community is carried out by both librarians and partners or volunteers who are willing to help the community participate in various activities from making products, producing food, to online marketing and practicing cultural performances – all of which are related to the local resources, historical roots, and local tradition.

ACHIEVEMENT OF PERPUSERU

The PerpuSeru project managed by Coca-Cola Foundation Indonesia was highly effective and reached 18 provinces of Indonesia until 2018. There were 104 county libraries and more than 1,000 rural public libraries joined PerpuSeru from 2011 until 2018. The PerpuSeru program was designated to achieve the following objectives: first, social welfare and development through poverty eradication and basic service improvement; second, the distribution of quality education and lifelong learning activities; third, literacy for social development.

By holding training for trainers for librarians, Coca-Cola Foundation Indonesia has been able to bring the librarians to learn how to persuade people and attract the community to attend activities in the public libraries; how to manage collaborative activities between librarians and the community; and to get closer to the community. The librarians practiced what they got from the training by inviting the community to come to the libraries to learn and practice just anything related to their needs and interests. Librarians felt that the programs held by Coca-Cola Foundation Indonesia gave them new experience, view, and ideas on how they could serve the community through their libraries because earlier library training programs usually only dealt with library management from managing collection, library services, library promotion, to library automation.

Indeed, PerpuSeru has been so successful in giving an impact to librarians and the librarians have better ideas to support the community's welfare, especially those living in the rural areas. The interesting point of the PerpuSeru program was that it also considered the situation and development. The programs do not only deal with traditional activities, but are also concerned with digital technology. The latter is an important tool for anyone nowadays. Unfortunately, the PerpuSeru project that began in 2011 finally ended in 2018. However, the end of PerpuSeru in 2018 did not mean the end of the library social inclusion program in Indonesia. The National Library of Republic of Indonesia appreciated Bill and Melinda Gates Foundation and PerpuSeru for having supported the library social inclusion program in Indonesia and National Library of Republic of Indonesia quickly responded this situation and decided to continue the program in an effort to empower public libraries to develop the communities as it was considered very beneficial for many people.

Beginning in 2019, the National Library took the turn to support the library social inclusion program. Supported by the National Development Planning Agency and the Parliament, the National Library of Republic of Indonesia replicates the PerpuSeru program so that the organizational change does not really affect the program. The change in management indeed does not affect much the enthusiasm of the librarians to continue their social inclusion program, including the librarians from Gunungkidul who currently play very important roles both in Gunungkidul and nationally.

GUNUNGKIDUL

Yogyakarta Special Region has a population of 3,689,000 and has an area of 3,178.79 km². Yogyakarta has one city, Yogyakarta, and four counties, namely Bantul, Gunungkidul, Kulon Progo, and Sleman. Among all four counties and the city, Gunungkidul is the largest county with the area of 1,485,36 km² (Bappeda, 2021). It is almost three times larger than the three other counties and the city in the province of Yogyakarta. Meanwhile, according to the local authority of Yogyakarta, the population of Gunungkidul is 747,161 in the year of 2020 (Badan Perencanaan Pembangunan Daerah, 2021). Gunungkidul has an active public library and 148 rural public libraries in the county. In all, 45 out of 148 rural public libraries are engaged in social inclusion programs. The Regency's public library has won several awards and the librarians are very active in empowering the community and have got national reputation and won librarian awards as well. Due to its reputation in empowering the community, Gunungkidul Regency Library received a grant for a new library building which was opened by the Director of National Library of the Republic of Indonesia on January 25, 2022. The rural public libraries continue to be active in engaging the community and bringing together the heads of the villages.

GUNUNGKIDUL, PUBLIC LIBRARY, AND RURAL LIBRARIES

Gunungkidul Public Library and PerpuSeru activities for library social inclusion have now been running for 11 years. As we all know, a public library is an organization that is established, supported, and funded by the community, either through local authorities, the government, or the community themselves. The community sometimes voluntarily builds a library for the community and they hold activities for the community too. The structure of public libraries in a county actually consists of a county library, sub-district libraries (in some counties), then rural public libraries. While IFLA (2001) stated that libraries provide access to knowledge, information, and various types of publications for all members of community regardless of race, nationality, age, sex, religion, language, disability, economic and employment status and educational attainment, but often times, public libraries can do even more than that.

The presence of PerpuSeru has created opportunities of entrepreneurship for the community and changed people's lives. As stated earlier, there were 586 rural public libraries and 104 county libraries that take part in the PerpuSeru library social inclusion program. One of them was Gunungkidul Public Library that later also trained rural public libraries in Gunungkidul to hold activities to empower the community.

THE SOCIAL INCLUSION ACTIVITIES IN GUNUNGKIDUL COUNTY

In the Regency Public Library of Gunungkidul, one of the activities carried out over the past few years is basic computer training. The training is provided to young people in the rural areas which has helped in addressing substance abuse by rural youth. The youth participating in this training program entered in a design competition and were recognized for their work.

Gunungkidul Public Library has also held programs on membatik (batik painting), all of which were very successful. Batik painting is an Indonesian technique of wax-resistant dyeing applied to whole cloth. In this batik painting workshop, all of the participants were from the local community and other nearby neighborhoods and learned how to do batik painting on the whole cloth. They were first introduced to the basic painting technique and then continued with practicing the painting and how to make batik. The result of batik making is shown in Fig. 2.

Fig. 2. Batik Clothes Made by the Community After Attending Batik-Making Training. *Source*: Ida Priyanto (2022).

In addition, participants also learned how to market their batik cloth using the Internet. It was surprising for them that one day there was a group of women from California who visited and were interested in buying batik that was earlier marketed online by the community. The community still continues the batik painting nowadays.

IFLA (1994) states that "the public library, the local gateway to knowledge, provides a basic condition for lifelong learning, independent decision-making and cultural development of the individual and social groups." Gunungkidul Public Library does so. To increase public interest in using the library and in order to make the library closer to the community, Gunungkidul Public Library applies the concept of library social inclusion, in which the community can visit the library to learn and practice making or doing things, besides reading. This activity is considered successful because finally the community takes part in activities organized by the library. Because of batik painting training and online marketing, the batik products made by the community reach the market not only locally but also overseas.

Another important role of the public library is providing a focus for cultural centers in the community and helping to shape and support the cultural identity of the community (IFLA, 2011). The public library is a key agent in the local community promotion of local culture. For example, there are storytelling, traditional dances, and traditional music. It can be concluded that the library has been successful in involving the community to learn and practice how-to activities through training held by the library.

The implementation of the PerpuSeru Program in Gunungkidul Public Library has many benefits, both in terms of output and outcome. It is stated by David Lankes (2011) that "the mission of librarians is to improve society through facilitating knowledge creation in their communities." At the core of this statement lies the importance and the essential role that librarians play toward the involvement of library users.

The physical library building includes the improvement of infrastructure in the library and improving the function of the library both recreationally and culturally. Mentoring training programs aim to improve the knowledge of library workers with respect to work planning strategies, excellent service, promotion, and information technology. The outcomes of this training were: work planning training resulting in library strategic plans; excellent service training resulting in library service innovations, promotional training resulting in increased library visits; and finally, information technology training resulting in the availability of services aimed at learning and access to information technology.

GUNUNGKIDUL PUBLIC LIBRARY ACTIVITIES DURING THE COVID-19 PANDEMIC

In Indonesia, the COVID-19 pandemic existed in March 2020 when two persons were confirmed to be positive of COVID-19. The first days of the pandemic people did not consider it a serious matter. With the rapid increase of cases, most institutions closed their activities and services. While offices were closed and business activities were limited, schools and universities halted their face-to-face teaching and learning activities, and shifted to online classes – with some adjustment and the available facilities. Public libraries experienced the same. They closed their physical spaces and only provided online resources for users to access. However, after several months, the public libraries were allowed to open with a limited number of users. Public libraries opened their physical services by considering health measures due to the COVID-19 pandemic such as compulsory mask wearing and physical distancing among users. The public library also limited the number of visitors.

After closing for several months due to the pandemic, the library social inclusion program began again. However, due to physical distancing and limitation of participants, the activities were held in the rural public libraries instead of the Public Library of Gunungkidul, which is the county public library. The activities were held in the rural public libraries because the librarians expected the community to stay in their own areas. Moreover, in principle, a library social inclusion is an approach and commitment of the library to develop life quality and welfare of the community through community's empowerment according to the Department of Library and Information Science, Airlangga University (2020).

Although it was held in the rural public libraries, the librarians continued their effort to develop their community by keeping some COVID-19 health measures, such as the number of participants allowed to take part in activities, physical distancing among participants, and the cleanliness of the place and participants. Due to the size of the rural public libraries, the librarians held the activities in several rural public libraries and they split the librarians from the Public Library of Gunungkidul so that they could manage the activities across multiple rural libraries. They also invited librarians from the rural public libraries to take part in the program so that they could learn to be trainers moving forward.

There were several rural public libraries chosen to hold library social inclusion activities including Sumber Ilmu Rural Public Library in Petir neighborhood, Rongkop sub-district; Kemadang rural library in Tanjungsari sub-district; Ngawu Rural Public Library in Playen sub-district; Purba Pustaka Rural Public Library in Nglanggeran neighborhood, Patuk sub-district; Sidoharjo Rural Public Library in Tepus sub-district; and Indika Rural Public Library in Ngawen sub-district. The Public Library of Gunungkidul regency becomes the coordinator of all activities in the rural public libraries.

Table 1 shows the social inclusion activities held by rural public libraries in Gunungkidul during the COVID-19 pandemic. Their activities varied from cultural performance, food and beverage practical workshops, online marketing, and creative writing. Each rural public library had its own activities that were different from the others but they welcome anyone from different neighborhoods to join in one library. Other practical workshops held in the rural public libraries in Gunungkidul included woodcut stamp (sablon cukil), Javanese choir (sholawat Jawi), verticulture, ecobrick. Each rural public library had an activity that attracted the community to learn and practice. After they finished one activity, they continued with another activity that the community considered as useful for them. So, the activities were decided by the community instead of the librarians.

According to the librarian of Gunungkidul Public Library, a team from Bill and Melinda Gates Foundation and a delegation from National Library Board of Singapore visited Gunungkidul Public Library and some of the rural public libraries including Indika Rural Public Library as they wanted to know the enthusiasm of the librarians and the engagement of the community in the social inclusion program.

In addition to library social inclusion, the Public Library of Gunungkidul continues empowering the librarians working in rural public libraries by way of training for librarians. Nowadays, the librarians from Gunungkidul have been

Table 1. Rural Public Libraries and Their Activities in 2021.

No.	Rural Public Library	Subdistrict	Activity
1	Sumber Ilmu	Rongkop	Woodcut stamp (Sablon cukil)
2	Kemadang	Tanjungsari	Javanese Choir (Sholawat Jawi)
3	Ngawu	Playen	Verticulture
4	Purba Pustaka	Patuk	Online marketing
5	Sidoharjo	Tepus	Ecobrick
6	Indika	Ngawen	Creative writing

Source: Ida Priyanto (2022).

invited to hold training not only in Gunungkidul Regency but also across the whole Special Region of Yogyakarta and in other provinces in Indonesia. The training in Gunungkidul Public Library itself varies but is related to the activities within the library, for example, training on collection development, training on library services, and so on. The training is then realized by conducting activities for library development and expansion.

A new phenomenon emerged after the training. For example, changing a nightwatch area into an open library space without a staff is called "Gardu Pintar" as shown in Figs. 3 and 4. In this nightwatch area, the librarians put a bookshelf and books, but no one librarian serves users. The bookshelf is not locked, so that anyone may find a book to read at any time for 24 hours a day. The people there call it a self-service reading area. The community may read books in the "nightwatch" library at any time. For those who want to donate books, they may do so, by putting the books in the bookshelf. The area also has Internet access for the community who need it. The community may also use the three available desktops.

Another social inclusion activity is seen at Perpustakaan Balai Pintar (Balai Pintar Library). In this library, the community and librarians grow various plants behind the library (Fig. 5), besides doing that in their own homes. The community and librarians grow ginger, cassava, peanut, moringa, lemongrass, turmeric, and some other plants. Before they grow the plants, they already got training

Fig. 3. Gardu Pintar Public Library for Social Inclusion Program.
Source: Ida Priyanto (2022).

Fig. 4. Another Side of Gardu Pintar Public Library. *Source*: Ida Priyanto (2022).

Fig. 5. Library Backyard. *Source*: Ida Priyanto (2022).

from experts in agriculture and food technology on how to produce food from those plants. Later, after the plants grow, they produce various products to sell. Products are then marketed in and sold by the library (Figs. 6–8).

Fig. 6. Herbal Products Sold at the Library. *Source*: Ida Priyanto (2022).

Fig. 7. Cassava Crackers Sold in the Library. *Source*: Ida Priyanto (2022).

Fig. 8. Tortilla Made by the Community. *Source*: Ida Priyanto (2022).

In other words, the library keeps developing their library skills, besides providing library services and library social inclusion activities. Darmawan (2019) stated that besides providing reading materials for information and knowledge, a library also provides training and other activities to empower the community's social and economic sectors. The Public Library of Gunungkidul and its rural public libraries have helped the community to develop their skills and practice various activities for the benefit of the community.

CONCLUSION

To sum up, public libraries and rural libraries in Gunungkidul have changed their communities by approaching and inviting the community to develop their skills and be productive and creative. Public libraries and even rural libraries hold activities to develop the community's skills such as graphic design, online marketing, and other technological or hard skills. The public libraries may help the community preserve their culture by inviting the community to learn and practice their own traditional dances. In addition, the libraries also help develop their economy by learning, practicing, and then producing any products from the local resources.

The COVID-19 pandemic has not been considered a barrier but a challenge for librarians to continue developing their communities. They continued supporting the community so that the community could keep the positive activities by taking some simple precautions, such as wearing a mask, physical distancing, and organizing a meeting with fewer people. The libraries may also divide the community into smaller groups when holding activities with the community. In addition, the strong support of librarians has enabled the community to enjoy the library as well as changing learning into practice for the benefit of the community.

REFERENCES

Badan Perencanaan Pembangunan Daerah, Daerah Istimewa Yogyakarta. (2021). Jumlah penduduk DIY. Dataku. https://bappeda.jogjaprov.go.id/dataku/data_dasar/index/361-jumlah-penduduk-diy?id_skpd=29

Darmawan, H. (2019). Sosialisasi Perpustakaan Berbasis Inklusi Sosial. https://www.perpusnas.go.id/news-detail.php?lang=id&id=190328065053IwHcN3x98C

International Federation of Library Associations and Institutions. (1994). IFLA/UNESCO Public Library Manifesto. https://repository.ifla.org/handle/123456789/168

International Federation of Library Associations and Institutions. (2001). The Public Library Service: IFLA/UNESCO Guideline for Development. https://www.ifla.org/wp-content/uploads/2019/05/assets/hq/publications/archive/the-public-library-service/publ97.pdf

Jayani, D. H. (2019). Berapa Jumlah Penduduk Perkotaan di Indonesia? https://databoks.katadata.co.id/datapublish/2019/09/11/berapa-jumlah-penduduk-perkotaan-di-indonesia

Kameke, L. V. (2022). Population of ASEAN region 2020, by age. https://www.statista.com/statistics/1026696/asean-population-by-age/#statisticContainer

Lankes, R. D. (2011). The atlas of new librarianship. Massachusetts Institute of Technology. https://davidlankes.org/new-librarianship/the-atlas-of-new-librarianship-online/

Mahatma, F. (2017, November 7). PerpuSeru, Program Pemberdayaan Perpustakaan Berbasis Teknologi Informasi. Tribunnews. https://wartakota.tribunnews.com/2017/11/07/PerpuSeru-program-pemberdayaan-perpustakaan-berbasis-teknologi-informasi?page=all

Majlis Dikdasmen PP Muhammadiyah. (2022). Dapokdimu jumlah sekolah. Retrieved November 14, 2022, from https://dikdasmenppmuhammadiyah.org/dapodikmu-jumlah-sekolah/

Priyanto, I. F. (2022). Community engagement through library outreach program. [powerpoint] presented at *Bridging the Spectrum Symposium* held by Catholic University of America, Washington, D.C. 18 February 2022.

Pustakawan, J. (2023). *Berapa Banyak Perpustakaan di Indonesia?* https://www.pustakawanjogja.blogspot.com/2019/07/berapa-jumlah-perpustakaan-di-indonesia.html

Suharyanto. (2022, March 13). Data Perpustakaan di Indonesia 2022. Kompasiana. https://www.kompasiana.com/mallawa/621ca06f87006426843a3972/data-perpustakaan-di-indonesia-2022

CHAPTER 5

APPLYING ESG TO MODERN LIBRARIANSHIP: LESSONS FROM THE BUSINESS WORLD

Samantha Connell and Micaela Porta

ABSTRACT

Responding to growing market demands for corporate social responsibility, the Asset Management Working Group of the United Nations Environment Programme's Finance Initiative created a legal framework in 2005 to integrate Environmental, Social, and Governance (ESG) issues in institutional investment. It challenged the business world to think beyond fiduciary responsibility, toward measurement of both tangible and intangible assets. As an institutional force committed to the triple bottom line (environmentally sound, socially equitable, and economically feasible), modern libraries serve by reaching outward, and can lead by looking inward. ESG practices enable libraries to clearly identify criteria, set goals, and measure and report progress for external and internal operations, and help garner support and sustain and fund broader programs and initiatives. Applying ESG thinking to library policies, strategic plans, and operational culture will create a sustainable efficiency for these goals, provide evidence-based support for all stakeholders, and generate effective intrapreneurship while fostering community partnerships. This chapter describes our tailored, real-time approach to this work at New Canaan Library. It is a road we are building one brick at a time, and there is value in paving it organically – drawing on and meeting the aptitudes and needs of employees and our

How Public Libraries Build Sustainable Communities in the 21st Century
Advances in Librarianship, Volume 53, 73–83
Copyright © 2023 by Samantha Connell and Micaela Porta
Published under exclusive licence by Emerald Publishing Limited
ISSN: 0065-2830/doi:10.1108/S0065-283020230000053006

community where we are – while also employing best practices borrowed from successful models.

Keywords: Environmental, Social, and Governance (ESG); triple bottom line; sustainability; social justice; Doughnut Economy; Design for Freedom; community asset mapping; land acknowledgment; ESG Coordinator; Sustainable Libraries Initiative

INTRODUCTION

Throughout history, libraries have safeguarded human knowledge – often for the privileged few. For modern librarians to fulfill a mission to "improve society through facilitating knowledge creation in their communities" (Lankes, 2011, p. 15), we must sustainably provide equitable access to resources and services. Applying Environmental, Social, and Governance (ESG) practices from the corporate world to library operations and governance can synergize a library's existing social capital with effective organizational change management, buttressing progress with a systemic process endorsed by leadership and stakeholders. Furthermore, as defenders of intellectual freedom, libraries can harness ESG's mainstream recognition and adoption to help garner support, sustain, and fund programs and initiatives, even when challenged by special interests. An institutional ESG approach normalizes and systematizes the work of elevating our libraries from informational hubs toward a connected community resource. ESG is a decades-long effort taking place in business and financial sectors and integrating these principles in our libraries ensures that progress on these fronts does not rest on the energy and commitment of a few passionate librarians and staff members, who are often working in committees outside of core library programming, lending, and services.

ESG PRACTICES

ESG began in the investment world as a response to growing market demands for corporate social responsibility. The Asset Management Working Group of the United Nations Environment Programme's Finance Initiative created a legal framework in 2005 to integrate ESG issues in institutional investment. It challenged the business world to think beyond fiduciary responsibility, to reconsider the value of degrees of returns for investors if

> the society in which they are to enjoy retirement and in which their descendants will live deteriorates. Quality of life and quality of the environment are worth something, even if not, or particularly because, they are not reducible to financial percentages. (Freshfield Bruckhaus Deringer, 2005, p. 3)

This idea, of measuring both tangible profit and intangible social and value assets, ignited a movement in the corporate world. Widely adopted by for-profit organizations, ESG helps businesses do good and make money, by following the triple bottom line of People, Planet, and Profit (Miller, 2020). A PIMCO analysis of earnings call transcripts demonstrated the significant growth of ESG through May of 2021 (Brown & Sundstrom, 2021).

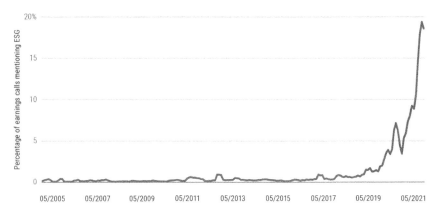

Fig. 1. ESG is a rapidly increasing topic in corporate earnings calls since 2019. *Source*: PIMCO "Mid-Cycle Investing: Time to Get Selective," Brown and Sundstrom (2021).

SUSTAINABILITY AND LIBRARIES

In parallel, national library organizations in the United States have broadened guiding tenets of librarianship to include values of sustainability and social justice. The American Library Association (ALA) Council adopted sustainability as a core value of librarianship in 2019 and made a commitment to the "triple bottom line" framework recommended by the ALA Special Task Force on Sustainability (ALA, 2019). ALA (2021) acknowledged the need for libraries to support racial and social justice initiatives by adopting a new principle to their Code of Ethics.

ESG defines an approach toward organizations that brings initiatives of sustainability and social equity together while applying measurability in governance and can result in an efficient and coherent systemwide application that integrates disparate energies. Many libraries are already invested in improving both People and Planet; in a nonprofit ESG framework, "Profit" is quantified by a human-forward, financially viable approach to governance. In *Sustainable Thinking*, Rebekkah Smith Aldrich (2018) illustrates this vision of sustainability for libraries as a Venn diagram in which all three goals overlap (Fig. 2) and further, suggests we look to Kate Raworth's Doughnut Economics to think like a future-forward economist, with "new economic principles designed to enable humans to thrive. These new economic principles are compatible with the core values of librarianship" and can help address environmental, social, and economic issues (Tanner et al., 2022, p. 130).

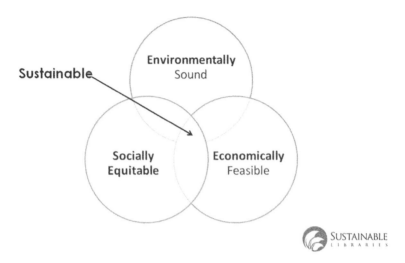

Fig. 2. Triple Bottom Line.
Source: Aldrich (2018). Used with permission.

INSTITUTIONAL TRANSFORMATION

Even with strategies in place, planned organizational change does not always result in institutional transformation. Creating a real shift in an organization's culture with a stable, if not permanent, impact

> requires the steadfast long-term commitment of organizational leaders, a strong commitment and desire by key influential champions, coupled with significant investment in the design and implementation of targeted people strategies that are specifically aimed at shifting the culture. (Mierke & Wiliamson, 2017, p. 2)

Effective change management toward embedded ESG principles will be unique for every library and should include "rigorous internal research from within the organisation on itself." An organization should look inward to identify assets and scope ways to "enhance intrinsic competencies for systemic change" (Baker-Shelley et al., 2020, 5.5.2), and also look at extrinsic factors.

Spanish poet Antonio Machado's (2013) assertion that "the road is made by walking" (p. 281) aptly characterizes our tailored, real-time approach to this work at New Canaan Library. Efforts undertaken by staff members in the past circle back to us today, joining current strides toward an institutional commitment to all forms of sustainability. It is a road we are building one brick at a time, and there is value in paving it organically – drawing on and meeting the aptitudes and needs of employees and our community where we are – while also employing best practices borrowed from successful models. The beginning of the journey toward meaningful and sustainable organizational change began with a policy review. Every bylaw, strategic plan, and policy was reviewed with an eye toward a values-based approach of organizational governance. Organizational change began with a vigilant exploration to identify missing or marginalized perspectives while concurrent efforts were made to build local partnerships based on asset-based community development concepts (McKnight & Kretzmann, 1993) which helped inform our progress.

NEW CANAAN LIBRARY

New Canaan Library serves a town population of about 20,000 and is currently constructing a new, world-class library – a 42,000 square foot transformational and sustainable space designed to inspire lifelong learning, cultural discovery, and community connection. These aspirations not only manifest in the building's beautiful architecture, but in the construction process itself. The library has partnered with Grace Farms Foundation, founder of the Design for Freedom movement to eliminate forced labor from the global building supply and construction chain. As Design for Freedom's first pilot project, we committed to raising awareness of this often-hidden problem, and to help develop a tracking system that ensures transparency in the manufacture and distribution of building materials (Aldrich, 2022). The construction of a new library space invites the opportunity to think of a public library as an organism with mind, body, and soul. Best practices to deliver modern information and cultural literacy through our collections, services, and programs are the mind, and our future-forward building creates the body. The real work is the soul of a library, and the effort to make every person in our community better, healthier, happier, and more connected. The townwide effort of building a new library coincided with select staff efforts of building a more equitable, inclusive, and sustainable institution. Responding to the need for coordinated responses for sustainability and equity, diversity, and inclusion, key committees were formed.

The Sustainability Committee is composed of staff members representing Facilities, Reader's Advisory, Collections, Family Services, Adult Services, Circulation, and Technology Support. In past years, it focused on generating internally developed environmental programming, as well as reaching out to local nonprofits to either co-create programs, or help amplify their messages and grow their organizations by using the library's platform. Today, as our new sustainable building nears completion, the Sustainability Committee is looking inward to examine whether our institutional practices align with our goals. Key areas of inquiry are waste management – designing a system incorporating waste reduction, industrial composting, and better recycling; purchasing – creating a policy to minimize transactions and trips, and support local businesses and vendors who share our values; and printing – starting interdepartmental conversations about printing needs, and experimenting with ways to print less, offset, and eventually go paperless.

Following the departure of a key member of our sustainability committee who innovated with programming around conservation and climate change, our organization scrambled to regroup. Working in parallel, an ad hoc group banded to create a committee to address equity, diversity, inclusion, and social justice issues both externally and internally. Led by an especially capable and devoted team of research, children, and adult services librarians, this committee was motivated by their own values, passion, and curiosity. They set their sights on intensive policy reviews, community asset mapping and engagement, diversity audits, own-voice land acknowledgment, and professional development and training – all in addition to their regular jobs.

This Equity, Diversity, and Inclusion (EDI) Committee has staff members representing Family Services, Adult Services, Community Partnerships, and Development. From the start their efforts were both internally and externally focused: making demonstrable strides to support EDI internally, while serving patrons and building community partnerships externally to walk the road more equitably together. From small interventions to those far thornier, this group has stuck with its research-driven game plan as it also seizes everyday opportunities to maintain forward momentum. The painstaking work of performing diversity audits in all parts of our collection, beginning with the children's classics; the reflective gestation toward an enduring, collaborative relationship with New Canaan's Indigenous people that focuses not just on the past but on contemporary presence; the push to help our staff and public better understand the breadth of gender identities; the detailed review of spaces, materials, and services through the lens of equity and accessibility, from policies concerning eating in the library and checking out museum passes to designing programs that are inclusive on all fronts – all are examples of work to which the group committed and assigned a timeline.

Based on rigorous asset mapping and our library's history of joining forces with town and local nonprofit initiatives, our EDI Committee also took the lead in convening the "Adult & Youth Social Justice Partnership" and "Multicultural Programming Advisory Committee" in New Canaan, to create spaces for collective local action aligned with these values. In these monthly meetings, chaired by our EDI team members, participants brainstorm, plan, support, and uplift one another to create fun and diverse learning experiences for all ages. New Canaan's first-ever (and wildly successful) Juneteenth Celebration, for example, was spearheaded by a local antiracism nonprofit, which got a huge boost from the combined efforts of all in the Adult & Youth Social Partnership.

Our library was making undeniable progress on sustainability and EDI initiatives both within our internal library culture and with community programming and education, but our leadership recognized the vulnerability of our achievements. By adopting an ESG framework, we could enshrine our commitment to sustainability, EDI, and social justice work throughout the library's full hierarchy and safeguard our efforts against future personnel changes and other upheavals. A part-time leadership role was therefore created to coordinate, measure, and evaluate all the library's efforts in these areas. The aim was to institutionalize and systematize the work, with accountability centralized in this role reporting directly to the executive director, and action decentralized across departments

Applying ESG to Modern Librarianship

and working groups. It was important for the ESG coordinator's role to pivot between leading on the delivery of progress and supporting staff engagement and empowerment, so that employees could take ownership of our achievements by learning, growing, and leading from where they stand.

ESG COORDINATOR ROLE

Our own work, together with the trend in job titles reflecting the core values of librarianship (Dankowski, 2022), led us to the creation of this role and framework, but every organization will have a unique set of internal and external assets that will map a unique road toward sustainable change. Recognizing and leveraging the capacity, experience, and relationships of our diverse team informed our next steps. The requirements for our ESG coordinator included reporting directly to the executive director, being trusted by staff members, collaborating across departments and management levels, and having nonprofit experience in sustainability-related areas. This staff member, who would function as a pivot point across tangible systemic rubrics of organization transformation for sustainability (Baker-Shelley et al., 2020), would further shape the job description while simultaneously researching and designing the framework.

Accountability is centralized in the role of the ESG coordinator, who oversees and co-creates with others on decentralized solutions (Scherer et al., 2022). Those solutions, also referred to as benchmarks or action items, relate to the three areas of the Triple Bottom Line. To establish goals in those areas, we are urged to look at trends and needs in our community, then execute action items.

As we had a significant amount of action taking place already (what we had lacked was the institutional structure to channel it), we found ourselves working backward, from specific action items in which many of us were already involved; to the broader goals under which those actions might be categorized; to the policies and mission that drive the goals. This grew out of an early and significant resource, Julie Edwards's (2021) "Diversity Plans for Academic Libraries," in which she gives a detailed description of steps her academic library took to create a diversity plan using the ALA's framework. Our existing working groups – the Sustainability Committee, the EDI Committee, Adult & Youth Social Justice Partnership, and Multicultural Programming Advisory Committee – are led by trained librarians and staff. The new ESG coordinator now meets and communicates with each group, not to supplant members or take charge of implementing action, but to support the staff by helping them draft policy and plans, and through advocacy within the various levels of our organization. According to Edwards, action items can be things the library is already doing, as well as others that are planned or aspirational, but they are tangible, detailed actions. We began by listing specific action items, then grouping these into common goals, which in turn are formulated by strategic choices informed by our mission – from granular detail to guiding principles.

LIBRARY ACTION ITEMS

Examples of action items are: off-site programs that go where people congregate, such as technology support outreach at the local senior center, and story times at local parks and public pools; partnerships with local nonprofits; and professional development and training for staff, encouraged by the executive director and department heads. These actions derive from a common goal: to provide equitable access to resources for all our members, staff, partners, and stakeholders, in a space where they feel welcome, supported, and included. The goal grew out of a four-pronged strategic plan (community and town engagement; streamline operations/processes; provide dynamic and rewarding workplace environment; fundraising and planning for new building), which was in turn informed by our mission: to be an essential place for lifelong learning and a vibrant hub for knowledge, culture, and connection for everyone in our community.

MEASURING IMPACT

From experience, we knew that measuring impact is as tricky as it is essential for making progress. Monthly energy usage is fairly straightforward, while a sparsely attended poetry circle, less so, and yet both are important bricks we must lay down to make our road. Turning to the business world's metrics for evaluating ESG (Brown & Nuttall, 2022), some big-picture questions are:

- Will it increase employee engagement or diversity?
- Will it improve community engagement?
- Will it reduce our carbon footprint?
- What will be the effects on well-being?

How to create a system for evaluation that is evidence-based and progress-driven, but does not run the risk of only considering one data point, like money, attendance, or patron complaints? How to avoid the pitfalls of spending too much time debating desired impact and not enough on how to achieve it? Or gathering scattershot data instead of investing in a handful of deep indicators that refer directly to our mission, policies, and strategic plan? ESG strategy applied to any organization can be a broad catch all for values-based planning, execution, and measurement. In the investment world, where ESG strategies have been developing for almost two decades, ESG is still considered a new way of responsible investing that continues to be refined and redefined. At the heart of an ESG strategy for any organization is the commitment to effect real positive change without performative banners and statements, however, clear applications of measurement can be elusive. In a critical review, "ESG and Responsible Institutional Investing Around the World," Matos (2020) notes that, "ESG implementation has not been defined consistently, partly because ESG investing is evolving" (p. 3). Our library's effort to incorporate ESG values in our organization is less about the invention of a one-size-fits-all measurement rubric and more about

Applying ESG to Modern Librarianship 81

a structured organization-wide commitment to an evidence-based path forward that will ensure that we are stewards of our environment, supporters of all individuals, and responsible to our community and stakeholders. We needed to find a small handful of specific targets that could help stakeholders understand what success looks like. Namely, evaluation must be not only a strategic tool toward the realization of our mission, or feedback taken from a self-selecting or narrow group, but a way of measuring the "expectations, needs, and wants of the broadest possible constituency" (Irwin & St-Pierre, 2014).

For measuring progress toward our current environmental goals, we landed on the following performance metrics: building-wide energy usage; tracking our waste; number of purchasing decisions that support sustainable suppliers and/or materials. Measuring progress toward our social goals is more nuanced, and therefore requires a broader assortment of metrics. Attendance and materials circulation numbers will always help us gauge popularity, though we know these never tell the whole story. Here, we must tread judiciously and flexibly, evaluating a given action by always referring to the goal it seeks to advance, asking ourselves, "Are we further on the road? Standing still? Going in reverse?" For an optional staff-wide training on gender inclusion, for instance, we might measure impact based on the combination of number of participants, responses to a short email survey, and a guided discussion of learning highlights during a staff meeting. We are not only after numbers but trying to get a clearer understanding of the ripple effect toward public benefit. Public Library Association's (PLA) "Project Outcome," a measurement guide for libraries that goes beyond the quantitative to the qualitative by not only evaluating outputs but also outcomes (ALA, 2016), launched a series of surveys tailored to outcome evaluation. The seven areas for which they launched surveys toward outcome measurement give an idea of the terrain and impact we seek to observe and assess going forward: civic and community engagement; digital inclusion; early childhood literacy; economic development; education and lifelong learning; job skills; and summer reading (Teasdale, 2015).

One of the most helpful decisions we made was pursuing certification with the Sustainable Libraries Initiative (SLI) (https://sustainablelibrariesinitiative.org/), co-founded by Rebekka Smith Aldrich who is also the founding board member of the ALA's Sustainability Round Table. In the financial and business world, ESG data reporting, analysis, and integration can be highly complex and granular. Joining SLI and undertaking their certification process, which will take 18–24 months to complete, gives us a proven and ongoing path toward the triple bottom line, with measures, mentors, and a network of practicing libraries. While not all data points may apply to our library, having this detailed, industry-specific roadmap of criteria helps us not only chart the course but also value our efforts, outcomes, and impact in a deep and meaningful way. This is especially important given the inconsistencies in defining outcome assessment (Lyons, 2012). In "Examining the 'Culture of Assessment' in Public Libraries," Ferguson (2022) describes outcome measurement as consistently focused on

> benefits to the library patron (e.g., parents who bring their children to storytime see increases in early literacy) versus benefits to the library (e.g., the library sees an increase in circulation of children's books).

Through SLI's certification process, we are pursuing 13 areas of action (i.e., social cohesion, energy, collections, financial sustainability); within each area there are approximately 20 action items we must perform, with dozens of others recommended (under the heading of social cohesion, for instance, are listed inclusive services assessment and guide, programs celebrating diversity, economic development education for staff, and employee recognition for service outside the library to name just a handful). We might initially measure progress based on the mere existence of a policy or procedure – in other words, creating one where none existed before, as with a purchasing policy we are developing to prioritize resource conservation and support for local and underrepresented businesses. Policies already in existence are being updated, with special attention given to language and practices that advance sustainability and EDI. A newly formulated "Climate and Equity Pledge" will be included with all of our policies, reports, and on our website, communicating in a brief, but highly visible way our commitment to environmental and social justice, and inviting engagement by stating that our work is ongoing, dynamic, and always inclusive. Moving forward, progress would be assessed according to positive momentum determined by quantifiable data together with a qualitative approach regarding our goals. Again, "Are we further on the road? Standing still? Going in reverse?" It is a holistic process, one in which we seek feedback on our progress – by not simply measuring the height of the trees but taking soil samples along the way to better understand how we cultivate ongoing positive change. Measuring with consistency and discernment is key to success, as is listening, clearly communicating, and educating our staff, stakeholders, and community members about the changes we endeavor to effect.

CONCLUSION

As an institutional force for good, modern libraries are mandated to serve by reaching outward and lead by looking inward. How are we serving as a platform for environmental education and climate action, and how are we leading regarding our own energy use and resource consumption? How are we serving by providing equity of access to information, and how are we leading by promoting equity in our employment policies and collections? ESG enables libraries to clearly identify criteria, set goals, and measure and report progress for all manner of external and internal operations. While many libraries seek solutions by hiring outside consultants, a systemic ESG approach as adopted by the for-profit world can create a symbiotic gestalt that ensures continuity of this work in a dynamic environment. It leverages each library's unique assets and community context as it codifies the values and progress of ESG in process and policy. Applying ESG strategy to library policies, strategic plans, and operational culture will create a sustainable efficiency for these goals, provide evidence-based support for our stakeholders at the highest level, and generate opportunities for effective, authentically representative intrapreneurship within the organization.

REFERENCES

Aldrich, R. S. (2018). *Sustainable thinking: Ensuring your library's future in an uncertain world*. American Library Association.

Aldrich, R. S. (2022). Sustainability: Living our values out loud. *Library Journal, 146*(9), 12.

American Library Association (ALA). (2016). *Project Outcome* [Website]. http://www.ala.org/pla/data/performancemeasurement

American Library Association (ALA). (2019). *ALA adding sustainability as a core value of librarianship* [Press release]. https://www.ala.org/news/press-releases/2019/05/ala-adding-sustainability-core-value-librarianship

American Library Association (ALA). (2021). *ALA Adopts new Code of Ethics principle on racial justice* [Press release]. https://www.ala.org/news/member-news/2021/07/ala-adopts-new-code-ethics-principle-racial-and-social-justice

Baker-Shelley, A., Van Zeijl-Rozema, A., & Martens, P. (2020). Pathways of organizational transformation for sustainability: A university case-study synthesis presenting competencies for systemic change and rubrics of transformation. *International Journal of Sustainable Development & World Ecology, 27*(8), 687–708. https://doi.org/10.1080/13504509.2020.1762256

Brown, S., & Nuttall, R. (2022). *The Role of ESG and Purpose* [Podcast]. Mckinsey & Company. https://www.mckinsey.com/business-functions/strategy-and-corporate-finance/our-insights/the-role-of-esg-and-purpose

Brown, E., & Sundstrom, G. (2021). Mid-Cycle Investing: Time to Get Selective. Retrieved June 15, 2022, from https://www.pimco.com/en-us/insights/economic-and-market-commentary/global-markets/asset-allocation-outlook/mid-cycle-investing-time-to-get-selective

Dankowski, T. (2022). *5 Library Jobs on the Rise: Emerging roles and titles reflect libraries' core values*. American Libraries. Retrieved June 15, 2022, from https://americanlibrariesmagazine.org/2022/06/01/5-library-jobs-on-the-rise/

Edwards, J. B. (2021). Diversity plans for academic libraries: An example from the University of Montana. *Library Leadership & Management, 29*(2), 1–15.

Ferguson, A. (2022). Examining the "Culture of Assessment" in public libraries. *Pathfinder: A Canadian Journal for Information Science Students and Early Career Professionals, 3*(1), 47–63.

Freshfield Bruckhaus Deringer. (2005). A Legal Framework for the integration of environmental, social and governance issues into institutional investment. Produced for the Asset Management Working Group of the UNEP Finance Initiative. Retrieved October 2005, from https://www.unepfi.org/fileadmin/documents/freshfields_legal_resp_20051123.pdf

Irwin, B., & St-Pierre, P. G. (2014). Creating a culture of meaningful evaluation in public libraries: Moving beyond quantitative metrics. *SAGE Open, 4*(4), 1–15.

Lankes, R. D. (2011). *The Atlas of new librarianship* (Vol. 16). MIT Press.

Lyons, R. (2012). Duck soup and library outcome evaluation. *Public Library Quarterly, 31*(4), 326–338.

Machado, A. (2013). *Border of a dream: Selected poems of Antonio Machado*. Copper Canyon Press.

Matos, P. (2020). ESG and responsible institutional investing around the world: A critical review. Charlottesville, VA: CFA Institute Research Foundation.

McKnight, J. L., & Kretzmann, J. P. (1993). *Building communities from the inside out: A path toward finding and mobilizing a community's assets*. Center for Urban Affairs and Policy Research, Northwestern University.

Mierke, J., & Wiliamson, V. (2017). A framework for achieving organizational culture change. Library Leadership & Management, *31*(2).

Miller, K. (2020). *The Triple Bottom Line: What It Is & Why It's Important* [Website]. Harvard Business School Online. Retrieved December 8, 2020, from https://online.hbs.edu/blog/post/what-is-the-triple-bottom-line

Scherer, J., Kropp, L., & Smith-Aldrich, R. (2022). *Sustainable Thinking Builds Strong Libraries and Resilient Communities* [Webinar]. American Library Association Core Webinar. Sustainable Library Initiative. Retrieved March 15, 2022, from https://sustainablelibrariesinitiative.org/events/ala-core-webinar-sustainable-thinking-builds-strong-libraries-and-resilient-communities

Tanner, R., Ho, A., Antonelli, M., & Aldrich, R. S. (2022). *Libraries and sustainability: Programs and practices for community*. ALA Editions.

Teasdale, R. (2015). *Project Outcome Launch – Seven Surveys to Measure Impact* [Website]. Public Libraries Online. Public Library Association. Retrieved May 28, 2015, from https://publiclibrariesonline.org/2015/05/project-outcome-launch-seven-surveys-to-measure-impact/

SECTION TWO

LIBRARIES ADVOCATING FOR SOCIAL JUSTICE

INTRODUCTION TO SECTION TWO: SUSTAINABLE COMMUNITIES AND THE ROLE OF THE PUBLIC LIBRARY

Kaurri C. Williams-Cockfield and Bharat Mehra

FRAMING OF SECTION TWO ["LIBRARIES ADVOCATING FOR SOCIAL JUSTICE"]

The case studies included in Section Two provide examples of programs that work toward ending poverty [SDG 1], ameliorating hunger [SDG 2], addressing food insecurity, supporting good nutrition, living healthy lives [SDG 3], promoting well-being, supporting community education, promoting life-long learning, empowering women and girls [SDG 4], achieving gender equality and reducing inequality within their service communities. Collectively, these SDGs are focused on addressing social inequities and with creating a world where everyone has value.

The chapters included in this section operationalize significant elements of the public library–sustainable communities (PLSC) framework visualized in the introduction to the book. In Chapter 6 ["Anti-Racism in Practice: The Development of a Black Community Public Library in Canada"], Amber Matthews and Pastor Sandie Thomas discuss the development of the Black Community Center in London, Ontario, which encompasses the first Black community public library designed to "reflect and include Black ideas, experiences, and knowledge." Reviewer Eric Ely-Ledesma, PhD candidate in the Information School at the University of Wisconsin-Madison states,

the case study of the Black Community Public Library provides valuable insight into how libraries can address historical marginalization and racism while simultaneously combating the enduring consequences of these historic processes.

How Public Libraries Build Sustainable Communities in the 21st Century
Advances in Librarianship, Volume 53, 87–89
Copyright © 2023 by Kaurri C. Williams-Cockfield and Bharat Mehra
Published under exclusive licence by Emerald Publishing Limited
ISSN: 0065-2830/doi:10.1108/S0065-283020230000053007

In Chapter 7 ["Public Library Pride: A Journey of Small Steps Toward Inclusivity"], Debra Trogdon-Livingston discusses the ways that public libraries support LGBTQ+ library employees, adult, and youth patrons. Reviewer Christopher Knapp, Youth Community Engagement Librarian with the Prince George Public Library, Prince George, BC, Canada writes:

> This manuscript and book is a valuable piece of professional literature that should be a staple in every public library's professional collection and every university or college with a library and information science program creating future librarians of the 21st Century. In a time where the LGBTQIA+ community is facing some of its worst socio-cultural pressures from people in the highest positions of power, it is more important than ever that the public library remain a symbol of hope, equity, inclusion, and safety.

In Chapter 8 ["A Call to Action: Libraries Leaning in for Unhoused LGBTGEQ+ Youth"], Julie Ann Winkelstein discusses public library support for unhoused LGBTQ+ youth.

In Chapter 9 ["Let's Learn Together Outside: Families Playing, Building Relationships, and Connecting with Their Community in Nature"], Emily Sedgwick and Wendee Mullikin discuss "Let's Learn Together Outside," a four part family literacy model featuring children's education time, parent time, parent education time, and parent and child together time which was developed through a partnership with the National Center for Families Learning (NCFL).

In Chapter 10 ["Sustainability, Outdoor Life, and Libraries"], Hilde Ljødal and Tordis Holm Kverndokk share programs and initiatives developed between public libraries in Norway and the National Library of Norway in observation of National Book Year 2019. These programs and initiatives combine books, literature, and outdoor life throughout Norway. Reviewer Amanda Harrison, Assistant Professor, University of Central Missouri, writes:

> The Norway National Library and public libraries in Norway provide an example of how libraries can provide literacy and programming in innovative ways and be embedded in their community while also meeting many of the UN sustainability goals. Their on-going Norwegian connection between reading and the outdoors serves as a reminder of how literacy can bring us together both locally and globally.

In Chapter 11 ["Older Adults, Public Libraries, and Sustainable Development Goals"], Nicole K. Dalmer and Meridith Griffin reflect on the contexts and social trends that impact how older adults interact with public libraries. Reviewer Joseph Winberry, PhD candidate, University of Tennessee, states:

> People sixty-five years and older represent the fastest growing demographic in most communities around the world. Public library researchers and practitioners must move quickly and purposely to meet the needs of older adults. This chapter – penned by gerontologists with years of experience at the intersection of aging and public libraries – provides a biblio-Ted Talk that can help our field think more theoretically and practically about how to identify and meet this population's needs.

STRATEGIC COLLECTIVE ACTIONS

The thematic threads flowing through the six chapters in this section highlight how different library case studies operationalize the following significant strategic collective actions:

Introduction to Section Two 89

- Use the public library as "place" to address racial inequity;
- Address gender inequity through library policies, programming, and staff support;
- Provide quality education programming that models parents teaching their children while experiencing nature;
- Enhance quality of life for patrons by providing library experiences outdoors;
- Reduce inequities by addressing the needs and practices of older adults through library staff, spaces, materials and programming.

These six chapters present case studies that showcase public library programs and partnerships with a focus on addressing social justice issues within local communities (Mehra, 2021). The programs and partnerships can be adapted for use in other communities and, thereby, provide a blueprint for replication.

KEY CONCEPTS AND TERMS

Active Mediation – Process of providing funding to Norwegian libraries to enact good measures for strengthening reading and to increase the borrowing of physical and digital materials from the collections.

Black Community Public Library – A safe and equitable space designed to represent Black excellence and a place in which Black cultures and knowledge can be taught, expressed, and celebrated.

Kindness by Design – Creating a welcoming space and environment for the LGBTQIA+ community.

Parent and Child Time (PACT) – Refers to a program established by the National Center for Families Learning that focuses on the importance of parents and their children spending time together learning.

REFERENCES

Mehra, B. (2021, October). Libraries reclaiming "Social Justice Warriors" during "Miss Rona's" Global Pandemic Crises. *The Library Quarterly: Information, Community, Policy, 91*(4), 385–401. https://doi.org/10.1086/715919

RESOURCES AND RELEVANT ORGANIZATIONS

American Library Association, Chicago, IL, US. https://www.ala.org/
Black Youth Action Plan, Ontario, CA. https://www.ontario.ca/page/black-youth-action-plan
Human Rights Campaign, Washington, D.C., US. https://www.hrc.org/
National Book Year 2019, Norway. https://naple.eu/mdocs-posts/national-strategy-for-libraries-2020-2023-english/
National Center for Families Learning (NCFL), Louisville, KY. https://www.familieslearning.org/
National Library of Norway, Rana, Norway. https://www.nb.no/
National Strategy for Libraries 2020–2023, Norway. https://naple.eu/mdocs-posts/national-strategy-for-libraries-2020-2023-english/
Where We Are Now Black (W.E.A.N.) Community Center, London, CA. https://weancommunitycentre.com/

CHAPTER 6

ANTI-RACISM IN PRACTICE: THE DEVELOPMENT OF A BLACK COMMUNITY PUBLIC LIBRARY IN CANADA

Amber Matthews and Sandie Thomas

ABSTRACT

Neutrality and diversity are the bedrock of public libraries. Yet, public libraries are also steeped in white privilege and many have yet to examine the effects of anti-Black racism. Amidst an ever-growing crisis of inequity, this chapter explores the development of the Black Community Public Library and its roots in Black-centered and community-based perspectives. It provides important insights into how public libraries can transgress the centrality of whiteness in traditional public libraries through community-led and community-based partnerships within collaborative anti-racism and justice frameworks. Opening in January 2022, the Black Community Public Library is the first of its kind to conceptualize and highlight the need for Black-centered services and collections in Canadian public libraries. Located in the Where We Are Now Black Community Centre, the library is the result of a year-long partnership between the Black Community Centre, local higher education institutions, and the municipal library system. It holds an initial circulating collection of 600 titles representing a variety of equity-seeking perspectives. Detailing the development and launch of the Black Community Public Library, this case study demonstrates how to re-envision library spaces with and for communities that have been historically under-represented and provides invaluable insight into how the public library sector can support and engage with Black communities through meaningful

How Public Libraries Build Sustainable Communities in the 21st Century
Advances in Librarianship, Volume 53, 91–103
Copyright © 2023 by Amber Matthews and Sandie Thomas
Published under exclusive licence by Emerald Publishing Limited
ISSN: 0065-2830/doi:10.1108/S0065-283020230000053008

partnership and collaboration. Furthermore, it will substantially contribute to the growing body of collaborative knowledge on advancing anti-racism in LIS.

Keywords: Anti-Black racism; Black Community Public Library; Canada; Black experiences; Black-centered services; Black-centered collections; underserved populations; community-led partnerships

With the backdrop of the resurgence in the Black Lives Matter movement and a rising national crisis of racial inequity, the Where We Are Now Black Community Center opened in December 2020 in London, Ontario, to begin addressing structural inequalities acutely felt in local Black communities. The center advocates for a truly inclusive approach to social and public library services for and about Black communities that begins with the recognition that anti-Black racism is a serious form of exclusion that impacts every measure of community health, well-being, and social support for Black Canadians. Founded by Pastor Sandie Thomas, a long-time city resident and advocate for London's Black communities, the center offers a holistic approach to social development and well-being that is locally informed and community directed to honor the plurality of Black experiences in Canada. Since its inception, the operation of the center has been informed through community decision-making in leadership and strategic directions, local input into program development through consultation and feedback sessions, and the use of community knowledge to the greatest extent possible in programs. Members of the center come from across the London area, a mid-sized city located halfway between Toronto and Detroit in southwestern Ontario, and its constituents are a wide representation of Canadian Black and African diasporic communities. It is located in a transit-accessible area of the city and houses a vibrant multipurpose space that includes technological resources, spiritual and community gathering spaces, and most recently, what is known to be Canada's first Black Community Public Library.

In collaboration with local higher education institutions and the municipal library system, the *Black Community Public Library* opened in January 2022 in response to the need for Black-led and Black-centered services and collections in Canadian libraries. It recognizes that local public libraries are uniquely positioned to support equity-seeking groups and that they have also faced long-standing challenges to reflect and include Black ideas, experiences, and knowledge. The library holds an initial circulating collection of 700 titles representing a variety of equity-seeking voices that have struggled to find their perspectives and lived experiences in other Canadian library collections. It offers a series of community-identified programs such as business development coaching, computer literacy and skills enhancement, and dedicated interventions for children and youth in areas where Black young people are historically under-represented such as Science, Technology, Engineering, and Medicine (STEM). The strong emphasis on young people is a targeted strategy to address the cyclical nature of racialized poverty and their differential access to community-based resources and services that leave many with feelings of isolation, a lack of belonging, and diminished self-esteem and self-confidence due to anti-Black racism in the local community (Anucha et al., 2017, p. 19). As a case study, the Black Community Public Library and its roots in Black-centered and community-based perspectives provides important insights into how the library sector can meaningfully adopt inclusive and anti-racist institutional responses to meet the localized needs of equity-deserving communities. It further offers invaluable experience on how the public library sector supports and engages underserved groups through community-led partnerships to further the growing body of collaborative knowledge on advancing anti-racist practice in librarianship.

ANTI-BLACK RACISM IN CANADA

Over 1.2 million people in Canada identify as Black and Ontario is home to over half of the Canadian Black population who are predominantly urban, multilingual, and ethnically and culturally diverse (Statistics Canada, 2019b). There has been rapid demographic change in the country over the last two decades as the number of Black Canadians has doubled to 3.5% of the total population and will nearly double again by 2036 (Statistics Canada, 2019b). While the London Black community had historically been demographically small compared to larger cities like Toronto or Montreal, the city has now become the fourth fastest growing Canadian metropolitan area (Statistics Canada, 2022) and roughly 15,000 London residents now identify as Black or mixed race with African heritage (Statistics Canada, 2017). This growth has placed a strong demand on already limited social services dedicated for the Black community and affordable housing resources are strained across the city. While 17% of the London population currently live in poverty, 29.8% of this population are self-identified as Black and a further 28.3% are self-identified as multiple identities of color (Colour of Poverty – Colour of Change, 2019, p. 1). In fact, London has the second highest rate of Black poverty in Ontario with rates 20% higher than the City of Toronto and the province of Ontario as a whole (Colour of Poverty – Colour of Change, 2019, p. 1). These high rates of racialized poverty in the city have resulted in limited economic opportunities, inadequate social and community services, and fewer indications of health and overall well-being for the London Black community (Colour of Poverty – Colour of Change, 2019).

Despite mounting evidence, there has been a persistent hesitancy to acknowledge anti-Black racism in Canada. Meanwhile, it has been identified by Black communities and multiple levels of government as prolific across social, cultural, and education institutions (Alberta, 2022; British Columbia, 2022; Canada, 2019; Foster et al., 2021; Nova Scotia Office of Equity and Anti-Racism Initiatives, 2022; Ontario, 2017). The Government of Ontario defines anti-Black racism as a two-part process of devaluing Black lives through widespread "prejudice, attitudes, beliefs, stereotyping and discrimination" experienced along with systemic forms of marginalization in social and institutional policies (Ontario, 2022, Anti-Black racism para. 1). Black young people have been particularly impacted with many suggesting that their most urgent needs are for social service institutions to examine practices of anti-Black racism that undermine their agency and limit their future outcomes (Anucha et al., 2017). For example, Black children and youth are taken from their homes up to five times the rate of white children and youth and they account for over 40% of Ontario minors in care (Contenta et al., 2014). Black males are two times more likely to be unemployed (Statistics Canada, 2020) and four times more likely to engage with police than their white peers (Wortley & Jung, 2020). Evidence from other areas of the province also suggests that Black young people are also less prepared for post-secondary education due to streaming into non-academic high-school classes that leave them unqualified for admission into higher education (James & Turner, 2017). To counter the rising consequences of systemic inequity, Canada's Anti-Racism Strategy (2019) has identified that enhancing capacity through collaboration, improving funding and resources, and increasing participation in social programs are key strategies to combat the dual forces of racialized poverty and systemic marginalization facing Black youth and their communities in Canada.

LIBRARY SECTOR RESPONSES TO ANTI-BLACK RACISM

A growing chorus of voices in library and information science (LIS) suggest that inattention to race, its roots in unacknowledged white cultural norms, and institutional reluctance to adopt justice-minded approaches in favor of neutrality has also rendered librarianship particularly susceptible to anti-Black racism (Cooke & Sweeney, 2017; Espinal, 2001; Espinal et al., 2018; Gibson et al., 2017 2021; Hathcock, 2015; Hudson, 2017; Leung & López-McKnight, 2021; Mehra, 2021; Mehra & Gray, 2020; Schlesselman-Tarango, 2017; Schmidt, 2019). The overwhelming point is that many diversity and inclusivity initiatives proffer the poignant fallacy that white is not racial and thereby fail to respond to and ameliorate systemic injustices (Espinal, 2001). Underscoring this point, Espinal et al. (2018) write that "acts of violence don't always look like a bullet" (p. 154). In fact, some of the most impactful forms of racial violence enacted on Black communities are the subtle and everyday messages of anti-Blackness that repeatedly convey that their lives, experiences, and perspectives are unimportant or irrelevant. In the context of public library services for youth, programs and services are often envisioned from a race-neutral perspective of needs derived from assumptions based on age (Bernier, 2019; Rothbauer, 2019). This practice has been problematized by LIS scholars who advocate for more responsive services attuned to youth lived experiences and needs (Agosto, 2019; Austin, 2016; Bernier, 2019; Rothbauer, 2019). Paulette Rothbauer (2019), a Canadian scholar in public libraries and young people, highlights how the overwhelming characterization of youth as "a chronological or generational age" ignores crucially important aspects of youth experiences such as the impacts of race, class, gender, sexuality, and other non-dominant experiences (p. 4). This works to "erase" the social and material realities youth face and also binds libraries and adjacent fields to "universal or essentialist" ideas about community needs (Rothbauer, 2019, p. 4). Research from

Anti-Racism in Practice   95

the United States suggests that youth are acutely sensitive to these messages and often react by disengaging with programs and services because they perceive them as unresponsive and unwelcoming spaces (Kumasi & Hughes-Hassell, 2017). However, as Denise E. Agosto and Sandra Hughes-Hassell (2010) pointedly note,

> if we want to foster positive outcomes for them, we must hear their voices, affirm their identities, validate their perspectives, see them as individuals, and find ways to help them get their voices heard. (p. 18)

LIS scholars highlight that this ought to be a guiding principle of all services in public libraries (Bernier, 2019; Rothbauer, 2019). Regardless, this is an expressly important mandate for Canadian Black young people who have identified how anti-Black racism in social programs and services leaves them feeling profoundly marginalized in education and other spaces of learning.

THE ROLE OF THE COMMUNITY CENTER IN ADDRESSING ANTI-BLACK RACISM

Guided by the principle of "by and about Black people for the whole community," the Black Community Center and Public Library is a volunteer run organization that relies on local investments of time and community financial support. While the center does not yet receive operating funds from the municipality, it has received financial and in-kind support from the local municipal library and other government programs to facilitate its library and youth programs. Incorporated as a non-profit entity, it is governed by a five-member board of community members representing a diverse range of London Black professionals in information technology, finance, sports rehabilitation and naturopathy, education, and medicine. Board members were identified through a community selection and nomination process. Members were selected that represented London's various Black and diasporic communities and specifically sought those who were able to provide strong mentorship and guidance to young people. Collectively, the volunteer board members and executive director have a rich history of participation in community-led advocacy with many having served on local committees and boards dedicated to addressing the effects of anti-Black racism and the promotion of local Black histories and cultures. Deeply grounded in ideas of the Black renaissance, the center is a vibrant, inclusive, and collaborative community space that features the spectrum of Black ideas and knowledge as a counternarrative to persistent societal marginalization.

The heartbeat of the center is the *Black Community Public Library* – a safe and equitable space designed to represent Black excellence and a place in which Black cultures and knowledge could be taught, expressed, and celebrated. The library collection has been curated to include materials that accurately feature Black histories and knowledges that are not often included in the Ontario school curriculum or in materials found the collections of other local libraries. The sole focus on "Eurocentric values, history, and worldviews" has been strongly critiqued within the province and Black communities have expressed how this erasure leaves them feeling ignored and excluded (Anucha et al., 2017, p. 30). In direct response to this chronic devaluing of

Black voices in education and learning environments, the collection centers the rich contribution of Black stories and storytellers in local and Canadian history. However, the library has also sought to strike a balance between materials that focus on struggles to obtain freedom or equity in society and those that demonstrate the fullness of Black histories and cultures. While equity and justice are an important part of Black histories and feature prominently in some areas of the library, the collection also includes the vast contributions of Black communities to areas such as STEM, Canadian literature and poetry, and practical knowledge areas such as self-discovery and cooking. It has also dedicated space for the breadth of equity-deserving identities and experiences and features a growing collection of LGBTQ2S+ materials and works by Canadian Indigenous peoples and communities.

PARTNERSHIPS WITH PUBLIC LIBRARIES

The Black Community Public Library was supported through a year-long collaboration with the local municipal public library. In the early stages, organizational leaders met frequently to consult on collection needs and identify opportunities for partnership. The municipal public library provided expertise on collection development, recommendations for library-specific technology such as TinyCat to manage constituents and circulation, and library design elements such as physical infrastructure donated for the space. Over the first year, the library collection has continued to grow steadily through contributions from the local municipal library, donations from the community, and direct library purchases from Ontario Black booksellers. It holds an initial circulating collection of 700 books and has recently moved to a new space to accommodate an additional 1,500 books donated from a personal special collection. The collection was developed through a consultation process that was led by the Black Community Center and supported by the municipal public library. The public consultation process began with an open call for book suggestions from the Center to the London Black community through email, social media, and word of mouth. The center also conducted a review of recommended book lists from Black booksellers and consulted with an Ontario-based children's publisher that specializes in works by diverse authors and/or with diverse characters and stories. The resulting list was shared with over 100 members of the London Black community that had signed up for library information or attended workshops as well as to the Black business community. To ensure the widest representation possible, the Executive Director also reached out to Black ethnic and diasporic community leaders for suggestions on titles that they felt represented their culture and communities. Three community meetings were held on Zoom (due to the COVID-19 pandemic) and between 5 and 30 people attended each session to review the book list and provide additional suggestions. Whenever possible, titles for the library collection were purchased from independent Black booksellers in Ontario to support locally owned Black businesses. The community consultation process also resulted in an additional 100 books by Canadian Black authors being purchased by the municipal library for their collection.

PARTNERSHIPS WITH HIGHER EDUCATION

The Black Community Public Library has also developed strong partnerships with various offices and faculties at Western University particularly the campus-wide Office of Equity, Diversity, and Inclusion and the graduate-level program in LIS. Graduate students enrolled in a course titled *Anti-Racism in Library and Information Science*, the first known Canadian MLIS course to directly address racial inequity and justice in librarianship, completed a semester-long community-engaged learning project with the library. Working alongside the course instructor and the Executive Director (both co-authors of this chapter), the class piloted a novel community-engaged learning partnership in which graduate students employed skills from the breadth of their MLIS education to solve real-world operational problems while furthering their understanding of anti-racist work and spaces. Student projects in the library included developing a volunteer guide to standardize TinyCat use (e.g., how to create and update patron records, create new collection records, manage circulation, and organize metadata), researching and developing a small-scale collection management system (e.g., instructions on how to find and assign call numbers, created an identification system for materials, and process for storage and retrieval), and developed a case for support to use in funding applications to support library programs. Following the course, some of the graduate students have continued to volunteer and have taken on new projects in the library to improve the library experience for patrons and ready the space for future growth in the collection.

OTHER COMMUNITY PARTNERSHIPS

In 2018, the Ontario Government launched a province-wide consultation with Black communities to draft the far-reaching Black Youth Action Plan (BYAP) (Anucha et al., 2017). The government conducted engagement sessions in four regions with over 1,500 Ontarians to identify challenges for Black youth as well as opportunities for support and intervention to address their needs (Anucha et al., 2017). The BYAP consultation identified several key structural challenges in the province: Black youth are disadvantaged in education, many are unable to obtain meaningful employment, they often work in precarious environments with limited support or stability, and they have challenges meeting their basic needs and improving social mobility (Anucha et al., 2017). In conjunction with the Black Community Centre, a series of programs have been developed to fill this gap and prepare Black youth to enter the workforce and succeed as adults. Community programs are offered in the library space and include financial literacy (budgeting, introduction to saving and investing, setting financial goals, and building credit) and employment readiness (resume writing, career counseling, interview skills, and job placement). The library has also developed a popular "Black Boys Coding" program that was supported through a federal grant program to hire and train youth leaders from the local Black community. This program has been wildly popular with participants expressing how the program has opened their eyes to opportunities for Black young people in STEM. For many Black youth, a key facet of their experiences with marginalization and social exclusion center around how their race and culture are framed as a single point of entry to their lives (Briggs, 2018; Kumasi, 2019). Research also shows that too strong of an emphasis on anti-Black racism has negative correlative effects such as shame associated with their identity and feelings of hopelessness due to barriers that they face (Briggs, 2018; Ginwright, 2010). Thus, the programs offered in the library place a strong focus on enabling Black youth to develop agency, confidence, and life skills that will support them to take actionable change to respond to structural constraints on their lives and communities as well as provide exposure to new opportunities.

Community-based research also shows that fostering strong ties to community is a key factor to achieving positive outcomes for Black children and youth and this is especially important in education and learning environments (Deschenes et al., 2010). As a result, the library has been committed to developing opportunities for the local Black community to mentor and engage with young people. For example, in partnership with the Congress of Black Women of Canada and Black Chamber of Commerce, youth can participate in mentorship programs with local Black professionals to build networks, develop employment and leadership skills, and grow their confidence in the job market. The library has also developed an intergenerational reading program for older adults and children in the community. The program was developed following the COVID-19 pandemic after older adults, affectionately and respectfully called "the Wisdom community," reported feeling isolated and lacking opportunities for emotional and social support due to the closure of social programs in the city. Through weekly early reading sessions and conversations, the Wisdom community shares their cultural knowledge, provides mentorship, and improves their connection to community and overall well-being. The program also breaks down age barriers and builds strong relationships to revive and pass along local Black history.

LEARNING OUTCOMES AND OPPORTUNITIES

During its early development, a key challenge faced by the library was conveying the need for *Black-led* and *Black-centered* programs and services to community partners and the public. Local organizations have typically partnered with the London Black community to further include culturally specific programming and advocacy in already existing spaces, collections, and programs (e.g., during Black History month). However, there was an initial reluctance to explore the idea of a dedicated space that would address concerns felt by Black communities such as bias-fraught services and interactions in the past. This lack of recognition of institutional anti-Black racism has been identified by Canadian governments who have recently undertaken significant policy measures to support social service institutions to understand how systemic racism functions and identify measures to address it (Alberta. 2022; Canada, 2019; Nova Scotia Office of Equity and Anti-Racism Initiatives, 2022; Ontario, 2017). While these efforts underscore how institutional practices can negatively impact the lives and well-being of Black communities, they also stress that the purpose is not to suggest that institutions or its workforce are purposefully racist (Canada, 2019; Ontario, 2017). Rather, these strategic and legislative policies focus attention on the harm that is caused by historic and contemporary practices that perpetuate white supremacy as normative and neutral. In the development of the Black Community Public Library, this challenge was overcome by sharing resources on the predominance of anti-Black racism in Canadian social institutions and opening dialogue on how it was experienced by members of the London Black community. Partner organizations were also encouraged to conduct institutional audits on cultural representation and participate in listening sessions. These inward-facing measures resulted in additional resources provided for the development of the dedicated library space and expanded offerings in existing library collections.

Funding and volunteer support remains challenging as the center and the library are entirely supported by voluntary contributions from the local community. For some in local Black communities, there was initial skepticism about the project coming to fruition and this resulted in lack of confidence and financial support. Others had feelings of mistrust and a lack of desire to participate in community partnerships with organizations that may have negatively impacted local Black communities in the past. This was expected given that Black communities have repeatedly expressed disillusionment with social and civic participation in institutions that adopt a "willful blindness" to their perspectives and lived experiences (Anucha et al., 2017, p. 30). The community-led and directed approach has increased participation over time as the library continues to demonstrate strong community involvement and maintains open communication. The community-engaged learning partnership with graduate students in LIS has also provided the library with tools to help bridge these challenges. In particular, the case for funding support will be utilized to fund new programs and services in the future. This includes plans to expand its service to the Black Francophone community in London.

UNITED NATIONS SUSTAINABLE DEVELOPMENT GOALS

Reflecting on the United Nations Sustainable Development Goals (SDGs), it is clear that inequitable access and services not attuned to community needs are a pronounced form of marginalization that prevent equity-deserving groups from achieving their full social and economic potential. This perspective is also cogently reflected in the suite of programs and services developed at the Black Community Public Library. Indeed, the spirit of SDG 10 (Reducing Inequities) is to draw attention to the need for targeted and preferential interventions that support historically marginalized groups to achieve equitable outcomes. The entrepreneurial and education programs for young people are an especially important contribution to this area as well as goals that endeavor to address gaps in education and training for young people (SDGs 4 and 8). The Black Community Public Library's commitment to supporting Black-owned local businesses is also a sustainable and replicable approach that benefits local communities, the local economy, and furthers efforts to identify more environmentally responsible business practices (SDG Goal 8). Finally, their work to address racial inequity in existing public library services and build strong Black community-based organizations neatly encapsulates the intent of SDG Goal 16 to build infrastructure to "ensure responsive, inclusive, participatory and representative decision-making at all levels" (UN, 2022). The development and success of the library demonstrates that there is a strong demand and desire for public library services in equity-seeking communities that have been historically under-represented. It also shows the need to transgress the centrality of white perspectives in Canadian public libraries and remedy unequal power relationships that have hindered participation. The SDG's provide a useful tool to measure the aims of future programs as well as underscore the importance of the work already done.

RECREATING THIS PROGRAM

Although the library is distinct in their approach to addressing community-identified needs for Black communities, it exemplifies the spirit of successful collective impact projects that draw on the strengths of partner institutions to further mutual goals, support each other's work, share knowledge and resources, improve organizations through effective communication, and ensure staff and resources are allocated where needed (Kania & Kramer, 2011). For example, while the Black Community Public Library is a stand-alone entity that functions independently from the municipal public library, the organizations have partnered at critical junctures to assist in the development and organization of the community library space. This partnership drew heavily on the knowledge of both organizations to develop a collaborative approach to library services that included best practices from the municipal public library within the dedicated library space for the London Black community. This model concisely demonstrates Kafi D. Kumasi's (2019) astute reflection that the remedy to anti-Black racism is not to simply insert Black or other equity-deserving communities into existing library practices and services. Rather, the challenge is working alongside those that have been under or ill-represented to identify what is needed locally to create "more culturally sensitive library spaces" with *and for* them (Kumasi, 2012, p. 33). Public libraries cannot address anti-Black racism without engaging and supporting communities seeking equity and inclusion in social services. Rather, this case study demonstrates how community-led engagement can provide insight into under-represented groups' feelings about their services, how they may or may not meet their needs or the ways that they might experience anti-Black racism and other forms of exclusion in library services and in interactions with staff.

CONCLUSION

Neutrality and diversity are often regarded as the bedrock of public libraries. Yet, they are also steeped in white cultural privilege and many have yet to examine the effects of anti-Black racism. While there are no studies that show that anti-Black racism impacts Black communities in Canadian public libraries, the conclusion ought not to be that it does not exist. There have been no inquiries into systemic racism in Canadian librarianship and there are no known race-based analyses to support that public libraries offer equitable and inclusive service to Black communities. Furthermore, there are no known studies on Black youth perceptions or experiences in Canadian public libraries. In response to the wide spread lack of institutional readiness to address the roots of anti-Black racial injustice, Gibson et al. (2021) rightfully declare that "the time has come to interfere" (p. 4). Their pointed response conveys the anger and frustration felt by Black members of the library community whose institutions have consistently failed to meet commitments made to address racial injustice (Gibson et al., 2021). This disturbing trend also raises serious issues for Canadian librarianship that will only increase as Black communities continue to grow and face increasing forms of marginalization. More significantly, this inattention leaves Canadian public libraries underequipped and may further disengage when communities feel like libraries are not responsive to their needs (Kumasi & Hughes-Hassell, 2017). As this case study demonstrates, community-led partnerships with Black communities can enable public libraries to begin to meet their needs by understanding and addressing ways they experience structural challenges and feel under-represented. As the Black Community Public Library looks to the future, the Executive Director and Board members are committed to long-term collaboration with education and social services organizations. While there have been challenges underscoring the need for dedicated services that maintain alignment with the mission and vision of the Black Community Public Library, community-building and trust require investments in both time and energy to maximize their full potential. Communityled partnerships with anti-racist approaches like distinct space and representation remain an important way for the public library sector to support Black communities with meaningful partnership and collaboration to share resources, ideas, and exchange cultural and practical knowledge.

REFERENCES

Agosto, D. E. (2019). Envisaging young adult librarianship from a teen-centered perspective. In A. Bernier (Ed.), *Transforming young adult services* (2nd ed., pp. 50–64). American Library Association.

Agosto, D. E., & Hughes-Hassell, S. (2010). *Urban teens in the library: Research and practice.* American Library Association.

Alberta. (2022). Taking action against racism. Retrieved August 3, 2022, from, https://www.alberta.ca/taking-action-against-racism.aspx

Anucha, U., Srikanthan, S., Siad-Togane, R., & Galabuzi, G.-E. (2017). Doing right together for black youth: What we learned from the community engagement sessions for the Ontario Black Youth Action Plan. In *Youth Research and Evaluation exchange (YOUTHREX)*.

Austin, J. (2016). Questioning "Positive Development": Toward Centering YA library practice on the lived realities of youth. In B. Mehra & K. Rioux (Eds.), *Progressive community action: Critical theory and social justice in library and information science* (pp. 249–282). Library Juice Press.

Bernier, A. (2019). Introduction: Making the case for transforming. In A. Bernier (Ed.), *Transforming young adult services* (2nd ed., pp. xxiv–xlviii). ALA Neal-Schuman.

Briggs, A. Q. (2018). Second generation Caribbean black male youths discuss obstacles to educational and employment opportunities: A critical race counter-narrative analysis. *Journal of Youth Studies, 21*(4), 533–549. https://doi.org/10.1080/13676261.2017.1394997

British Columbia. (2022). Anti-Racism Data Act. Retrieved August 3, 2022, from https://engage.gov.bc.ca/antiracism/

Canada. (2019). *Building a foundation for change: Canada's Anti-Racism Strategy 2019–2022.* Canadian Heritage.

Colour of Poverty – Colour of Change. (2019). 2019 Colour of Poverty Fact Sheets: Understanding the Racialization of Poverty in Ontario, Canada. Retrieved August 3, 2022, from https://colourof-poverty.ca/fact-sheets/

Contenta, S., Monsebraaten, L., & Rankin, J. (2014). *Why Are So Many Black Children in Foster and Group Homes?* Toronto Star. Retrieved August 3, 2022, from https://www.thestar.com/news/canada/2014/12/11/why_are_so_many_Black_children

Cooke, & Sweeney, M. E. (2017). *Teaching for justice: Implementing social justice in the LIS classroom.* Library Juice Press.

Deschenes, N., Arbreton, A., Little, P., Herrera, C., Grossman, J., & Weiss, H. (2010). *Engaging older youth: Program and city-level strategies to support sustained participation in out-of-school time.* Harvard Family Research Project.

Espinal, I. (2001). A new vocabulary for inclusive librarianship: Applying Whiteness theory to our profession. In L. Castillo-Speed (Ed.), *The Power of Language/El Poder de La Palabra; Selected Papers from the Second REFORMA National Conference* (pp. 131–149). Libraries Unlimited.

Espinal, I., Sutherland, T., & Roh, C. (2018). A holistic approach for inclusive librarianship: Decentering whiteness in our profession. *Library Trends, 67*(1), 147–162. https://doi.org/10.1353/lib.2018.0030

Foster, L., Park, S., McCague, H., Fletcher, M.-A., & Sikdar, J. (2021). *Black Canadian National Survey Interim Report 2021.* 32.

Gibson, A. N., Chancellor, R. L., Cooke, N. A., Park Dahlen, S., Patin, B., & Shorish, Y. L. (2017). Libraries on the frontlines: Neutrality and social justice. *Equality, Diversity and Inclusion: An International Journal, 36*(8), 751–766. https://doi.org/10.1108/EDI-11-2016-0100

Gibson, A. N., Chancellor, R. L., Cooke, N. A., Park Dahlen, S., Patin, B., & Shorish, Y. L. (2021). Struggling to breathe: COVID-19, protest and the LIS response. *Equality, Diversity and Inclusion. An International Journal, 40*(1), 74–82. https://doi.org/10.1108/EDI-07-2020-0178

Ginwright, S. A. (2010). Peace out to revolution! Activism among African American youth: An argument for radical healing. *YOUNG, 18*(1), 77–96. https://doi.org/10.1177/110330880901800106

Hathcock, A. (2015). White librarianship in Blackface: Diversity initiatives in LIS. *In the Library with the Lead Pipe, 7.* Retrieved October 30, 2020, from http://www.inthelibrarywiththeleadpipe.org/2015/lis-diversity/

Hudson, D. J. (2017). On Diversity as anti-racism in library and information studies: A critique. *Journal of Critical Library and Information Studies, 1*(1). https://doi.org/10.24242/jclis.v1i1.6

James, C. E., & Turner, T. (2017). *Towards race equity in education: The schooling of black students in the Greater Toronto Area.* York University.

Kania, J., & Kramer, M. (2011). Collective impact. *Stanford Social Innovation Review, 9*(1), 36–41. https://doi.org/10.48558/5900-KN19

Kumasi, K. (2019). "The Library Is Like Her House": Reimagining youth of color in LIS discourses. In *Transforming young adult services* (2nd ed., pp. 103–113). ALA Neal-Schuman. https://digitalcommons.wayne.edu/slisfrp/95

Kumasi, K., & Hughes-Hassell, S. (2017). Shifting lenses on youth literacy & identity. *Knowledge Quest, 45*(3), 12–21.

Leung, S., & López-McKnight, J. R. (2021). *Knowledge justice: Disrupting library and information studies through critical race theory.* The MIT Press.

Mehra, B. (2021). Enough crocodile tears! Libraries moving beyond performative antiracist politics. *The Library Quarterly (Chicago), 91*(2), 137–149. https://doi.org/10.1086/713046

Mehra, B., & Gray, L. (2020). An "Owning Up" of White-IST Trends in LIS to further real transformations. *The Library Quarterly (Chicago), 90*(2), 189–239. https://doi.org/10.1086/707674

Anti-Racism in Practice   103

Nova Scotia Office of Equity and Anti-Racism Initiatives. (2022, March 23). Equity and anti-racism legislation engagement: What we heard report. Retrieved August 3, 2022, from Novascotia.ca website: https://beta.novascotia.ca/documents/equity-and-anti-racism-legislation-engagement-what-we-heard-report

Ontario. (2017). Ontario's anti-racism strategic plan. Retrieved August 3, 2022, from Ontario.ca website: http://www.ontario.ca/page/ontarios-anti-racism-strategic-plan

Ontario. (2022). Data Standards for the Identification and Monitoring of Systemic Racism: Glossary. Retrieved August 3, 2022, from https://www.ontario.ca/document/data-standards-identification-and-monitoring-systemic-racism/glossary

Rothbauer, P. (2019). Imagining today's young adults in LIS: Moving forward with critical youth studies. In *Transforming young adult services* (2nd ed., pp. 151–162). ALA Neal-Schuman.

Schlesselman-Tarango. (2017). *Topographies of whiteness: Mapping whiteness in library and information science*. Library Juice Press.

Schmidt. (2019). Perspectives: White fragility and privilege in librarianship. *Canadian Journal of Academic Librarianship, 4*, 1–7. https://doi.org/10.33137/cjal-rcbu.v4.32166

Statistics Canada. (2017). London [Census metropolitan area], Ontario and Ontario [Province] (table). In *Census Profile. 2016 Census. Statistics Canada Catalogue no. 98-316-X2016001*. Ottawa. Retrieved August 3, 2022, from https://www12.statcan.gc.ca/census-recensement/2016/dp-pd/prof/details/page.cfm?Lang=E&Geo1=CMACA&Code1 = 555&Geo2=PR&Code2 = 35&Data=Count&SearchText=london&SearchType=Begins&SearchPR=01&B1=All&TABID=1

Statistics Canada. (2019a). *A Portrait of Canadian Youth: March 2019 Updates*. Statistics Canada. https://www150.statcan.gc.ca/n1/pub/11-

Statistics Canada. (2019b). *Diversity of the Black population in Canada: An overview*. Retrieved August 3, 2022, from https://www150.statcan.gc.ca/n1/pub/89-657-x/89-657-x2019002-eng.htm

Statistics Canada. (2020). *Canada's Black population: Education, labour and resilience*. Retrieved August 3, 2022, from https://www150.statcan.gc.ca/n1/pub/89-657-x/89-657-x2020002-eng.htm

Statistics Canada. (2022, February 9). *Canada's fastest growing and decreasing municipalities from 2016 to 2021*. Retrieved August 3, 2022, from https://www12.statcan.gc.ca/census-recensement/2021/as-sa/98-200-x/2021001/98-200-x2021001-eng.cfm

Wortley, S., & Jung, M. (2020). *Racial disparity in arrests and charges: An analysis of arrest and charge data from the Toronto Police Service*. Ontario Human Rights Commission.

CHAPTER 7

PUBLIC LIBRARY PRIDE: A JOURNEY OF SMALL STEPS TOWARD INCLUSIVITY

Debra Trogdon-Livingston

ABSTRACT

LGBTQIA+ community members have a history of viewing public libraries as safe spaces. Having this resource is especially important as public policy has shifted away from supporting the LGBTQIA+ community. In this chapter, hear how public libraries have responded to this need. Learn about innovative programming and responsive policies which serve the needs of a wide swath of the LGBTQIA+ community. Discover how libraries can be even more impactful in the lives of the LGBTQIA+ community through a refinement of services, policies, procedures, and collective action.

Explore how library pride recognition is meaningful to the LGBTQIA+ community but needs expansion throughout the year and a more intersectional and inclusive approach. Learn the steps libraries have taken to support youth members of the LBTQIA+ community, from programming to innovative use of technology during pandemic isolation. Discover the importance of using and normalizing pronouns. Hear how my experiences as a public library worker, leader, and member of the LGBTQIA+ community impacted the work done in my libraries. Discover how public libraries can become more inclusive for LGBTQIA+ employees.

Re-think how public libraries can create welcoming spaces and environments for the LGBTQIA+ community. Discover how communities have embraced

---

How Public Libraries Build Sustainable Communities in the 21st Century
Advances in Librarianship, Volume 53, 105–111
Copyright © 2023 by Debra Trogdon-Livingston
Published under exclusive licence by Emerald Publishing Limited
ISSN: 0065-2830/doi:10.1108/S0065-283020230000053009

LGBTQIA+ programming and innovative certification programs to create spaces for and relationships with the LGBTQIA+ community. Consider how LGBTQIA+ equity work fits into the 17 Goals of the United Nations to create a better world for everyone. Discover areas for impact and future growth as public libraries work toward creating meaningful relationships with the LGBTQIA+ community.

Keywords: Collective impact; inclusivity; LGBTQIA+; library workers; policies; pride; public libraries

INTRODUCTION

I spent more than four decades in public libraries as a patron, volunteer, and employee; during that time I have seen small steps and big strides taken toward LGBTQIA+ inclusivity. Public libraries respond to the call for safe spaces through innovative programs, policy changes, displays, and partnerships. This work has become especially difficult as the political tide has turned away from supporting LGBTQIA+ rights (Baer et al., 2019). This chapter will explore how public libraries embed themselves in communities to create change and build strong, sustainable, and inclusive communities.

PRIDE

Fig. 1. Debra Trogdon-Livingston at Charlotte Pride (2019).

One of the first ways people think to support the LGBTQIA+ community is by celebrating pride. Public libraries are no different. As a patron and employee, I always check to see how my public library is celebrating pride. I observe whether there are displays and inclusive programming. I look for signs of LGBTQIA+ inclusivity before applying to a job. In libraries in southern cities, I have often seen little acknowledgment or positive reinforcement of the LGBTQIA+ community. As seen in Figure 1, I get a great sense of peace and joy from attending pride and it is especially meaningful when I see pride celebrated in libraries.

Libraries celebrating pride can create a sense of welcome if they are as inclusive as possible. It is important to note that pride celebrations are commercialized, whitewashed, and often silence minority populations (Trogdon-Livingston, 2022). Barriers to access like incorrect terminology use, personal safety concerns, no access to affirming restrooms, poor collection locations, and privacy concerns are areas for improvement (Trogdon-Livingston, 2022).

EMPLOYEES

Advocating for the LGBTQIA+ community includes advocating for employees. Often, we are asked to advocate for equity we do not experience. There is a scarcity of LGBTQIA+ work–life balance research (Stavrou & Ierodiakonou, 2018). To meet the needs of LGBTQIA+ employees, we need more data. All too often, studies exclude gender and sexuality. LGBTQIA+ employees deserve to be part of the library story.

The American Library Association (2020) gives a clear direction to use pronouns in introductions, hold consistent equity trainings, and use language signaling welcoming workplaces for transgender applicants. Baer et al. (2019) note that libraries using neutrality as a stance can be harmful to library workers and that there is a need to offer stronger support and policies to counter their lack of political support. They suggest offering inclusive health care policies, stronger social support, diversity training, and better overall workplace environments.

RESPONSIVE POLICIES

One of the most visible ways libraries can work for LGBTQIA+ equity is through inclusive policies and procedures. Sweden set the bar high by making equitable libraries a legal concern and by creating measures like LGBTQIA+ workplace certification (Karlsson, 2021). These types of innovative systematic changes have the power to re-create spaces and relationships with the LGBTQIA+ community.

Revising policies to remove barriers and create an inclusive experience takes time. The American Library Association Rainbow Round Table (2022) suggests removing titles indicating gender, making name and gender changes an easier process, not assuming parents are a mother and father, offering single stall gender-inclusive bathrooms, and including LGBTQIA+ books in all displays. Currier and White (2019) advocate for not only offering bathrooms for all genders with clear signage but creating a statement about why this is important. Having policies in place can help with potential backlash. Each of these policy choices is a manageable change with a big impact.

Utilizing gender-neutral language and using pronouns with everyone, not just the LGBTQIA+ community, creates an environment where people begin to feel safe to be themselves. The power librarians have when people need to change gender, pronouns, driver's license, etc. is immense. Libraries already manage custody arrangements and change from a minor card to an adult card. This process can be just as easy.

Jensen (2016) pointed out problematic procedures like shelving LGBTQIA+ materials in the same section as materials about sexual deviancy. *Voices of Youth*

Advocates has reviewed materials as mature based solely on a character's sexuality, which controls its placement on the shelf (Ollis, 2017). Library material placement and location can limit access. Isolating and stickering LGBTQIA+ materials can be problematic. Libraries that are contentious about how they label, shelve, and market materials make a visible statement about their support of the LGBTQIA+ community.

Ollis (2017) encourages libraries to have strong policies in place and to be aware of avenues of support before they face forced policy changes contrary to library ethics and values. This is sound wisdom. I have heard tales from librarians who were able to face a challenge because of a strong collection development policy or offer LGBTQIA+ programming because inclusive programming was written into their mission statement.

PARTNERSHIP

Effective partnership helps public libraries to build momentum toward better services. As resources have become scarce, libraries have aligned with partner organizations to make a bigger impact. I have seen successful partnerships with LGBTQIA+ youth organizations, pride organizations, and LGBTQIA+ school groups. To make deeper connections, libraries must be as intentional about reaching out to the LGBTQIA+ community as they have other underserved communities.

Often LGBTQIA+ gains have centered around large issues and served the most privileged sections of the LGBTQIA+ community (Adam, 2017). Adam (2017) argues that often partnerships don't outlast a specific movement and the money and resources don't trickle into BIPOC communities. Libraries have great potential to better serve LGBTQIA+ communities through partnerships, but it is important that they include voices from the LGBTQIA+ community and intentionally focus on intersectionality and underrepresented communities.

One example of thoughtful partnership is when Cleveland Public Library donated LGBTQIA+ themed materials to the Beyond Identities Community Center, an organization who serves LGBTQIA+ BIPOC youth (Young, 2022). It is important that they selected a partner organization serving LGBTQIA+ youth who are also BIPOC. This chips away at the notion that the LGBTQIA+ population is a homogeneous group. If they involved the LGBTQIA+ community in the decision to partner with this group, which they may have, they would be creating more equitable partnerships.

YOUTH

Public libraries have taken strides toward supporting LGBTQIA+ youth. Including gender-diverse programming and using innovative technology to create social connections during pandemic isolation are the two ways through which libraries created a change. Finding information can be tricky when there is a fear of stigma. Libraries are finding creative solutions. Amrein (2021) praised "the Queer Gabby teen reference tool provided by the Cincinnati and Hamilton County Public Library" (para. 5–7) as a safe way to get reliable answers. This platform allows teens to find trusted information through casual interaction (Amrein, 2021).

One step that libraries have taken is learning the names and pronouns of LGBTQIA+ youth and being open to fluidity. Library staff sharing their pronouns consistently opens the door for youth to share theirs. Restroom equity will always be meaningful, but for youth with limited power and choices, having a safe restroom regardless of gender or sexuality can be life-changing.

Up to 40% of the homeless youth population identify as LGBTQIA+ versus up to 7% of the non-LGBTQIA+ youth population (Winkelstein, 2021). This dramatic difference indicates the need of support for LGBTQIA+ youth. They need education, employment, housing, social services, entertainment, technology, policy flexibility, and a place to relax and be invisible (Winkelstein, 2021).

Winkelstein (2021) advocates that we challenge stereotypes traditionally associated with people experiencing homeless such as assuming someone is unsheltered or unclean. Avoiding these stereotypes with a vulnerable population like LGBTQIA+ youth is especially important to prevent them from feeling judged and isolated. Creating policies and an atmosphere of support allows LGBTQIA+ youth experiencing homelessness to thrive in libraries.

PROGRAMMING

Public libraries become more inclusive when they enhance LGBTQIA+ programming. Incorporating LGBTQIA+ elements builds inclusivity from the ground up. Utilizing LGBTQIA+ themed materials, those by LGBTQIA+ authors, and using family neutral terminology in program titles and advertisements signals acceptance.

Successful programs include drag story time, rainbow family story time, gender expansive crafting, and hosting LGBTQIA+ authors (Naidoo, 2018). During the pandemic, a colleague utilized Discord to engage with LGBTQIA+ youth. Another colleague created a gender-inclusive recycled runway program where participants utilized recycled materials to create fashion pieces to walk the runway. I have seen successful virtual LGBTQIA+ book clubs. The most important part of programming is involving the community in planning and implementation.

MOMENTUM

To gain the most impact from LGBTQIA+ library services, programs, and policies, libraries need to be embedded into the fabric of their communities. A clear path to this outcome is to follow the "Five conditions of collective impact" set forth by Kania and Kramer (2011, para. 15). In library work, having a "common agenda" (Kania & Kramer, 2011, para. 16) starts with acknowledging the existence of differences in interpretation and objectives and coming to a common agreement about a larger goal. Libraries have begun working toward this goal by having equity-driven goals and embracing cultural humility.

"Shared measurement systems" (Kania & Kramer, 2011, para. 18) are vital in a world of increasing misinformation and disinformation. Having the same means of measuring outcomes allows for accountability and quick pivot time if data indicate the need. This skill is crucial when utilizing "mutually reinforcing activities" (Kania & Kramer, 2011, para. 21). Being strategic allows each partner to use their niche skills to benefit the success of the entire group. As resources have become scarce, libraries have become more focused on outcomes and are utilizing shared measurement systems to maximize partnerships.

When working with a variety of groups with their own interests, "continuous communication" (Kania & Kramer, 2011, para. 25) is necessary to build group trust. This involves frequent meetings with the highest level leaders and a clear plan. Each group must be able to trust that their own interests are being considered alongside the greater good. One outcome I have seen from COVID is the ability to have meetings with all levels of leaders more often. That access can be the start of building foundations of trust.

It may be difficult for public libraries to find a "backbone support organization" (Kania & Kramer, 2011, para. 28). While libraries focus on partnerships, they often partner with organizations that also lack resources. Public libraries try to be the backbone but are understaffed, underfunded, and overstretched. Collective impact needs "supporting infrastructure" (Kania & Kramer, 2011, para. 30) to succeed. Finding those partnerships is vital to making sure the work lasts beyond a single project. As organizations recover from the impacts of COVID-19, it may become easier to find partners who have their own strong infrastructure. When libraries combine these elements, they amplify the work community partners accomplish together, help each group involved stay focused on the work and outcomes, and utilize resources effectively.

KINDNESS BY DESIGN

Libraries who serve the LGBTQIA+ community well model how intentionality creates a welcoming environment. Building design, inclusive restrooms, and kind staff interactions have a strong impact. Remembering that LGBTQIA+ people can feel incredibly visible and invisible at the same time and allowing space for both creates safety. Libraries use building design and interactions to model kindness that people do not see anywhere else.

Quality education, clean water, sanitation, and reduced inequalities as priorities are included in The 17 Goals (2022) of the United Nations. By offering inclusive education, access to gender affirming bathrooms, and offering access to water, libraries are meeting those needs. We work toward a more equitable world with each step libraries have taken to be more inclusive for the LGBTQIA+ community. Each of the steps helps the LGBTQIA+ community, every other patron, and employee.

CONCLUSION

I am grateful to public libraries that work diligently to create safety for the LGBTQIA+ community. The investment into creating inclusive policies that honor gender expression and removing barriers are worth it. The time spent building connections with the LGBTQIA+ community pays off in programs and services built on the foundation of LGBTQIA+ people's input. Public libraries that are intentional and inclusive in their treatment of LGBTQIA+ library workers are changing the world one employee at a time. Using principles of collective action can extend the scope of this equity work and keep the momentum going in public libraries.

REFERENCES

Adam. (2017). Intersectional coalitions: The paradoxes of rights-based movement building in LGBTQ and immigrant communities. *Law & Society Review*, 51(1), 132–167. https://doi.org/10.1111/lasr.12248

American Library Association. (2020). *Libraries respond: Protecting and supporting transgender staff and patrons*. Advocacy, Legislation & Issues. https://www.ala.org/advocacy/diversity/libraries-respond/transgender-staff-patrons

American Library Association Rainbow Round Table. (2022). *Open to all: Serving the LGBTQIA+ community in your library*. https://www.ala.org/rt/sites/ala.org.rt/files/content/RRT/rrt-open-to-all-toolkit-2022.pdf

Amrein, C. (2021). *Improving virtual reference services for LGBTQIA+ users*. Public Libraries Online. http://publiclibrariesonline.org/2021/12/improving-virtual-reference-services-for-lgbtqia-users/

Baer, A., Cahoy, E. S., Schroeder, R., Cope, J., Fisher, Z., Patillo, E., Goodfellow, R., & Krueger, S. (2019). What it means to be out: Queer, trans, and gender nonconforming identities in library work. *Libraries promoting reflective dialogue in a time of political polarization*. Association of College & Research Libraries, a division of the American Library Association.

Currier, B. D., & White, T. (2019). *Creating the trans inclusive library*. https://doi.org/10.31229/osf.io/re8gf

Jensen, K. (2016). *Queer phobia and the public library*. Book Riot. https://bookriot.com/public-libraries-you-owe-your-queer-patrons-better/

Kania, J., & Kramer, M. (2011). *Collective impact*. Stanford Social Innovation Review. https://ssir.org/articles/entry/collective_impact#

Karlsson, T. (2021). *LGBTQ+ education for library personnel: Examples from Swedish public libraries*. IFLA LGBTQ Users. https://iflalgbtqusers.wordpress.com/2021/08/16/lgbtq-education-for-library-personnel-examples-from-swedish-public-libraries/

Naidoo, J. C. (2018). A rainbow of creativity: Exploring drag queen storytimes and gender creative programming in public libraries. *Children & Libraries*, 16(4), 12–22. https://doi.org/10.5860/cal.16.4.12

Ollis, C. (2017). Standing up for our communities. *American Libraries Magazine*. https://americanlibrariesmagazine.org/2017/06/21/standing-up-lgbtq-youth-communities/

Stavrou, E., & Ierodiakonou, C. (2018). Expanding the work-life balance discourse to LGBT employees: Proposed research framework and organizational responses. *Human Resource Management*, 57(6), 1355–1370. https://doi.org/10.1002/hrm.21910

The 17 Goals. (2022). https://sdgs.un.org/goals#goals

Trogdon-Livingston, D. (2022, March). *Take pride in your library: Working towards LGBTQIA+ inclusivity in public libraries* [Paper presentation]. Southeast Collaborative Online Conference.

Winkelstein, J. A. (2021). *LGBTGIQ+ youth, homelessness, and libraries*. IFLA LGBTQ Users. https://iflalgbtqusers.wordpress.com/2021/10/18/lgbtgiq-youth-homelessness-and-libraries/

Young, M. (2022). Cleveland Public Library's Rainbow Readers donates LGBTQIA+ themed books to the Beyond Identities Community Center. https://cpl.org/cleveland-public-librarys-rainbow-readers-donates-lgbtqia-themed-books-to-the-beyond-identities-community-center/

CHAPTER 8

A CALL TO ACTION: LIBRARIES LEANING IN FOR UNHOUSED LGBTGEQ+ YOUTH

Julie Ann Winkelstein

ABSTRACT

Libraries must acknowledge their role as gatekeepers for lesbian, gay, bisexual, transgender, gender expansive queer and questioning (LGBTGEQ+) young people on their journey to home. By exploring the intersections of community, identity, accessible information, equitable practices, and leadership commitment, this chapter calls on the profession to lean in and no longer look away (K. Strowder, personal communication, 2022).

Keywords: LGBTGEQ+ youth; homelessness; public libraries; identity; narrative inquiry; experience; intersectionality; National Runaway Safeline; Point Source Youth

INTRODUCTION

In this chapter, I offer my perspective on the intersection of libraries and LGBTGEQ+ youth who are unhoused. I hope this personal narrative will provide insights into the lives of the youth, and the work that could be and is being done.

I also point out that this topic supports many of the United Nations Sustainable Development Goals (SDGs), in particular SDG 1 No Poverty, SDG 2 Zero Hunger, and SDG 17 Partnerships for the Goals (United Nations, n.d.). I stress these in particular, as all three contribute to the youth stories that are told, as well as the essential library responses.

How Public Libraries Build Sustainable Communities in the 21st Century
Advances in Librarianship, Volume 53, 113–123
Copyright © 2023 by Julie Ann Winkelstein
Published under exclusive licence by Emerald Publishing Limited
ISSN: 0065-2830/doi:10.1108/S0065-283020230000053010

ABOUT THE AUTHOR

I worked as a public librarian for 20 years and during that time I worked in jails and prisons, on a bookmobile serving low-income childcare programs, as a family literacy program coordinator and in a branch as both a young adult and children's librarian. I fell into my current work as a researcher, teacher, and writer after completing my PhD at the University of Tennessee, Knoxville, where my dissertation was on the role of libraries in addressing LGBTGEQ+ youth homelessness.

I created and teach a library school class on homelessness and libraries, some years specifically focusing on unaccompanied youth ages 12–24. The work I do to teach this class has changed me. The materials I gather each year, the guest speakers, and especially my students offer me continuing opportunities to look more deeply at my assumptions, my knowledge and lack thereof, and what part libraries play in the lives of the youth.

METHODOLOGICAL INSIGHTS

The author uses narrative inquiry to describe observations and thoughts about LGBTGEQ+ unhoused/home-free/street-based youth and the role of libraries in their lives. Narrative inquiry can be defined as "a way of understanding experience. It is a collaboration between a researcher and participants, over time, in a place or series of places…" (Clandinin & Connelly, 2000). Or as Lindsay and Schwind (2016) put it:

> Experience happens in a place or places over time, in a relationship, which may be within oneself or others. Consequently, when studying experience, narrative inquirers consider four directions: inwards, outwards, forwards, and backwards. (p. 15)

I have chosen this method because this is my story, based on what I've heard from youth I have either interacted with or had the privilege of learning about through their writings and presentations. These interactions have not only provided me with insights into their lives but they have also changed me – changed my story, as I hear and share theirs.

LITERATURE REVIEW

Extensive literature reviews on this topic can be found in Winkelstein (2012, 2017, 2019).

STIGMA AND STEREOTYPE

In her TED talk "The Danger of the Single Story," Ngozi Adichie Chimamanda (2009) says: "The single story creates stereotypes, and the problem with stereotypes is not that they are untrue, but that they are incomplete." This statement beautifully sums up the barriers for both unhoused LGBTGEQ+ youth and libraries.

Assumptions are made that become a single story: LGBTGEQ+ youth experiencing homelessness are viewed, by the very definition of their housing status – i.e., "homeless" – to be unkempt, living with a mental health challenge that makes them unstable, unpredictable, potentially violent, unreliable, uneducated and without anything of value to contribute to society. This is the single story attached to the word "homeless."

Libraries and library staff are seen as controlling, disinterested in social justice, committed to maintaining hushed buildings that are full of pristine books, quietly checked out by housed, whispering community members. Library workers who read this may scoff or laugh or be angry, because you know we are so much more than that. But that is frequently our image, to the detriment of both the library profession and the communities we serve, and we struggle to move away from our single story.

As Adichie (2009) points out so well in her talk, it is by learning more about those who are defined by a single story that we are able to move beyond our assumptions and our stereotypes. We must take in the full story – not the abridged version so easily accessed. It is in this full story that we can find our path to addressing societal challenges like LGBTGEQ+ youth homelessness.

INTERSECTIONALITY/OVERLAP

As many know, Kimberlé Crenshaw coined the term "intersectionality" in her 1989 article "Demarginalizing the Intersection of Race and Sex: A Black Feminist Critique of Antidiscrimination Doctrine, Feminist Theory and Antiracist Politics" (Crenshaw, 1989). In the more than 30 years since that publication, intersectionality has been applied, interpreted, and re-interpreted by the media, the public, and Crenshaw herself. In a 2017 Columbia Law School interview, Crenshaw is asked about what is meant by this term so many years later. Her answer includes a definition that aptly applies to the lives and experiences of the youths' lives:

> Intersectionality is a lens through which you can see where power comes and collides, where it interlocks and intersects. It's not simply that there's a race problem here, a gender problem here, and a class or LBGTQ problem there. Many times that framework erases what happens to people who are subject to all of these things. (Columbia Law School, 2017)

Crenshaw's definition fits well with the danger of the single story. The intersection or overlap of the many identities and experiences of our lives is directly linked to our present and our future. That is, we must take into account the overlap of our numerous identities, much like a Venn diagram. Each of us lives at the center of that overlap and what that means to us is unique. In a world where identities are generalized, stigmatized, or exalted, we must remember there is no generic person and no one LGBTGEQ+ youth story that lets us know what it's like to be a young person who is living an unstable and unpredictable life, that yet may be preferable to living in a situation where they are not free to be themselves. Make no assumptions is an excellent motto to keep in mind with the youth, as with any of our library users. We don't know until they tell us.

DEFINING YOUTH HOMELESSNESS

Unlike many assumptions about homelessness, there are many ways youth qualify as "homeless." These include:

- Sleeping at a friend's house or couch surfing
- Riding the subway or staying on the street
- Trading work or sex for a place to stay or other needed resources
- Living in a car, sleeping in parks, abandoned buildings, or other public places
- Staying in a crisis shelter or transitional shelter
- Staying at someone else's…supportive housing apartment although not allowed to be there
- Forced to leave their homes with no place to go (Safe Horizon, n.d.).

The McKinney-Vento Act definition of homelessness also includes:

- Individuals who lack a fixed, regular, and adequate nighttime residence
- Children and youths who are sharing the housing of other persons due to loss of housing, economic hardship, or a similar reason; are living in motels, hotels, trailer parks, or camping grounds due to the lack of alternative adequate accommodations
- Children and youths who are living in…substandard housing (NCHE, n.d.).

You can see from these definitions that you may already be encountering youth who fit one of them, whether or not you realize it. Unlike the visibility of the small percentage of adults who experience chronic homelessness, youth on the whole are able to remain invisible. This fact makes it even more important that you know more about their lives and create a place that feels safe enough to divulge their housing status to you, so your library can offer resources, support, and connections, and can be part of "helping them put down roots, helping them feel a part of a community, helping them see the value that they can contribute to their community" (Samuels, 2021). This is critical to the work we must all do, as we examine our power and position, as we dislodge our assumptions and open ourselves to an expanded awareness of how our libraries may or may not be welcoming places, where unhoused LGBTGEQ+ youth can let down their guard and be themselves.

STATISTICS AND OVERLAPPING FACTORS

Even beginning to describe the challenges experienced by home-free youth can immediately bring up feelings of being overwhelmed (as my students will attest to) or pity or a tendency toward being a "savior." So while I briefly list some of the systems that lead to youth homelessness, please set these reactions aside. These statistics offer insights into the factors that led to their housing instability, not to burden or even inspire. "Know your community" is where you can start, by

A Call to Action   117

listening, asking questions, and listening more. Sometimes listening to one young person may be all you can do at the moment and that simple gift will likely be noted and even cherished.

Having said that, here are some of the ways in which the youth end up unstably housed.

- LGBTGEQ+ youth

Each year in the United States, as many as 4.2 million youth experience homelessness (True Colors United, n.d.). On a single night in 2020, 34,210 unaccompanied youth, ages 12 to 24, were reported to be experiencing homelessness in the United States (Henry et al., 2021, p. 42), although due to the challenges of the pandemic that began in 2020 and other factors, these numbers are universally acknowledged to be undercounts. Up to 40% of the youth are LGBTQ+, as compared to approximately 7% of the overall youth population (True Colors United, n.d.).

- Exiting the foster system

According to McDonald (2021):

- Many young people who enter homelessness, including young parents with children, do so after exiting foster care. Researchers have found that between 31% and 46% of youth exiting foster care experience homelessness by the age of 26. A study conducted in Washington State found that approximately one-quarter of youth that exited foster care at the age of 17 or older became homeless within 12 months of exit. The risk of homelessness was particularly acute for Black youth exiting foster care and for parenting youth.

- Incarceration

As Wenzel (2020) explains:

  - On average, adolescents incarcerated before they're 18 years old experience literal homelessness for the first time 9.8 years earlier than those incarcerated after age 24.
  - Transitional-age youth (TAY) incarcerated between the ages of 18 and 24 experience literal homelessness for the first time 5.1 years earlier.
  - Those incarcerated as adolescents spent an average of 3,095 days experiencing literal homelessness, those incarcerated as TAY spent an average of 1,853 days literally homeless, and those incarcerated greater than age 24 spent an average of 1,598 days in literal homelessness.

- Youth of color

In their research, Chapin Hall (Gonzalez et al., 2021) found:

- o The challenge of youth homelessness and housing instability is more pronounced among **BIPOC** youth ages 13 to 25, with 11% of American Indian and Alaskan Indian youth experiencing homelessness during a year, 7% of Black youth, and 7% of Hispanic [Latinx] youth relative to 4% of White, non-Hispanic youth.
- o The intersection of different marginalized identities compounds inequities among youth of color, with Black youth identifying as LGBTQ experiencing especially high rates of homelessness and adversity.

As you can imagine, there are many other factors that affect the youth, including generational poverty, health, trauma, lack of family support, lack of socially acceptable life skills and education.

The other factor is of course housing. What I call "truly" affordable housing (as opposed to the more common term of affordable, which is so frequently unaffordable for those who are experiencing homelessness) is becoming more and more difficult to find and when that lack is combined with a need for the life skills related to finding and retaining housing, the legal records of those who are punished for being unhoused, the need for an ID, references, and an adequate income – all of these and more create barriers.

However, barriers create opportunities for libraries. As we consider our role in addressing LGBTGEQ+ youth homelessness and as we ask questions through partnerships and individual interactions, and as we listen, we can begin to see what part we could play in lowering or removing the impediments the youth experience, so they have equitable access to the resources and spaces provided by libraries. This requires a commitment on the part of leadership, it requires honesty, humility, and a willingness to engage not as managers but as supporters and allies.

When I was conducting the phenomenological qualitative methods research for my dissertation on the role of libraries in the lives of LGBTGEQ+ youth experiencing homelessness (Winkelstein, 2012), I had multiple conversations with unhoused youth and the service providers who were involved in their lives. In addition, I talked with youth services librarians, as well as library administrators. I came away from the conversations with a strong sense of the importance of libraries being involved and the barriers to this involvement.

One theme in particular was the concept of safety. As I discovered through the stories shared with me, the youth wanted to feel safe, the service providers wanted the youth to feel safe and the library staff wanted safety for both their housed library users as well as themselves. This common thread was particularly notable since the feeling of safety for one group – the library users and library staff – seemed to be in direct contradiction to the safety for the youth. The mere presence of someone who was perceived to be unstably housed or who acknowledged their housing status, despite not fitting into the stigmatized stereotype of homelessness, made the housed library staff and community members uncomfortable and the discomfort by the white community members and library staff is frequently exacerbated if the youth are Black or Brown.

This discomfort creates a significant barrier to the services, connections, and resources that could be made accessible to the youth. In addition, the reliance on policing – hiring uniformed security guards, calling the police, implementing rules and policies that enable library staff to be over vigilant when specific library users are present – creates an environment that feels unwelcoming and unsafe to the youth.

We can take this knowledge and look at our library practices. We can understand that what we don't know is going to affect the way our buildings and services are received and experienced. We can look directly at the youth and challenge ourselves to learn more about their lives and their needs so when we listen, we begin to understand.

LIBRARIES TAKING ACTION

For three years, through an Institute of Library and Museum Services (2013) grant, I provided workshops and training materials to library staff in both California and Tennessee on serving unhoused LGBTQ+ youth. These workshops offered insight into the need for connections between library staff and local, state and/or national organizations. Since then, I've seen the power of partnerships when they do happen and how these partnerships are beneficial for everyone: the youth, the service providers and non-profits, the community, and the libraries themselves.

This last fact is one that is too often overlooked. Libraries can frequently be inward-focused. Concerns about funding, staffing, scheduling, and balancing the stated desires of their housed community members can lead to creating programs, collections, and resources that serve these members. Without hearing directly from the youth and those who support them, it is impossible to truly understand the impact and trauma of living with housing and food insecurity and not being accepted for simply being themselves in the community and at the library. Voice is crucial to dispelling stereotypes so we can provide appropriate and relevant services that acknowledge power differentials and work to dismantle them.

In 2022, the National Runaway Safeline (NRS) hosted an online webinar that brought together the voices of youth who have experienced homelessness. Each young person told their story – of being not being accepted, of living with a disability, of enduring two and a half years of conversion therapy that included electric shocks, of wanting to make a difference, of defining advocacy as a wellness project, of what it means to have support and be listened to, acknowledged and welcomed for being themselves (NRS, 2022). The stories the youth told reinforced the mission of NRS: "The mission of the National Runaway Safeline (NRS) is to keep America's runaway, homeless and at-risk youth safe and off the streets" (NRS, n.d.).

Another organization that offers youth voices is Point Source Youth, dedicated to scaling-up "affirming youth centered solutions" to end the crisis of youth homelessness (Point Source Youth, n.d.). At a 2021 webinar called "Radical Collaboration: Co-Creating Programs with Youth" (Point Source Youth, 2021), the panelists described the difference between tokenization and meaningful youth collaboration. As Guttierrez III (2021) explained: "Tokenism is when young people appear to be given a voice but in fact have little to no choice about what they do or how they participate." Jacobs (2021) described meaningful youth collaboration as the need to "integrate youth voice into every process of the organization... youth-led, for youth, by youth." Jacobs also stressed including more than one youth perspective, so all youth are able to be engaged and have their voices represented, respected, and acted on.

It cannot be emphasized enough how these stories of lived experience are crucial for understanding the needs and challenges being faced by unhoused LGBTGEQ+ youth. Nothing can replace hearing a person's story, firsthand. Each personal story invites library staff to listen and care and then support conversations, programs, collections, environments that directly reflect the lives of the youth, without judgment or taking control. The disconnect between library staff and youth, by not bringing in youth or by tokenizing their voices, means library staff either don't include the concerns and needs of the youth or they're under the impression they are doing that despite the lack of youth leadership and the outcomes.

Another action many libraries are taking is to eliminate fines on library materials, and reconsider public conduct policies, such as no sleeping, no eating, bathroom restrictions and requiring a permanent address for a library card. All of these policies impact unhoused youth and create an atmosphere of fear not safety. In addition, libraries can provide staff training, created and presented by the youth themselves who are paid for their expertise, so staff can hear directly from their community members and work toward an environment that tells unhoused LGBTGEQ+ youth "this space is for you."

Some libraries provide curated lists of LGBTGEQ+ books, as well as books related to the lives of unhoused teens (e.g., The Seattle Public Library, n.d.) and Oak Park Public Library hosted a restorative justice peace circle for youth (OPPL, 2018). These are examples of the efforts by libraries across the United States to truly serve all youth in their communities.

ONE STORY

For seven years I worked with a local public librarian to bring books and other resources to an emergency shelter for TAY, ages 18 to 24. I brought the materials and the librarian brought the library laptop, so she could register the youth for library cards, as well as clear their records of any fines or fees. We purposely chose to be there on the weeknight when they held their community meetings, because in addition to talking with the youth one on one about books, we could then also hear about the topics that were of importance to them. The insights we were able to get by interacting and by listening were invaluable.

During the community meeting one night, several of the youth pointed out that the job announcement flyer they had received the previous day required access to the internet and the applications were due in two days. The shelter had no public access computer with internet and so the librarian offered to reserve a bank of internet computers at the library the following day. Even though we were there weekly and even though the youth regularly used the library, no one

A Call to Action

thought of asking if the library could do this – because they didn't know library staff would listen, because they weren't used to asking library staff for exceptions, because they didn't think of the library as a partner.

This is a barrier – and one that can be overcome.

CONCLUSION

In this chapter, I ask libraries to lean in and not avert their attention from LGBTGEQ+ youth homelessness (K. Strowder, personal communication). It can seem daunting for library staff to directly look at this topic, so it's important to emphasize that libraries are not responsible for the lives of the youth, just as they are not responsible for anyone's lives. However, they *are* responsible for focusing on the needs and lives of all their community members, including unhoused/home-free/street-based LGBTGEQ+ youth. Partnerships can and do provide libraries with the opportunity to take action on the challenges in the lives of so many young people and I encourage all library staff to actively engage with local, state, and national organizations. Libraries bring with them the respect of the community and the privilege that comes with that respect. Retired librarian Mayo (personal communication, 2022) put it like this:

> Being involved in these groups [local CBOs] helped us identify specific community needs and niches that we could fill, gave us credibility in our county, and allowed us to help other groups shine through their association with the library. Small non-profits need our endorsement, especially when many of us are addressing big problems that need broad support. The library systems get plenty of recognition (and will be around year after year) but some smaller ones (with tight budgets) need the boost and support that we can help provide.

Partnerships also enable libraries to bring in youth voices that are not tokenized but are instead respected, included, and considered necessary leadership in the work that can and should be done to address the multiple challenges for the young people, while celebrating who they are and their contributions to the library and the community.

Low expectations related to partnerships between libraries and youth-serving organizations run both ways. As library staff, we can do our part by being willing to listen and persist. The library, the organization, and the community all gain through these opportunities.

As Point Source Youth says: "As an organization, we believe in the power of community. Together we can end youth homelessness" (Eventbrite, 2022). Samuels adds to this in his Chapin Hall video on youth homelessness by concluding with:

> Reducing or eliminating youth homelessness would require a multi-level approach to making change happen, so young people have different experiences in their families, they have different experiences in their community, and that they have access to the resources and supports that they need from the larger system. (Samuels, 2021)

Libraries can be part of this multi-level approach, by partnering, listening, providing staff training, and creating myriad connections. We can do this.

ACKNOWLEDGMENT

I'd like to acknowledge my students, guest speakers, Point Source Youth, and Kevin Strowder, whose writing helped me find some of the words to perfectly express my thoughts and viewpoint.

REFERENCES

Chimamanda, N. A. (2009). "The danger of the single story." *TED.* https://www.ted.com/talks/chimamanda_ngozi_adichie_the_danger_of_a_single_story

Clandinin, D. J., & Connelly, F. M. (2000). *Narrative inquiry: Experience and story in qualitative research.* Jossey-Bass Publishers.

Columbia Law School. (2017, June 8). "Kimberlé Crenshaw on intersectionality, more than two decades later." *Columbia Law School.* https://www.law.columbia.edu/news/archive/kimberle-crenshaw-intersectionality-more-two-decades-later

Crenshaw, K. (1989). "Demarginalizing the intersection of race and sex: A Black feminist critique of antidiscrimination doctrine, feminist theory and antiracist politics." *University of Chicago Legal Forum,* 1989, 1, Article 8. http://chicagounbound.uchicago.edu/uclf/vol1989/iss1/8

Eventbrite. (2022). "6th annual Point Source Youth national symposium on solutions to end youth homelessness." *Point Source Youth.* https://www.eventbrite.com/e/the-national-symposium-on-solutions-to-end-youth-homelessness-registration-267711862387

Gonzalez, S. B., Morton, M., Patel, S., & Samuels, B. (2021). "Youth of color disproportionately impacted by housing instability." *Chapin Hall.* https://www.chapinhall.org/research/youth-of-color-disproportionately-impacted-by-housing-instability/

Guttierrez, A. III (2021). "Radical collaboration: Co-creating programs with youth." *Point Source Youth.* https://vimeo.com/656305037

Henry, M., Watt, R., Mahathey, A., Ouelette, J., & Sitler, A. (2020). The 2019 annual assessment report (AHAR) to Congress. Retrieved from https://www.hudexchange.info/resource/5948/2019-ahar-part-1-pit-estimates-of-homelessness-in-the-us/

Institute of Museum and Library Services. (2013). "Library Anchor Models for Bridging Diversity Achievements (LAMBDA)." Laura Bush 21st Century Librarian Program. University of Tennessee, Knoxville. Log Number: RE-06-13-0051-13. https://www.imls.gov/grants/awarded/re-06-13-0051-13

Jacobs, Z. (2021). "Radical collaboration: Co-creating programs with youth." *Point Source Youth.* https://vimeo.com/656305037

Lindsay, G. M., & Schwind, J. K. (2016, March). Narrative inquiry: Experience matters. *Canadian Journal of Nursing Research,* 48(1), 14–20.

McDonald, S. (2021, January 26). "Preventing homelessness for youth and young families in foster care: FY2021 updates." *National Alliance to End Homelessness.* https://endhomelessness.org/blog/preventing-homelessness-for-youth-and-young-families-in-foster-care-fy2021-updates/

National Center for Homeless Education (NCHE). (n.d.). "The McKinney-Vento definition of homeless." https://nche.ed.gov/mckinney-vento-definition/

National Runaway Safeline (NRS). (2022). "The intersection of LGBTQIA2S+ identity and youth homelessness: A youth advisory board panel discussion." *NRS Pride Panel 2022.* https://www.1800runaway.org/events/nrs-pride-panel-2022

National Runaway Safeline (NRS). (n.d.). "Mission." https://www.1800runaway.org/about-us#mission

Oak Park Public Library (OPPL). (2018, December 2). "What grows with restorative justice?" https://www.oppl.org/news-events/learn-connect/what-grows-with-restorative-justice/

Point Source Youth. (2021). "Radical collaboration: Co-creating programs with youth." https://vimeo.com/656305037

Point Source Youth. (n.d.). "About." https://www.pointsourceyouth.org/what-we-do

Safe Horizon. (n.d.). "Youth homelessness statistics & facts." https://www.safehorizon.org/get-informed/homeless-youth-statistics-facts/#description/

Samuels, B. (2021). "Youth experiencing homelessness in Cook County Illinois." *Chapin Hall*. https://www.chapinhall.org/research/youth-of-color-disproportionately-impacted-by-housing-instability/

The Seattle Public Library. (n.d.). "Teens and homelessness." https://www.spl.org/programs-and-services/social-justice/social-justice-series/homelessness/teens-and-homelessness

True Colors United (n.d.). "Our Issue." True Colors United. https://truecolorsunited.org/our-issue/

United Nations. (n.d.). "Make the SDGs a reality." Department of Economic and Social Affairs. https://sdgs.un.org/#goal_section

Wenzel, S. (2020). "Do people incarcerated before age 25 experience a longer duration of homelessness?" *Housing Matters*. https://housingmatters.urban.org/research-summary/do-people-incarcerated-age-25-experience-longer-duration-homelessness

Winkelstein, J. A. (2012). *Public libraries and homeless LGBTQ youth: Creating safe spaces through cultural competence* [Unpublished doctoral dissertation]. University of Tennessee, Knoxville.

Winkelstein, J. A. (2017). Libraries and LGBTQ* youth experiencing homelessness: Creating safe spaces through ethical librarianship. In T. Samek & L. Shultz (Eds.), *Information ethics, globalization and citizenship: Essays in ideas to praxis* (pp. 156–168). McFarland & Company, Inc., Publishers.

Winkelstein, J. A. (2019). Chapter 8: The role of public libraries in the lives of LGBTQ+ youth experiencing homelessness. In B. Mehra (Ed.), *LGBTQ+ Librarianship in the 21st century: Emerging directions of advocacy and community engagement in diverse information environments* (pp. 197–221). Emerald Publishing Limited.

CHAPTER 9

LET'S LEARN TOGETHER OUTSIDE: FAMILIES PLAYING, BUILDING RELATIONSHIPS, AND CONNECTING WITH THEIR COMMUNITY IN NATURE

Emily Sedgwick and Wendee Mullikin

National Center for Families Learning

ABSTRACT

Libraries provide ideal learning spaces within communities. By partnering with them, families are able to access equitable programming that promotes Family Engagement with the library and beyond. The program – Let's Learn Together Outside (LLTO) – was implemented by libraries to provide support to low-income caregivers and their preschool-age (3–5 years) children during vocabulary- and conversation-building activities created to promote outdoor learning and increase participants' sense of wonder, imagination, and creativity during play. This free programming scaffolded caregivers' understanding of early literacy and oral language skills while they learned alongside their children about exploring nature. The three stand-alone, interactive sessions utilized a consistent structure and were implemented at eight libraries, located in Kentucky, Ohio, and Michigan. With thorough, practical training experiences and professionally designed materials, staff were able to connect with families in ways that sustained learning outside the library walls.

How Public Libraries Build Sustainable Communities in the 21st Century
Advances in Librarianship, Volume 53, 125–136
Copyright © 2023 by Emily Sedgwick and Wendee Mullikin
Published under exclusive licence by Emerald Publishing Limited
ISSN: 0065-2830/doi:10.1108/S0065-283020230000053011

Keywords: Programming; family engagement; equity; early literacy; oral language skills; nature; materials

Learning consistently takes place in public libraries, and by offering multigenerational educational opportunities through these institutions, "we support families to help them thrive" (Lopez & Caspe, 2021, p. 3). Through the implementation of Let's Learn Together Outside (LLTO), a regional nature-based, three-part learning series, multigenerational learning takes place through purposeful interactions between caregivers and children. By using a consistent learning format forged in Family Engagement, caregivers have the opportunity to practice research-based literacy strategies with children aged three to five years and are provided with outdoor, community, and real-world connections to learning specific to their region. Through the use of concurrent Children's Education and Parent Education time, children and caregivers are introduced to the concepts and learning strategies for the session's lesson. During Parent and Child Together (PACT) Time® (Jacobs et al., 2019), caregivers and children have the opportunity for supported practice of literacy strategies – including conversational turns, expanding responses, and expanding vocabulary. Participants also engage in outdoor activities designed to promote language and literacy engagement. A Debrief/Wrap-Up before the session ends allows caregivers to share their experiences and ask questions while facilitators provide suggestions for use or extension of the activity at home or in other community venues as well as providing a glimpse at the next session's contents. Ultimately, caregivers should realize, through participation in the program, that learning can take place anytime and anywhere.

Funded by the Caplan Foundation through Family Engagement grants to qualifying libraries, who self-identified as either rural or urban and serve a low-income population, seven sites implemented programming in three states. Evaluation of three sites in Kentucky was completed in 2018.

The National Center for Families Learning (NCFL) supports family success by partnering with communities on initiatives where families develop their literacy and leadership skills through education. NCFL's founder pioneered the four-component Family Literacy model in 1985. Since that time, the components of Children's Education, Parent Time, Parent Education, and PACT Time, have been combined in different ways to support Family Engagement and Family Learning programming.

> Family Engagement programming includes [multi]-generation learning opportunities, events, activities, and strategies that support children's academic achievement [...] Program supports provided are often less intensive and with shorter duration than family literacy or family learning programs. (Jacobs et al., 2019, pp. 5–6)

A main tenet of Family Engagement in educational settings honors parenting adults as their children's first and most influential teachers (Hart & Risley, 1995 as cited in Kaiser & Hancock, 2002). *"Parenting adults" are referred to more inclusively throughout this chapter as "caregivers."* As children grow and enter school, caregivers can be advocates for and participants in children's learning; they can partner with school staff and have the opportunity to build relationships with educators and school leaders (Henderson et al., 2007, pp. 28–39). NCFL's LLTO initiative targets low-income families to improve academic results, as research in the United States confirms this group's achievement gap – although they disagree on the explanation (Renth et al., 2015).

STRUCTURE OF THE PROGRAM

Free for participants, LLTO's design reduces inequalities and encourages families to think about public outdoor spaces in their community where they can explore and enjoy nature. From building good health and well-being to developing literacy skills through quality education, the program creates not only educational opportunities but also intentional family time in addition to developing social capital as families forge connections with one another and the library staff. Intended to take place once per week for three consecutive weeks, caregivers and preschool-aged children (three to five years) engage in vocabulary- and conversation-building activities which promote outdoor learning. A goal of the initiative is for participants to practice the skills introduced in the program on their own, in whatever spaces they choose, and during the time between sessions – as well as after the program concludes. All participant-facing content is available in both English and Spanish, allowing families to engage with materials through one or both languages. Additionally, the content text intentionally encourages participants' sense of wonder, imagination, and creativity through play (Bluiett, 2018). The program utilizes NCFL's Family Engagement structure and includes Parent Time, Children's Education, and PACT Time (Jacobs et al., 2019, pp. 5–6; NCFL, 2014).

Library program facilitators greet families as they enter. Caregivers and children engage in concurrent 45-minute (minimum) sessions, ideally held in separate spaces to allow learners, especially caregivers, to focus on participation and discussion. After the Parent Time and Children's Education sessions, families reunite for 45 minutes of PACT Time (Jacobs et al., 2019, pp. 7–11). The entire day's LLTO experience wraps up with a debrief and any closing invitations or reminders. Fig. 1 shows the sample agenda from the LLTO Facilitator Guide, p. 9.

Parent Time

The main purpose of Parent Time is to offer support to caregivers in their role as primary teachers for their young children (Jacobs et al., 2019, p. 8). This segment also provides caregivers with time and space to practice learning strategies they will use with children during PACT Time – which is one of the goals of LLTO, intended to support transfer to other environments, such as the home or the community. Caregivers learn new strategies to enhance language and literacy interactions with children. Throughout the regularly scheduled sessions, they

Sample Agenda

Let's Learn Together Outside

Family Arrival (10-15 mins.)
• A staff member should be available to greet families as they come in and escort them to the event. Have a plan for where parents will drop off children for Children's Time and where parents will gather for Parent Time. Also, direct parents to sign in and make them feel comfortable as they wait for the event to begin.

Parent Time/Child Time (45 mins.)
• Parents will learn the strategies for the week and prepare for Parent and Child Together (PACT) Time* with their children.
• Children will participate in story time and an activity to use in PACT Time with their parents.

PACT Time (45 mins.)
• Parents and children will go outside together to participate in the PACT Time activities for the week.
• Families should be given the opportunity to practice the activities/strategies modeled by presenters.

Debrief (10 mins.)
• Families are given the opportunity to share the strategies they practiced and how it went for them.
• Discuss any questions or concerns parents have about carrying out the strategy.
• Families share their plan for using the strategy/activity at home.

Closing (5 mins.)
• Summarize the event for families.
• Make connections to home.
• Provide materials for families to use at home.
• Incorporate food at this time.

Fig. 1. Sample agenda for Let's Learn Together Outside.

have various opportunities to practice explicit skills in both indoor and outdoor locales.

Within the context of LLTO, caregivers receive direct instruction and scaffolding for early literacy strategies such as using open-ended questioning (Strasser, 2018), expanding vocabulary (Colker, 2014), and storytelling (Nicolopoulou et al., 2015; Raising Children Network, 2020). These oral language skills are essential building blocks related to literacy acquisition and kindergarten readiness skills (U.S. Department of Health & Human Services, Administration for Children & Families, Head Start [ECLKC], n.d.-a). Facilitators provide information to help caregivers understand why each skill is important. Another goal of LLTO is for caregivers to realize that learning can happen anytime, anywhere as the outdoors becomes a new and adventurous learning space. Lastly, adults spend time in community with their peers. They have the opportunity to build relationships and social connections through the three-session experience, as well as through a community mapping exercise focused on the locations of outdoor activity resources.

Children's Education

This portion of the initiative provides high-quality early childhood experiences and interactions to support children's language and literacy skill development – an essential part of kindergarten readiness (ECLKC, n.d.-b). Children receive

Let's Learn Together Outside 129

experiential background knowledge which acts as a "warm-up" for the PACT Time activity that follows.

Specifically, LLTO provides children with intentional and dynamic learning opportunities while experiencing nature. An important aspect of Children's Education, within the context of the programming, is that children have the opportunity for social interaction with others from their age group (Bagdi & Vacca, 2005; Hay et al., 2004; Sheridan et al., 2003; Vandell et al., 2006) – which is important, as many young children are not attending preschools where this might otherwise happen (National Center for Education Statistics & U.S. Department of Education [NCES], 2021; Sparks, 2021).

Parent and Child Together (PACT) Time®

The purpose of PACT Time is to give caregivers the opportunity to build stronger relationships with a child through working, playing, reading, and learning. Positive outcomes in language, literacy, emotional growth, and cognitive development of children are also benefits of PACT Time (Jacobs, 2004 as cited in Jacobs et al., 2019, p. 10).

After their separate learning experiences, participants reunite during PACT Time to support one another as they complete the activities and practice new skills. As applied in the LLTO initiative, children and caregivers spend intentional time together working on a common activity. Caregivers learn alongside children while exploring nature and flowers, trees and plants, and wildlife. Caregivers model lifelong learning and curiosity for children during this time as well.

Debrief/Wrap Up

At the end of each LLTO session, facilitators offer adult participants the opportunity to engage in conversation about their PACT Time experience and how they might plan to use the language or literacy strategy in another space. This process reinforces the skill of adult goal setting and increases the likelihood that caregivers will continue to practice the new skills they have learned long after the end of the program (Traugott, 2014).

PRACTICAL APPLICATION: LLTO

Implementation Training

NCFL provides in-depth instruction focused on strategies for library programming staff to support caregivers and their preschool-age children. Trainers go step-by-step through literacy-building skills, all activities, planning, recruiting, and other aspects of the LLTO initiative. The three-week family engagement project provides materials, reading lists, and suggestions for extensions. Libraries receive designed handouts for participants that include a fill-in community resource map, laminated plant and animal scavenger hunt cards for use with dry-erase markers, and take-home sheets with ideas for reinforcing at-home interactions with opportunities to practice skills learned in Parent Time.

Adult and children's library staff and administrators receive hands-on experiences with all included materials. This method of training was designed to increase their comfort level for facilitating nature-based activities, which they lead during the three program sessions. Facilitators are also offered ongoing technical assistance.

Response to Implementation Training

Feedback from three Kentucky counties included in a 2018 evaluation (Levesque) indicated strong and positive responses from the seven respondents, with all strongly agreeing (mean score of five on a Likert scale – with five being the highest) with the statements:

- The facilitator(s) were knowledgeable about parents' understanding of nature and outdoor play.
- The facilitator(s) were knowledgeable about the ways young children learn about nature.
- The facilitator(s) offered useful feedback and practical suggestions to support this training in future programs.
- This training will help me improve my work with families.

Mean scores of 4.7 (on the same Likert scale) measured responses to the questions:

- The content was relevant to the needs and interests of the families that frequent our library.
- My comfort level with outdoor nature-based family learning is stronger as a result of this training.

Open-ended comments supported staff satisfaction with the training content and applicability. Respondents mentioned they appreciated the thought and preparation in the program design. Another appreciated practicing caregiver icebreakers and how they were linked to the Parent Time sessions, corroborated by another participant mentioning how the first-hand experience with the activities prepared them for sessions with caregivers and children. Another significant response indicated that the staff felt this program could help show ways to share a book without intimidating low-literate caregivers (Levesque, 2018, pp. 3–4).

Session 1: Storytelling

During this session, caregivers choose cards with prompts, like "Tell a story about when you planted something." Through this storytelling practice, caregivers explore using descriptive vocabulary to build children's oral language (National Research Council, 2000, pp. 140, 142, 146–152; Nicolopoulou et al., 2015; Raising Children Network, 2020; Weisleder & Fernald, 2013). Caregivers also learn about and practice responsive communication. For example, when taking a nature walk, a child sees a flower and says, "Look! A flower!" The caregiver can respond with additional information, such as, "I see a yellow flower and a blue one up next to the sidewalk. What other colors of flowers can we find?" The take-home sheet for this session gives examples for adults to practice asking questions or expounding on observations when reading with a child (What Works Clearinghouse, 2007). Caregivers also discuss their background in spending time outdoors and how to feel comfortable with their children in natural surroundings. A mapping activity (see Fig. 2) supports identification of free outside play areas in their communities. Participants revisit the map during the third session to collaboratively expand their knowledge of available resources.

Session 2: Understanding the Importance of Meaningful Conversation

Facilitators encourage caregivers to think about everyday opportunities for rich discussion. With nature photographs, everyone takes turns building out descriptive words and phrases for the image. This activity introduces the idea that common family practices provide easy ways to engage children in conversation (Raising Children Network, 2020). Through their practice together in Parent Time, caregivers increase their experience encouraging children to build vocabulary by scaffolding descriptive language in a variety of situations.

Session 3: Open-Ended Questions

Caregivers begin by discussing the difference between yes/no/one-word-response questions and open-ended questions. In a game similar to 20 Questions, caregivers work in teams to guess objects from provided cards displaying single-word items found in nature. In round one, only yes/no questions are allowed. In round two, participants are encouraged to ask open-ended questions. When reviewing the difference between the rounds, caregivers can see how rich information and conversation can be by moving away from only asking yes/no questions to asking open-ended ones (Massachusetts Department of Early Education, 2014). The handout for this session provides examples of how to use this conversation-building strategy, particularly when reading with children. The suggested PACT Time activity for the third session includes an animal scavenger hunt, which connects with caregivers practicing open-ended questions (What kinds of animals do you see? Can you tell me how the birds are the same [or different]?) and activities from Children's Education time.

Participating Libraries

Public libraries are an ideal place to host programming of this nature – they historically have knowledgeable staff and are interested in building community through learning and/or activities (Wiegland, 2015 as cited in Lopez & Caspe, 2021, p. 3). Libraries were invited to apply for this opportunity. Sites self-identified as serving a low-income population and indicated willingness to implement the programming. Selected demographics for the counties in which the participating systems are located are represented in Table 1 and indicate communities met the grant requirements based on poverty rates and adult literacy rates.

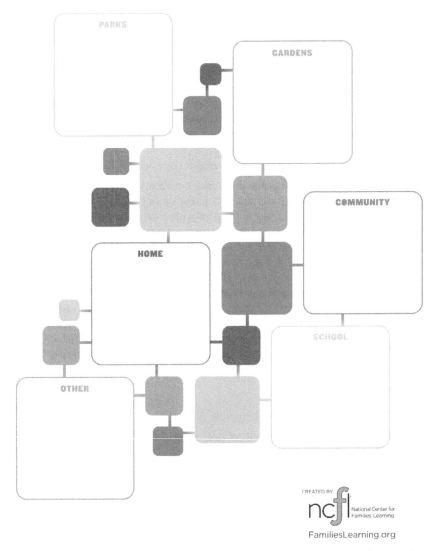

Fig. 2. Outdoor Resources Web activity template from Let's Learn Together Outside.

Let's Learn Together Outside

Table 1. Population Demographics by Library Location.

Location	Population[a]	Poverty Rate[a]	Adult Literacy Rate[b]
Kentucky			
Bell County	24,097	31.3	21
McCracken County	67,875	15.2	38
Muhlenberg County	30,928	14.7	28
Pike County	58,669	25	29
Michigan			
Van Buren County	75,677	27.3	44
Washtenaw County	367,601	29.7	65
Ohio			
Cuyahoga County	1,264,817	17.1	46

[a]data.census.gov.
[b]Level 3 nces.ed.gov.

RESPONSES TO LLTO

Evidence of LLTO Program Success

Open-ended responses from caregivers completing the post survey "included many statements of appreciation and positive affirmations… (Levesque, 2018)." Of the Kentucky participants evaluated by Levesque (2018), a total of 32 caregivers completed the initial survey, compared to 28 analyzed post-participation. According to librarians interviewed for the evaluation,

> … all of the patrons in their individual programs who completed the final survey expressed in person their great satisfaction with the LLTO program and asked that it be offered again the following summer.

Other comments indicated:

- "We had a great time getting to learn new things and meet new people."
- "I like the motivation to get outside. I only attended the last session, but I am excited to visit the parks I didn't know about."
- "The project is really good for my children. The library has done a great job."

Two caregivers suggested programs for older children.

Responses from Implementing Libraries

Sites were excited and creative about the sessions in the LLTO initiative and thought the programming was a playful way for families to interact during stories followed by a related outdoor activity (personal communication, Summer 2018). Using their own audiences and spaces as a guide, one library – which already had an outdoor patio area – planned to hold sessions in that space and talk about gardening as a potential extension activity. Another site decided against the suggested activity of capturing insects (to be released after the activity) for observation and instead ordered ladybugs for release into their onsite garden area, encouraging lessons on the importance of pollinators in their community.

Yet another library leveraged community connections to bring in county extension agents and state wildlife staff to interact with families.

Working in nature was an exciting concept for many; others were reluctant to leave the building. Providing a thorough, practical training experience and "out-of-the box" materials made the programming very accessible and well-received by the staff (Levesque, 2018). Story time ideas and craft suggestions were included in the training, but trainers were clear with facilitators that they were free to adapt to the library staff's comfort, the goals and interests of the families, and the energy level of the children as long as there was fidelity to the learning framework for each session.

Advice for Future Program Implementation

Overall, LLTO was well received and participating library staff thought it would add value to their programming (Levesque, 2018). Through interactions with library staff, NCFL honed its approach for training. Library staff who are customarily "siloed" in their departments, working with a targeted band of age groups, were not accustomed to the idea of multigenerational learning – which encouraged them to work together (E. Sedgwick, personal communication, Summer 2018).

Although consistent attendance in the series was encouraged, not all families were able to attend all three sessions. The concept of persistent Family Engagement does not match libraries' typical drop-in programming; therefore, a host of recruitment and especially retention strategies which promote ongoing weekly attendance may need to be employed.

In reviewing recommendations from Levesque's 2018 project evaluation, they suggest:

- Continuing to provide libraries with programming that takes participants outside; promote children's development via interactive learning outside and in their communities.
- Building a collection of family activities that bridge story times with sensory learning out of doors, engaging caregivers and young children.
- Review survey responses from caregivers in the participating programming. Apply these responses to future programming, including session topics, types of resource materials, and unanticipated outcomes.

Additionally, a few libraries sustained programming related to LLTO in meaningful ways. For example, one library acquired additional funding and expanded outdoor offerings (Trivisonno & Van Der Schalie, 2021) and another offered the content in a take-home packet of interactive activities during the COVID-19 pandemic.

CONCLUSION

LLTO is a successful example of a quality multigenerational education opportunity for libraries to implement. Caregivers and children were afforded time to

Let's Learn Together Outside 135

strengthen their relationships both within their families and as members of their communities while becoming more aware of library programming options in an effort to reduce inequalities. Children were presented with opportunities to socialize and engage with peers outside of the formal education landscape. Ultimately, LLTO provides libraries with family engagement opportunities that are rich in necessary language acquisition and social networking skills that support a family's overall growth, good health, and well-being.

For more information on LLTO and how to implement it in your library, contact the authors. For more information on the National Center for Families Learning and free Family Literacy and Family Engagement resources, visit their website: www. familieslearning.org.

REFERENCES

Bagdi, A., & Vacca, J. (2005). Supporting early childhood social–emotional well being: The building blocks for early learning and school success. *Early Childhood Education Journal, 33*, 145–150. https://doi.org/10.1007/s10643-005-0038-y

Bluiett, T. (2018). Ready or not, play or not: Next steps for sociodramatic play and the early literacy curriculum – A theoretical perspective. *Reading Improvement, 55*(3), 83–88. https://eric.ed.gov/?id=EJ1191124

Colker, L. J. (2014). *The word gap: The early years make the difference*. NAEYC. Retrieved January 3, 2023, from https://www.naeyc.org/resources/pubs/tyc/feb2014/the-word-gap

Hay, D., Payne, A., & Chadwick, A. (2004). Peer relations in childhood. *Journal of Child Psychology and Psychiatry, 45*(1), 84–108.

Henderson, A. T., Mapp, K. L., Johnson, V. R., & Davies, D. (2007). *Beyond the bake sale: The essential guide to family/school partnerships* (pp. 28–39). The New Press.

Jacobs, K., Cramer, J., Noles, T., & Lovett, P. (2019). *Defining our work: Families learning together*. National Center for Families Learning. https://www.familieslearning.org/uploads/media_gallery/NCFL-Defining_Our_Work_F3.pdf

Kaiser, A. P., & Hancock, T. B. (2002). Teaching parents new skills to support their young children's development. *Infants & Young Children, 16*(1), 9–21.

Levesque, J. A. (2018). *Let's learn together outside in Kentucky: A project at three Kentucky public libraries program evaluation*. Unpublished.

Lopez, M. E., & Caspe, M. (2021). Know, partner, lead: Family engagement in public libraries. In M. E. Lopez, B. Mehra, & M. Caspe (Eds.), *A librarian's guide to engaging families in learning* Libraries Unlimited.

Massachusetts Department of Early Education. (2014). *Engaging children in meaningful conversation*. Resources for Early Learning. Retrieved January 4, 2023, from http://resourcesforearlylearning.org/educators/module/20/7/18/

National Center for Education Statistics, U.S. Department of Education (NCES). (2021). *Fast facts: Preprimary education enrollment*. Retrieved June 24, 2022, from https://nces.ed.gov/fastfacts/display.asp?id=516

National Center for Families Learning (NCFL). (2014). *Family engagement brief*. National Center for Families Learning. Retrieved January 3, 2023 from https://www.familieslearning.org/pdf/NCFL_Family_Engagement_Brief_.pdf

National Research Council. (2000). *From neurons to neighborhoods: The science of early childhood development* (J. P. Shonkoff & D. A. Phillips, Eds.; 1st ed.). National Academies Press. https://nap.nationalacademies.org/catalog/9824/from-neurons-to-neighborhoods-the-science-of-early-childhood-development

Nicolopoulou, A., Cortina, K. S., Ilgaz, H., Cates, C. B., & de Sá, A. B. (2015). Using a narrative- and play-based activity to promote low-income preschoolers' oral language, emergent literacy, and social competence. *Early Childhood Research Quarterly, 31*, 147–162. https://doi.org/10.1016/j.ecresq.2015.01.006

Pahigiannis, K., & Glos, M. (2020). Peer influences in self-regulation development and interventions in early childhood. *Early Child Development and Care*, *190*(7), 1053–1064. https://doi.org/10.108 0/03004430.2018.1513923

Raising Children Network. (2020, December 14). *Reading and storytelling with babies and children*. https://raisingchildren.net.au/babies/play-learning/literacy-reading-stories/reading-storytelling

Renth, B. A., Buckley, P., & Puchner, L. (2015). Academic performance gaps and family income in a rural elementary school: Perceptions of low-income parents. *Education Leadership Review of Doctoral Research*, *2*(1), 70–84. https://files.eric.ed.gov/fulltext/EJ1105743.pdf

Sheridan, M., Buhs, E. S., & Warnes, E. D. (2003). *Childhood peer relationships in context*. University of Nebraska – Lincoln, Educational Psychology Papers and Publications. 21. https://digitalcommons.unl.edu/edpsychpapers/21

Sparks, S. D. (2021, October 26). Preschool enrollment has plunged: What that means for school readiness. *Education* Week. Retrieved June 16, 2022, from https://www.edweek.org/teaching-learning/preschool-enrollment-has-plunged-what-that-means-for-school-readiness/2021/10#

Strasser, J. (2018). *Conversations with children! Questions that spark conversations and deepen understanding*. NAEYC. Retrieved January 3, 2023, from https://www.naeyc.org/resources/pubs/tyc/apr2018/conversations-with-children

Traugott, J. (2014, August 26). *Achieving your goals: An evidence-based approach*. Michigan State University Extension. Retrieved June 29, 2022, from https://www.canr.msu.edu/news/achieving_your_goals_an_evidence_based_approach

Trivisonno, M., & Van Der Schalie, B. (2021). The blossoming of the library garden: How one library is engaging families outdoors. *Children & Libraries: The Journal of the Association for Library Service to Children*, *19*(1), 13–15. https://doi.org/10.5860/cal.19.1.13

U.S. Census Bureau. (2022, June 14). *Population*. Census.Gov. U.S. Census Bureau. Retrieved June 24, 2022, from https://www.census.gov/topics/population.html

U.S. Department of Education. (n.d.). *U.S. PIAAC skills map*. U.S. Skills Map: State and County Indicators of Adult Literacy and Numeracy. Retrieved June 27, 2022, from https://nces.ed.gov/surveys/piaac/skillsmap/

U.S. Department of Health & Human Services, Administration for Children & Families, Head Start (ECLKC). (n.d.-a). *How parents and families support oral language and vocabulary*. Head Start Early Childhood Learning & Knowledge Center. Retrieved January 3, 2023, from https://eclkc.ohs.acf.hhs.gov/sites/default/files/pdf/big5-strategies-parents-families-oral-language-eng.pdf

U.S. Department of Health & Human Services, Administration for Children & Families, Head Start (ECLKC). (n.d.-b). *School readiness: News you can use – Foundations of school readiness: Language and literacy*. Head Start Early Childhood Learning & Knowledge Center. Retrieved January 4, 2023, from https://eclkc.ohs.acf.hhs.gov/school-readiness/article/news-you-can-use-foundations-school-readiness-language-literacy#

Vandell, D. L., Nenide, L., & Van Winkle, S. J. (2006). Peer relationships in early childhood. In K. McCartney & D. Phillips (Eds.), *Blackwell handbook of early childhood development* (pp. 455–470). Blackwell Publishing. https://doi.org/10.1002/9780470757703.ch22

Weisleder, A., & Fernald, A. (2013). Talking to children matters. *Psychological Science*, *24*(11), 2143–2152. https://doi.org/10.1177/0956797613488145

What Works Clearinghouse. (2007). *WWC intervention report*. U.S. Department of Education, Institute of Education Sciences, What Works Clearinghouse, Early Childhood Education. Retrieved January 4, 2023, from https://ies.ed.gov/ncee/wwc/Docs/InterventionReports/WWC_Dialogic_Reading_020807.pdf

CHAPTER 10

SUSTAINABILITY, OUTDOOR LIFE, AND LIBRARIES

Hilde Ljødal and Tordis Holm Kverndokk

ABSTRACT

In 2015, the UN adopted 17 goals for the Agenda for Sustainable Development. The library's work is visible in all the primary goals, particularly with respect to public access to information, technology, and lifelong learning. Libraries are at the intersection between culture, education and lifelong learning, public health, and social work.

The Norwegian Parliament adopted the Sustainable Development Goal (SDG) as a foundation for regional and municipal planning. SDGs are also incorporated in the Strategy for Libraries (2020–2023). In connection with the Strategy, the National Library of Norway (NB) allocating funding for projects aimed at the development of public libraries and special libraries.

The authorities want people to enjoy and participate in outdoor life and trials. This improves health and quality of life, and it is a central part of the Norwegian cultural heritage.

In the last years, it has become popular to bring the library to people enjoying the outdoors. People can encounter both books and literary activities when out in nature or at a cabin far from the public library. Through the project and development funds and the celebration of National Book Year 2019, and measures related to the Strategy, the NB has supported projects for open-air libraries. This makes public libraries more visible and available to people and will reach new user groups and promote a sustainable society. Several of the

---

How Public Libraries Build Sustainable Communities in the 21st Century
Advances in Librarianship, Volume 53, 137–152
Copyright © 2023 by Hilde Ljødal and Tordis Holm Kverndokk
Published under exclusive licence by Emerald Publishing Limited
ISSN: 0065-2830/doi:10.1108/S0065-283020230000053012

SDGs are utilized through the development and use of new methods for creating open-air libraries.

14 projects are presented to show the importance of bringing the library to people enjoying the outdoors.

Keywords: Cottages; open-air libraries; National Library of Norway; Norwegian cultural heritage; public health; quality of life; mini-libraries; Strategy for Libraries; Sustainable Development Goals (SDGs); trials; Book Year 2019

INTRODUCTION

In the last few years, it has become popular to bring the library to people enjoying the Norwegian outdoors. Residents can encounter both books and literature mediation when they hike outside in nature, or when they reach day outing cottages far from the closest public library. Many libraries have gradually gained experience with establishing and operating open-air and trail libraries. In some cases, there are players other than the libraries involved in running the open-air libraries. The book collections may be strategically placed at a tourist cottage, or there may be curated book collections at specially constructed cottages for day outings or collections that circulate in specially built boxes and mini-libraries out in nature. In some places, these activities are highlighted or established as a separate project, and in other places, open-air libraries are an extension of the library's services. A common consideration for all these services is the desire to bring literature out to where people are going on trips in nature.

Through the project development funds and the observation of National Book Year 2019 (The National Library of Norway, 2019) and activities related to *The National Strategy for Libraries 2020–2023* (The Ministry of Culture and the Ministry of Education and Research, 2020), the National Library of Norway has financed several projects to support the development of library services located out in nature, to strengthen the active promotion of literature, and to help contribute to an increased desire to read. We have examined the background of this investment in trail and open-air libraries in Norway, and how the government has, through the National Library, provided financial support for many of these projects and activities. Meanwhile, it is interesting to examine how these projects positively contribute to the achievement of different sustainable development goals, to the increased active promotion of literature, and to the renewal of library development. The health aspects of these projects and activities, which contribute to enhancing people's quality of life by encouraging them to go on trips, are also clearly a key component. Several of the projects and activities discussed here have also received financial support from other institutions and organizations. Cooperation between different players is a key aspect of library development and in the activities contributing to sustainable development. This chapter presents an overview of the theme sustainability, outdoor life, and libraries and provides information on case studies implemented over the past few years.

BACKGROUND

Sustainability Goals

In 2015, United Nations (UN) member states adopted 17 goals for the 2030 Agenda for Sustainable Development. These goals integrate the economic, social, and environmental dimensions of sustainable development. Through the International Federation of Library Associations and Institutions (IFLA, 2018), the library field contributed to the discussion of sustainability goals at the UN. Library activities are visible in all the primary goals, especially with respect to public access to information, technology, and lifelong learning. Libraries are at the intersection of culture, education and lifelong learning, public health, and social work. Due to their many visitors, libraries have a unique opportunity to reach out with a message involving sustainability goals and to contribute to the creation of a sustainable society. The government adopted the sustainability goals as the basis for all regional and municipal planning going forward. The sustainability goals are also included in the *National Strategy for Libraries 2020–2023*, which was presented by the government in 2019.

National Library Policy

According to the mandate, the National Library contributes to the reinforcement of the library sector as a mediator of literature, knowledge, and cultural heritage, and to facilitate the public libraries as relevant and independent meeting spots and arenas for public discourse and debate. The goal of the strategy is to further develop the libraries as relevant and important institutions of knowledge, that are to contribute to public information and education among the population. Through this strategy, the government supports the development of libraries as visible institutions in municipalities, schools, and educational institutions. The strategy provides an overview of governmental responsibility and tasks to contribute to the development of future-oriented public libraries. An important measure for library development is project and development funding that the libraries can apply to receive.

About Development Funding

> One of the most important measures for contributing to the development of the public libraries are project and development funding, which are at the disposal of the National Library. The National Library is to be active in its administration of the development funding to achieve the best possible impact. The National Library may itself take the initiative for larger development projects, initiate cooperation, and coordination of projects that can and should be viewed in context. (The Ministry of Culture and the Ministry of Education and Research, 2020, p. 15)

Based on the guidelines in the strategy, the National Library grants funding to projects and activities aimed at the development of public and academic libraries.

The scope of the project and development funding are determined by the Ministry of Culture and are financed through lottery profits from Norsk Tipping.

About Funding for Active Mediation

> Each year, the National Library shall issue funding for active mediation, so that public libraries and county libraries across the country can enact good measures for strengthening reading and increase the borrowing of physical and digital materials from the collections. (The Ministry of Culture and the Ministry of Education and Research, 2020, p. 21)

The goal is to reach new library users, gain more readers, and increase borrowing. The broader goal is for public libraries to build experiences, competence, and to test out new methods for mediation, which in the long term may enter the library's daily operations. Reading, literature, and the library are to be made visible in arenas where it is possible to reach the groups that do not read or use the library's services. The projects in the establishment of trail and open-air libraries can be good examples of how libraries can drive active mediation in new arenas and contribute to sustainable societies.

The National Book Year 2019

The Book Year was a celebration of the 500th anniversary of the first printed Norwegian books. A key goal of the granting support was that 500 events in 500 public libraries would encourage enthusiasm and interest in books and literature, renewing a love of reading. 15 million was granted to libraries and 12 million to literary institutions that wanted to observe the Book Year. Several of the 95 libraries that received support involved library services and mediation out in nature, where people went on trips (National Library, 2019).

Outdoor Life and Health Aspects

In Norway, to "go on trips" is a concept we grow up with as part of our cultural heritage. Outdoor life is an important part of people's culture and identity, and outdoor life is often viewed as being "typically Norwegian." Outdoor life can be defined as spending time and being physically active outdoors during leisure time for a change of environment and experiencing nature (Report No. 18 to the Storting, 2015–2016). In Norway, outdoor life has the status of intangible cultural heritage. Norwegian outdoor life has roots in the villages' traditional harvesting and use of nature through the millennia, as well as in nationalist romanticism. The term outdoor life was likely first used by Henrik Ibsen in the poem *On the Heights* (1859) (Store Norske Leksikon, n.d.-a).

Public authorities wish for people to seek out and participate in outdoor life as part of a health perspective. Outdoor life has a documented effect on health and is a key factor in the population's quality of life. The combination of physical activity and natural experience is unique. Furthermore, an active outdoor life can give the individual a relationship with nature, which can again lead to an increased will to make environmentally friendly choices (Report no. 18 to the Storting, 2016). Over the past years, Norwegian authorities and organizations have chosen to prioritize

Sustainability, Outdoor Life, and Libraries 141

outdoor life in local communities, so that everyone can have the opportunity to be physically active and experience nature, also in their daily lives. Outdoor life can be enjoyed by all, regardless of the place of residence and independently of physical condition, mobility, and knowledge. The health and quality of life of the population have an impact on the development of society, and are affected by changes in society. The government will contribute to a sustainable welfare society through cross-departmental public health efforts. Norway will follow through with the UN's sustainability goals, and good public health efforts are needed to achieve the goals (Report no. 19 to the Storting, 2019).

Through the right to roam, everyone has the right to wander freely in undeveloped nature without having to pay for it. This is the fundamental prerequisite for Norwegian outdoor life. Furthermore, many outdoor life activities require little to no special equipment or financial resources. Everyone can go on a trip in the local park or in green areas in their local environment. "Going on a trip" is practically a common good for all, much like how "going to the library" is a common good for everyone living in Norway.

The Library in Nature

The National Strategy for Libraries 2021–2023 included active mediation as one of three key areas, while the other two key areas of cooperation, development, and infrastructure are to contribute to supporting the active mediation. The idea of developing library services out in nature, such as in cottages for day trips, came from the environment surrounding the county library in the former Sogn og Fjordane County in 2016. The notion was to make the public libraries more visible and accessible to all. Such a library service could also reach new groups of users and help promote a sustainable society. Several of the sustainability goals can be recognized regarding development and use of new methods to create a library for outdoor life and active mediation where people are going on trips. The sustainability goals 3: Good health and well-being, 10: Reduced inequality, 11: Sustainable cities and communities, 17: Partnerships for the goals. All these goals mentioned can be recognized in many of the projects. This chapter presents several different projects to show the importance of connecting library services to various forms of open-air libraries, to again promote active mediation, an interest, and a love of reading, which again promotes public education, public health, and a sustainable society.

PRESENTATION OF PROJECTS AND ACTIVITIES

New-Norwegian Trail Library

The establishment of cottages for day trips with library services has primarily taken place in Western Norway. This area consists of a wild, beautiful coastline with deep fjords, tall mountains, and small local societies, and is a well-known and frequently used area for hiking and outdoor life. One of the largest development projects, development projects, which can be described as the start of the establishment of the trail and open-air libraries, is the project the New-Norwegian Trail Library. They received support from the National Library in 2017–2019. In the former Sogn og Fjordane County, there was a major investment in cottages for day trips in all municipalities in 2016, and the public library participated in the development of a library concept suited for the cottages. In total, 26 cottages were established with libraries and books written in New Norwegian, which is the most written standard in Western Norway. New Norwegian and Bokmål are two equalized written standards of Norwegian (Store Norske Leksikon, n.d.-b). The library shelves were made visible and an integrated component of the design of the cottages. This has become a good service for different user groups that stop by to rest and relax during their trip. This is particularly for children as a target group. The books are not for circulation and are only for use at the cottages. Dissemination of the books was part of this service during the project period through several events in and around the cottages for day trips. According to the plan, a total of 56 cottages for day trips will be established in Vestland County during spring 2022, all of which will include a New-Norwegian Trail Library. Investments in cottages for day trips have spread across Vestland County as a popular service. This is a well-funded project that aligns with both active mediation of literature and innovative library development where people wander. Through this project, the public library has succeeded in making the library visible for people in new arenas. The cottages for day trips have become popular trip destinations for both residents and visitors. Over the course of one year, approx. 70 events were held with over 1,600 children, youths, and multicultural participants. For the library, additional investments are needed regarding labor hours, resources, and follow-up, while the library employees have received new knowledge and experience. Cottages for day trips with trail libraries are in line with the intentions of the Strategy for Libraries. We are aware that counties such as Agder and Rogaland are set to follow along with establishing cottages for day trips and that libraries have become a natural, included part of the concept.

One precursor to this project could be Literature trails which was organized by the Hedmark County Library in Eastern Norway in 2014 and involved the development of a digital hiking app. The goal was to mediate literature in a new way, in which people travel and establish collaborations with new collaboration partners with an emphasis on trails linked to nationally renowned authors such as Alf Prøysen, Hans Børli, and Vidar Sandbeck, and their authorships in their home county. Experiences from the project showed that the librarians thought it was good to try digital mediation aimed at hikers to disseminate well-known authorships while taking a trip through the authors' own homelands. This was an early project which was testing digital skills using tablets, but these were locked to a proprietary data system and today this project has been shut down.

Library On the Go

This was another early project that brought the library in Stordal Municipality out of its premises. This included the use of what were termed Stub poem travels. The goal was to make the library an active, visible part of the local community, while also including the public health aspect in its services to adults in a new manner. When the revised *Public Libraries Act* was adopted in 2014 (The Public Libraries Act, 1985), requirements were issued stating that the libraries had to operate active mediation, encourage civil discourse, and become a meeting place

Sustainability, Outdoor Life, and Libraries

for conversation and debate and encourage civil discourse. The project was also aimed at public health, and the municipality participated in Good Health[1] a partnership for public health activities in Møre og Romsdal Municipality. The library arranged trips in cooperation with local associations and organizations out in nature, as the head librarian, the mayor, and others invited people along and read poems at the tree stumps along the way. Attendance at these trips was good. There was also Headlamp safari, in which children and adults went on a trip in the dark to a bonfire, where fairy tales were read aloud. The good collaboration between the cultural team at the municipality and the volunteers allowed this work to continue. The Library on the go is just one example of a project that brought together many good causes in a small municipality, driven by the head librarian as project manager and enthusiast for making the library visible, as well as in compliance with the National Library's grant of project funding, as well as for the action plan at the municipality and the county.

Local History Hikes in Froland, Physical and Digital Trails

Froland Library, Agder County, seeks to disseminate its local history collection through digital mediation in local trail areas. Through the library's earlier project, The Books Are Off: The Open-Air Library, which was supported by the National Library in 2019 and in 2020–2021, the staff have made book boxes with history books labeled the open-air library. The book boxes are small and can easily be moved around the terrain and are hung up in different places in nature. This way, more and more popular hiking areas can be reached, and readers can be tempted and stimulated with good reading experiences along their way. The library developed the services further to ensure it becomes a digital participant of outdoor life by tying the books to the library through QR codes, and by contributing to the active public health efforts in the municipality.

THE NATIONAL BOOK YEAR 2019

The Minister of Culture wished to observe the Book Year, to celebrate the 500-year anniversary of the first printed Norwegian books. The National Library was given the task of issuing funds to the public libraries and reading organizations that wanted to celebrate this event. A key goal in granting support was that 500 events in 500 public libraries would encourage enthusiasm and interest in books and literature, and a renewed love of reading. 15 million was granted to libraries and 12 million to literary institutions, reading organizations, and others who wanted to observe the Book Year. Several libraries opted to observe the Book Year by seeking out nature trails and providing activities there. A total of NOK 1,315,000 was issued for dissemination projects of this type.

Literature Trail: All of Nordland Reads

Twenty-five libraries participated in this project. The Nordland County Library wished to involve the population in the Book Year through a county-municipal relay race, which centered on a love of reading and outdoor life. All participating libraries observed the Book Year through the year, ending up with an outdoor event with readings. Two texts were performed on a trip for residents of the municipalities. One of the texts was selected by the residents of Nordland. The other text was selected in the individual municipality. Contact was established with the public health department of the county municipality, which was highly interested in participating in the project, hoping not least to connect the project to a public health week, in which the goal was to establish an event that would promote public health in the municipalities. Collaboration was initiated between the county's health department and the municipalities' public health coordinators to collaborate with their own public library to complete the Literature trail. The following information was sent to the public libraries and published on the county library's website:

> We have entered a collaboration with the county municipality's section for public health. They have a very positive view of this project and are eager to get the library and residents of the municipality out in nature. The local outdoor recreation councils have received a memo that explains this project, and that encourages them to participate in it. We are particularly interested in bringing public health coordinators and the outdoor recreation councils along for the trail day in autumn. It would be good if you could have a meeting early, so that you can distribute tasks, find a suitable trail area, and set the date for this trip. The first two weeks of September will otherwise be well-suited for the trail day, because week 36 is the Outdoor Life Week, and week 37 is the Public Health Week in Nordland.

One prerequisite was that the trail had to be easily accessible to everyone, and that it should go to a known trail destination in the municipality. The trail was advertised in local newspapers and online. The library's impression has later been that the project led to contact with new collaborating partners and new users in unfamiliar surroundings. The book and trail were a success for all municipalities. The most successful part of the project for most of the libraries was the Literature trail event itself. Feedback from the libraries shows major commitment in the municipalities with many collaborating partners such as the public health coordinator, volunteer centers, cultural departments, literary communities, the Red Cross, the outdoor recreation councils, museums, coastal communities, hiking communities, village councils, friends, and family. This is an example of a project that builds relationships and cooperation in society at many levels, strengthening libraries, sustainability goals, and health.

Troms Reads North Norwegian and Literary Trail Destinations

Troms County Library in Northern Norway received funding to observe the Book Year on behalf of all the public libraries in the county. The goal was to inspire to the love of reading through encounters with literature. They wished to create interest in a conversation surrounding literature, and to create synergy by bringing the libraries closer to local readers and reader groups, making the library visible as a good arena for meetings in the local community, expanding its services in stimulating reading and discussion, as well as increasing book borrowing numbers. They opened the new year with a day of reading and they started the Book Year in all municipalities with the vignette: With the northern lights as a reading light. 18 of the libraries in the county took the challenge to hold their own opening events, most of which took place in varying weather in North Norwegian nature.

Sustainability, Outdoor Life, and Libraries

Literary Trail Destinations in Troms County

The libraries wanted to give people on trails a literary experience by forming a campaign that would highlight the Book Year using authors from Troms and the local public libraries by setting up posters with information about trail destinations on the different trails. In total, 25 trail destinations were selected in 14 municipalities in Troms. The posters included excerpts from books by local authors, as well as a greeting from the local library. The county library received good feedback from the libraries, participants, the authors involved, and contributors. The goal was to inspire to the love of reading through encounters with fiction. This was achieved in both projects.

The Book Is Off – Open-Air Library in Froland, Agder County

During the Book Year, the Froland Library sought to give books and literary mediation a space in outdoor life arenas across the municipality. The goal was to reach out to new user groups in new arenas where people did not expect to encounter library services. Smaller book boxes were placed out in nature with information on how this worked. The library's encouragement was: "Enjoy a book while you catch your breath." The borrowed book could be returned to another open-air library or to the public library. The book boxes are to continue circulating around the municipality in different places to tempt hikers with reading experiences on the go.

Mini-Library

Horten Library in Vestfold og Telemark County opted to set up mini-libraries to promote interest in reading by making literature available out in the city environment, as well as in nature trails. A mini-library aimed at families with children was placed near a playground. Another was placed along a nature trail along the coast, and a third was placed at a central bus stop, so that one can read while waiting or bring the book on the bus. Many have taken books with them, and new books have been put into the mini-libraries. The goals of making books and libraries visible, encouraging a love of reading both in and outside the library, and of giving access to books on trails were all achieved. The feedback has been positive.

MEASURES FOR ACTIVE MEDIATION SUPPORTED BY THE NATIONAL LIBRARY

The National Library's funding for active mediation at public libraries also led to various outreach initiatives where people were hiking. The goal of this funding is described in the strategy:

> Each year, the National Library shall issue funding for active mediation, so that public libraries and county libraries across the country can enact good measures for strengthening reading and increase the borrowing of physical and digital materials from the collections. (The Ministry of Culture and the Ministry of Education and Research, 2020 p. 21)

The goal is to reach new library users, get more people to read, and increase borrowing. Furthermore, it is to get the employees at the public libraries to acquire experience and skills, and to test out new methods for mediation, which in the long term may enter the library's daily operations. Reading, literature, and the library are to be made visible in arenas where it is possible to reach the groups that do not read or use the library's services. There are some examples of initiatives that have been given support in 2021.

Literary Trails in World Heritage

Røros Library started the initiative Literary trails in world heritage. The goal is to make the library visible in new ways and to increase the use of library services. The target group is residents, cottage owners, and tourists. An emphasis is also placed on the library's contribution to Røros as a World Heritage site in cooperation with the Museum. The library arranges literary trails in Røros, where librarians read excerpts from books that are related to Røros, such as the books of the author Johan Falkberget. All the trails end at the library. An example of bringing literature, local history, and people out hiking to an initiative that helps achieve the goal in the call for active mediation. It simultaneously contributes to knowledge and information, also considering the sustainability goals.

Reading Trip – With the Fox, the Loom – and Perhaps the Stars

At Gloppen Library, Vestland, the "Reading Trip Project – With the Fox, the Loom – and Perhaps the Stars" is one of several initiatives related to mediation out on the trips. With the Bonfire crackling under the stars initiative, they collaborate with village associations and hold events in lean-tos. There are readings around the bonfire and connections are drawn to the lives of previous generations. The children's librarian cooperates with a Children's Trial organization "The fox goes on a trip," for several events. They visit for example, the day trip cottage Draumekvila, which is one of the New Norwegian trail libraries.

Words at Tyrielden

Eidskog Library is testing out the initiative Words at Tyrielden. The library is collaborating with hiking associations in the municipality, and the libraries join these trips with a backpack library. The backpack library includes the books that are to be mediated, and they are loaned out using a scanner and loaning options via tablet. With the tablet, digital library services can also be marketed and demonstrated during the trip. Technology becomes a key aid to make the backpack library work.

The Children's Exercise

The Exercise takes place in the summer and is a fun competition for children aged 0–10 at Meløy Municipality, Nordland. The trails are easy and even the youngest can join in. It has 16 trail destinations in the municipality. Each trail destination has a red waterproof bag with a children's book. There is a new book at each post of the trail. Some trail destinations have a trail box, others do not. The trial code must be registered on the child's trial account, and the child must be signed up for the trial competition. All children who are signed up for the competition and who complete 10 or more hours of children's exercise trails receive a nice prize. This initiative is a collaboration between the cultural office, the volunteer center, and the library, with funding from the Nordland County Library.

These are some examples of libraries that operate library services out in nature, around the bonfire, at day trip cottages, on mountain peaks, and along hiking trails.

BENEFITS

The benefits of the various projects can be described as a positive full package for everyone involved, in different ways. By following the intention in the National Strategy for Libraries to operate active, outreach mediation in where people can be found, the libraries can test out new ways to mediate the libraries' collections. The librarians can boost their competence by mediating new arenas out in nature. On trips, the population can experience a new dimension in addition to the trail experience itself, namely access to literature and books. People can read and borrow books at the open-air library, or meet up for a shared event for readings, alongside other hikers. The sustainability goals can be recognized in many of the projects regarding goals such as 3: Good health and well-being. To go on a hike promotes both physical and mental health. 10: Reducing inequality. Everyone gets access to literature and information on this trails. 11: Sustainable cities and communities. Shared experiences in nature build bridges between people. 17: Partnerships for the goals. Many different forms of partnerships are a fundamental principle to establish the various trail and open-air library projects. This becomes a "win-win situation," in which the library services and health aspects complete each other in a manner that again contributes to the creation of a stronger, sustainable society.

Fig. 1.   The Cottage "Klettenhytta" at Kinn in Deknedalen in Møre og Romsdal County. Photo: Siw Merethe Hatlem.

Fig. 2. The Cottage «Sjøbua» in Alver in Vestland County with the Theater Company "Eventyr i parken" (Fairytale in the Park in English). Photo: Sigrid Furnes.

Fig. 3. The Cottage "Vardetangen" in Austrheim, Norway's Most Western Point in Vestland County. Photo: Geir Åge Nesbø.

Sustainability, Outdoor Life, and Libraries   149

Fig. 4. The Cottage "Larsbulia" in Øygarden, Vestland County. Photo: André Marton Pedersen/Bergen og Hordaland turlag.

Fig. 5. From the Opening of the Cottage "Orrebu" in Leikanger in Vestland County. Photo: Silje Engeland.

CONCLUSION

The primary goal of the projects is, from the library's side, to reach out to the population with an active mediation of literature, promoting a love of reading, increasing borrowing figures, and contributing to knowledge and culture where people can be found. Library services out in nature combined with outdoor life and hiking can also positively contribute to an improved quality of life. It may also lead more people to consider the relationship between the environment and the climate. In total, each point contributes to the social capital of society. This is a key factor in creating a sustainable society going forward.

NOTE

1. Collaboration agreement for Good Health Folkehelse (mrfylke.no).

REFERENCES

Froland Municipality, Library. (2020). *Boken går – friluftsbibliotek: rapport*. Final report submitted to the National Library, case number 2019/178.

Horten Library. (2020). *Minibibliotek: rapport for Bokårsmidler Horten bibliotek*. Final report submitted to the National Library, case number 2019/192.

IFLA. (2018). *Libraries and the sustainable development goals: A storytelling manual* [Brochure]. https://www.ifla.org/wp-'content/uploads/2019/05/assets/hq/topics/libraries'-development/documents/sdg-storytelling-manual.pdf

Nordland County Library. (2020). *LitteraTUR – hele Nordland leser: rapport*. Final report submitted to the National Library, case number 2019/216.

Nordland County Library. (2021). *Barnetrimmen i Meløy*. Application to Nordland County Library.

Report no. 18 to the Storting. (2015–2016). *Friluftsliv – Natur som kilde til helse og livskvalitet*. Meld. St. 18 (2015–2016) – regjeringen.no.

Report no. 19 to the Storting. (2018–2019). *Folkehelsemeldinga – Gode liv i eitt trygt samfunn*. The Ministry of Health and Care Services. https://www.regjeringen.no/n'o/dokumenter/meld.-st.-19-20182019/id2639770/?ch=1

Store Norske Leksikon. (n.d.-a). *Friluftsliv*. Retrieved June 30, 2022, from https://snl.no/friluftsliv

Store Norske Leksikon. (n.d.-b). *Nynorsk*. Retrieved June 30, 2022, from https://snl.no/nynorsk

The Ministry of Culture and the Ministry of Education and Research. (2020). *Rom for demokrati og dannelse: nasjonal bibliotekstrategi 2020-2023*. Bibliotekutvikling. Retrieved May 05, 2023 from https://bibliotekutvikling.no/content/uploads/2020/05/Rom-for-demokrati-og-dannelse-Nasjonal-biblioteksstrategi-2020-2023-Engelsk.pdf

The National Library. (n.d.-a). Bokåret 2019. Retrieved June 01, 2022, from https://www.nb.no/bokaret-2019/

The National Library. (n.d.-b). *Biblioteket i farta!* Retrieved May 31, 2022 from https://bibliotekutvikli'ng.no/prosjektbank/prosjekt/biblioteketet-i-farta/

The National Library. (n.d.-c). *Lesetur – med reven, veven – og kanskje stjernene*. Retrieved May 31, 2022, from https://bibliotekutvikling.no/prosjektbank/a'ktiv/lesetur-med-reven-veven-og-kanskje-stjernene/

The National Library. (n.d.-d). *Litteraturer*. Retrieved May 31, 2022, from https://bibliot'ekutvikling.no/prosjektbank/prosjekt/litteraturer/

The National Library. (n.d.-e). *Litterær vandring i verdensarven*. Retrieved May 31, 2022, from https://bibliotekutvikling.no/pro'sjektbank/aktiv/litteraer-vandring-i-verdensarven/

The National Library. (n.d.-f). *Lokalhistoriske vandringer i Froland – fysiske og digitale turer*. Retrieved May 31, 2022, from https://bibliot'ekutvikling.no/prosjektbank/prosjekt/lokalhistoris'ke-vandringer-i-froland-fysiske-og-digitale-turer/

The National Library. (n.d.-g). *Nynorske turbibliotek i Sogn og Fjordane*. Retrieved May 31, 2022, from https://bibliotekutvikling.no/prosjektbank/'prosjekt/nynorske-turbibliotek-i-sogn-og-fjordane/

The National Library. (n.d.-h). *Ord ved Tyrielden – på tur med ryggsekkbiblioteket*. Retrieved May 31, 2022, from https://bibliotekutvikling.no/prosjektbank/akt'iv/ord-ved-tyrielden-pa-tur-med-ryggsekkbibliotek/

The Public Libraries Act. (1985). *Lov om folkebibliotek* (LOV-1985-12-20-108). Lovdata. Retrieved July 04, 2022 from https://lovdata.no/dokument/NL/lov/1985-12-20-108

The UN Sustainable Development Goals. (n.d.). Retrieved July 04, 2022 from https://www.un.org/sustainabledevelopment/

Troms County Library. (2020). *Rapport for prosjekt «Bokåret 2019» i Troms fylkesbibliotek*. Final report submitted to the National Library, case number 2019/296.

Vestland County Municipality. (n.d.). *Dagturhyttebrosjyre*. Retrieved June 01, 2022, from https://www.vestlandfylke.no/idrett'-og-friluftsliv/dagsturhytta/dagsturhyttebrosjyre/

APPENDIX: ASSIGNMENT OF FUNDING

Development Projects Funded by the National Library

Nynorske turbibliotek/New Norwegian Trail Library	NOK 800,000
Biblioteket i farta/Library on The Go	NOK 130,000
Lokalhistoriske vandringer i Froland, fysiske og digitale turer/Local History Hikes in Froland, Physical and Digital Trails	NOK 200,000
Litteraturer, Prøysenvandringer/Literature trails, Prøysen Hikes	NOK 960,000
Total amount	**NOK 2,090,000**

The National Book Year 2019 Funded by the National Library

LitteraTUR: hele Nordland leser/Literature Trail: All of Nordland Reads	NOK 800,000
Troms leser nordnorsk og Litterær turmål/Troms Reads Northern Norwegian and Literary Trail Destinations	NOK 450,000
Boken går – friluftsbiblioteket i Froland/The Book Is Off – Open-Air Aibrary in Froland	NOK 25,000
Minibibliotek/Mini-library	NOK 40,000
Total amount	**NOK 1,315,000**

Active Mediation 2021 Funded by the National Library

Nå ut!/Reach out!	NOK 75,000*
Litterær vandring i verdensarven/Literary Trails in World Heritage	NOK 55,000
Lesetur med reven, veven og kanskje stjernene/Reading Trip – With The Fox, The Loom and Perhaps the Stars	NOK 75,000
Ord ved Tyrielden/Words at Tyrielden	NOK 75,000

Friluftsbibliotek på Barnas dag, Maihaugen/Open-Air Library for Children's Day, Maihaugen	NOK 50,000*
Mellom linjene – formidling/Between The Lines – Mediation	NOK 50,000*
#ditt bibliotek – i hele byen/#Your Library – all Across Town	NOK 75,000*
Kul tur med biblioteket/Cool Trail with the Library	NOK 100,000*
Tid og spor/Time and Traces	NOK 75,000*
Litterær stolpejakt/Literary Post Hunt	NOK 75,000*
Gatelangs med Larviks litterære høydepunkter på øret!/Streetside with Larvik's Literary Highlights in Your Ear!	NOK 50,000*
LesLittPåTur/ReadSomethingOnTheTrial	NOK 75,000*
Total amount	**NOK 830,000**

This project is not discussed in the article.

New mediation forms funded by Nordland County Library

Barnetrimmen i Meløy/Children's Exercise in Meløy	NOK 25,000

CHAPTER 11

OLDER ADULTS, PUBLIC LIBRARIES, AND SUSTAINABLE DEVELOPMENT GOALS

Nicole K. Dalmer and Meridith Griffin

ABSTRACT

By 2030, one in six people in the world will be aged 60 years or over. As the average age of population increases, governments are increasingly called upon to implement policies to address the needs and interests of older people, including those related to housing, employment, health care, social protection, and other forms of intergenerational solidarity. Public libraries, as trusted community hubs, have the opportunity to serve as an environment for reflection and dialogue on age and aging. In this chapter, the authors reflect on the broader contexts and social trends that are shaping older adults' engagement with public libraries and identify those older adults-focused public library practices that align with specific UN Sustainable Development Goals: Goal 3: Good Health and Well-Being, Goal 4: Quality Education, Goal 8: Decent Work and Economic Growth, Goal 10: Reduce Inequalities, and Goal 16: Peace, Justice, and Strong Institutions. While public libraries are already meeting many facets of UN Sustainable Development Goals, to ensure that libraries can responsively meet older adults' changing needs and expectations, the authors conclude with suggestions to enhance public libraries' cross-sector coordination for maximum reach and impact on older patrons' everyday lives.

Keywords: Older adult; aging; public library; aging in place; UN Sustainable Development Goals; outreach

---

How Public Libraries Build Sustainable Communities in the 21st Century
Advances in Librarianship, Volume 53, 153–160
Copyright © 2023 by Nicole K. Dalmer and Meridith Griffin
Published under exclusive licence by Emerald Publishing Limited
ISSN: 0065-2830/doi:10.1108/S0065-283020230000053013

INTRODUCTION

Public libraries are trusted sociocultural hubs that foster community relationships (Grace & Sen, 2013; Scott, 2011; Sørensen, 2021). As public facing organizations that are open to the widest range of individuals, libraries seek to create safe and welcoming spaces for individuals of different socioeconomic statuses, ethnic and cultural backgrounds, sexual and gender identities, and of particular interest to us, ages (Audunson et al., 2019; Martell, 2008; Mehra & Davis, 2015). As gerontologists, one of whom is a former librarian (Dalmer) and both of whom have experience in conducting research with and about public libraries (e.g., Dalmer, 2017; Dalmer & Griffin, 2022; Dalmer et al., 2020; Dalmer & Mitrovica, 2022; Griffin et al., 2022; Wynia Baluk et al., 2021), we are especially interested in understanding, identifying, and highlighting the many intersections of gerontology and public libraries. In this chapter, we draw on an iterative process of critical, reflective inquiry (Lyons, 2010) regarding the contexts and social trends that are shaping older adults' engagement with public libraries and identify, broadly, the landscape of older adult-focused public library programs, services, and spaces adults that align with UN Sustainable Development Goals. To do so, we first provide some important age-related context and then connect pertinent UN Sustainable Development Goals to the changing aging landscape and to public library practice.

MAPPING THE LANDSCAPE: AGING WITH PUBLIC LIBRARIES

Population aging – or the shift in distribution of the population toward older ages[1] – is a major global trend,[2] demonstrated by census data, surveys, and statistical projections the world over. By 2030, one in six people in the world will be aged 60 years or over, and older people are expected to account for over 25% of the population in Europe and Northern America (Dugarova, 2017; WHO, 2021). As the average age of population increases, there has been a call for governments to implement policies to explicitly address the needs and interests of older people, including those related to housing, employment, health care, social protection, and other forms of intergenerational solidarity (United Nations, 2017). The reasoning is that by anticipating this demographic shift, countries can proactively enact policies to adapt to an aging population, which will be essential to fulfill the pledge of the 2030 Agenda for Sustainable Development that "no one will be left behind."

Public libraries' engagement with older adults is evolving – in part due to certain social and economic trends, such as aging in place. Governments at all levels have embraced "aging in place" policies and strategies to empower older adults to remain in their homes and communities as they age, instead of relocating to costly hospitals or long-term care facilities (Oswald & Wahl, 2005; Vasunilashorn et al., 2012). In addition to fulfilling an economic imperative, aging in place aligns with the preference of 85% of Canadian older adults who intend to remain in their homes to maintain their independence and remain strongly connected to their communities (Canadian Mortgage & Housing Association, 2015). An overwhelming percentage of older Americans express a similar desire to age in place, with numbers ranging from 65% to "nearly 90%" (AARP, 2018; Fresenius Medical Care, 2020), although many express a lack of confidence in being able to do so due to various factors (i.e., concerns about mobility and health, finances [including housing and food], social isolation and loneliness). As a result, older adults' homes and local communities (including their public library branches) are especially pivotal in their lives.

In addition to the impact of broader social trends, public libraries' engagement with older adults is also shaped by library culture and education. While library services for children and teens have traditionally been overemphasized in LIS education, practice, and research (thus inevitably displacing library services for and research about older adults; Angell, 2009; Dalmer, 2017), the growing proportion of older adults in most countries around the globe necessitates a refocusing on older public library patrons' needs and practices. With growing emphasis on aging in place, public libraries' staff, spaces, materials, and programming are even more crucial for its older adult patrons. As older adults want and plan to age in the right place *for them*, connections to a community public library branch can help maintain a sense of identity, facilitating adjustments into older age (Dalmer et al., 2020; Wiles et al., 2009).

WHERE DO PUBLIC LIBRARIES ALIGN WITH SUSTAINABLE DEVELOPMENT GOALS?

Global population aging provides opportunities for sustainable development, associated with the active participation of older generations in the economy, labor market and society at large in addition to older adults' experience, knowledge, and skills. Accordingly, we draw on our own research findings to identify the ways in which different facets of public library initiatives support and align with the implementation of specific UN Sustainable Development Goals. In doing so, we intend for this chapter to initiate important conversations to ensure that older adults are included in conversations with those who promote economic, political, and social development and related policy responses (Stakeholder Group on Aging, 2020; United Nations Development Programme, 2016).

Goal 3: Good Health and Well-Being. This third goal is centered on healthy living and the promotion of wellbeing. As health and wellness resources are increasingly decentralized or are only accessible virtually, public library staff, spaces, resources, and collections become especially valuable spaces for those older adults who may be uncertain where to turn with their health-related questions or who may not have the necessary technological infrastructure to access and assess online health information.

There are a number of existing public library programs that also support this third goal. For example, Griffin et al.'s (2022) project engaged with older adults who participated in a writing/memoir program at their local public library. In speaking with older participants, the writing sessions contributed to feelings of wellbeing. Their work highlighted the role of the public library as a key third place for older adults:

> a public gathering place, offering accessible, interactive leisure pursuits, actively drawing people together in physical space and with the capacity to contribute to the strength of community as a destination for sociability. (Griffin et al., 2022, p. 863)

Lenstra's ongoing work at the intersection of movement, fitness, and the public library (e.g., Lenstra et al., 2022) further elucidates the role of the public library in supporting healthy (including active) aging, revealing that exercise programs for older adults at the public library support older patrons' physical, mental, and social health and wellbeing. Other programming examples demonstrate the valuable collaborations that can be forged between public libraries and public health partners, particularly regarding guiding older patrons to locate helpful, accurate, and understandable online health information (Eriksson-Backa, 2010; Schwartz et al., 2002; Xie & Bugg, 2009).

Goal 4: Quality Education. The fourth goal seeks to ensure inclusive and equitable quality education and to promote lifelong learning opportunities. A large portion of Nicole's research has documented the range of public library programming for older adults, uncovering that public libraries develop a wide range of educational programming for older adults, ranging from digital, health, financial, cultural, recreational, and environmental topics – which often simultaneously generate opportunities for intergenerational and social connections (e.g., Dalmer, 2017; Dalmer et al., 2020; Dalmer & Mitrovica, 2022). Importantly, library programming is provided without expectation of payment, enhancing its accessibility for older patrons. Specific library programming (e.g., digitally focused programming and training) may also support *Goal 8: Decent Work and Economic Growth*, supporting those increasing numbers of older patrons who are continuing in or are returning to the workforce.

Wynia Baluk et al. (2021) identified public libraries as community hubs that can help to create more age-inclusive and socially connected communities and societies. And so, the final sustainable development goal we highlight in this section is *Goal 10: Reduce Inequalities.* This particular goal is accomplished as other goals take place. Library programming, spaces, and materials can prompt reflection and dialogue on age and aging. Intergenerational programming, hiring staff members to specifically develop relationships with older community members, or educational events focused on ageism can, for example, stimulate conversations about aging. By presenting, (re)interpreting, and even challenging stereotypical representations of later life, public libraries have the capacity to "counter traditional stereotypes and promote awareness of the historical and cultural circumstances that determine our attitudes about aging" (Dow Schull & Thomas, 2010, p. 64). As "age-based conceptions of human experience are deeply entrenched in libraries" (Rothbauer, 2013, p. 183), to engage in these (re)interpretations of later life, LIS scholars and practitioners must move toward reflecting on the constructions and representations of age within library spaces, programming, and collections and the impact this construction has on library services and patrons. In

Older Adults, Public Libraries, and Sustainable Development Goals 157

doing so, public library workers and library scholars can simultaneously contribute to *Goal 16: Peace, Justice and Strong Institutions*, supporting the flourishing of sustainable communities and boosting social capital for older public library patrons who so often experience inequalities.

CONCLUSIONS: MOVING FORWARD

Our process of reflection has simultaneously invited an identification of opportunities for change and growth. As we have identified trends in public library engagement with older adults, it is apparent that programs, resources, and innovative initiatives are typically isolated to specific library systems or geographic locales. This is counter to the underlying ethos of the "five conditions of collective impact" as outlined by Kania and Kramer (2011), in which large-scale social change (which we argue includes the needed change in public library education, culture, and administration to responsively support older library patrons commensurate with their growing and changing demographics) is only possible through responsive, cross-sector coordination. Public libraries are increasingly understood as social infrastructures[3] (physical places and organizations that shape communities' resilience and the way people act and interact) as they are called upon to serve as public squares, community hubs, think tanks, community centers, and makerspaces, among others. As public library staff and systems navigate these changing roles, cross-sector coordination is necessary to ensure that libraries are responsively meeting older adults' changing needs and expectations.

Accordingly, in this section, we briefly highlight those salient conditions from Kania and Kramer (2011) that we envision will produce larger-scale impact for public library engagement with older adult populations. We propose that the primary importance is firmly establishing the condition of "backbone support organizations" in which "a separate organization and staff with a very specific set of skills ... serve[s] as the backbone for the entire initiative" (Kania & Kramer, 2011, p. 40). For example, the already-existing Library Services to an Aging Population Committee of the Reference Services Section (RSS) of the Reference and User Services Association (RUSA) of the American Library Association could be reimagined to serve as this backbone support organization, providing national-level planning, support, management, and coordination of initiatives. Similarly (or perhaps in tandem), the IFLA Public Libraries Section could create a committee to provide international-level support and guidance about broader issues impacting older patrons (working with, for example, HelpAge International). Establishing this backbone support organization would enable other "conditions of collective impact" to more organically occur, such as ensuring continuous communication and establishing and nurturing a common agenda in addition to increasing opportunities for communication and engagement, reducing redundancies, and ensuring more effective and impactful collaboration with national-level stakeholders (e.g., AARP, Senior Planet). To ensure that decisions and initiatives at the national level resonate with and reflect the challenges and opportunities that arise at the more local level, library systems may elect to designate a point person who liaises with RUSA and communicates news with colleagues. This also necessitates a commitment of resources (time, finances, staffing, etc.) among library systems to ensure that local public library systems can responsively serve as backbone support anchors for RUSA.

As we have highlighted, a number of specific public library activities/initiatives, as reported in available research, clearly support a number of UN Sustainable Development Goals. However, without the creation or a reimagining of a governing "backbone support organization," existing and forthcoming public library initiatives that engage with older adult populations will not be able to realize their full impact beyond their locale or beyond the short window of available funding for a particular project.[4] We hope to convey a degree of urgency with this statement. Without an overarching infrastructure that can proactively and sustainably share pertinent research about older adults, circulate creative programming ideas and related resources or curriculum, or easily make known collection development strategies for older patrons (among other tasks), public library offerings risk a sense of being fractured or being piecemeal – existing briefly for a small number of older patrons in a particular locale.

NOTES

1. In understanding the complexities of later life, it is key to note that the concept of "older age" is multidimensional, including chronological, psychological, biological, and social age.

2. Population aging is not an isolated event, but is occurring in tandem with other megatrends, including poverty, climate change and ongoing conflicts and migration, which necessarily impact both local and more global conditions under which people age and how they experience their age (see, for example, Moody and Sasser [2020]).

3. For further conversations about public libraries as social infrastructure, see: Audunson et al. (2019), Dalmer and Mitrovica (2022), Klinenberg (2018), and Mattern (2014, 2021).

4. The Transforming Life after 50 (TLA50) is a prime example of this – the TLA50 initiative (https://transforminglifeafter50.org), supported by the U.S. Institute of Museum and Library Services and undertaken by the California State Library, was a comprehensive, innovative program designed to help libraries better serve and engage with older adults. The initiative's activity and reach have dwindled as the funding period has ended.

REFERENCES

AARP. (2018). 2018 home and community preferences: A national survey of adults ages 18-plus. https://www.aarp.org/research/topics/community/info-2018/2018-home-community-preference.html

Angell, K. (2009). Boom or bust: The need for senior services librarians. *Progressive Librarian*, (*32*), 29–35.

Audunson, R., Aabø, S., Blomgren, R., Evjen, S., Jochumsen, H., Larsen, H., Rasmussen, C. H., Vårheim, A., Johnston, J., & Koizumi, M. (2019). Public libraries as an infrastructure for a sustainable public sphere. *Journal of Documentation*, *75*(4), 773–790.

Canadian Mortgage and Housing Association. (2015). Housing for older Canadians: The definitive guide to the over-55 market. http://www.cmhc-schl.gc.ca/odpub/pdf/67514.pdf

Dalmer, N. K. (2017). Mind the gap: Towards the integration of critical gerontology in public library praxis. *Journal of Critical Library and Information Studies*, *1*(1) 1–23.

Older Adults, Public Libraries, and Sustainable Development Goals 159

Dalmer, N., & Griffin, M. (2022). "Still Open and Here for You": News media's framing of Canadian public libraries during COVID-19. *The Library Quarterly, 92*(2), 129–150.

Dalmer, N., Griffin, M., Baluk, K. W., & Gillett, J. (2020). Aging in (third) place with public libraries. *Public Libraries, 59*(4), 22–30.

Dalmer, N. K., & Mitrovica, B. L. (2022). The public library as social infrastructure for older patrons: Exploring the implications of online library programming for older adults during COVID-19. *Library & Information Science Research, 44*(3), 101177.

Dow Schull, D., & Thomas, S. (2010). Reconsidering age: The emerging role of cultural institutions. In P. Rothstein & D. Dow Schull (Eds.), *Boomers and beyond: Reconsidering the role of libraries* (pp. 63–70). The American Library Association.

Dugarova, E. (2017). Ageing, older persons and the 2030 agenda for sustainable development. https://www.un.org/development/desa/ageing/wp-content/uploads/sites/24/2017/07/UNDP_AARP_HelpAge_International_AgeingOlderpersons-and-2030-Agenda-2.pdf

Eriksson-Backa, K. (2010). Elderly people, health information and libraries: A small scale study on seniors in a language minority. *Libri, 60*(2), 1181–1194.

Fresenius Medical Care. (2020). Aging in place in America. https://fmcna.com/content/dam/fmcna/live/aging-in-place/Aging-In-Place-in-America-Research-Report-FINAL.pdf

Grace, D., & Sen, B. (2013). Community resilience and the role of the public library. *Library Trends, 61*(3), 513–541.

Griffin, M., Harvey, K., Gillett, J., & Andrews, G. (2022). Writing as/about leisure: Connecting with oneself and others through creative practice. *Leisure Sciences, 44*(7), 862–880.

Kania, J., & Kramer, M. (2011). Collective impact. *Stanford Social Innovation Review, 9*(1), 36–41.

Klinenberg, E. (2018). *Palaces for the people: How social infrastructure can help fight inequality, polarization, and the decline of civic life.* Crown.

Lenstra, N., Oguz, F., D'Arpa, C., & Wilson, L. S. (2022). Exercising at the library: Small and rural public libraries in the lives of older adults. *The Library Quarterly, 92*(1), 5–23.

Lyons, N. (Ed.). (2010). *Handbook of reflection and reflective inquiry: Mapping a way of knowing for professional reflective inquiry.* Springer.

Martell, C. (2008). Fresh start at a neighborhood library. *Public Library Quarterly, 27*(2), 134–138.

Mattern, S. (2014). Library as infrastructure. *Places Journal.* https://doi.org/10.22269/140609

Mattern, S. (2021). *A city is not a computer: Other urban intelligences.* Princeton University Press

Mehra, B., & Davis, R. (2015). A strategic diversity manifesto for public libraries in the 21st century. *New Library World, 116*(1/2), 15–36.

Moody, H. R., & Sasser, J. R. (2020). *Aging: Concepts and controversies.* Sage Publications.

Oswald, F., & Wahl, H.-W. (2005). Dimensions of the meaning of home in later life. In G. D. Rowles & H. Chaudhury (Eds.), *Home and identity in late life: International perspectives* (pp. 21–46). Springer.

Rothbauer, P. (2013). Imagining today's young adults in LIS: Moving forward with critical youth studies. In A. Bernier, A. (Ed.), *Transforming young adult services* (pp. 171–188). Chicago: Neal-Schuman.

Schwartz, D. G., Mosher, E., Wilson, S., Lipkus, C., & Collins, R. (2002). Seniors Connect: A partnership for training between health care and public libraries. *Medical Reference Services Quarterly, 21*(3), 1–19.

Scott, R. (2011). The role of public libraries in community building. *Public Library Quarterly, 30*(3), 191–227.

Sørensen, K. M. (2021). Where's the value? The worth of public libraries: A systematic review of findings, methods and research gaps. *Library & Information Science Research, 43*(1), 101067.

Stakeholder Group on Aging. (2020). Position paper submitted to the high-level political forum 2020. https://sustainabledevelopment.un.org/content/documents/26444Stakeholder_Group_on_Ageing.pdf

United Nations. (2017). World population ageing. https://www.un.org/en/development/desa/population/publications/pdf/ageing/WPA2017_Highlights.pdf

United Nations Development Programme. (2016). *Leave no one behind: Ageing, gender and the 2030 Agenda.* Issue Brief. UNDP.

Vasunilashorn, S., Steinman, B. A., Liebig, P. S., & Pynoos, J. (2012). Aging in place: Evolution of a research topic whose time has come. *Journal of Aging Research.* https://doi.org/10.1155/2012/120952

WHO. (2021). *Ageing and health*. https://www.who.int/news-room/fact-sheets/detail/ageing-and-health

Wiles, J. L., Allen, R. E., Palmer, A. J., Hayman, K. J., Keeling, S., & Kerse, N. (2009). Older people and their social spaces: A study of well-being and attachment to place in Aotearoa New Zealand. *Social Science & Medicine, 68*(4), 664–671.

Wynia Baluk, K., Griffin, M., & Gillett, J. (2021). Mitigating the challenges and capitalizing on opportunities: A qualitative investigation of the public library's response to an aging population. *Canadian Journal on Aging/La Revue canadienne du vieillissement, 40*(3), 475–488.

Xie, B., & Bugg, J. M. (2009). Public library computer training for older adults to access high-quality Internet health information. *Library & Information Science Research, 31*(3), 155–162.

SECTION THREE

LIBRARIES MOBILIZING CLIMATE CHANGE

INTRODUCTION TO SECTION THREE: SUSTAINABLE COMMUNITIES AND THE ROLE OF THE PUBLIC LIBRARY

Kaurri C. Williams-Cockfield and Bharat Mehra

FRAMING OF SECTION THREE ["LIBRARIES MOBILIZING CLIMATE CHANGE"]

The three case studies included in Section Three provide examples of programs that work toward increasing and/or supporting environmentally sound consumption and production of goods and services [SDG 12], ameliorating the impacts of climate change [SDG 13], and sustainable use of terrestrial ecosystems including forests, land degradation, and biodiversity [SDG 15]. Personal narratives focus on experiences in library work environments by library staff, administration, library users, and other key library stakeholders including library board members and volunteers covering the same topics. These three SDGs are grouped together given their focus on actions needed to ensure the sustainability of Earth's natural resources.

The chapters in this section operationalize significant elements of the public library – sustainable communities (PLSC) framework visualized in the introduction to the book. In Chapter 12 ["Inspiring Climate Action: A Collaborative Effort and a Perfect Partnership"], Lynn Blair, Andrea Bugbee, and John Meiklejohn discuss partnerships between Hampden and Hampshire County Libraries in Massachusetts and climate change organizations (Voices 4 Climate Change and Communities Responding to Extreme Weather) that resulted in the development of the Pioneer Valley Library Collaborative to empower communities and spread awareness of climate change year round.

In Chapter 13 ["How Repair Events in Libraries Can Create Socially and Ecologically Compassionate Culture and Resilient Communities"], Gabrielle

---

How Public Libraries Build Sustainable Communities in the 21st Century
Advances in Librarianship, Volume 53, 163–164
Copyright © 2023 by Kaurri C. Williams-Cockfield and Bharat Mehra
Published under exclusive licence by Emerald Publishing Limited
ISSN: 0065-2830/doi:10.1108/S0065-283020230000053014

Griffis discusses a case study on hosting repair events in a public library and presents information on how other libraries can implement this type of program. Reviewer Rachel Fenningsdorf, Community Engagement Coordinator, Jackson District Library, writes:

> The text in this chapter provides a modern-day look at an age-old problem...teaching practical skills needed for life. At the same time, it acknowledges the need for sustainability in our "throwaway" culture and provides an attainable solution grounded in current research. Any librarian could begin to plan a successful program like this today with the framework provided.

In Chapter 14 "A Small Library Making Big Changes: A Case Study of the Baramsup Library"], Yong Ju Jung presents a case study on the Baramsup Picturebook Library in South Korea. This picturebook library was developed to address the creation of a book culture, to empower children's ecological sensitivity, and to support the building of school libraries for children in Laos.

STRATEGIC COLLECTIVE ACTIONS

The thematic threads flowing through the three chapters in this section highlight how different library case studies operationalize the following significant strategic collective actions:

- Partner with key local and state organizations to educate the community on climate change;
- Foster a socially and ecologically compassionate culture by teaching community members how to repair malfunctioning consumer products;
- Encouraging ecological sensitivity through literature and outdoor experiences.

These case studies illustrate ways that public libraries are combining literacy with the ecological world and creating a teaching/learning environment that builds community connections between different groups of people.

KEY CONCEPTS AND TERMS

Right-to-Repair Movement – Formed as a reaction to tech and automotive companies increasing legal restrictions and barriers to personal and third-party repair of consumer products.

Voices for Climate (V4C) – A volunteer group of environmental activists whose mission is to create non-partisan community conversations around climate change.

RESOURCES AND RELEVANT ORGANIZATIONS

Climate Preparedness Week, MA Library System, MA. https://guides.masslibsystem.org/ClimatePrepWeek
Communities Responding to Extreme Weather (CREW), US. https://www.climatecrew.org/
Fixit Clinic, US. https://fixitclinic.blogspot.com/
Massachusetts Library System, MA. https://masslibsystem.org/
Voices Rising Together, Indivisible Mass Coalition, Granville, MA, US. https://indivisible-ma.org/find-a-group/voices-rising-together/

CHAPTER 12

INSPIRING CLIMATE ACTION: A COLLABORATIVE EFFORT AND A PERFECT PARTNERSHIP

Lynn Blair, Andrea Bugbee and John Meiklejohn

ABSTRACT

In the context of the risks inherent in global warming, public libraries can partner with each other, community-based environmental groups and/or other institutions to enhance community resilience and sustainability. This chapter presents a case study of an ongoing experiment to address this opportunityand challenge. In April 2021, six Western MA libraries formed a collaborative in conjunction with a local citizens' group, Voices for Climate [V4C], to expand public education opportunities relating to understanding, mitigating, and adapting to climate change. In its initial year, this effort yielded 13 separate programs serving more than 110 patrons, all within the 7 days of Climate Preparedness Week, a state-wide program held annually. Subsequently, this Pioneer Valley Library Collaborative [PVLC] has grown to 10 library partners and continues its close alliance with V4C. In describing the programs offered in the first year, the challenges met, limitations encountered, and lessons learned, the chapter provides one model for how libraries can jointly choose to become hubs of climate conversation and education as a means to promote their communities' quality of life, sustainability, and resilience.

Keywords: PVLC; climate change; public libraries; collaboration; climate preparedness; hubs of climate conversation; education

---

How Public Libraries Build Sustainable Communities in the 21st Century
Advances in Librarianship, Volume 53, 165–174
Copyright © 2023 by Lynn Blair, Andrea Bugbee and John Meiklejohn
Published under exclusive licence by Emerald Publishing Limited
ISSN: 0065-2830/doi:10.1108/S0065-283020230000053015

INTRODUCTION

Libraries are trusted community institutions well positioned to serve the common good by providing a "civic commons" (Kranich, 2012) where citizens can not only learn but also come together to collaborate in ways that foster the development, sustainability, and resilience of their communities. In other words, libraries are, and can be, "platforms of civic engagement" (Coward et al., 2018). At a local, state, national, and global level, society currently faces an urgent need to develop ways to mitigate and adapt to the growing threats posed by earth's changing and warming climate (IPCC, 2022; USGCRP, 2018). As a "civic commons," libraries are well-suited to be hubs of non-partisan, scientifically based educational programming that foster informed and rational engagement by individuals and community organizations in addressing this looming danger to the public good. Indeed, in 2019, the American Library Association added "sustainability" to its list of core values (ALA, 2019).

As a consequence of the existential threats posed by climate change, it can be argued that if libraries are to effectively serve as vehicles for their communities to develop in sustainable and resilient ways, then libraries need to become platforms for engaging the topic of climate change. To this point, the most recent report from the United Nations (UN) Intergovernmental Panel on Climate Change (IPCC) states that the achievement of the UN's 17 Sustainable Development Goals (SDGs) (UN, 2015) must be framed now within the concept of "Climate Resilient Development" (IPCC, 2022). Thus, the ALA's core value of sustainability needs to be nurtured through policies and actions that promote climate resilience (ALA, 2020).

In 2021, with the goal of empowering communities and spreading awareness of climate change, a collaboration was initiated between a community-based committee and local libraries in the Pioneer Valley of Western Massachusetts. Voices Rising Together (VRT), a grassroots activist group that works on a range of political and social issues, has been around since 2017 and is a chapter of the Indivisible Massachusetts Coalition (https://indivisible-ma.org/). Within VRT, a small group of individuals came together in late 2020/early 2021 to form a committee, Voices for Climate (V4C). This community-based citizens' committee set itself a two-fold mission: first, at the local level, creating non-partisan climate conversations geared to raising awareness of what individuals and communities can do to reduce the risks associated with climate disruption; and, second, advocating for equitable climate legislation at the state level in conjunction with other climate advocacy groups. The five-member V4C committee began to meet and discuss how they could focus their energies on climate issues both within VRT as well as outside their organization to create climate-related educational opportunities for the public. In the spring of 2021, inspired by climatologist Dr Katharine Hayhoe's view that the single most valuable act for any individual wishing to address climate change is to talk about it (Citizens' Climate Lobby, 2021), V4C began preparing for the national September 2021 Climate Preparedness Week (https://guides.masslibsystem.org/ClimatePrepWeek) by

Inspiring Climate Action 167

seeking out local libraries interested in becoming hubs of climate conversation and public education.

V4C COMMITTEE PARTNERSHIPS

In 2021, V4C also learned about Communities Responding to Extreme Weather (CREW). CREW describes themselves as "a network of local leaders building grassroots climate resilience through inclusive & hands-on education, service, and planning" (CREW, n.d.-b). In 2019, the Massachusetts Library System began partnering with CREW to inspire Bay State libraries to participate in Climate Preparedness Week, a CREW event held annually from September 24 to 30. Libraries are natural conduits for community education, and Climate Preparedness Week has been particularly instrumental in disseminating important climate information at the local level. In 2021, over 100 organizations across the Eastern United States – most of them libraries – joined in making Climate Preparedness Week a success. Inspired by Katharine Hayhoe's message (Citizens' Climate Lobby, 2021), and fortified by CREW's free framework (CREW, n.d.-b), the five members of V4C set a goal: each would tell their local library director about CREW and Climate Preparedness Week. Then, they'd ask if their library would participate in forming a local library climate collaborative.

THE LIBRARY COLLABORATIVE

Initially, V4C members reached out to Lise LeTellier, director of the Granville Public Library in Granville, MA. Lise, in turn, reached out to other libraries. Thus, the Pioneer Valley Library Collaborative (PVLC) was born. The PVLC is a partnership of Hampden and Hampshire County public libraries united in presenting climate related programming throughout the year, particularly during the annual Climate Preparedness Week. In the true spirit of public libraries everywhere, this partnership exists to share, for free, its combined ideas, materials, and resources in order to more broadly inspire, educate, and assist their communities. The original cohort included the Agawam Public Library (Agawam, MA), the Granville Public Library (Granville, MA), the SPL (Southwick, MA), the Tolland Public Library (Tolland, MA), the West Springfield Public Library (West Springfield, MA), and the Westfield Athenaeum (Westfield, MA). Presently, as of January 2023, the collaborative has expanded to welcome the Emily Williston Memorial Library (Easthampton, MA), the Westhampton Public Library (Westhampton, MA), the Williamstown Public Library (Williamstown, MA), and the Forbes Library (Northampton, MA).

Librarians have long been on the forefront of public issues and, in 2019, "sustainability" became one of the ALA's Core Values of Librarianship. The ALA announcement stated, "Libraries play an important and unique role in promoting community awareness about resilience, climate change and a sustainable future" (ALA, 2019). Just as librarians are aware of the needs for reliable information and resources, library partnerships with community organizations are nothing new. Libraries have long been collaborating with local groups to offer programs and services to their patrons. As many patrons' interests and concerns are turning toward climate change, such partnerships have become more prevalent and are getting national interest.

The partnership between V4C and the public libraries provided an opportunity for each group to collaborate and thereby address their organizational strengths and weaknesses. V4C had funds to provide for programs as well as knowledge of the topic and community connections. They lacked the space to provide programs and the means of reaching a wide and varied audience. Libraries are used by many patrons and could easily spread the word, and most libraries have a space designated for programs or areas for educational displays. However, libraries are often constrained by tight budgets and understaffing. The collaborative took the best of what each had to offer to create the means to provide programs with funding in the appropriate and accessible meeting spaces, as well as the means to reach a wide audience. A full roster of programs was presented during Climate Preparedness Week, yielding 13 programs serving 110 patrons, all within a week. Since the completion of that programming, participating libraries have continued to offer programs and services on the topic, with the collaborative planning several meetings during the spring and summer to discuss Climate Preparedness Week 2022 and 2023.

A PLANNING MODEL FOR LIBRARIES AND COMMUNITY ORGANIZATIONS

Presented below is a chronology of V4C's and the local libraries' combined efforts to create a collaborative offering programs and resources for their patrons and communities. The model can easily be replicated in other communities by libraries and local organizations wishing to make a difference.

Stage One: Initial Meetings with V4C Members: V4C members took their information learned and met with individual library directors about potentially collaborating. In Southwick, Andrea Bugbee, a V4C member, met with Lynn Blair, director of the SPL. SPL was enthusiastic about collaborating; the library had long intended to offer programs on climate change, but did not have the contacts to look for qualified presenters on such topics. As various members of V4C met with their local library directors, the collaborative grew to include many other area libraries.

Recommendations for Beginning: Whether you are a librarian or a community member interested in starting such a collaboration, anyone can begin this process. Look around your community – are there groups that already exist? Can you join them and discuss your ideas? Maybe you need to create such a group. Reach out among your community and gauge the interest level. As seen with V4C, you only

Inspiring Climate Action 169

need a small group to make a big difference! If you are a community organization, reach out to your local library. As mentioned before, libraries and community groups can complement each other's strengths and bolster each other's shortcomings. Your library may have some ideas for programming or may have space to offer. If you are a library, look outwards to your community. Librarians are aware of the power of outreach and this is an excellent way to reach more members of the community. Does your community already have a climate action group? Maybe the library can begin such a program and get the conversation going.

Stage Two: Meeting with the Collaborative Group: Once V4C had several libraries on board, the members of the collaborative met multiple times via Zoom to brainstorm event possibilities. Libraries were able to co-sponsor events, and smaller libraries that may not have had the meeting space were able to team up with larger libraries to present programs.

Recommendations for Meeting: Assign one or two people (or more, depending on your group size) as "facilitators." If possible, have these facilitators be from different organizations such as one community member and one library representative. Assign one person to draft an agenda and send out a request to all participating members for any topics for the agenda. Have the agenda ready for the meeting. Assign one person to manage the meeting scheduling (whether it be creating a Zoom room and sending out the link or booking a physical meeting room). If you have an agenda and a plan for the meeting, the discussion will be efficient and beneficial for all. Have one participant either take minutes or jot down topics discussed in the meeting so you can go back and review as needed. Assign someone to write up a meeting summary and send it to all collaborative partners.

Stage Three: Joining CREW as a Climate Resilience Hub: This step is completely optional depending on your organization's capabilities. According to CREW, Climate Resilience Hubs can be any "community institutions – libraries, churches, schools, nonprofits, local businesses and others – that help educate residents about extreme weather preparedness and other impacts of climate change" (CREW, n.d.-a). As a Hub, your organization is expected to have the Climate Resilience Hub signage on display as well as having materials for patrons to access. CREW has a plethora of brochures and ready-to-print resources. Additionally, Hubs should host one event annually on a related topic. CREW also has three different levels of Hubs that an organization can join (CREW, n.d.-a). For more information on becoming a Hub or the levels, visit CREW's website: https://www.climatecrew.org/resilience_hubs?locale=en. The SPL joined CREW as a Level 1 Hub. An ongoing display is offered to patrons in the main area of the library with resources and brochures for patrons to take home. SPL proudly displays CREW's Climate Resilience Hub decal in the entryway and is committed to providing at least one event related to emergency preparedness at the library each year. CREW offers regular virtual meetings with other resilience hubs, and there is a great deal of discussion and idea sharing. For Southwick, both working with CREW and being a Climate Resilience Hub have been positive experiences.

Recommendations for Joining CREW: Research CREW to see if their goals align with yours. Take a look at what is required to become a Climate Hub and whether it is appropriate for your organization. There may also be other climate-related organizations out there, either local or national, with which you can partner.

Stage Four: Putting Together the Schedule of Events and Related Challenges: After several PVLC brainstorming sessions, the calendar of events started to come into fruition. The COVID-19 pandemic was still underway, presenting a challenge for in-person events. Many events were planned to be virtual. Each library and V4C coordinated the advertising effort. Flyers with programs were posted at libraries and a complete listing of programs was available as a handout. Many events brought new and exciting topics to the participating libraries (for program details, see Table 1).

Recommendations for Putting Together the Schedule: Try to have a variety of events, including events for youth, but don't overwhelm yourself! Think quality over quantity. Put together a handout for patrons that each organization can post with the complete listing of events, and make sure the location and registration requirements are clearly described. A keynote address or commencement event is recommended not only to get the ideas and interest flowing at the beginning of the week, but to highlight themes to make participants excited for what's to come in the future.

Table 1. PVLC's Programming for 2021 Climate Preparedness Week.

Date	Program Name	Sponsoring Library
All Week	Make & Take Herb Garden	West Springfield
Friday, September 24	How to Prepare for Climate Change w/ David Pogue	Massachusetts Library System
	Chasing Ice Film and Discussion	Westfield Athenaeum & Granville
	Science Rocks: Making Biodegradable Plastic (kids)	West Springfield
Saturday, September 25	Hawk Watch with the Allen Bird Club	Southwick
	Children's Story Hour	Granville
Monday, September 27	Code Red for Humanity: Understand Global Warming's Risks & What Each of Us Can Do with Dr Carsten Braun	V4C
Tuesday, September 28	Mini Make & Take Planters	Agawam
	Teens Outsmart Disposables for a Better World	Southwick
	Teen Trivia Night on Zoom	Agawam
	Cookbook Club	Southwick
Wednesday, September 29	Mindful Outdoor Experience with Colleen Mollica	Granville
	Becoming an Outdoor Citizen with John Judge, AMC President	Granville & Simsbury, CT Library
Thursday, September 30	Resilience & Preparedness in a Changing Climate panel discussion	Agawam & Granville

Source: Lynn Blair (2023).

Inspiring Climate Action

Stage Five: Implementing the Programs: The keynote of the week was "How to Prepare for Climate Change" with David Pogue (2021), hosted by the Massachusetts Library System and was offered state-wide as well as to the local audiences. The program was well attended and got the rest of the week in gear for the whole range of programs offered. "Code Red for Humanity" with Westfield State University Professor Carsten Braun drew a large attendance and went over the allotted time with Q&A which Braun generously stayed to answer.

The SPL offered its first off-site program with a Hawk Watch at Blueberry Hill in Granville, Massachusetts. The watch was led by the Allen Bird Club. Participants signed up in advance and the group met at the base of Blueberry Hill to take the 10-minute hike to the top. Although few hawks were seen, attendees were able to enjoy beautiful views as well as sightings of other birds and even a moose! The event was attended by individuals of all ages. Due to the success, the SPL aims to offer more off-site programs in the future.

Recommendations for the Week's Programming: Coordinate your advertising efforts. Spread the word about your events. If all participating libraries and organizations share the events and happenings on their respective social media pages (and through other means), you will have the best chance of reaching a wider audience. For example, in our case, V4C was able to provide funding for a front page banner ad in a local weekly newspaper reaching 21,000 households. You don't always have to reinvent the wheel to offer new programs; think about your existing programs! Climate Preparedness Week occurred in the same week that the SPL's regular cookbook club met, so SPL decided to combine both the regular event and Climate Preparedness Week by having participants select recipes out of the cookbook *In the Green Kitchen: Techniques to Learn by Heart* by Alice Waters (2010).

See Table 1 for the listing of events offered during Climate Preparedness Week 2021.

Discussion: Lessons Learned: If you've made it this far, it means that you've finished a successful week of events – take a breath and reflect on your collaboration. By the end of Climate Preparedness Week, the PVLC team learned several valuable lessons.

Lesson 1: Schedule a Wrap-Up Meeting: Schedule a wrap-up meeting with your participants to discuss how the week went, what changes can be made for the future, and how to keep the ball rolling throughout the year. The PVLC participants took some time to reflect on the week. While Climate Preparedness Week was a success, after it was over, participating libraries and V4C members were able to look back and evaluate how the program ran and what could be improved. One of the major strengths of the program was that events reached a wide variety of audiences.

Lesson 2: Don't try to do it all! Lise Letellier, director of the Granville Public Library stated, "It was a week of lots of energy and enthusiasm, but there were too many options." Focus on quality over quantity – there may be lots of events that sound wonderful, but focus on having a core group of strong events.

Lesson 3: The Show CAN Go On! Programs don't need to stop because Climate Preparedness Week is over. Continue programs all year long. Not everything needs to be crammed into one week. Choose programs that reflect the values of

Climate Week or that might get the most patron attention so you can create a core audience of attendees who will attend more events throughout the year – and hopefully tell their friends.

Planning for the Future: The collaborative's efforts during Climate Preparedness Week have had many positive outcomes. Libraries have gained additional contacts for potential future programs as well as new community partnerships with V4C and other organizations that were introduced through the collaborative, such as Springfield MA's Allen Bird Club. V4C has gained a partnership with local libraries and a wider reach for their climate change awareness efforts. An incredibly valuable resource, created by V4C's Andrea Bugbee, is a running list of local programs and presenters that librarians can pull on to offer programs at their library during Climate Preparedness Week and throughout the year.

The combined efforts of V4C and the PVLC helped create a successful week of programs and a sustainable group that will continue to work together for future Climate Preparedness Weeks and throughout the year. John Kania and Mark Kramer (2011) describe the importance of collaboration and a group mindset in achieving results. The pair identified "Five Conditions of Collective Success": (1) Common Agenda; (2) Shared Measurement Systems; (3) Mutually Reinforcing Activities; (4) Continuous Communication; and (5) Backbone Support Organizations (Kania & Kramer, 2011). These five conditions are apparent in the collaborative's efforts. PVLC came together with a common agenda: to inform and educate the public about climate change and climate preparedness. Having a "Common Agenda" (Kania & Kramer, 2011) and a group of passionate individuals created a powerhouse collaborative that we hope will be strong for years to come. This being the first year of the collaborative, a "Shared Measurement System" (Kania & Kramer, 2011) is something that can be developed with the next years' efforts. Having completed the first year, PVLC will take the data and engagement numbers from last year's Climate Preparedness Week and compare them to 2022's. With each successive year, we will be able to discover if there are certain needs that are not being met or areas where program topics should be developed. PVLC members participated in "Mutually Reinforcing Activities" (Kania & Kramer, 2011). PVLC members all had roles to perform that contributed to the greater effort of having a successful Climate Preparedness Week. PVLC members, including V4C members and library staff, each brought diverse experiences and perspectives to the collaborative efforts. If there is one of the five conditions the group succeeded in particularly well, it was "Continuous Communication" (Kania & Kramer, 2011). PVLC members had several brainstorming and planning sessions and communicated by email regularly during the planning process. Lastly, V4C provided the "Backbone Support" (Kania & Kramer, 2011) for the collaboration. John Meiklejohn and Andrea Bugbee were essential in providing support to the libraries who were planning, preparing for, and hosting multiple programs throughout the week. While the libraries focused on all aspects of hosting events, John and Andrea helped with the logistical side of the project, including keeping track of statistics and managing shared documents. The enthusiasm of John and Andrea, as well as their dedication, has helped the collaborative effort remain strong into 2023.

Inspiring Climate Action

On a larger scale, PVLC's collaborative efforts support the implementation of the UN Sustainable Development Goals.

The 2030 Agenda for Sustainable Development, adopted by all United Nations Member States in 2015, provides a shared blueprint for peace and prosperity for people and the planet, now and into the future. At its heart are 17 Sustainable Development Goals (SDGs), which are an urgent call for action by all countries – developed and developing – in a global partnership. (United Nations Department of Economic and Social Affairs, n.d.)

The collaborative's efforts are intended to provide education to anyone interested in learning about climate change and climate preparedness. PVLC's efforts exemplify a large portion of the UN's SDGs. However, the efforts were distinctly tied into the following goals: Good Health and Well-Being (SDG 3); Quality Education (SDG 4); Sustainable Cities and Communities (SDG 11); Responsible Consumption and Production (SDG 12); Climate Action (SDG 13); Life on Land (SDG 15); Peace, Justice and Strong Institutions (SDG 16); and Partnerships for the Goals (SDG 17) (United Nations Department of Economic and Social Affairs, n.d.). In the coming years of Climate Preparedness Week, PVLC will keep their efforts attuned to the SDGs listed by the United Nations and see if additional goals can be achieved with programs offered by the collaborative.

CONCLUSION

In summary, think local, but also think global. There may be other organizations, both locally and globally, that are working toward the same goals as yours. There is always something we can learn from another organization. If your organization is able, expand your collaboration. Even if you don't directly work with an outside group, the sharing of ideas and experiences is always a valuable tool.

The collaborative efforts of PVLC and V4C, including all member organizations and individuals, helped make the 2021 Climate Preparedness Week a success. We hope this chapter will provide an inspirational and instructional primer if your organization wishes to begin a similar collaboration. To keep up to date with the latest PVLC happenings and events, visit forbeslibrary.org/pvlc.

REFERENCES

American Library Association. (2019). ALA adding sustainability as a core value of librarianship. May 14, 2019. Retrieved January 7, 2023, from http://www.ala.org/news/press-releases/2019/05/ala-adding-sustainability-core-value-librarianship. Document ID: febd2792-a7fc-4c4a-90b4-23ab823344f7

American Library Association (ALA). (2020). Resilient communities: Libraries respond to climate change. February 4, 2020. Retrieved January 3, 2023, from http://www.ala.org/tools/programming/climatechange. Document ID: c165e7df-93be-44ed-8fef-86af381d5c9d

Citizens' Climate Lobby. (2021). Dr. Katharine Hayhoe: Talking Climate in a Polarized Environment | CCL Feb 2021 Regional Conferences. https://www.youtube.com/watch?v=uA2Fyy0a_U0

Communities Responding to Extreme Weather (CREW). (n.d.-a). Climate Resilience Hubs. https://www.climatecrew.org/resilience_hubs?locale=en

Communities Responding to Extreme Weather (CREW). (n.d.-b). More About Crew. https://www.climatecrew.org/?locale=en

Coward, C., McClay, C., & Garrido, M. (2018). *Public libraries as platforms for civic engagement.* Technology & Social Change Group, University of Washington Information School. http://hdl.handle.net/1773/41877

IPCC. (2022). Summary for policymakers In H.-O. Pörtner, D. C. Roberts, E. S. Poloczanska, K. Mintenbeck, M. Ignore, A. Alegría, M. Craig, S. Langsdorf, S. Löschke, V. Moller, & A. Okem (Eds.), *Climate change 2022: Impacts, adaptation, and vulnerability. Contribution of Working Group II to the Sixth Assessment Report of the Intergovernmental Panel on Climate Change* (pp. 3–33). Cambridge University Press. https://doi.org/10.1017/9781009325844.001

Kania, J., & Kramer, M. (2011). Collective impact. *Stanford Social Innovation Review, 9*(1), 36–41. https://doi.org/10.48558/5900-KN19

Kranich, N. (2012). *Libraries and civic engagement.* Rutgers University Community Repository. https://doi.org/10.7282/T3VX0DWS

Pogue, D. (2021). *How to prepare for climate change: A practical guide for surviving the chaos.* Simon & Schuster.

USGCRP. (2018). Impacts, risks, and adaptation in the United States: Fourth national climate assessment, Volume II. In D. R. Reidmiller, C. W. Avery, D. R. Easterling, K. E. Kunkel, K. L. M. Lewis, T. K. Maycock, & B. C. Stewart (Eds.), *U.S. Global Change Research Program*, Washington, DC, USA, 1515 pp. doi: 10.7930/NCA4.2018

United Nations (UN). (2015). *Transforming our world: The 2030 agenda for sustainable development.* UN Publishing.

United Nations Department of Economic and Social Affairs. (n.d.). Sustainable Development: Do You Know All 17 SDGs? https://sdgs.un.org/goals

Waters, A. (2010). *In the green kitchen: Techniques to learn by heart: A cookbook.* Clarkson Potter Publishers.

Special Thanks to:

Colin Battis, CREW
Kira Bingemann, Williamstown Public Library
Becky Blackburn, Westfield Athenaeum
Cher Collins, Agawam Public Library
Bernard Davidow, Wilbraham Public Library
Michelle Eberle, Massachusetts Library System
Antonia Golinski-Foisy, West Springfield Public Library
Jacklyn Hart, West Springfield Public Library
Jessica Kelmelis, Tolland Public Library
Benjamin Kalish, Forbes Library
Lise LeTellier, Granville Public Library
Stephanie Levine, Emily Williston Memorial Library
Guy McLain, Westfield Athenaeum
Heather Paparella, Southwick Public Library
Meaghan Schwelm, Westhampton Public Library
Paula Sharon, V4C
Rev. Vernon Walker, CREW

Thank you to all of our presenters and panelists for your participation.

CHAPTER 13

HOW REPAIR EVENTS IN LIBRARIES CAN CREATE SOCIALLY AND ECOLOGICALLY COMPASSIONATE CULTURE AND RESILIENT COMMUNITIES

Gabrielle Griffis

ABSTRACT

This chapter examines how libraries can help create socially and ecologically compassionate culture by hosting repair events. The introduction provides a general overview of repair events, as well as how they fit into the mission of public libraries and support sustainability goals. This chapter explores the impacts of repair events through the lens of the five conditions of collective success, doughnut economics, the right-to-repair movement, education, cultural practices, accessibility, and social infrastructure. The second part of the chapter provides a case study of Wellfleet Public Library on Cape Cod, Massachusetts, a library that has successfully implemented repair events. The final section offers an overview and step-by-step guide of how libraries can implement repair programs.

Keywords: Repair events; right-to-repair movement; cultural practices; Fixit Clinic; donut economics; public libraries

---

How Public Libraries Build Sustainable Communities in the 21st Century
Advances in Librarianship, Volume 53, 175–184
Copyright © 2023 by Gabrielle Griffis
Published under exclusive licence by Emerald Publishing Limited
ISSN: 0065-2830/doi:10.1108/S0065-283020230000053016

INTRODUCTION

Hosting repair events can help libraries build sustainable culture in their communities. A repair event is an intergenerational program in which patrons bring their broken items to the library, to be mentored by a person with fixing skills, to hopefully mend their malfunctioning items (Griffis et al., 2021). This chapter will examine how repair events can foster a more socially and ecologically compassionate culture, teach fixing skills, create more resilient communities, bridge social divides, and offer valuable services. This chapter will examine repair events through the lens of the five conditions of collective success, doughnut economics, the right-to-repair movement, education, cultural practices, accessibility, and social infrastructure. The second part of the chapter will provide a case study of Wellfleet Public Library on Cape Cod, Massachusetts, a library that has successfully implemented repair events. The final section will provide an overview and step-by-step guide of how libraries can implement repair programs.

SUSTAINABLE COMMUNITIES AND REPAIR EVENTS

As co-directors of the global nonprofit social advisory firm FSG, John Kania and Mark Kramer identified the five conditions of collective success to help create large-scale social change through the coordination of private and public organizations (Kania & Kramer, 2011). These conditions are: having a common agenda, using shared measurement systems, mutually reinforcing activities, continuous communication, and having backbone support organizations.

Libraries share a common agenda with the right-to-repair movement. The right-to-repair movement was formed as a reaction to tech and automotive companies increasing legal restrictions and barriers to personal and third-party repair of consumer products. In 2019, the American Library Association, having established sustainability as a core value stated that, "Libraries play an important and unique role in promoting community awareness about resilience, climate change and a sustainable future" (ALA Media Relations, 2019). In addition to sustainability, repair events uphold other core values of librarianship including: intellectual freedom, the public good, access, education and lifelong learning, service, preservation, and social responsibility (ALA Council, 2019). Libraries, as backbone support organizations, are helping assert citizen rights and actualize sustainability goals by providing a space in which communities can not only learn how to fix broken items, but also engage in conversation about reimagining waste systems and cultural practices.

According to the Intergovernmental Panel on Climate Change, current landfill and pollution statistics are historically unprecedented, and the negative impacts improper waste management has on our ecosystems and climate is worsening (IPCC, 2019). Public libraries have an important role to play in helping their communities deal with pollution and climate-related problems, as such issues are systemic, and require behavioral change in all aspects of society. As public centers for information and cultural enrichment, libraries are specifically structured to provide their communities with essential information and programming. Like all other institutions, libraries must adapt to the changing needs of communities confronted with the realities of improper waste management and climate change. Kania and Kramer, in putting together the five conditions of collective success, contend that individual organizations cannot solve such complex and massive global problems alone, but rather, require cross-sector collaboration to enact any form of large-scale change. Being a multi-sector problem, it is important to consider the root causes of waste and pollution. Repair events, although helpful and important, cannot solve all the social, economic, and environmental flaws of current manufacturing systems, however, they can bring attention to systemic flaws and promote alternative practices to ways of thinking that have historically exploited people and the environment. They can also help communities reassess access to vital services and how communities can be more equitable by catalyzing conversations around issues of repair and the fixing of essential items such as technology and medical equipment.

Librarians focused on sustainability are using a multidisciplinary approach to reimagine our systems and integrate new practices into their communities through hands-on programs such as repair events. The importance of introducing communities to alternative economic paradigms, such as doughnut economics, is an essential focus of *Libraries and Sustainability: Programs and Practices for Community Impact* (Antonelli et al., 2021). Doughnut economics is a mindset that considers the conditions necessary for social equity relative to the planet's ecological carrying capacity and uses these two conditions as the bedrock for policy (Raworth, 2017). As Kania and Kramer note, shared measurement systems are an essential part of the five conditions of collective success. While public and environmental health seem like logical measures of collective wellbeing, not every country uses these metrics and to what degree they are used, varies. Measurement systems impact cultural values and practices. Powerful countries such as the United States, consume disproportionately more planetary resources to the detriment of other nations, and have also historically correlated national wellbeing with gross-domestic product (Weeks, 2019). Doughnut economics asserts that in order to combat the root causes of social inequity, climate change and pollution, economic measurement systems must prioritize social and environmental health, not just relentless growth, which is ultimately not just impossible, but harmful to human survival. Using social and environmental health as measurement systems should be common sense, but becomes difficult in a society that does not guarantee that peoples' basic needs such as clean water, food, shelter, education, or healthcare will be met. In this context, basic needs are commodified and value is placed on control of resources instead of care for people and our shared environment. Doughnut economics is a useful tool for librarians to re-contextualize their practices and role in their communities.

The British economist Kate Raworth, who created the theory of doughnut economics, describes linear-degenerative economic systems in which consumer goods, rather than being designed to be fixed and reused, are designed to be thrown away. Raworth's economic theory resists normalizing the view that objects, people, or places are disposable, and puts the value of human and environmental life at its core. Fixing and stewarding broken things is one way to start addressing exploitative manufacturing systems, as this practice helps lessen the demand for cheaply made goods destined for the landfill. Repair events promote the circular and regenerative paradigm of doughnut economics, and asserts that every person has the right to safe, quality, and repairable goods, free from socially and environmentally destructive methods of production. Libraries, by hosting repair events and related programming, can introduce community members to human and environment-centric concepts, but also provide a way to implement these practices. At the bare minimum, library collections can offer literature and resources on these topics.

Since economics impacts every aspect of people's lives, it is necessary to consider how economic theory influences and creates culture. Culture, being socially expressed customs, institutions, art, and practices is mutable (Merriam-Webster, n.d.). When considering sustainability, the question arises, how do economic systems and practices impact culture when those systems are incompatible with sustainability? Economic and manufacturing systems that exploit people and the health of their environments are inherently unsustainable. Such a system can and should be reformed, but what does that look like in practice? Repair events are an opportunity to help communities consider and implement alternative forms of commerce especially because libraries are a successful example of the sharing economy. The library model, in which resources are collectively owned and shared by everyone, is being expanded by many libraries and communities to include tools, seeds, and other useful items. By participating in repair events, community members are sharing information, resources, skills, and building connections, which promote stewardship and resilience. Rigid economic systems that function exclusively on for-profit models and do not consider human and environmental wellbeing will inevitably fail. If a person has destructive habits, those habits must be replaced with healthy ones to preserve their life, in the same way that communities and cultures with socially and ecologically destructive habits need to change in order to survive, but alternative practices are necessary for change.

Social responsibility is one of the core values of the American Library Association, which is defined as helping to ameliorate or solve

> [...] the critical problems of society; support for efforts to help inform and educate the people of the United States on these problems and to encourage them to examine the many views on and the facts regarding each problem.... (ALA Council, 2019)

There is no greater threat to human survival than the ones posed by climate change caused by environmental destruction. Public libraries should take an active role in connecting communities to information and resources that help build social and environmental resilience.

Social resilience has been defined as "the ability of groups or communities to cope with external stresses and disturbances as a result of social, political, or environmental change" (Adger, 2000). Social infrastructure, which is the many places people go beyond work and home to socialize and find enrichment, such as libraries, is necessary to build social resilience (Klinenberg, 2018). Social infrastructure plays an integral role in the manifestation of culture and cultural values. A community that regularly shares resources such as tools and information, and helps teach one another valuable fixing skills, is going to be more resilient to certain challenges than communities where people are isolated and do not build strong social connections.

The following sections will provide a case study of how Wellfleet Public Library has implemented repair events on Cape Cod, Massachusetts. The study illustrates how libraries can work with different community groups as outlined in the five conditions of collective success, and also introduce communities to environmentally-minded cultural practices and ideas. The case study will follow with a step-by-step guide on how libraries can host their own repair events.

CASE STUDY: WELLFLEET PUBLIC LIBRARY'S FIXIT CLINIC

In Wellfleet, Massachusetts, located on Cape Cod, a peninsula that juts off the east coast, Wellfleet Public Library started hosting an annual Fixit Clinic in 2018, after being approached by the Wellfleet Recycling Committee. Fixit Clinic is a type of repair event founded by technologist and right-to-repair advocate, Peter Mui. A major goal of the Fixit Clinic is for participants to do the hands-on work of repairing their items with the assistance of a repair coach, rather than just bringing a broken item and passively having it fixed. The Fixit Clinic website provides a framework by which libraries and other community members can host their own repair events (Fixit Clinic, 2014). The free online resources on the Fixit Clinic website include tool lists, step-by-step instructions, as well as intake and exit forms for broken items brought to a repair event. Fixit Clinic is one example of a repair event, as are Repair Cafes.

INTENT OF PROGRAM

The intent of the Wellfleet Public Library's Fixit Clinic was to provide the community with a hands-on, interactive program that brought people together, taught participants fixing skills, helped keep items out of the landfill, and facilitated conversations and new approaches to problems surrounding waste.

PROGRAM STRUCTURE

At the Fixit Clinic, tables were set up around the library's auditorium near electrical outlets. For three hours, repair experts sat at tables with their tools and a sign that indicated their area of fixing expertise. A greeter sat at a table in the auditorium entrance with in-take and exit forms, and paired participants with the appropriate coaches. Participants, who had heard about the Fixit Clinic, through the library's various forms of outreach, were assisted on a first-come first-serve basis, with no prior registration required. During the three hours, coaches helped participants troubleshoot, disassemble, and many times fix their broken stuff. A bell was rang to celebrate successful repairs.

IMPLEMENTATION

Wellfleet Library provided the space and some of the resources essential to implement each Fixit Clinic. The Fixit Clinic webpage contains all the essential information and resources needed to host a Fixit Clinic. The webpage was created and is managed by Fixit Clinic Founder, Peter Mui. Mui has overseen hundreds of Fixit Clinics and voluntarily mentored Wellfleet Library, in starting their Fixit Clinic. The town of Wellfleet's recycling committee members volunteered their time and skills, to organize the clinic with the assistance of the library. Working with committee members, the library's outreach coordinator created and implemented the publicity and outreach necessary to recruit repair volunteers.

With the guidance and resources provided by Peter Mui, the committee and library recruited coaches, and acquired the necessary tools to successfully execute a repair event. Some of these tools included: testing batteries, electrical outlets, extension cords, toolkits, needle nose pliers, scissors, glue, tape, paintbrushes, tables, in-take and exit forms, signage, and more.

A week before each Fixit Clinic, a repair coach meeting was held to explain the objectives of the clinic, as well as inventory the tools each coach would bring. The day of the clinic, a greeting table, and stations were organized around the library's meeting room to help direct participants to the appropriate coach. Recycling committee members also set up a refreshment table for coaches and attendees. Around the room, participants worked together to try and fix a range of items: jewelry, sewing machines, lamps, wooden stools, books, fans, children's toys, kitchen appliances, and so on.

OUTCOMES

At Wellfleet Public Library's Fixit Clinic, coaches helped participants, from several neighboring towns, troubleshoot items such as sewing machines, espresso makers, blenders, lamps, cd players, electric razors, and computers. Participants learned fixing skills, engaged in conversations around sustainability, and positively interacted with their community. In total, there were more than 40 items repaired, with a handful of items that were not fixed. The anonymous information from the intake and exit forms were submitted to the Fixit Clinic item report form on the Fixit Clinic website.

While many items brought into a repair event are non-essential, many people are adversely impacted by a lack of access to repair of essential items, such as wheelchairs and medical equipment. This raises the question, for all the items brought in and documented at a repair event, what types of items are not brought in due to barriers such immobility and legal restrictions? For some people, the repair of a medical device such as a wheelchair, can be the difference between life or death due to health complications that result from immobility. This is further complicated by medical device monopolies that inhibit individuals or third-party services from repairing essential equipment. Some states, such as Colorado, have passed right-to-repair laws that permit third-party repair services and owners to access tools, parts, embedded software, maintenance, and other components necessary to repair wheelchairs (Hawryluk, 2022; Kaiser Health News, 2022).

While many companies try to make right-to-repair an issue of intellectual property, the reality is that they are mostly interested in making consumers dependent on them to repair devices to maximize their profits. With complete control over repair, companies can maintain monopolies, charge individuals exorbitant repair fees, and leave consumers with little choice but to purchase new items. In this way, corporations have subtle, and not so subtle, ways of controlling individual and collective behavior. In capitalist economic systems, companies have a shared goal of maximizing their profits, and because of their structure and focus, are successful at increasing their revenue regardless of the true social and environmental costs. Gone unchecked, profit maximizing practices have disastrous effects on society and the environment. Libraries are essential when it comes to mutually reinforcing activities that promote human-centered, rather than profit-driven, values such as: equity, sustainability, education, lifelong learning, intellectual freedom, the public good, access, service, preservation, and social responsibility. By hosting repair events, libraries are doing all that and more.

In this way, the benefits of acquiring information regarding broken materials at a Fixit Clinic are multifold. A major part of the repair movement's objective is to better understand what types of items are most frequently brought to repair events, how easy or difficult it is to repair them, and whether there are any local services that actually do repair such items. The ease of repairing an item is dependent on many factors such as location, the complexity of an item, affordability, and whether an object was made to be repaired in the first place. Some repairs can be done at home, while some services are more difficult to obtain.

Wellfleet, being further away from the mainland of Massachusetts, is relatively remote. Like many of the more rural towns in Massachusetts, access to certain repair services for different items is more difficult to obtain. One such vital service is electronic repair for devices such as phones and laptops. There are a few computer repair services on Cape Cod for individuals who have access to transportation and can afford such services, and despite Wellfleet being remote, it is still closer to computer and other repair services than many rural towns.

Many libraries that offer technology assistance, without being explicitly clear about the parameters of their tech assistance, receive community members who require help troubleshooting and fixing devices beyond the scope or capability of even the savviest technology librarian. Access to repair services is contingent on many factors, which are often beyond the control of individuals. This access decreases the less able-bodied and financially stable a person is. Repair events, invite communities to consider how accessibility to repair services can, and should, be increased for everyone. Repair events encourage people to consider the many points of system failure, which includes economics.

Being a coastal town, Wellfleet Public Library serves a community confronted with unique challenges relative to climate change. Rising sea levels, increased temperatures, and extreme weather threaten the long-term survival of Cape Cod. Fixit Clinics are one way libraries are helping bring community members to forge

182   GABRIELLE GRIFFIS

stronger social bonds and sustainable values. With increasing commercialization and less public gathering spaces, libraries are playing an increasingly important role in helping define community social life. Repair events provide an additional space where people can access resources, receive help, and share information free of cost. In this way, repair events also promote tolerance and a sense of social trust, in which community members from dissimilar backgrounds can meet and learn not just valuable fixing skills, but about people and cultures that might be different from their own. All communities have their own unique problems, which require multi-sector collaboration and creative solutions outlined by Kania and Kramer in their five conditions for collective success.

When implemented successfully, repair events can help create socially and ecologically compassionate culture and resilient communities by providing alternative group practices, learning opportunities, and context to discuss and reimagine cultural systems and behaviors.

They have both individual and communal benefits, and provide life-long positive outcomes, especially when it comes to young people and education. Repair events help instill the importance of environmental stewardship and civic engagement, as well as help young people gain new skills, build confidence, and form new friendships. These opportunities are especially important as inequality increases and the cost of education continues to rise. Every person has the right to education, and yet, most advanced degree programs are prohibitively expensive unless a young person has parents who can pay the cost or they receive scholarships and loans. The impact of inflated college tuition costs can be seen in declining enrollment rates (Saul, 2022). This is not to suggest that repair events can replace a college education, but they can help connect young people to opportunities, resources, and ideas, which would not occur otherwise. Repair events can help instill people and planet-centric values in the next generation of young people. Libraries, by hosting repair events, can help create socially and ecologically compassionate culture by promoting the view that no person, place, or thing, is truly disposable.

STEPS FOR HOLDING A REPAIR EVENT

Source: Griffis (2023)

- Determine what kind of repair event the library will host. Fixit Clinic and Repair Cafe provide existing models and directions on their websites. A generic name such as "repair event" can also be used. Libraries can get creative with event titles, or host smaller events focused on specific types of repair such as a repair event just for sewing machines or bicycles.
- Appraise library event space relative to program needs such as tables, electrical outlets, and traffic flow. Pop-up events can be done at libraries without large program rooms or outside.
- Choose the date and length of the program, with consideration for event setup and cleanup, which is typically an hour before and after – five hours total is sufficient.

- Assess program budget. A large budget is not needed to host repair events and can rely on donated tools as well as coaches bringing their own tools. If a library has a larger budget, then that money can be used to purchase tools, refreshments, and other resources.
- Recruit co-hosts. Co-hosts are not necessary, but collaborating with local organizations such as conservation commissions, recycling committees, schools, makerspaces, and other groups can improve the planning process and implementation.
- With the planning committee, allocate tasks: outreach, snacks, repair coach coordination, greeting table, publicity and event documentation.
- Enlist coaches three to two months in advance of the event. Best practice is to have one person as repair coach coordinator. Enlisting repair volunteers can be done through word-of-mouth, flyers, local media, and social media. Announcements should include contact information, fixing abilities sought, and date/time of program.
- Begin outreach for programs two to one month prior to events in library newsletter, publicity, social media, and other platforms.
- Host meeting for repair coaches one week in advance of the program. This meeting is intended to answer the coaches' questions, inventory tools, and outline event goals/expectations. Important to note that coaches should be guiding participants in item repair.
- On the day of the event, prepare the room an hour or more before start time. Make sure tables are positioned near electrical outlets with appropriate tables for greeting and signage, as well as chairs for waiting.
- During the repair event, greeters should welcome attendees, give them in-take/liability and exit forms, provide an overview of the event, and connect attendees with appropriate coaches.
- Volunteers and library staff can share responsibilities of event photography, hospitality, snacks (if offered), and clean up.
- In-take and exit forms should be taken by library staff. Anonymous repair information can be submitted to right-to-repair databases, such as Fixit Clinic.
- With permission, photos of the event can be shared to social media.
- A good rule of thumb is to send thank notes to volunteers and coaches.

CONCLUSION

Libraries, by hosting repair events and related programming, can help create socially and ecologically compassionate culture and build resilience. This chapter has sought to examine how repair events can foster a more socially and ecologically compassionate culture, teach fixing skills, create more resilient communities, bridge social divides, and offer valuable services. Using the five conditions of collective success identified by John Kania and Mark Kramer, mindsets such as doughnut economics and the right-to-repair movement, this chapter has provided some examples of how and why linear-degenerative economic systems impact culture, accessibility, education, and overall planetary and social health. Ultimately, technological progress without social and environmental equity is unsustainable. While current systemic problems are massive and require cross-sector collaboration, change cannot happen without alternative behaviors and practices. Repair events can provide insight into alternative paradigms and have a ripple effect for individuals and communities. As free public spaces for learning, repair events align with library values and beliefs in basic human rights. In this way, repair events challenge current social norms which treat some people, environments, and objects as being expendable, and provide the alternative view that on planet earth, stewardship and repair are essential to survival.

REFERENCES

Adger, W. N. (2000). Social and ecological resilience: Are they related? *Progress in Human Geography*, 24(3), 347–364.

ALA Council. (2019). *Core values of librarianship*. https://www.ala.org/advocacy/intfreedom/corevalues

ALA Media Relations. (2019). *ALA adding sustainability as a core value of librarianship*. https://www.ala.org/news/press-releases/2019/05/ala-adding-sustainability-core-value-librarianship

Antonelli, M., Ho, A., Smith Aldrich, R., & Tanner, R. (2021). *Libraries and sustainability: Programs and practices for community impact*. ALA Editions.

Fixit Clinic. (2014). *Start a clinic*. https://fixitclinic.blogspot.com

Griffis, G. (2021). Libraries and sustainability: Programs and practices for community impact. In M. Antonelli, A. Ho, R. Smith Aldrich, & R. Tanner (Eds.), *How Repair events at libraries can build social infrastructure and create sustainable culture* (p. 176). ALA Editions.

Griffis, G. (2023). *25 ready-to-use sustainable living programs for libraries. Kroski, Ellyssa* (pp. 71–75). ALA Editions.

Hawryluk, M. (2022, August 18). *Colorado passes the first bill for wheelchairs*. Silver Century Foundation. https://www.silvercentury.org/2022/08/colorado-passes-the-first-right-to-repair-bill-for-wheelchairs/

IPCC. (2019). In P. R. Shukla et al. (Eds.), *Climate Change and Land: An IPCC special report on climate change, desertification, land degradation, sustainable land management, food security, and greenhouse gas fluxes in terrestrial ecosystems*. In press.

Kaiser Health News. (2022). Despite a First-Ever 'Right-to-Repair Law, There's No Easy Fix for Wheelchair Users. https://khn.org/news/article/power-wheelchair-users-right-to-repair-law-no-easy-fix/

Kania, J., & Kramer, M. (2011). *Collective impact*. Stanford Social Innovation Review. https://ssir.org/articles/entry/collective_impact#bio-footer

Klinenberg, E. (2018). *Palaces for the people*. Penguin Random House.

Merriam-Webster. (n.d.). Culture. In *Merriam-Webster.com dictionary*. Retrieved September 26, 2022, from https://www.merriam-webster.com/dictionary/culture

Raworth, K. (2017). *Doughnut economics*. Chelsea Green Publishing.

Saul, S. (2022, May 26). College Enrollment Drops, Even as the Pandemic's Effects Ebb. *New York Times*. https://www.nytimes.com/2022/05/26/us/college-enrollment.html

Weeks, J. (2019). *GDP: Origin, uses and abuses*. Prime Policy Research in Macroeconomics. https://www.primeeconomics.org/articles/gdp-origin-uses-and-abuses/

CHAPTER 14

A SMALL LIBRARY MAKING BIG CHANGES: A CASE STUDY OF THE BARAMSUP LIBRARY

Yong Ju Jung

ABSTRACT

How rural libraries influence their communities' development is shown in a number of studies, and many of those rural libraries have focused on their roles in increasing the accessibility of technology for their local community. However, few focused on how rural libraries are immersed in their surrounding natural environment to empower the community members' learning about and with nature. Also, there have been rare examples of rural libraries that support not only their local community but also another country's sustainable development. The Baramsup Picturebook Library, located in a rural area in South Korea, is an exemplary case because it has provided a large range of programming and services for diverse groups of people (i.e., from children to older adults) from diverse levels of communities – from the local communities around the library to the global communities of a developing country, Laos. Through qualitative content analysis of an interview with the library's director as well as their official blog and articles and reports from magazines, this chapter presents a case study of this library. The library's services and programs are demonstrated under three themes: (1) rural, local communities: cultivating the book culture; *(2) local and regional communities: empowering children's* ecological sensitivity; *(3) with global communities: building school libraries for children in Laos. This case study of the Baramsup Picturebook Library provides conceptual and practical insights into how rural and small libraries*

How Public Libraries Build Sustainable Communities in the 21st Century
Advances in Librarianship, Volume 53, 185–195
Copyright © 2023 by Yong Ju Jung
Published under exclusive licence by Emerald Publishing Limited
ISSN: 0065-2830/doi:10.1108/S0065-283020230000053017

initiate changes in people and communities, thereby impacting sustainable social changes in larger communities.

Keywords: Rural public libraries; environmental education; nature; book culture; local and global communities; picture books; school libraries

INTRODUCTION

Rural libraries have been contributing to the economic, social, and technological development of communities (Hoq, 2015; Samsuddin et al., 2020). In particular, rural libraries usually serve communities of low socioeconomic status and with limited information literacy, so their roles in mitigating the digital and economic divide have been increasingly highlighted (Mehra et al., 2017). Accordingly, small and rural libraries mainly provide services and programs related to digital literacy and access (i.e., Internet, maker tools) for technologically marginalized populations in local communities as well as physical space and facilities for community people (e.g., Chase, 2021; Reid & Howard, 2016).

There is no doubt that such efforts for infrastructural and technological support are crucial. However, it is also important to note that rural libraries also provide other varied services and programming; their roles are not limited to the monotonous type of support. Beyond this, rural libraries have the potential to make a positive influence on the culture and mindset of community people, which are critical for any sustainable transformation. However, few studies focus on how rural libraries utilize the surrounding natural environment – considering their geological locations – to empower people's learning and change attitudes. Little attention has been paid to if and how a rural library assists not only their local community but also larger and global communities. Accordingly, this chapter presents a case study demonstrating a small library located in a rural area in South Korea – the Baramsup Picturebook Library – and how it has driven social and cultural changes in diverse communities.

ABOUT THE BARAMSUP PICTUREBOOK LIBRARY

Baramsup Grimchaek Doseoguan (Baramsup Picturebook Library; BPL) is a private–public library in Ganghwa, an island in a rural area of Incheon. Baramsup means wind forest in Korean. As the name indicates, this library is in the middle of a forest in Ganghwa. The library being private–public means that it was built by a private unit rather than a government, but it has served diverse populations of the public and has been officially registered as one of the "private–public-small libraries" by the Incheon city government. As this library is not "public–public," the support from the city government has been very limited, but more space for flexibility and creativity is allowed in terms of programming and services.

The director[1] of the library had worked in different types of libraries in South Korea and Paris, France, for almost 40 years; in particular, she had worked as the director of a couple of public libraries. Building on her passion for picture books and experiences across various libraries, she started the Bramsup Picturebook Library in 2014 – with the visions of "making a better world through picture books, growing diverse dreams of people through picture books, and making their hearts warm through picture books" (Baramsupai, 2014). The library initially started with 3,000 books, but currently holds around 10,000 volumes (Library Director, Personal Correspondence, February 24, 2022). In response to increasing demands, in 2019, the library renovated its facility and built a new building (Fig. 1). The new building was architecturally inspired by nature, so it includes physical spaces, symbolic of fields, mountains, and forests.

The registered small libraries by the Incheon city government are assessed and categorized into different ranks every year; depending on their ranks, they are provided different amounts of financial support to be used for programming and equipment purchases (Incheon City Government, 2021). BPL has been keeping the highest rank. The support from the city government, however, is not much and not allowed to be used for employee payment and utility fees; much of the library operation has relied on donations and earnings from a café in the library. There have been volunteers helping run programs and manage the library facility. After experiencing operational and financial challenges due to COVID-19, the library has adopted an online appointment system that requires people to book their visits in advance and pay a small fee (₩5,000 in South Korean won; about $4 in USD) (Shin, 2022).

BPL started as the first library specializing particularly in picture books in South Korea; it should be noted that being a picture book library is different from being a children's library, so they have patrons of all age ranges from children to older adults. The majority of the library's patrons have been from local communities in Ganghwa, including individuals and groups from nearby towns, community-based groups, and schools. Also, there are patrons who purposefully visit the library from other regions (Shin, 2021a). Ganghwa is about two hours

Fig. 1. The Baramsup Picturebook Library (New Building).

away from Seoul, the Capital of South Korea and one of the largest metropolises in the world, and has numerous historical remains and sites from ancient Korean countries along with forests and sea (Encyclopedia of Korean Culture, 2011). These attractors are likely one factor in bringing people from other areas into the library. In addition to services for local and regional communities within the country, the library has initiated a movement for building school libraries in Laos, one of the developing countries in South Asia.

CASE STUDY METHODOLOGY

This chapter presents a case study (Stake, 1995) of the Baramsup Picturebook Library as an exemplary case for its local and global contributions to sustainable community changes. To investigate BPL's services and programming, a qualitative content analysis (Hsieh & Shannon, 2005) was conducted with an interview with the library's director as well as news and magazine articles about the library and its official blog pages (https://blog.naver.com/baramsupai). The interview with the director was conducted virtually through Zoom for about an hour and then transcribed; the interview data was the main data source. The articles included six reports written by reporters from news and magazines (e.g., *Happy Education*, a magazine published by the Ministry of Education; the *School Library Journal* of South Korea) and six essays written by the library's director and staff members (e.g., Shin, 2021a, 2021b). Using various sources helped with data triangulation. Data collection and analysis were conducted in Korean; the coding schemes, findings, and some key excerpts from the interview were translated into English.

Data were read first word by word and noted with initial notes. Then, 11 labels were created for coding, such as regions (local, other regions in Korea, other countries), patrons (children from schools, children and families, adults, older adults), and topics (humanities, environment/ecology, reading, picture book-making). Coded contents were clustered and summarized into three themes: (1) with rural, local communities: cultivating the *book culture*; (2) with local and regional communities: empowering children's *ecological sensitivity*; (3) with global communities: building school libraries for children in Laos. More details and examples of each theme are demonstrated in the following section.

FINDINGS: COMMUNITY CHANGES FROM THE SMALL LIBRARY

Rural, Local Communities: Cultivating the Book Culture

The Baramsup Picturebook Library has provided various programs and services to promote community people's learning in humanities, reading, and the natural environment using picture books. BPL also holds community events, such as concerts, movie nights, puppetries, and exhibitions for community populations. By doing so, the library has become a core space for social and cultural activities of the local communities and cultivated the *book culture* in the communities. The book culture fostered by this library means the atmosphere where people feel the picture books are familiar; the ways of thinking about the books and the world through picture books; and ways of making interactions and sharing feelings with others through picture books.

The first and foremost service has been "selecting good picture books and helping those books meet readers well," according to the director. Every month, the director and staff members choose a topic of the month and select several topic picture books. They organize the majority of picture books based on topics rather than common library classification systems, such as Korean Decimal Classification (KDC). They display picture books by showing each cover from the front and exhibit character toys if related to certain picture books (Fig. 2). This way helps people easily find books more attractive and meaningful to them (Lee, 2014; Seo, 2016).

Also, BPL put efforts into supporting its community people to read picture books. In particular, considering that age groups of 60 and above are the largest populations of Ganghwa (like many other rural areas in South Korea), the library offers various supports for older adults, especially to help them familiarize themselves with picture books. When the library was first opened, most community people saw the library as very strange. Sometimes, older adults from the area stopped by and said, "aren't picture books only for children?" and left (Library Director, Personal Correspondence, February 24, 2022). However, the director's philosophy was that picture books are for all stages of life – from birth to the very last moment of life. Below is one episode from her:

> One day, two grannies sisters came into the library and said that they were traveling in Ganghwa for the birthday of one of them and just noticed the library by chance. They got so curious about why there's a library here and stopped by, but said "there will be no books for us [because the library is for picture books]." So I introduced them to a picture book about life ["*Hundred: What You Learn in a Lifetime*" by Heike Faller and Valerio Vidali]. The book starts from 1 year old to 100 years old. One lady who was 78 years old opened the page about age 78, and another lady who was 80 years old opened the page about age 80, and

Fig. 2. Inside of the Baramsup Picturebook Library Showing How Picture Books Are Displayed.

then their eyes got wet and said this book illustrated their life so well. They said they were so thankful to come to the library and get a chance to meet this book. Because of their limited eyesight [due to presbyopia] they could not read texts easily even with glasses, so they said, "instead of books full of texts, picture books having both illustrations and texts can be a good friend, and this is a great gift for my birthday gift." Hearing their conversations, my eyes got wet too, and thought that yes, picture books have such power! (Library Director, Personal Correspondence, February 24, 2022)

Like this episode, BPL has tried to mitigate prejudice about picture books and helped older adults newly find the value of picture books. In addition, by collaborating with local nursing homes in Ganghwa, the library offers outreach services by visiting them, reading picture books, and providing some programs with picture books, such as writing essays or making artifacts related to a picture book (Seo, 2016). Older adults in their 80s and 90s (and some with Alzheimer's disease) learn how to communicate their thoughts and feelings through picture books.

In terms of programming, BPL runs several picture book-making programs for children's and adults' groups. Periodically, the library accepts applications and makes cohorts for weekly classes, through which people learn about picture books, make their own stories, and design and draw their own picture books. *Eorinee Jakga Gyosil* (Children Author Class) is a program for children to develop not only storytelling skills but also facilitate their empathy and sympathy skills through making picture books. *Naega Mandunun Grimchaek* (Picture Book Made by Me) is a program for adults, especially women (i.e., "mothers" from the local town), supported by the Incheon city's project for empowering the regional culture (Shin, 2021b). This program has helped women reflect on themselves, show their voices, and connect with others through picture books and stories. After classes, BPL has hosted exhibitions of patrons' picture books, collaborated with publishers on printing (or publishing), and displayed them in the library.

Regarding their services and programs for picture books, the director mentioned that:

[...] picture books helped people enjoy reading and expanded skills in not only humanities but also affective aspects. Also, image-based media is particularly important in the 21st century, I would argue that picture books could make a more impact. By doing so, [people] can have a healthy mentality, and the growth of the economy can occur in a healthy way. (Library Director, Personal Correspondence, February 24, 2022)

In other words, BPL ultimately aims to support the inner growth of people's minds and the book culture in the local communities beyond sparking short-term interests in picture books.

Local and Regional Communities: Empowering Children's Ecological Sensitivity

Along with picture books, another emphasis of BPL has been on the natural environment and ecology of the natural world. What the director envisioned when planning to start this library was "a library in the middle of a natural forest," and for this, the current location was deliberately selected (Seo, 2016). The library has been surrounded by forests and mountains, and has its own yard and garden. With the hope to help children enjoy nature while reading books, the library offers programs. The *Baramsup Jayeon Hakgyo* (Baramsup Nature School) is a monthly, regular program for registered children. Also, similar one-day workshops have been provided to field-trip students from nearby elementary schools. Each month our workshop has a topic related to the natural environment, such as birds, insects, or plants, and children spend time reading related picture books together. And then, they explore the outside world using their five senses (e.g., observing, touching). With such sensory experiences, they create drawings or write poems (Library Director, Personal Correspondence, February 24, 2022). For instance, when their topic was bird migration (which is a particularly relevant topic to the library's location because during the fall seasons, the Ganghwa region is along the migratory flyways of birds from the Northern regions such as Siberia, Russia), children read picture books about this topic, walked outside with binoculars, and closely investigated the bird migrations. For the topic of woodpeckers (as they live in the mountain next to the library), children read and then went to the mountain and found holes in trees created by woodpeckers. For the topic of acorns, children read and picked up acorns from the nearby forest. After reading about biological life, children planted lettuce seeds in the library's garden. In the spring seasons, children read about and collected dandelions from the yard, made dandelion salad, and ate it together. All these programs help children integrate picture book reading and hands-on learning with nature in various ways.

Furthermore, the library offers programs of hands-on making with ingredients from nature, such as wood and plants (Lee, 2014). One prominent program has been *Dulpul Jongeechaek Mandulgi* (Wild-plant-paperbook-making). In this program, children and families are engaged with the slow, Korean traditional process of making papers with wild plants – from steaming, mincing, and filtering, to drying wild plants. Then, combined with the concept of the picture book-making programs, they also create small books using their own wild-plant papers. The library also provides programs, such as crafting flowers and insects with wood and making herb soaps with natural oils. Perhaps due to the uniqueness of these programs, there have been patrons from not only the local communities but also other nearby towns and urban communities (Lee, 2014).

For these programs, the library takes the advantage of their geological and environmental conditions and helps patrons immersed in nature. Children learn how to breathe and live together with the natural environment and connect their learning from reading with the sensory, hands-on experiences in nature, which is critical for children's environmental science learning (Jung et al., 2019). Such affective experiences with picture books and nature at this library possibly promote children's *ecological sensitivity* – as also reported in Lee (2014). Ecological sensitivity (Noh, 2013) means children's creativity, attitude, understanding, and sympathy for the natural environment and ecology of the world, according to children's environmental science education literature, and is critical to building and maintaining sustainable community development. This approach of the library appears different from the focus of other rural libraries, such as on information and technology access; instead, this library has more centered on meaningful access to nature.

WITH GLOBAL COMMUNITIES: BUILDING SCHOOL LIBRARIES FOR CHILDREN IN LAOS

In addition to the regional contributions within the country, BPL has broadened its impacts on the global world. Notably, BPL has initiated the project for building libraries in schools in rural areas in Laos. In 2016, the director, staff members, and volunteers from BPL flew to Laos and created the first library in a school in Xayaboury province; they named it *Wind Forest Library*. Since the first Wind Forest Library in Laos, they have received requests from other schools in Laos. In response to such needs, they made three more school libraries in Xayaboury and Xiangkhouang provinces. From 2016 to 2019, a total of four Wind Forest Libraries were created in schools in particularly underdeveloped areas of the provinces. (The project has stopped since the COVID-19 pandemic, but the director was hoping to resume this project in the near future.) The basic infrastructure of the schools was very limited as they had not had electricity at that time. Thus, the very first step of this project was setting up solar photovoltaics and lighting up the bulbs in the school. Empty classrooms of each school were cleaned, re-organized, painted, and furnished with shelves, tables, and chairs, and then turned into school libraries (Fig. 3). Each of the Wind Forest Libraries had three sections for books written in Lao, Korean, and English, respectively. Books in Lao were collected and purchased locally, but not many picture books and children's books were available in Laos, according to the director. Thus, some books and picture books in Korean and English were brought from South Korea.

Along with BPL's contributions and efforts, the cooperation and support from other organizations and individuals were also crucial for the success of this project in Laos. In the initial two years, this project was supported by financial and non-cash donations mainly from non-government organizations, such as publishing companies and volunteer groups, and individuals from the library's local and

Fig. 3. Wind Forest Library Built in a School in Laos.

regional communities in South Korea. Adding to that, in 2018 and 2019, the project was partially funded by South Korea's Ministry of Foreign Affairs. With this additional fund, BPL invited two professional picture book writers and had them lead book-making programs for children in Laos while the school libraries were under construction. In the programs, children designed and drew picture books (Fig. 4); due to the limited technology in local printing and publishing, those drawings and designs were brought to South Korea, turned into printed picture books, and sent back to the school libraries in Laos. The director said,

Fig. 4. Picture Books Made by Children in Laos.

[…] when they [children] saw that their own books were on the stack in their own school library, they got so proud of themselves. They could read their own books, and their friends read their books. Also, there were not many books accessible [in Laos], the schools and children felt so precious about these books. By doing so, they could nurture self-efficacy and seed new hope. (Library Director, Personal Correspondence, February 24, 2022)

Through building the school libraries and providing the book-making programs, BPL has contributed to a better learning space for children and supported their affective/emotional states (e.g., "self-efficacy," "hope"). Such small changes in the schools and children potentially drive sustainable changes (Brosch & Steg, 2021).

DISCUSSION AND CONCLUSION

Despite the small size and rural location, the Baramsup Picturebook Library has offered various programs and services for local, regional, and global communities, particularly by focusing on picture books, nature, and children. Their programs and services have initiated multidimensional changes across the different levels of communities. First, BPL has brought in spatial and infrastructural changes by placing the library in a rural area (i.e., Ganghwa) and school libraries in an underdeveloped country (i.e., Laos). The existence of BPL in the rural area in Ganghwa has improved the community populations' accessibility to books. Also, the school libraries in Laos have provided safer and brighter spaces for children. Second, BPL has initiated the cultural changes by promoting the book culture and the ecological sensitivity of the community populations. BPL has become a core space for such cultural changes, through which people – from children to older adults – have engaged with sustainable learning about picture books and nature. Third, BPL has led the societal movement by inviting collective efforts from various groups on different levels (e.g., individual, organizational, national, and global) – beyond the boundary of its rural town. The library has actively communicated with its local and regional communities (e.g., nursing homes, schools, printing and publishing companies) for services and programs. The library has also worked with government organizations. Especially for the project in Laos, BPL has built a national partnership with various individuals and groups, including the Ministry of Foreign Affairs. Lastly, but perhaps most importantly, BPL's programs and services aim to make individual changes in each patron's mind by "seeding new hope." For example, what children in the *Baramsup Nature School* program experience with birds, plants, and trees may change a small thought and emotion about nature, which is expected to promote the larger community's ecological sensitivity and sustainable growth. Also, from the project in Laos, small changes in the confidence of each child may become the foundation of sustainable economic development in their country.

This case study has some limitations because it does not include direct reports or any measurements from patrons who have participated in the library's programs and services. Also, because this case study is mainly focused on describing what BPL did, a theoretical investigation of the phenomenon surrounding the library has not been fully conducted. Still, this exemplary case of BPL provides conceptual and practical insights into how rural and small libraries initiate changes in people and communities, thereby impacting sustainable social changes in larger communities.

ACKNOWLEDGMENT

The author fully appreciates the director, Jeehye Choi, and staff members from the Baramsup Picturebook Library for providing resources, participating in an interview as well as making a better world with picture books.

NOTE

1. The director was also the owner who founded the library, but she preferred to be called the director.

REFERENCES

Baramsupai. (2014). BaramsupGrimchaekDoseoguaneun [About the Baramsup Picturebook Library]. https://blog.naver.com/baramsupai/10189770020

Brosch, T., & Steg, L. (2021). Leveraging emotion for sustainable action. *One Earth, 4*(12), 1693–1703. https://doi.org/10.1016/j.oneear.2021.11.006

Chase, S. (2021). Innovative lessons from our small and rural public libraries. *Journal of Library Administration*, *61*(2), 237–243. https://doi.org/10.1080/01930826.2020.1853473

Encyclopedia of Korean Culture. (2011). Ganghwado [Ganghwa Island]. http://encykorea.aks.ac.kr/Contents/Item/E0001507

Hoq, K. M. G. (2015). Rural library and information services, their success, failure and sustainability: A literature review. *Information Development*, *31*(3), 294–310. https://doi.org/10.1177/0266666913515693

Hsieh, H. F., & Shannon, S. E. (2005). Three approaches to qualitative content analysis. *Qualitative Health Research*, *15*(9), 1277–1288. https://doi.org/10.1177/1049732305276687

Incheon City Government. (2021). JakeunDoseoquan Jiwon Hyunhwang [The current status of supporting small libraries]. https://www.incheon.go.kr/open/OPEN010201/beffatInfoPublictDetail?bbsNo=1988462

Jung, Y. J., Zimmerman, H. T., & Land, S. M. (2019). Emerging and developing situational interest during children's tablet-mediated biology learning activities at a nature center. *Science Education*, *103*(4). https://doi.org/10.1002/sce.21514

Lee, S. (2014). BaramsupGrimchaekDoseoguan: Yaedula, supeseo chaekhago nolja [The Baramsup Picturebook Library: Children, play with books in a forest]. *Happy Education*, *10*, 40–41.

Mehra, B., Bishop, B. W., & Partee II, R. P. (2017). Small business perspectives on the role of rural libraries in economic development. *Library Quarterly: Information, Communit, Policy*, *87*(1), 17–35.

Noh, H. J. (2013). Saengtaehakjeok jaaheui jeongripgua saengtaehakjeok gamsuseong jungjineul wihan gyoyuk [Establishment of ecological self and education for promoting ecological sensitivity]. *Environmental Philosophy*, *16*, 61–81.

Reid, H., & Howard, V. (2016). Connecting with community: The importance of community engagement in rural public library systems. *Public Library Quarterly*, *35*(3), 188–202. https://doi.org/10.1080/01616846.2016.1210443

Samsuddin, S. F., Shaffril, H. A. M., & Fauzi, A. (2020). Heigh-ho, heigh-ho, to the rural libraries we go! – A systematic literature review. *Library and Information Science Research*, *42*(1). https://doi.org/10.1016/j.lisr.2019.100997

Seo, J. (2016). Jayeonsure ilkko shigo Baramsup Geurimchaek Doseoguan [Naturally read and rest, Baramsup Picturebook Library]. *School Library Journal*, *6*, 110–115.

Shin, A. (2021a). Mueoteul chaja chaekbangyeohaengeul danilkka? [For what people travel to bookstores?]. http://www.incheonin.com/news/articleView.html?idxno=81970

Shin, A. (2021b). Seoro gonggamhameo jijiga deonun gonggan [A space for people to feel empathy and support each other]. https://www.smalllibrary.org/program/bestPractice/1443?libraryName=&currentPage=5

Stake, R. E. (1995). *The art of case study research*, Thousand Oaks, CA: Sage.

Shin, A. (2022). Jakeundoseoguan, ilsangeui hwabokeul ggumgguda [Small libraries, dreaming the recovery to the normal]. *School Library Journal*, *1*, 50–53.

SECTION FOUR

LIBRARIES PROMOTING ECONOMIC DEVELOPMENT

INTRODUCTION TO SECTION FOUR: SUSTAINABLE COMMUNITIES AND THE ROLE OF THE PUBLIC LIBRARY

Kaurri C. Williams-Cockfield and Bharat Mehra

FRAMING OF SECTION FOUR ["LIBRARIES PROMOTING ECONOMIC DEVELOPMENT"]

Section Four features three case studies that provide information about programs which promote sustainable economic growth [SDG 8], advance workforce development and employment opportunities, support individual advancement and innovation [SDG 9], and support the establishment of safe and resilient communities. These SDGs are grouped together given their combined focus on building a sustainable economy rich with employment and advancement opportunities as well as innovation (Mehra, 2017; Mehra et al., 2017).

The chapters in this section operationalize significant elements of the public library – sustainable communities (PLSC) framework visualized in the introduction to the book. In Chapter 15 ["Public Libraries as Key Knowledge Infrastructure Needed to Empower Communities, Promote Economic Development, and Foster Social Justice"], Sarah E. Ryan, Sarah A. Evans, and Suliman Hawamdeh discuss the role of public libraries in the knowledge economy and their contribution to sustainable development. This chapter includes narrative on three case studies which demonstrate ways rural public libraries impact the knowledge economy.

In Chapter 16 ["Libraries as Public Health Partners in the Opioid Crisis"], Kendra Morgan, based on her prior research for OCLC, reflects on the ways that public libraries support the opioid crisis across the United States.

In Chapter 17 ["Partnering for Social Infrastructure: Investigating the Co-Location of a Public Library in an Affordable Housing Building"], Kaitlin Wynia

---

How Public Libraries Build Sustainable Communities in the 21st Century
Advances in Librarianship, Volume 53, 199–201
Copyright © 2023 by Kaurri C. Williams-Cockfield and Bharat Mehra
Published under exclusive licence by Emerald Publishing Limited
ISSN: 0065-2830/doi:10.1108/S0065-283020230000053018

Baluk, Ali Solhi, and James Gillett share a case study about a public library located within an affordable housing building in Ontario, Canada. Reviewer Alicia K. Long, University of Missouri, writes:

> The authors expertly mapped the results of this partnership between a public library and a housing development to the U.N. Sustainable Development Goals, demonstrating the impact that libraries can have in building sustainable communities and strengthening their social infrastructure.

STRATEGIC COLLECTIVE ACTIONS

The thematic threads flowing through the three chapters in this section highlight how different library case studies operationalize the following significant strategic collective actions:

- Provide a platform for citizen engagement, community development, and economic growth;
- Leverage library assets and community partnerships in response to health and other community crises;
- Build networks and programs that support people in their efforts to improve their life;
- Create library service points in locations that serve marginalized populations.

These case studies focus on libraries as social infrastructure resulting from both their role within a community and the subsequent network. Public libraries meet people at their point of need regardless of the type and level of said need.

KEY CONCEPTS AND TERMS

Redistributive Technology – The idea of libraries as part of a community's network of social infrastructure.

REFERENCES

Mehra, B. (2017). Mobilization of rural libraries towards political and economic change in the aftermath of the 2016 Presidential Election. *The Library Quarterly: Information, Community, Policy* (Special Issue: Aftermath: Libraries, Democracy, and the 2016 Presidential Election), *87*(4), 369–390.

Mehra, B., Bishop, B. W., & Partee, R. P. II (2017). How do public libraries assist small businesses in rural communities? An exploratory qualitative study in Tennessee. *Libri International Journal of Libraries and Information Studies, 67*(4), 245–260.

RESOURCES AND RELEVANT ORGANIZATIONS

American Medical Association, US. https://www.ama-assn.org/

Blount County Recovery Court Life Skills Program, Blount County, TN, US. https://bcpl.populr.me/life-skills

Center for Disease Control and Prevention, US. https://www.cdc.gov/

Introduction to Section Four 201

Center for Racial and Ethnic Equity in Health and Society, University of North Texas, Denton, TX, US. https://creehs.unt.edu/

CLX Connected Learning Guide, Chicago Learning Exchange, Chicago, IL, US. https://chicagolx.org/resources/connected-learning-guide

Indwell Hope and Homes Charity, Hamilton, Ontario, Canada. https://indwell.ca/

National Library Board, Singapore. https://www.nlb.gov.sg/main/home

National Science Foundation, Alexandria, VA, US. https://www.nsf.gov/

OCLC.Org, Dublin, OH, US. https://www.oclc.org

Parkdale Branch, Hamilton Public Library, Hamilton, ON, Canada. https://www.hpl.ca/parkdale

Peer Navigators Program, Kalamazoo Public Library, Kalamazoo, MI, US. https://www.kpl.gov/about/dei/peer-navigators-western-michigan-university-social-work-interns-at-kpl/

Public Libraries Respond to the Opioid Crisis with Their Communities, OCLC, Dublin, OH, US. https://www.oclc.org/research/publications/2019/oclcresearch-public-libraries-respond-to-opioid-crisis/supplemental.html

Raise Up Radio Libraries, UNT College of Information, Denton, TX, US. https://rurl.ci.unt.edu/

Recovery Institute of Southwest Michigan, Kalamazoo, MI, US. https://www.recoverymi.org/

United Nations Office on Drugs and Crime. https://www.unodc.org/

CHAPTER 15

PUBLIC LIBRARIES AS KEY KNOWLEDGE INFRASTRUCTURE NEEDED TO EMPOWER COMMUNITIES, PROMOTE ECONOMIC DEVELOPMENT, AND FOSTER SOCIAL JUSTICE

Sarah E. Ryan, Sarah A. Evans and Suliman Hawamdeh

ABSTRACT

Public libraries are incubators for collective action in the knowledge economy. As three case studies from the United States and Singapore demonstrate, public libraries can serve as influential champions that garner financial resources, communicate an urgent need for change, and respond to the unmet information and economic needs of marginalized individuals and communities. In the Raise Up Radio (RUR) *case, public librarians engaged schools, museums, youth, and families in rural communities to develop and deliver STEM (science, technology, engineering, and math) content over local radio stations. In collaboration with organizational partners,* RUR *librarians created a model for library-community-radio projects for the rural United States. In the* What Health Looks Like (WHLL) *case, public librarians engaged senior citizens in discussions of health and the creation of health comics. In partnership with an interdisciplinary health research team,* WHLL *librarians developed a pilot for library-community-public health projects aimed at information dissemination and health narrative generation.*

How Public Libraries Build Sustainable Communities in the 21st Century
Advances in Librarianship, Volume 53, 203–218
Copyright © 2023 by Sarah E. Ryan, Sarah A. Evans and Suliman Hawamdeh
Published under exclusive licence by Emerald Publishing Limited
ISSN: 0065-2830/doi:10.1108/S0065-283020230000053019

In the Singapore shopping mall libraries case, the National Library Board (NLB) created public libraries in commercial spaces serving working families, senior citizens, and the Chinese community. The NLB developed an exportable model for locating information centers in convenient, popular, and useful business spaces. These case studies demonstrate how libraries are nodes in the knowledge economy, providing vital services such as preservation of cultural heritage, technology education, community outreach, information access, and services to working families, small- and medium-size businesses, and other patrons. In the years to come, public libraries will be called upon to respond to shifting social norms, inequitable opportunities, emergencies and disasters, and information asymmetries. As the cases of RUR, WHLL, and the shopping mall libraries show, public librarians have the vision and capacities to serve as influential champions for collective action to solve complex problems and foster sustainable development and equitable participation in the knowledge economy.

Keywords: Collective action; health disparities; knowledge economy; rural libraries; shopping mall libraries; working families

In the 1990s, governments around the world launched National Information Infrastructure (NII) initiatives to support a global knowledge economy (Brown et al., 1995; Cordeiro & Al-Hawamdeh, 2001; McLoughlin, 1995; Shin, 2007). Individual countries recognized that technology and knowledge work would drive future development, and that they had to have sound infrastructure in place to participate in the new knowledge economy (Al-Hawamdeh, 2002). They responded in various ways, including: Canada's Information Highway Advisory Council, Japan's Info-communications in the twenty-first Century white paper, South Korea's IT839 strategy, Malaysia's Multimedia Super Corridor 2020 plan, Singapore's Intelligent Island strategy, and the United States' High-Performance Computer Act (HPCA) of 1991 (Brown et al., 1995; Cordeiro & Al-Hawamdeh, 2001; Hallowell et al., 2001; Shin, 2007). This new infrastructure changed the nature of information, work, development, and access to resources globally. It introduced new opportunities and inequities.

The knowledge economy fueled exponential growth in digital information, highly skilled knowledge workers, globalization, and increased competition (Powell & Snellman, 2004). National efforts drove worldwide developments in physical (e.g., hardware, networks, and fiber optics) and human infrastructure (e.g., education systems, talent development, and information literacy). In the United States, the HPCA was part of a broader effort that included National Science Foundation investment in digital libraries and federal funding for advanced telecommunications networks (McLoughlin, 1995; Pomerantz et al., 2008). In Singapore, the Intelligent Island strategy included $6 billion in new spending on information technology (IT), education, and training, of which $1 billion was earmarked for the NLB (Hallowell et al., 2001). Together, these and other efforts paved the way for cellular telephone advancements, application development, e-commerce, and a host of technologies that transformed the way people interact with each other and conduct business (Pomerantz et al., 2008). The digital transformation of business and commerce brought about fundamental societal changes and revolutionized the way people access, use, manipulate, and interact with information. The use of mobile devices, learning technologies, and Internet of Things (IoT) devices eroded territorial boundaries and expanded the participation of people from around the world in the new knowledge economy (Shafique et al., 2020).

The knowledge economy soon provided services such as education, job placement, and medical information via the Internet and Web technologies (Al-Hawamdeh, 2003). Web-based services increased efficiencies for corporations, governments, and some citizens (Powell & Snellman, 2004). But these gains largely accrued to wealthier countries and individuals (Cullen, 2001; Korovkin et al., 2022). For decades, many struggled to adapt to digitized work, services, and information. Libraries have helped to level the playing field in equitable information access and economic participation in the knowledge economy (Bryson, 2001; Hayes, 2004).

THE ROLE OF LIBRARIES IN THE KNOWLEDGE ECONOMY AND SUSTAINABLE DEVELOPMENT

Library staff gather, analyze, evaluate, and disseminate material in line with their mission: to provide equitable information access, promote literacy and community education, offer culture and recreation, steward resources, and facilitate the intellectual empowerment of all people (Chatterjee et al., 2020; Fraser-Arnott, 2022). With the digital transformation and the shift toward a knowledge society, public libraries have been reinventing themselves, expanding services, and hiring staff with knowledge in specialized areas such as data science and knowledge management. As nodes in the knowledge economy, libraries provide vital services such as the long-term preservation of cultural heritage, technology education, community outreach, and information access. Public libraries subscribe to proprietary digital scholarship and host open-access repositories, allowing people to make their work available through an EPrint Archive, DSpace, OpenDOAR, DRUM, Deep Blue, Knowledge Bank, or another platform (Albert, 2006; Cullen & Chawner, 2011). Libraries provide physical and intellectual spaces for in-person and virtual research and debate, fostering the information access and intellectual exchange necessary for preserving democracy (Gibson et al., 2017).

Public libraries also contribute to economic development in several ways. First, libraries create information service jobs and purchase resources for their communities. An Indiana Business Research Center report estimated that public libraries accounted for approximately 9,000 jobs in the state of Indiana, for instance (Indiana Business Research Center, 2007). Second, libraries provide early childhood programming that advances literacy, language learning, and other skills needed in the knowledge economy (Cahill & Ingram, 2022; The Urban Libraries

Council, 2007). Third, libraries support small businesses and individual workers (The Urban Libraries Council, 2007).

Small- and medium-size businesses use libraries to research laws, recruit workers, access data, and more (Arendt et al., 2018; Bingman-Forshey & Gibbons, 2020; Harmon et al., 2018). Individual workers use libraries for Internet access, to search for jobs, and to gain technical skills (The Urban Libraries Council). Libraries have quantified the impact of this support in numerous ways. In 2010, the Philadelphia Free Library reported an annual circulation of nearly 200,000 workforce-related volumes worth more than $2 million (Fels Institute of Local & State Government, 2010). In 2020, the Baltimore County Public Library enrolled 200 prospective business owners in its Entrepreneur Academy (Poon & Joshua, 2022). That same year, the American Library Association announced a $2 million grant from Google for Libraries Build Business, a national investment in additional local library support for low-income and underrepresented entrepreneurs (American Library Association, 2022). This support aims to promote equitable and sustainable economic development in local communities throughout the United States.

SUSTAINABLE DEVELOPMENT AND COLLECTIVE ACTION IN LOCAL COMMUNITIES

Broadly, sustainable economic development refers to the ability to create and sustain economic growth without damaging or compromising the resources that are fundamental to our existence and the stability of future generations (Giddings et al., 2002; Omotola, 2006). In knowledge economies, where innovation and knowledge creation are the driving forces of progress, open data, government transparency, citizen participation, and freedom of expression are indispensable for sustainable development (Ukachi, 2012).

United Nations (2015) adopted a framework for achieving sustainable development, or "free[ing] the human race from the tyranny of poverty and want and… heal[ing] and secur[ing] our planet" (p. 3). To realize intergenerational equity, the world's countries and stakeholders would need to act in collaborative partnership (United Nations, 2015). Their work would be guided by sustainable development goals (SDGs) ranging from ending poverty (SDG 1) and ensuring decent work (SDG 8) to promoting good health (SDG 3), quality education (SDG 4), and access to industry, innovation, and infrastructure (SDG 9) (United Nations, 2015). The SDGs also focused on gender equality (SDG 5) and reducing social inequality (SDG 10). The goals meshed with existing library efforts to educate and train individuals, support families and communities, and contribute to local and national economies (Ochôa & Pinto, 2020; Pinto & Ochôa, 2017). The SDGs also responded to a broad conversation about how to solve perennial social problems collectively.

John Kania and Mark Kramer (2011) summarized decades of research and nonprofit experience on collective action for social change. Kania and Kramer (2011) found that actors from multiple sectors must make long-term commitments. Those partners must maintain a common agenda, shared measurement system, mutually reinforcing activities, ongoing communication, and oversight by a separate backbone organization (Hanleybrown et al., 2012; Kania & Kramer, 2011). Each actor can play a different role in the initiative, but they must have the same vision for change (Kania & Kramer, 2011). It takes time, resources, and an early champion to achieve collective impact.

Hanleybrown et al. (2012) described the preconditions for collective action. Before launching a broad initiative, an influential champion must lay the groundwork, including obtaining financial resources and communicating an urgent need for change (Hanleybrown et al., 2012). The influential champion must have deep experience, dynamic leadership, and "a willing[ness] to let the participants figure out the answers for themselves...." (Hanleybrown et al., 2012, p. 3). Furthermore, the champion must understand that advancing equity in opportunities, outcomes, and representation is a prerequisite to collective impact (Kania et al., 2022).

Public library scholars have characterized Kania and Kramer's collective model as "place-based" (Field & Tran, 2018, p. 124). As Field and Tran (2018) explained, leaders of place-based collective action bring together existing but fragmented resources. Public libraries act as trusted local institutions that bring together groups of youth, parents, entrepreneurs, and civic leaders. Before the COVID-19 pandemic, the prototypical public library was "a community connector – a central organ that connect[ed] government agencies, community organizations, [and] education programs so that they [could] work together to achieve shared outcomes" (Field & Tran, 2018, p. 125). Since then, libraries have proved pivotal to emergency management, disaster recovery, and information access (Yang & Ju, 2021). As the following case studies show, libraries contribute to local sustainable development through science education, health education and narrative cultivation, and family and community support services located in business-enterprise spaces.

CASE STUDIES: PUBLIC LIBRARIES AS COLLECTIVE ACTION AND DEVELOPMENT INCUBATORS

The past few decades have witnessed unprecedented changes in the nature of work, family life, civic participation, and information access. During this time, marginalized groups have struggled to make a living, care for their children, and support older relatives (Heath, 2012). Public libraries have adapted to meet these needs through expanded services and partnerships, particularly during the COVID-19 pandemic. Three case studies demonstrate the ways that public libraries have worked to support rural communities, older adults, and working families. The first shows how libraries are working to enhance science education in the rural southern United States. The second demonstrates how libraries are contributing to health literacy and health storytelling in rural and urban US communities. The third illustrates how libraries are creating new locations to serve working families, senior citizens, and minority groups in Singapore. All three projects required synergistic partnerships among community members, public library staff, and outside partners from universities and the government. These cases demonstrate how public libraries can serve as incubators for sustainable development. The case studies also highlight potential roadblocks for librarians as collective action leaders.

RUR: Family and Youth Engagement in Library-Supported Learning Via Radio

For years, US educators and researchers have voiced concerns about the widening digital divide in communities, most notably "the homework gap" for youth without reliable access to computer technology, Internet services, back-up power sources, and skilled support at home (Centers for Disease Control and Prevention [CDC], 2021a, 2021b; Lee, 2020a, 2020b; Tyler-Wood et al., 2018). The COVID-19 pandemic exacerbated inequitable digital access, learning outcomes, and disconnection from school, particularly in the sciences (Maestrales et al., 2022). The *RUR* program sought a sustainable solution to this problem.

Utilizing public libraries as community anchors, *RUR* connected schools, museums, libraries, youth, and families in rural communities through rural radio programming. The pilot project focused on the development and delivery of STEM content over local radio stations. Rural radio continues to be a significant access point for community news and information and an effective tool for community learning and empowerment (Chávez & Soep, 2005; Gobir, 2020; Kretz, 2017; Richardson et al., 2019; Soep & Chávez, 2010). Radio also provides a lower barrier for access and engagement than the Internet (Waldman, 2011).

With funding from the Institute of Museum and Library Services, the project started in high-need communities in rural Alabama and Texas. These areas were selected because Alabama and Texas consistently rank below the national average on both key economic and technology access indicators (Institute of Museum & Library Services, 2019, 2020; United States Census Bureau, n.d., 2010, 2016, 2020; U.S. News & World Report, 2020). In Year 1, library staff from two rural-serving libraries – Pottsboro Area Library in Texas and Tuscaloosa Public Library in Alabama, which serves rural towns such as Coaling and Coker – formed a learning community with researchers from the University of Alabama and University of North Texas. Through regular online group meetings and visits to each library, the group explored the Connected Learning (CL) framework as the model for the unmet learning needs of local families. The CL framework is built on the premise that meaningful learning takes place at the intersection of interests, relationships, and opportunities (Chicago Learning Exchange, 2019), but also that learning takes place within the shared purpose and practices of a group or community (Widman et al., 2020). The learning community also met with an advisory board of nationally-recognized family learning scholars to guide their program design.

During the first year of the program, local families and library staff developed locally-produced STEM radio programs using best practices for equitable engagement in learning (Bang & Vossoughi, 2016; Bell et al., 2012; Caspe & Lopez, 2018; Coppens et al., 2014; Hoffman et al., 2016; Ishimaru et al., 2016; Ito et al., 2013; Roque & Stamatis, 2019). They also created science kits with activities that reinforced the radio content and distributed the kits to local families to use while listening to the STEM episodes. In the coming year, four more rural-based libraries will join the learning community. Library staff who started in the first year will mentor the next set of staff in learning, planning, and implementing the program with more families in more communities.

Beyond year two, these six libraries, in partnership with the university researchers, will form the backbone of a national rural library network for staff interested in radio programming and STEM. It will build upon an existing information network for rural libraries, created by researchers unaffiliated with *RUR*, but also funded by the Institute for Museum and Library Services. As a national initiative, *RUR* could foster scientific discovery, STEM entrepreneurship and economic opportunities in rural communities.

WHLL: Community Knowledge Creation via Graphic Medicine Library Programs

Health disparities are prevalent in the United States. Health researchers have long known that Blacks, Latinos, Asian Americans, Native Americans and Alaska Natives, rural residents, and people of lower socioeconomic backgrounds lack equitable access to health care and health information (Venkatesan & Murali, 2022). Because these populations receive less information and care, their health experiences remain underrepresented in medical research (Williams & Cooper, 2019). Health systems and biomedical treatments are then designed without their perspectives and are inherently biased against them (Williams & Cooper, 2019). Researchers and public health officials cannot reduce the nation's persistent health inequalities without the perspectives and experiences of marginalized groups. Graphic medicine offers one tool for addressing both access and representation deficits.

Graphic medicine refers to health narratives and medical information created and shared via the comics medium (Gessell, 2016). Graphic communication has proven effective for spreading information in marginalized communities (Singhal et al., 2003; Singhal & Rogers, 1999), including in outreach to Latino populations through fotonovelas from the Rural Women's Health Project, in partnership with government agencies and universities (King, 2017). Using graphic medicine to address health disparities, the WHLL project began as a small-scale pilot research study. The program expanded the use of graphic medicine in public libraries, which have been underutilized in graphic medicine research and practice. The pilot study was funded by a university seed grant.

The *WHLL* project was conceived by an interdisciplinary research team united through the Center for Racial and Ethnic Equity in Health and Society (CREEHS) at the University of North Texas. The team included scholars from learning sciences, information science, Black literary and cultural studies, journalism, and health and public services. In collaboration with library partners, the team identified underserved communities in three locations in rural and urban areas. Through each library, community members were invited to participate in an eight-week comics program that included discussions of two graphic novel narratives of health and illness relevant to the targeted population, followed by the creation of their own health experience comics. Participants and researchers met online via Zoom for one hour each week of the program.

At the first project site, library staff requested that *WHLL* be tailored to senior citizens in their rural community. Like much of rural America, the location has an increasing percentage of older residents, many of whom struggle to find ways to "age in place," or remain in their private homes as their health declines. Eight older adults, aged 60–79 years, participated in the pilot. While initially apprehensive about their ability to create a comic, they all reported feeling capable after coaching from a member of the research team. In the penultimate session, the researcher asked participants to reflect on a moment from their experiences early in the pandemic in order to create a storyboard. As they shared their drawings, common themes of anxiety and its impact on the body arose. Program feedback from the participants included words like "pleasure," "fun," and "enjoyment" in reference to the drawing section of the program.

At the second and third pilot sites, which are part of a large urban library system, a number of roadblocks have created delays. Project organization has proved more difficult given the complexity of the library systems. Organizational challenges from both the research team side and the library management side have compounded to delay of the project. As the team strives to launch the second and third sites, it is also seeking additional funds to test 10 more sites over 2 years. For that project, a postdoctoral researcher will analyze public health data and conduct needs assessments in order to identify communities with the greatest health needs.

The end goal of the *WHLL* project is a network of community experts, public libraries, and CREEHS researchers. In keeping with Community Based Participatory Research and Community Engagement Studio models (Joosten et al., 2015), the local expert panels will shape the *WHLL* programs in their communities. Public librarians and university researchers will provide support for the community-run graphic medicine projects. In the years to come, the university team will engage new library partners and seek additional funding for new sites where the program can be conducted feasibly and with cultural integrity. As a national initiative, *WHLL* could foster health equity, and health science innovation and entrepreneurship.

Shopping Mall Libraries: Working Family and Community Engagement in Commercial Spaces

In the early 1990s, Singapore's Intelligent Island strategy focused attention on public libraries (Hallowell et al., 2001). Patron surveys showed that library facilities were dated, offered anachronistic collections and services, and employed insufficient and under-skilled staff (Choh, 2014; Hallowell et al., 2001). "Only 12% of the population visited a library at least once a year and membership was shrinking" (Hallowell et al., 2001, p. 2). Simultaneously, family dynamics were changing due to the graying of the broader population and a dramatic rise in women's labor force participation (Choo, 2015; Yeoh & Huang, 1995). Childcare centers and kindergartens were not widely accessible (Choo, 2015; Yeoh & Huang, 1995). Working women faced new time pressures and criticism for spending less quality time with their families (Yeoh & Huang, 1995). In all of this, the NLB saw an opportunity to relocate public libraries to better serve families, senior citizens, and minority communities (Choh, 2014; Hallowell et al., 2001). With funds from the national government, the NLB launched its first shopping mall library (Choh, 2014).

The first site was not ideally located because the mall had rented out all of the spaces on its escalator floors, leaving only elevator-served floors (Choh, 2014). Still, the library soon flourished because parents could take their children there while grocery shopping (Choh, 2014). Soon after, the NLB created shopping mall libraries to serve young adults (e.g., library@orchard), families (e.g., Bukit Panjang Public Library, Sengkang Public Library, and Yishun Public Library), and the Chinese community (e.g., library@chinatown) (Matthews, 2021). The library@chinatown was co-developed with the Chinese community and was Singapore's first self-service library staffed by volunteers, first privately-funded public library, and first Chinese arts and culture library (Matthews, 2021; Ng, 2013). The shopping mall libraries have exceeded expectations.

"Today, more than half of the NLB's libraries are in shopping malls or co-located with other agencies" (Choh, 2014), and half of Singaporeans are public library members (Hallowell et al., 2001). The shopping mall libraries have met community needs, including emerging digital needs (Choh). Family-oriented libraries such as the Sengkang Public Library feature early literacy programs, story times, and dedicated children's and tween/teen spaces (NLB, 2022a, 2022b). The Bukit Panjang Public Library has a "Little Stage" (NLB, 2022b), and the Sengkang Public Library has TumbleBookLibrary stations for children's e-book reading (NLB, 2022a). To serve a different need, the library@chinatown features audio-visual and print collections on Chinese performance arts, chess, calligraphy, and painting (Ng, 2013). The library's initial collection was selected in consultation with Chinese educators and academics (Ng, 2013). Today, more than two-thirds of the collection is in Chinese and the Kwan Im Thong Hood Cho Temple funds collection development (NLB, 2022c).

While the shopping mall libraries were the product of central planning, they responded to the needs, feedback, and contributions of working families, senior citizens, and minority community members. Singapore's shopping mall libraries located family learning spaces near grocery stores and offered the Chinese community a place to come together. In addition, some evidence suggests that the shopping mall libraries served sustainable development by fostering digital access and literacy (Dresel et al., 2020) and supporting the nation's smart city initiatives. Smart cities can increase economic equity by enabling families to trade and sell household goods and find other sources of support (Lee et al., 2020). But smart cities can also exacerbate digital divides and increase citizen surveillance (Aizeki & Richardson, 2021; Peng, 2019). As a result, Singapore's libraries should remain focused on the needs and privacy of their diverse patrons.

LESSONS LEARNED FROM PUBLIC LIBRARY INCUBATORS IN THE UNITED STATES AND SINGAPORE

These three case studies show how public libraries can be incubators for collective action by serving as influential champions, garnering financial resources, communicating an urgent need for change, and focusing on the unmet needs of marginalized individuals and communities (Hanleybrown et al., 2012). Despite this great potential, public libraries also face challenges as collective action leaders.

Lesson 1: Public Libraries Can Serve as Influential Champions for Sustainable Development

In Singapore, the NLB embraced 1990s criticisms of the public library system and used them to reinvent libraries to support women's labor force participation (SDG 5), family education (SDG 4), and minority group inclusion (SDG 10). In rural Alabama and Texas, library leaders known for innovative services and strong community ties formed a learning community with university researchers to support STEM learning that could incubate scientific discovery and entrepreneurship (SDGs 4, 10). In *WHLL* library leaders recruited senior citizen participants and connected them with interdisciplinary health researchers to test the efficacy of graphic medicine projects, promote health literacy (SDG 3), bring community narratives to health researchers, and foster innovation in health care (SDG 10). Each of these projects required library leaders to exercise dynamic leadership and then cede control to participants (Hanleybrown et al., 2012). As a result, community members contributed to library design, educational programs, and health materials that reflected their experiences and met their needs. Every project integrated emerging technologies and encouraged community innovation (SDG 9).

Lesson 2: Public Libraries Can Secure Financial Resources

In the case of *RUR*, rural libraries and library science researchers won a two-year grant for community-developed STEM programming. The ongoing grant offers library staff the resources to launch an untested program while retaining their existing community services. For *WHLL*, public libraries donated staff time and a university provided a seed grant to test the efficacy of an interdisciplinary graphic medicine program. These investments yielded a successful pilot test that will be used to secure additional funding. In Singapore, the NLB secured government funding for the first shopping mall library and cultivated donor funding for the library@chinatown. In each of these projects, public libraries served as connectors among agencies, universities, research communities, community organizations, and funders (Field & Tran, 2018).

Lesson 3: Public Libraries Can Communicate an Urgent Need for Change

For the *RUR* and *WHLL* projects, the global pandemic created an urgent need for change. Public library staff witnessed communities in crisis, leading to a desire for new solutions and the commitment to put these solutions in place. Library leadership communicated with library staff and university researchers and then urged community members to find the energy to address education and health issues during a pandemic. In Singapore, the NLB pushed the national government to make significant investments in the public library system to ensure the nation's place in the global knowledge economy. In all three cases, library leaders used uncertainty to galvanize individual and institutional support for pro-social change and community development. Community development is often a precursor to sustainable development, particularly when it supports low-income and marginalized children, families, and entrepreneurs.

Lesson 4: Public Libraries Can Serve Equity

In Singapore, working women, older adults, and the Chinese community faced barriers to full social and economic inclusion. In Alabama and Texas, rural communities struggled to provide remote science instruction during a pandemic. In the rural town that hosted *WHLL*, senior citizens lacked information and social supports for aging in place and effectively managing their health. Public libraries recognized these needs and worked to find support for under-supported individuals and communities (Kania et al., 2022).

Lesson 5: Public Libraries Will Face Program Sustainability and
Leadership Challenges

At this time, the *RUR* project is moving forward while the *WHLL* project is at a standstill. This highlights a difficulty in the collective action model for public libraries. As the size and complexity of the library territory increase, it can become more difficult to launch and sustain projects. The libraries that participated in RUR have a relatively small administrative layer. This enables their leaders to adopt innovative approaches and quickly pivot when adjustments are needed. The *WHLL* project was successfully launched in a small rural library. Yet efforts to pilot the same program in a large library system have been significantly delayed. Library staff and community members in both settings recognize the urgent need for equity-focused programs. But the additional administrative layers in larger library organizations make change more difficult. The Singaporean case might seem to cut against this finding, but Singapore has a highly-centralized parliamentary republic structure incomparable to most other countries. And even in Singapore, libraries have yet to ensure full access to digital technologies and full participation in the knowledge economy (Peng, 2019).

While the 1990s changed the course of human history, so too did the COVID-19 pandemic. In the years to come, libraries will be called upon to respond to shifting social norms, inequitable opportunities, emergencies and disasters, and information asymmetries. As the cases of *RUR, WHLL,* and the shopping mall libraries show, public librarians have the vision and capacity to serve as influential champions for collective action to solve problems and achieve sustainable development. Often, this work will be place-based because public libraries have strong ties to the local communities they serve (Field & Tran, 2018). Still, the world's nearly 3 million libraries (IFLA, 2022) have the collective wisdom and capacity to foster sustainable development and equitable participation in the global knowledge economy.

CONCLUSION

This chapter has illustrated the importance of public libraries in building and sustaining a knowledge society and knowledge-based economy. Three case studies from the United States and Singapore demonstrated how libraries can serve the unmet information and social needs of marginalized individuals and communities, thereby supporting technology literacy and economic development. The *RUR* case study illustrated how public librarians can engage schools, museums, youth, and families in rural communities to develop and deliver STEM content over local radio channels. The *WHLL* case study showed how librarians can engage patrons in graphic art projects that promote health literacy, discussion, and storytelling. The Singapore shopping mall libraries case study described how the NLB and librarians created information centers in commercial spaces serving working families, senior citizens, and diverse communities. The shopping mall project brought Singaporeans back to the libraries, an important goal of the nation's Intelligent Island – or knowledge-based society – strategy.

In the knowledge-based economy, information is power. Public libraries are a vital knowledge infrastructure because they preserve cultural heritage, deliver technology education, lead community outreach, gather the stories of underrepresented people, and provide information access to working families, small- and medium-size businesses, and other patrons. Public libraries build sustainable communities through resource sharing and communal stewardship. They leverage existing resources to engage citizens, cultivate free expression, and facilitate knowledge sharing for future generations. Through this work, libraries empower people, support equitable development, and advance social justice.

REFERENCES

Aizeki, M., & Richardson, R. (2021). *Smart-city digital ID projects: Reinforcing inequality and increasing surveillance through corporate 'solutions.'* Immigrant Defense Project.

Albert, K. M. (2006). Open access: Implications for scholarly publishing and medical libraries. *Journal of the Medical Library Association, 94*(3), 253–262.

Al-Hawamdeh, S. (2002). Knowledge management: Re-thinking information management and facing the challenge of managing tacit knowledge. *Information Research, 8*(1), 143–163.

Al-Hawamdeh, S. (2003). *Knowledge management: Cultivating knowledge professionals.* Elsevier.

American Library Association. (2022). Libraries build business: Initiative highlights. https://www.ala.org/advocacy/sites/ala.org.advocacy/files/content/Workforce/LBB%20Initiative%20Highlights%20Report%20-%20072322_final.pdf

Arendt, A., Morris, A., & Stephens, M. (2018). Public library use of geographic information systems in the United States. *Journal of Library Administration*, *58*(8), 779–805. https://doi.org/10.1080/01930826.2018.1516946

Bang, M., & Vossoughi, S. (2016). Participatory design research and educational justice: Studying learning and relations within social change making. *Cognition and Instruction*, *34*(3), 173–193. https://doi.org/10.1080/07370008.2016.1181879

Bell, P., Tzou, C., Bricker, L., & Baines, A. D. (2012). Learning in diversities of structures of social practice: Accounting for how, why and where people learn science. *Human Development*, *55*(5–6), 269–284. https://doi.org/10.1159/000345315

Bingman-Forshey, H., & Gibbons, P. (2020). Behind the wall: Service challenges at a prison library. *Public Services Quarterly*, *16*(1), 65–69. https://doi.org/10.1080/15228959.2019.1677200

Brown, R., Irving, L., Prabhakar, A., & Katzen, S. (1995, February). *The global information infrastructure: Agenda for cooperation. Information Infrastructure Task Force*. National Telecommunications and Information Administration.

Bryson, J. (2001). Measuring the performance of libraries in the knowledge economy and society. *Australian Academic & Research Libraries*, *32*(4), 332–342. https://doi.org/10.1080/00048623.2001.10755171

Cahill, M., & Ingram, E. (2022). Extratextual talk in public library storytime programs: A focus on questions. *Journal of Early Childhood Research*, 1476718X221098662.

Caspe, M., & Lopez, M. (2018). Preparing the next generation of librarians for family and community engagement. *Journal of Education for Library and Information Science*, *59*(4), 157–178. https://doi.org/10.3138/jelis.59.4.2018-0021

Centers for Disease Control and Prevention. (2021a, March 19). *Operating schools during Covid-19: CDC's Considerations*. Retrieved March 25, 2021, from https://www.cdc.gov/coronavirus/2019-ncov/community/schools-childcare/schools.html

Centers for Disease Control and Prevention. (2021b, March 19). *Operational strategy for k-12 schools through phased prevention*. Retrieved March 26, 2021, from https://www.cdc.gov/coronavirus/2019-ncov/community/schools-childcare/operation-strategy.html?CDC_AA_refVal=https%3A%2F%2Fwww.cdc.gov%2Fcoronavirus%2F2019-ncov%2Fdaily-life-coping%2Foperational-strategy-k-12-phased-mitigation.html

Chatterjee, S., Samanta, M., & Dey, S. (2020). Role of public libraries in providing community information services. https://ssrn.com/abstract=3535051. https://doi.org/10.2139/ssrn.3535051

Chávez, V., & Soep, E. (2005). Youth radio and the pedagogy of collegiality. *Harvard Educational Review*, *75*(4), 409–434. https://doi.org/10.17763/haer.75.4.827u365446030386

Chicago Learning Exchange. (2019). *CLX connected learning guide*. Retrieved March 24, 2021 from https://chicagolx.org/resources/connected-learning-guide

Choh, N. L. (2014). Innovations in the National Library Board Singapore: A journey. *IFLA Journal*, *40*(3), 150–156.

Choo, E. (2015). Dynamic marriage matching: An empirical framework. *Econometrica*, *83*(4), 1373–1423.

Coppens, A. D., Silva, K. G., Ruvalcaba, O., Alcalá, L., López, A., & Rogoff, B. (2014). Learning by observing and pitching in: Benefits and processes of expanding repertoires. *Human Development*, *57*(2–3), 150–161.

Cordeiro, C. M., & Al-Hawamdeh, S. (2001). National information infrastructure and the realization of Singapore IT2000 initiative. *Information Research*, *6*(2).

Cullen, R. (2001). Addressing the digital divide. *Online Information Review*, *25*(5), 311–320.

Cullen, R., & Chawner, B. (2011). Institutional repositories, open access, and scholarly communication: A study of conflicting paradigms. *The Journal of Academic Librarianship*, *37*(6), 460–470. https://doi.org/10.1016/j.acalib.2011.07.002

Dresel, R., Henkel, M., Scheibe, K., Zimmer, F., & Stock, W. G. (2020). A nationwide library system and its place in knowledge society and smart nation: The case of Singapore. *Libri*, *70*(1), 81–94.

Fels Institute of Local and State Government. (2010). *The economic value of the Free Library in Philadelphia*. Fels Institute of Local and State Government.

Field, N., & Tran, R. (2018). Reinventing the public value of libraries. *Public Library Quarterly, 37*(2), 113–126. https://doi.org/10.1080/01616846.2017.1422174

Fraser-Arnott, M. (2022). Exploring public library identity through mission statements. *Public Library Quarterly, 41*(3), 236–256. https://doi.org/10.1080/01616846.2021.1893568

Gessell, P. (2016). Guru of graphic medicine. *Canadian Medical Association Journal, 188*(17–18), E541–E542. https://doi.org/10.1503/cmaj.160027

Gibson, A. N., Chancellor, R. L., Cooke, N. A., Dahlen, S. P., Lee, S. A., & Shorish, Y. L. (2017). Libraries on the frontlines: Neutrality and social justice. *Equality, Diversity and Inclusion: An International Journal, 36*(8), 751–766. https://doi.org/10.1108/EDI-11-2016-0100

Giddings, B., Hopwood, B., & O'Brien, G. (2002). Environment, economy and society: Fitting them together into sustainable development. *Sustainable Development, 10*(4), 187–196. https://doi.org/10.1002/sd.199

Gobir, N. (2020, May 11). YR media's storytelling tools keep students connected during COVID-19 pandemic. *The Connected Learning Alliance.* https://clalliance.org/blog/yr-medias-storytelling-tools-keep-students-connected-during-covid-19-pandemic/

Hallowell, R., Knoop, C.-I., & Siong, N. B. (2001). *Transforming Singapore's public libraries* [Harvard Business School case 9-802-009]. Harvard University.

Hanleybrown, F., Kania, J., & Kramer, M. (2012, January 26). Channeling change: Making collective impact work. *Stanford Social Innovation Review.* https://doi.org/10.48558/2T4M-ZR69

Harmon, M. G., Grzybowski, S., Thompson, B., & Cross, S. (2018). Remaking the public law library into a twenty-first century legal resource center. *Law Library Journal, 110*(1), 115–118.

Hayes, H. (2004). The role of libraries in the knowledge economy. *Serials, 17*(3), 231–238.

Heath, S. B. (2012). *Words at work and play: Three decades in family and community life.* Cambridge University Press.

Hoffman, K., Subramaniam, M., Kawas, S., Scaff, L., & Davis, K. (2016). *Connected libraries: Surveying the current landscape and charting a path to the future.* The ConnectedLib Project. https://papers.ssrn.com/sol3/papers.cfm?abstract_id=2982532

IFLA. (2022). *Library map of the world.* https://librarymap.ifla.org/

Indiana Business Research Center. (2007). *The economic impact of libraries in Indiana.* Indiana Business Research Center.

Institute of Museum and Library Services. (2019). *IMLS public data.* Metrics. https://www.imls.gov/sites/default/files/publicdata_imls_metrics.xlsx

Institute of Museum and Library Services. (2020). *IMLS indicators workbook.* Users Guide. https://www.imls.gov/sites/default/files/users_guide_imls_nofo_metrics.pdf

Ishimaru, A. M., Torres, K. E., Salvador, J. E., Lott, J., Williams, D. M. C., & Tran, C. (2016). Reinforcing deficit, journeying toward equity: Cultural brokering in family engagement initiatives. *American Educational Research Journal, 53*(4), 850–882. https://doi.org/10.3102/0002831216657178

Ito, M., Gutiérrez, K., Livingstone, S., Penuel, B., Rhodes, J., Salen, K., Schor, J., Sefton-Green, J., & Watkins, S. C. (2013). *Connected learning: An agenda for research and design.* Digital Media and Learning Research Hub.

Joosten, Y. A., Israel, T. L., Williams, N. A., Boone, L. R., Schlundt, D. G., Mouton, C. P., Dittus, R. S., Bernard, G. R., & Wilkins, C. H. (2015). Community engagement studios: A structured approach to obtaining meaningful input from stakeholders to inform research. *Academic Medicine, 90*(12), 1646.

Kania, J., & Kramer, M. (2011, Winter). Collective impact. *Stanford Social Innovation Review,* 36–41.

Kania, J., Williams, J., Schmitz, P., Brady, S., Kramer, M., & Juster, J. S. (2022, Winter). Centering equity in collective impact. *Stanford Social Innovation Review,* 38–45.

King, A. J. (2017). Using comics to communicate about health: An introduction to the symposium on visual narratives and graphic medicine. *Health Communication, 32*(5), 523–524. https://doi.org/10.1080/10410236.2016.1211063

Kirchner, L. (2020, June 25). Millions of Americans depend on libraries for Internet. Now they're closed. *The Markup.* https://themarkup.org/coronavirus/2020/06/25/millions-of-americans-depend-on-libraries-for-internet-now-theyre-closed

Kretz, C. (2017). What can libraries learn from the future of public media? *Urban Library Journal, 23*(2), 1–10.

Korovkin, V., Park, A., & Kaganer, E. (2022). Quantifying the second-level digital divide on subnational level. *International Journal of Computer and Information Engineering, 16*(5), 185–195.

Lee, N. T. (2020a, March 2). *Bridging digital divides between schools and communities.* The Brookings Institution. https://www.brookings.edu/research/bridging-digital-divides-between-schools-and-communities/

Lee, N. T. (2020b, March 17). *What the coronavirus reveals about the digital divide between schools and communities.* The Brookings Institution. https://www.brookings.edu/blog/techtank/2020/03/17/what-the-coronavirus-reveals-about-the-digital-divide-between-schools-and-communities/

Lee, J. Y., Woods, O., & Kong, L. (2020). Towards more inclusive smart cities: Reconciling the divergent realities of data and discourse at the margins. *Geography Compass, 14*(9), e12504.

Li, C. (2021, October 11). *Worsening global digital divide as the US and China continue zero-sum competitions.* Brookings. https://www.brookings.edu/blog/order-from-chaos/2021/10/11/worsening-global-digital-divide-as-the-us-and-china-continue-zero-sum-competitions/

Maestrales, S., Marias Dezendorf, R., Tang, X., Salmela-Aro, K., Bartz, K., Juuti, K., Lavonen, J., Krajcik, J., & Schneider, B. (2022). U.S. and Finnish high school science engagement during the COVID-19 pandemic. *International Journal of Psychology, 57*(1), 73–86. https://doi.org/10.1002/ijop.12784

Matthews, J. R. (2021). The remaking of Singapore's public libraries. *Public Library Quarterly, 40*(3), 183–184.

McLoughlin, G. J. (1995). The national information infrastructure: The federal role. *Journal of Academic Librarianship, 21*(5), 390–397.

Mngutyo, J., Dennis, A., & Gbuushi, J. A. (2020). Engaging the government in library services for sustainable national development: The case of public library and information systems in Nigeria. *International Journal of Research and Innovation in Social Science, 4*(9), 70–74.

National Library Board (NLB). (2022a). Sengkang public library. https://www.nlb.gov.sg/main/visit-us/our-libraries-and-locations/libraries/sengkang-public-library

National Library Board (NLB). (2022b). Bukit Panjang public library. https://www.nlb.gov.sg/main/visit-us/our-libraries-and-locations/libraries/bukit-panjang-public-library

National Library Board (NLB). (2022c). Library details: library@chinatown. https://www.nlb.gov.sg/files/pdfs/Library%20Details%20CNPL%20March%202022.pdf

Ng, E. (2013, June). library@chinatown: By the people, for the people. *Urban Solutions, 3*, 38–45.

Ochôa, P., & Pinto, L. G. (2020). Gathering evidence for sustainable development goals. *Evidence Based Library and Information Practice, 15*(1), 164–169. https://doi.org/10.18438/eblip29638

Omotola, S. J. (2006). No democracy, no development or vice versa? In H. A. Saliu, J. F. Olorunfemi, U. Lateef, & S. B. Oludoyi (Eds.), *Democracy and development in Nigeria: Conceptual issues and democratic practice* (Vol. 1). Concept Publication.

Peng, N. (2019). Inequality and the social compact in Singapore. *Journal of Southeast Asian Economies, 36*(3), 355–379.

Pinto, L. G., & Ochôa, P. (2017). Public libraries' contribution to Sustainable Development Goals: Gathering evidences and evaluating practices. Paper presented at the 83rd IFLA World Library and Information Congress, Warsaw, Poland. http://library.ifla.org/id/eprint/1946/1/190-pinto-en.pdf

Pomerantz, J., Choemprayong, S., & Eakin, L. (2008). The development and impact of digital library funding in the United States. In D. A. Nitecki & E. G. Abels (Eds.), *Influence of funding on Advances in Librarianship (Advances in Librarianship)* (Vol. 31, pp. 37–92). Emerald Group Publishing Limited. https://doi.org/10.1016/S0065-2830(08)31002-2

Poon, L., & Joshua, J. (2022). As entrepreneurship grows, public libraries fill the gap. Bloomberg. https://www.bloomberg.com/news/articles/2022-01-28/libraries-expand-resources-to-support-diverse-entrepreneurs

Powell, W. W., & Snellman, K. (2004). The knowledge economy. *Annual Review of Sociology, 30*(1), 199–220. https://doi.org/10.1146/annurev.soc.29.010202.100037

Richardson, L. M., Renner, B. R., Ottosen, T., & Goldstein, A. O. (2019). A library and a radio show: The story of a successful partnership at 10 years and counting. *Journal of Library Administration, 59*(4), 395–408. https://doi.org/10.1080/01930826.2019.1593713

Roque, R., & Stamatis, K. (2019). It's about relationships: Examining facilitation as a relational practice. In R. Kalir & D. Filipiak (Eds.), *Proceedings in the 2019 Connected Learning Summit.* Carnegie Mellon University/ETC Press.

Shafique, K., Khawaja, B. A., Sabir, F., Qazi, S., & Mustaqim, M. (2020). Internet of Things (IoT) for next-generation smart systems: A review of current challenges, future trends and prospects for emerging 5G-IoT scenarios. *IEEE Access, 8*, 23022–23040. https://doi.org/10.1109/ACCESS.2020.2970118

Shin, D.-H. (2007). A critique of Korean national information strategy: Case of national information infrastructures. *Government Information Quarterly, 24*(3), 624–645. https://doi.org/10.1016/j.giq.2006.06.011

Singhal, A., Cody, M. J., Rogers, E. M., & Sabido, M. (Eds.). (2003). *Entertainment-education and social change: History, research, and practice*. Routledge.

Singhal, A., & Rogers, E. (1999). *Entertainment-education: A communication strategy for social change*. Routledge.

Soep, E., & Chávez, V. (2010). *Drop that knowledge: Youth radio stories*. University of California Press https://www.worldcat.org/title/drop-that-knowledge-youth-radio-stories/oclc/340961369&referer=brief_results

Tyler-Wood, T. L., Cockerham, D., & Johnson, K. R. (2018). Implementing new technologies in a middle school curriculum: A rural perspective. *Smart Learning Environments, 5*(1). https://doi.org/10.1186/s40561-018-0073-y

Ukachi, N. B. (2012). Knowledge societies and sustainable development: The roles of libraries. *Madonna University Journal of Research in Library and Information Science, 2*(1), 88–109.

United Nations. (2015). *Transforming our world: The 2030 agenda for sustainable development*. United Nations.

United States Census Bureau. (n.d.). Texas – Census Bureau Profile. Retrieved June 20, 2022, from Explore Census Data website: https://data.census.gov/cedsci/profile?g=0400000US48&hidePreview=true&tid=ACSDP1Y2018.DP03&q=Texas#

United States Census Bureau. (2010). *Revised estimates of the population by county, 1980–1989 [Computer file]*. U.S. Census Bureau.

United States Census Bureau. (2016). *Measuring America: Our changing landscape* [Infographic]. U.S. Census Bureau. https://www.census.gov/library/visualizations/2016/comm/acs-rural-urban.html

United States Census Bureau. (2020). *Alabama*. Profiles. https://data.census.gov/cedsci/profile?g=0400000US01&hidePreview=true&tid=ACSDP1Y2018.DP03&q=Alabama#

The Urban Libraries Council. (2007). *Making cities stronger: Public library contributions to local economic development*. The Urban Libraries Council.

U.S. News & World Report. (2020). *Education*. Best states rankings index. https://www.usnews.com/news/best-states/rankings-index

Venkatesan, S., & Murali, C. (2022). Graphic medicine and the critique of contemporary U.S. healthcare. *Journal of Medical Humanities, 43*(1), 27–42. https://doi.org/10.1007/s10912-019-09571-z

Waldman, S. (2011). *Information needs of communities: The changing media landscape in a broadband age*. Diane Publishing.

Widman, S., Penuel, W., Allen, A. R., Wortman, A., Michalchik, V., Chang-Order, J., Podkul, T., & Braun, L. (2020). *Evaluating library programming: A practical guide to collecting and analyzing data to improve or evaluate connected learning programs for youth in libraries*. Connected Learning Alliance.

Williams, D. R., & Cooper, L. A. (2019). Reducing racial inequities in health: Using what we already know to take action. *International Journal of Environmental Research and Public Health, 16*(4), 606. https://doi.org/10.3390/ijerph16040606

Yang, S., & Ju, B. (2021). Library support for emergency management during the time of natural disasters: Through the lens of public library Twitter data. *Library & Information Science Research, 43*(1), 101072. https://doi.org/10.1016/j.lisr.2021.101072

Yeoh, B. S., & Huang, S. (1995, July). Childcare in Singapore: Negotiating choices and constraints in a multicultural society. *Women's Studies International Forum, 18*(4), 445–461.

CHAPTER 16

LIBRARIES AS PUBLIC HEALTH PARTNERS IN THE OPIOID CRISIS

Kendra Morgan

ABSTRACT

Public libraries are respected local institutions that connect community members to credible information and services, and support lifelong learning. The nature of these libraries means that they are open to all, including individuals who may be experiencing a physical or mental health crisis. A critical way that libraries in the United States are now supporting their communities is by leveraging their assets and their mission to respond to the opioid crisis. These responses have ranged from providing access to information and resources on addiction, prevention, treatment, and recovery support, to training staff and the public to use the drug naloxone to help reverse overdoses. Public libraries have found allies in this work in community organizations including nonprofits and public health departments, and are often working together with these partners toward common goals to bring about collective impact.

Through their programming efforts in response to the opioid crisis, public libraries are also demonstrating the ability to support the Sustainable Development Goals (SDGs) identified by the United Nations (UN) as a call to action for the global community. These goals include ensuring healthy lives, equitable education and lifelong learning, and decent work and economic growth. Public libraries are actively supporting people in their efforts to improve their lives and the lives of those around them. It is important and valuable work, and truly necessary for a functioning society.

Keywords: Libraries; public libraries; partnerships; collaboration; opioids; opioid crisis

---

How Public Libraries Build Sustainable Communities in the 21st Century
Advances in Librarianship, Volume 53, 219–228
Copyright © 2023 by Kendra Morgan
Published under exclusive licence by Emerald Publishing Limited
ISSN: 0065-2830/doi:10.1108/S0065-283020230000053020

Public libraries are respected local institutions that connect community members to credible information and services. The nature of these libraries means that they are open to all, including individuals who may be experiencing a physical or mental health crisis. A critical way that libraries are now supporting their communities is by leveraging their assets in response to the opioid crisis. This public health crisis has had a global impact but, in particular, has gripped the United States. As concerns over opioid misuse continued to grow, high-profile news stories and research from the project Public Libraries Respond to the Opioid Crisis with Their Communities (OCLC, 2020) have featured libraries' responses to the crisis. These responses have ranged from providing access to information and resources on addiction, prevention, treatment, and recovery support, to training staff to use the drug naloxone to help reverse overdoses (Allen et al., 2019a). This chapter highlights examples of programming from the public library community in the United States, the collective impact benefits that may be achieved through partnership with other organizations invested in healthy community outcomes, and how these efforts align with the UN SDGs.

A NATIONAL AND GLOBAL HEALTH CRISIS

The opioid epidemic was declared a national public health emergency in the United States in 2017 (Centers for Medicare & Medicaid Services, 2021). Library staff witnessed this unfold firsthand in their local communities, with substance misuse and overdoses occurring on or around library property (Graff, 2018). While the COVID-19 pandemic became the primary public health focus in communities in early 2020, with many libraries closing their doors to mitigate the spread of COVID-19, the opioid crisis continued to rage unabated. The Centers for Disease Control's National Center for Health and Statistics reported an estimated 107,622 drug overdose deaths in the United States in 2021, an increase of nearly 15% from the 93,655 deaths estimated in 2020 (Centers for Disease Control & Prevention, 2022). In March 2021, the American Medical Association reported that more than 40 states indicated recent increase in opioid-related deaths (American Medical Association, 2021a) and, as before the pandemic, rural areas continue to be impacted heavily (Jenkins et al., 2021). Despite successful efforts to decrease opioid prescribing rates in the United States, the overdose rate continues to increase (American Medical Association, 2021b); this issue will not resolve quickly and will continue to impact communities, individuals, and libraries.

While the United States has seen the most dramatic impacts of the opioid crisis, the international community is also affected. Globally, the UN Office on Drugs and Crime launched the Opioid Strategy in 2018 and subsequently released the UN Toolkit on Synthetic Drugs (UN, n.d.-a), which offers practical tools and guidance to help health practitioners, forensic experts, and policymakers tackle threats posed by the most harmful, persistent, and prevalent synthetic drugs (UN, 2021). This global need to address opioid misuse successfully connects public libraries to the UN SDGs in several ways. These goals, which are a call to action

Libraries as Public Health Partners in the Opioid Crisis 221

for the international community to promote prosperity while protecting the planet, provide a framework for global development through 17 key areas (UN, n.d.-b). The strongest alignment with the SDGs and public libraries and their responses to the opioid crisis is with SDG 3: Ensure healthy lives and promote well-being for all at all ages (UN, n.d.-c), and the specific target to strengthen the prevention and treatment of substance abuse. Library efforts and contributions are also connected to SDGs around education, work, and economic growth.

Communities are the clear beneficiaries when libraries become involved in public health initiatives, particularly with the support of partner organizations that bring subject matter expertise and other resources. Through partnerships and coalitions, libraries can align their strengths in service of a focused effort. The opioid crisis has garnered attention among a range of organizations and entities at the local, state, and federal levels, which given the severity and impact of the effects, is both critically needed and necessary. Joining other organizations' work is one way for libraries to harness the power of collective impact, which is a style of collaboration championed by John Kania and Mark Kramer. They also identify five conditions that are present with a collective impact approach: a common agenda, shared measurement systems, mutually reinforcing activities, continuing communication, and backbone support organizations (Kania & Kramer, 2011). The common agenda requires a shared vision for change among the collaborating organizations, including an understanding of the problem and a joint approach to solving it through agreed upon actions (Kania & Kramer, 2011).

The Denver Public Library has participated in a program framed on the collective impact model which serves as a coordinated response to the opioid epidemic. The effort brought together more than 100 organizations and agencies to work together to address the opioid crisis in the community. Through this work, the coalition agreed that the problem facing the community as a result of the opioid crisis required a highly coordinated response and an increased need for resources (Denver Department of Public Health & Environment, 2018). In communities around the country, public libraries can contribute to and support local needs through resources such as staffing and space, which can be powerful additions to response efforts. The opioid crisis is a problem that requires a multi-faceted approach to connect people to resources and information that can be lifesaving. Janosky et al. (2013) assert in their research that coalitions and collective impact efforts can "result in significant measurable changes in community infrastructure, financial and material resources, and health outcomes by improving the overall quality of life."

PARTNERSHIPS

In 2019, OCLC published research from Allen et al., including eight case studies featuring public libraries responding to the opioid crisis with public programming through the help of community partners. This research was done in partnership with the Public Library Association and funded by the Institute of Museum and Library Services through a National Leadership Grant (IMLS, 2022) called

"Public Libraries Respond to the Opioid Crisis with Their Communities" (OCLC, 2020). The research highlights include emphasizing the value and importance of partnerships with other community agencies to address a public health crisis. The libraries that participated in the research were in communities with varying demographics and were selected to represent a diverse range of programming responses and partnerships. The study's findings indicate that through partnerships with community agencies, the library was able to also amplify its partner's work by providing additional reach and access to the community. These partnerships included both new and existing relationships that strengthened throughout implementation. Health departments, in particular, were ideal partners for opioid-related work because of their local public health expertise and interest in operating within the community.

In responding to the opioid crisis, the research from Allen et al. (2019a) indicated that organizations such as those in public health and nonprofits who worked with libraries found great value in the partnerships and would seek out those partnerships again. Most organizations also reported that they had not previously partnered with the library, and that the library usually initiated the relationship. Elevating and promoting the strength of libraries as vital community partners in the public health response efforts can benefit the growth and development of the library's relationships and services to the community. Still, it is often dependent on the library making the initial connection. The importance of these partnerships is also evident in research interviews by Lenstra and McGehee (2022) who reported that organizations that partnered with public libraries on health programs saw libraries as trusted connectors, community experts, and as professionals that share goals.

LIBRARIES OFFER TRAINING AND SPACE

The Blount County Public Library (BCPL) case study in Blount County, Tennessee stands out for its approach to recovery for individuals dealing with opioid use disorder. The library director understood that the opioid crisis had a powerful and devastating impact on the community, including those in recovery, and sought out areas where the library could help. This was a consideration and view that other library stakeholders shared. In a research interview, a BCPL Board member articulated the library's call to action:

> The need is there. The crisis is there. We always ask ourselves, "So what can the library do? How can we, within our mission, contribute to this? And who do we need to partner with?"

A synergistic partnership opportunity arose, and the library responded (Allen et al., 2019b).

In Blount County, Recovery Court is an alternative sentencing program offered to nonviolent offenders with a history of drug and alcohol abuse to lower habitual criminal activity by providing treatment, monitoring, random drug screens, required employment, community service, education, and payment of fines. In a meeting with the library director, the Recovery Court staff shared that they were looking for classes in soft skills and space to provide the training. The skills include communication, personal finance, job skills, nutrition, and personal appearance. The library director proposed that the library could fulfill both needs in partnership with the Recovery Court, starting with an existing curriculum the library had already developed (Baker, n.d.). BCPL staff collaborated with Recovery Court to adapt the curriculum and build the Life Skills Curriculum program, which teaches participants the skills necessary to succeed as contributing members of the community (Blount County Recovery Court, n.d.).

The Life Skills Curriculum program is maintained with library funds, and a staff member is designated to manage the program. Holding the sessions at the library was intentional – this encouraged a sense of ownership in the library and aided in the transition to life after Recovery Court. As one BCPL staff member reflected,

> I've had students who have realized what an asset a library can be in terms of employment. For example, they can take practice tests for career exams at the library. One of the students applied for a job at a local manufacturer. She needed to take a mechanical and spatial test, so we got her set up with a practice test at the library. She got the job. It was the connection for her that you can find other resources you need to make a life at the library. (Allen et al., 2019b)

Through their efforts, the library is directly addressing the UN's SDG 4, which aims to "ensure inclusive and equitable quality education and promote lifelong learning opportunities for all" (UN, n.d.-d). The public library is a crucial resource for many people around lifelong learning needs – this is core to the work.

Additionally, the library's engagement with these activities is relevant to SDG 8 – Decent Work and Economic Growth – with a particular focus on 8.5,

> By 2030, achieve full and productive employment and decent work for all women and men, including for young people and persons with disabilities, and equal pay for work of equal value. (UN, n.d.-e)

Encouraging people in recovery from substance use disorder to engage in meaningful work by developing their soft skills to help them succeed in interviews and manage their time are critical factors to gainful employment.

Various modules of the BCPL curriculum introduce opportunities to engage with community partners, such as the local health department and other educational organizations. Some partners, such as the Pellissippi State Community College admissions counselors, help participants move into higher education by pursuing two-year or technical degrees. Partners like the American Job Center assist with job placement, and local realtors explain the differences between renting and owning and how to find housing with a felony offense (Allen et al., 2019b).

Developing and strengthening relationships with agencies like the health department and higher education institutions enables library staff to connect with these partners to support individual needs and help that may be needed in the future. For most community partners throughout all eight case studies, this was the first time they had worked with their local library. They noted that they would seek out future opportunities based on the success they experienced.

SUCCESS ALONG THE WAY

During research interviews, Recovery Court participants shared that participating in the program improved their lives significantly, including building confidence and gaining employment. Since joining the program, participants shared that they feel more connected to the community as a result of the relationships they have made with the library and the other community organizations involved. The Recovery Court and library staff also noted that other positive outcomes have occurred as a result of the program, including reduced recidivism rates, increased awareness of the library's role in the community, and improved lives for Recovery Court participants. As BCPL has welcomed all in its community, including those with felony offenses and those struggling with substance use disorder, it has embraced a role in SDG 10 – Reducing Inequality – with particular focus on 10.2, "By 2030, empower and promote the social, economic and political inclusion of all, irrespective of age, sex, disability, race, ethnicity, origin, religion or economic or other status" (UN, n.d.-f).

The BCPL's involvement in the Recovery Court program is a powerful and robust model for what is possible with the support of trusted partners, shared missions, and dedicated individuals. It is an example of what Kania and Kramer (2011) describe as mutually reinforcing activities – encouraging each participant to undertake the specific set of activities at which it excels in a way that supports and is coordinated with the actions of others. The library had the expertise, space, and mission which made providing soft skills training to Recovery Court participants a good fit, and it aligned with an existing community solution. Not every library can offer such a deep level of programming, but there is an entry point for all libraries. Whether it is choosing a book display that highlights books, authors, and topics connected to substance use disorder, or bringing in guest speakers and offering programs on the importance of healthy responses to stressful situations and periods – these activities are fulfilling needs for information, the core service of libraries. The stigma attached to substance use disorder is a strong deterrent to addressing these issues both among ourselves and in our libraries. But libraries can lead in this critical public health need and connect people to life-saving information and resources.

COMMUNITY COALITIONS AND EXPERTISE

A second example of a successful partnership shared in the OCLC Public Libraries Respond to the Opioid Crisis research is found at the Kalamazoo Public Library in Michigan, and its partnership with the Recovery Institute of Southwest Michigan (the Institute). This partnership involves peer navigators from the institute being on-site in the library to serve as a resource to help the public. Peer navigators are individuals who are themselves in recovery from substance use disorder or have other related lived experiences. They can connect patrons to a range of community services, recovery organizations, and even offer direct support (Kalamazoo Public Library, n.d.). The partnership was initiated when library managers noted that there had been an increase in patrons experiencing homelessness and substance misuse.

Libraries as Public Health Partners in the Opioid Crisis

Staff from the library participated in a Kalamazoo County Opioid Coalition meeting to discuss the epidemic's impact, where they learned about the Recovery Institute as a local resource (Allen et al., 2019b).

To start, the peer navigators from the institute were available in a relatively limited capacity, with just three service hours per week. As a result of the demonstrated success of the initial engagement, hours were subsequently increased to 40 per week. The introduction of the peer navigators to the library included training for the library staff to talk about the roles of the peer navigators, what they could assist with, and how they would interact with patrons. Library staff subsequently recognized that the availability of peer navigators helped the library serve the community better by providing direct assistance to patrons with specific needs with their expertise in recovery and social service resources (Allen et al., 2019b). Building and leveraging local experts can provide a critical path to success for libraries and organizations of all sizes in meeting goals.

Health-related community coalitions such as the one in Kalamazoo are increasingly common. They can be a strong connection point for libraries to seek out opportunities to support a broad range of community health needs, including those related to the opioid crisis. Joining the work that other organizations are doing is one way for libraries to amplify the power of collective impact, the model championed by Kania and Kramer (2011), who write that large-scale social change comes from better cross-sector coordination rather than from the isolated interventions of individual organizations. Research by Riley et al. (2021) demonstrated that community-led collective action that leverages all intervention types from community engagement and activation, strategic use of programming and large-scale built-environment and policy change together can improve health and well-being at scale. Library staff can champion their strengths by participating in meetings and forums and talking about the reach, resources, expertise, and capacity available in the library. It is an extension of the library's services through both outreach and engagement, exploring, and responding to needs outside of the library walls. It means connecting to people and potential partners where they are and introducing them to all that the library has to offer. The result of these connections is often a recognition that there are clear, shared goals to support an informed community and the importance of leading healthy, productive lives.

GETTING STARTED

In addition to the case study research featuring the BCPL and the Kalamazoo Public Library, OCLC also published a Call to Action (Allen et al., 2020) to help libraries navigate possible opioid responses for their community. The Call to Action was supported by the research findings and an advisory group of subject matter experts in libraries, public health, government, and nongovernmental agencies. There are five actions outlined that library staff can take:

- **Explore your community data**: Understand the health concerns that impact your community.

226   KENDRA MORGAN

- **Consider community assets and connect with partners**: Partnerships increase capacity and funding, including through programming opportunities and an ability to connect with nonlibrary users.
- **Increase awareness and knowledge of the issue among staff and the community**: Learning and training opportunities can increase understanding and confidence in addressing the opioid crisis.
- **Focus on library staff care**: Acknowledge that supporting patrons through the opioid crisis or other health epidemics can lead to compassion fatigue for staff. Plans also need to be in place to respond when staff experience a traumatic event.
- **Offer community engagement and programming options**: Increase awareness of the opioid crisis and increase the confidence of library staff in patrons in responding to needs.

As library staff are introduced to opioid-related programming, they will come with a range of readiness and willingness to participate. The research from OCLC found that several factors contribute to the success of the partnerships and programming. One was having champions within the library to drive the work forward, usually a person in a position of leadership. Other factors included allowing the work to start small and grow naturally, along with prioritization and support from local government agencies (Allen et al., 2019). The Call to Action was designed to help address key concerns raised during the project research and create a path to implementation. In dynamic and diverse communities, libraries are faced with endless opportunities and topics to engage. Some of these opportunities can be viewed as more accessible or closely aligned with the library's core mission, particularly when resources are limited. There needs to be a willingness to "meet people where they are" when it comes to their interest in this topic; issues connected to stigma were noted as the biggest challenge to pursuing opioid-related programming. Aspects of this work can be emotional and complicated, and individuals can carry deep personal feelings about substance use disorder. The step outlined in the Call to Action to "Focus on Library Staff Care" stresses the importance of acknowledging and addressing those challenges in a way that is respectful and compassionate, and also allows for the space to discuss and explore the library's role in supporting these community needs.

CONCLUSION

The role of libraries in supporting information needs around healthy individual and community outcomes is well established. From addressing food insecurity (Freudenberger, 2021), to providing access to online databases and resources to learn about medical conditions (Hodges, 2022), to programs that encourage movement and exercise (Miller & Chandra, 2018), libraries have long served as valuable access points. Health-focused programs can be undertaken with the assistance of community partners who can serve as subject matter experts, provide funding, or access to resources not generally available at the library (Allen et al., 2019a). The opioid crisis is no exception and exemplifies what libraries and partners can

Libraries as Public Health Partners in the Opioid Crisis 227

achieve together in service of healthy outcomes. There are even broader-reaching impacts that align with the global UN SDGs, including work, economic growth, lifelong learning, and ensuring healthy lives. Looking at the collective impact model championed by Kania and Kramer (2011), libraries can consider how to align with other organizations and contribute resources and expertise in reaching the community to address the opioid crisis. Supporting people in their efforts to improve their lives and the lives of those around them is important and valuable work, and truly necessary for a functioning society.

REFERENCES

Allen, S., Clark, L., Coleman, M., Connaway, L., Cyr, C., Morgan, K., & Procaccini, M. (2019a). *Public libraries respond to the opioid crisis with their communities: Summary Report*. https://doi.org/10.25333/qgrn-hj36

Allen, S., Clark, L., Coleman, M., Connaway, L., Cyr, C., Morgan, K., & Procaccini, M. (2019b). *Public libraries respond to the opioid crisis with their communities: Case Studies*. https://doi.org/10.25333/cx18-1p87

Allen, S., Clark, L., Coleman, M., Connaway, L., Cyr, C., Morgan, K., & Procaccini, M. (2020). *Call to Action: Public Libraries and the Opioid Crisis*. https://doi.org/10.25333/w8sg-8440

American Medical Association. (2021a). *Issue brief: Reports of increases in opioid- and other drug-related overdose and other concerns during COVID pandemic*. https://www.hsdl.org/?abstract&did=847256

American Medical Association. (2021b). *Report shows decreases in opioid prescribing, increase in overdoses*. https://www.ama-assn.org/press-center/press-releases/report-shows-decreases-opioid-prescribing-increase-overdoses

Baker, A. (n.d.). Libraries as the community partner [Blog post]. https://www.ala.org/advocacy/diversity/odlos-blog/Libraries-as-the-community-partner

Blount County Recovery Court. (n.d.). *Blount County Recovery Court life skills program*. Retrieved December 12, 2022, from http://bcpl.populr.me/life-skills

Centers for Disease Control and Prevention. (2022). *U.S. overdose deaths in 2021 increased half as much as in 2020 – But are still up 15%*. https://www.cdc.gov/nchs/pressroom/nchs_press_releases/2022/202205.htm

Centers for Medicare & Medicaid Services. (2021). *Ongoing emergencies & disasters*. https://www.cms.gov/About-CMS/Agency-Information/Emergency/EPRO/Current-Emergencies/Ongoing-emergencies

Denver Department of Public Health & Environment – Community Health Division and Denver Human Services – Office of Behavior Health Services. (2018). Opioid epidemic collective impact summary report. https://www.denvergov.org/content/dam/denvergov/Portals/771/documents/CH/Substance%20Misuse/Opioid%20Impact%20Summary%20Report%20final.pdf

Freudenberger, E. (2021). *Program Model: Farm-2-Library*. https://programminglibrarian.org/programs/farm-2-library

Graff, S. (2018). *The critical role your neighborhood library could be playing in public health*. https://www.pennmedicine.org/news/news-blog/2018/june/the-critical-role-your-neighborhood-library-could-be-playing-in-public-health

Hodges, M. (2022). Public libraries as community health partners. *Certified Public Manager Applied Research*, *3*(1). https://scholarworks.sfasu.edu/cpmar/vol3/iss1/2

Institute of Museum and Library Service (IMLS). (2022). *National leadership grants for libraries*. https://www.imls.gov/grants/available/national-leadership-grants-libraries

Janosky, J. E., Armoutliev, E. M., Benipal, A., Kingsbury, M. A., Teller, J. L. S., Snyder, K. L., & Riley, P. (2013). Coalitions for impacting the health of a community: The Summit County Ohio, Experience. *Population Health Management*, *16*(4), 246–254. http://doi.org/10.1089/pop.2012.0083

Jenkins, W. D., Bolinski, R., Bresett, J., Van Ham, B., Fletcher, S., Walters, S., Friedman, S. R., Ezell, J. M., Pho, M., Schneider, J., & Ouellet, L. (2021). COVID-19 during the opioid epidemic

– Exacerbation of stigma and vulnerabilities. *The Journal of Rural Health, 37*(1), 172–174. https://doi.org/10.1111/jrh.12442

Kalamazoo Public Library. (n.d.). *Peer Navigators & Western Michigan University Social Work Interns at KPL*. Retrieved December 12, 2022, from https://www.kpl.gov/about/dei/peer-navigators-western-michigan-university-social-work-interns-at-kpl/

Kania, J., & Kramer, M. (2011). Collective impact. *Stanford Social Innovation Review*. https://doi.org/10.48558/5900-kn19

Lenstra, N., & McGehee, M. (2022). How public health partners perceive public librarians in 18 US Communities. *Journal of Library Outreach & Engagement, 2*(1). https://doi.org/10.21900/j.jloe.v2i1.883

Miller, C. E., & Chandra, A. (2018). *Measuring progress toward a culture of health...At the library*. https://www.healthaffairs.org/do/10.1377/forefront.20181119.551788

OCLC. (2020). Public libraries and the opioid crisis. https://www.oclc.org/research/public-libraries-opioid-crisis.html

Riley, C., Roy, B., Lam, V., Lawson, K., Nakano, L., Sun, J., Contreras, E., Hamar, B., & Herrin, J. (2021). Can a collective-impact initiative improve well-being in three US communities? Findings from a prospective repeated cross-sectional study. *BMJ Open, 11*(12). http://doi.org/10.1136/bmjopen-2020-048378

United Nations (UN). (2021). *UN responds to the global opioid crisis*. https://www.un.org/en/delegate/un-responds-global-opioid-crisis

United Nations (UN). (n.d.-a). *Synthetic drugs*. https://syntheticdrugs.unodc.org/

United Nations (UN). (n.d.-b). *17 Goals to transform our world*. https://www.un.org/sustainabledevelopment/

United Nations (UN). (n.d.-c). *Goal 3: Ensure healthy lives and promote well-being for all*. https://www.un.org/sustainabledevelopment/health/

United Nations (UN). (n.d.-d). *Goal 4: Ensure inclusive and equitable quality education and promote lifelong learning opportunities for all at all ages*. https://sdgs.un.org/goals/goal4

United Nations (UN). (n.d.-e). *Goal 8: Decent work and economic growth*. https://www.un.org/sustainabledevelopment/economic-growth/

United Nations (UN). (n.d.-f). *Goal 10: Reduce inequality within and among countries*. https://www.un.org/sustainabledevelopment/inequality/

CHAPTER 17

PARTNERING FOR SOCIAL INFRASTRUCTURE: INVESTIGATING THE CO-LOCATION OF A PUBLIC LIBRARY IN AN AFFORDABLE HOUSING BUILDING

Kaitlin Wynia Baluk, Ali Solhi and James Gillett

ABSTRACT

In 2021, a public library in Ontario, Canada established a branch in an affordable housing building. Using interviews with library and support workers who work in the building ($n = 8$) and an analysis of media that describes the partnership ($n = 16$), this chapter explores how their partnership may create social infrastructure for tenants. Social scientists have positioned strengthening social infrastructure, a community's network of systems and spaces that facilitate social relationships, as an antidote to many of society's most pressing social issues, such as social inequity. An understanding of this partnership, its purpose, and how it intends to serve neighborhood members provides insight into how public libraries and non-profit and community organizations together provide social infrastructure for those living in affordable housing. Strengthening a community's social infrastructure may be a vital step toward building socially sustainable communities in the twenty-first century.

Keywords: Public library; social infrastructure; homelessness; stigma; affordable housing; UN Sustainability Goals

---

How Public Libraries Build Sustainable Communities in the 21st Century
Advances in Librarianship, Volume 53, 229–242
Copyright © 2023 by Kaitlin Wynia Baluk, Ali Solhi and James Gillett
Published under exclusive licence by Emerald Publishing Limited
ISSN: 0065-2830/doi:10.1108/S0065-283020230000053021

INTRODUCTION

Hamilton, Ontario's Parkdale neighborhood is shaped by the city's industrial sector. Home to the shores of Lake Ontario, it is bordered by steel and chemical factories. Picturing the neighborhood, what comes to our minds, are images of commercial box stores, shipping containers, the busy Barton Street that cuts across the city, smokestacks, and a few residential blocks. While it's not a neighborhood that attracts many outsiders and can be described as underserved, as of 2021, it made the news with its new 1,500-square-foot Hamilton Public Library (HPL) branch located in McQuesten Lofts – a 4-storey affordable and energy-efficient housing building with architecture that honors Parkdale's industrial vibes (see Fig. 1). Notably, 20% of units are reserved for Indigenous peoples.

McQuesten Lofts is located next to another affordable housing building, Parkdale Landing. The space between them forms a courtyard designed in collaboration with Indigenous organizations. McQuesten Lofts and Parkdale Landing are operated by Indwell, "a Christian charity that creates affordable housing communities that support people seeking health, wellness, and belonging" (Indwell, 2022). HPL is a library system that serves a large geographic region with 2 bookmobiles and 23 branches, Parkdale being its newest. This chapter explores how the library's co-location in affordable housing and the Indwell–HPL partnership impact the neighborhood's social infrastructure. It then considers how strengthening social infrastructure via a co-located public library can support the United Nations (UN) 2030 Agenda for Sustainable Development.

Fig. 1. Photograph of McQuesten Lofts and HPL's Parkdale Branch. *Source*: This photograph was provided by HPL, Indwell, and Invizij Architects Inc. The photograph was taken by Tom Ridout of Industrious Photography.

PUBLIC LIBRARIES AS SOCIAL INFRASTRUCTURE

Social infrastructure refers to a community's networks of systems and spaces that facilitate social encounters (Latham & Layton, 2019). Examples include public libraries, ice rinks, and public parks (Horgan et al., 2020; Layton & Latham, 2021; van Melik & Merry, 2021). Infrastructure, in a broad sense, helps to facilitate collective activities (Mattern, 2014). For example, public transit allows for travel, and school systems allow for education. Social infrastructure facilitates sociability (Latham & Layton, 2019; Mattern, 2014). Strengthening a community's social infrastructure is a strategy for addressing social issues, such as social inequities and natural disasters (Aldrich & Meyer, 2015). A thesis in sociologist Eric Klinenberg's (2018) book, *Palaces for the People*, is that social infrastructure helps address social issues because it fosters social capital and community resilience. When referring to social capital and resilience, we are referring to the trust and reciprocity in social networks that support groups in overcoming challenges (Putnam, 2000; Vårheim, 2017). When individuals build relationships via social infrastructure, they are more likely to have others to rely on and support during difficult times and to have positive encounters with those who embody social differences (Klinenberg, 2018). This sociability may support individuals in diverse communities in establishing a sense of connectedness (Anderson, 2011).

In this chapter, we use Latham and Layton's (2019) description of strong social infrastructure to investigate how HPL's Parkdale branch supports sociability. Latham and Layton (2019) describe strong social infrastructure as accessible to all community members, well-maintained, responsive to the community, democratic so that all members have collective agency in the space, and abundant in the community. Likewise, they describe how a community should ideally have diverse types of social infrastructure to serve diverse groups. In contrast, weak social infrastructure is often "private" or is laden with financial, social, legal, and cultural barriers that exclude or reinforce systems of inequality (Liinamaa et al., 2021; Radice, 2016). While social infrastructure may help facilitate social encounters, some encounters may potentially reinforce unequal power relations even when ostensibly positive (Derr, 2017; Liinamaa et al., 2021). Social infrastructure may thereby benefit some more than others. For example, accessible social infrastructure is typically in public spaces, yet few public spaces exist where people who are homeless are welcomed (Staeheli & Mitchell, 2007). Stigmas attached to homelessness inflect social encounters (Gerrard & Farrugia, 2015). Many communities criminalize homeless behaviors, use anti-vagrant architecture, or have few public spaces that are free to access (Staeheli & Mitchell, 2007). This group is thereby marginalized from the social capital afforded by social infrastructure.

Fortunately, there are exceptions; public libraries and non-profit organizations have a history of providing social spaces for marginalized groups (Hodgetts et al., 2008; Trussell & Mair, 2010). HPL's location in Indwell presents an opportunity to examine how these two types of social infrastructure coalesce to provide social spaces for people who may be marginalized. Public libraries that share a space with another organization are not a new or an exceptional one-off phenomenon (Palmer, 2022). To serve communities equitably, local governments in the United States have been establishing public libraries in strategic community locations, such as retail buildings and civic centers since the late 1800s (Koontz, 2007). Two recent examples in Miami, Florida and Cornelius, Oregon are affordable seniors' housing that incorporates a public library along with other community amenities (McCormick, 2019; Nelson, 2022). Despite the history of such partnerships, there is little research that focuses on the practice of co-locating a public library in affordable housing.

This book chapter contributes to both the literature on social infrastructure and on the co-location of library services by exploring how a public library and non-profit housing organization can together strengthen a community's social infrastructure. Considering whether a community's social infrastructure is well-maintained, abundant, diverse, democratic, and responsive to the community's changing needs and interests can reveal who might be missing from sociable public spaces (Latham & Layton, 2019). These considerations may also reveal the elements of public spaces that make them suitable for bringing together diverse groups into equitable sociable encounters and thereby fostering sustainable communities in the twenty-first century.

METHODS

This case study explores the institutional goals and elements of the Parkdale branch that allow it to serve as a social infrastructure. The guiding research questions are (1) What are the goals shaping the HPL–Indwell partnership? (2) How does the branch create opportunities for equitable and meaningful social encounters? An understanding of the HPL–Indwell partnership provides insight into how non-profit organizations and public libraries can partner to strengthen social infrastructure for marginalized members of society, such as those that have recently experienced homelessness, poverty, mental illness, addiction, and/ or the various forms of trauma associated with these life circumstances. Our case study consists of a thematic analysis of online news articles and web pages about McQuesten Lofts and/or the HPL-Parkdale branch, and interviews with HPL and Indwell staff who work in the building. The media provide a glimpse into the institutional aspirations shaping the branch, and thus supported us in responding to our first research question. Via staff interviews, we gather insight into how top-down goals are played out on the ground. The interview analysis was instrumental in responding to our second research question.

Data collection occurred in February and March 2022. We used purposive sampling to select sources and recruit participants who could address our research questions (Creswall & Poth, 2016). Using the search terms, "McQuesten Lofts, Parkdale Landing, Indwell, Hamilton Public Library, HPL, and Parkdale Branch," we searched Google and Nexis Uni, a search engine for news, business, and legal sources. Removing duplicates and irrelevant media, we included 16 sources. After achieving ethics clearance from McMaster University's Research

Partnering for Social Infrastructure

Ethics Board, we recruited participants by asking HPL and Indwell leadership to invite staff to contact us about the study. We recruited four HPL staff and four Indwell staff. Our small sample size is reflective of the small target population of staff who work in Parkdale regularly.

We analyzed both sets of data with Braun and Clarke (2006) thematic coding method. In adherence to this method, we familiarized ourselves first with the data by developing initial codes that relate to the research questions, looked for and compared patterned responses among the codes, and considered how these patterns form a coherent response to our research questions. We used Latham and Layton (2019) description of strong social infrastructure to consider how the branch creates opportunities for social encounters.

It is important to preface our discussion by highlighting this study's limitations. While this study provides insight into how the library and its co-location in affordable housing can strengthen social infrastructure, it does not show definitively that this is the case. Our case study provides a single example of a co-located library. To capture the library's role as a social infrastructure more fully, we need to hear directly from the Parkdale community. Our results, however, provide a basis for exploring how the library's co-location can strengthen social infrastructure for marginalized groups. It likewise provides a platform for considering how the library's potential to create social infrastructure might help advance the UN's 2030 Agenda for Sustainable Development.

RESULTS AND DISCUSSION

Our analyses indicated that the Parkdale branch is intended to provide community resources to an underserved neighborhood and can facilitate various forms of social encounters between library workers, Indwell staff, tenants, and community members. We begin by describing the goals of the branch to respond to our first research question: *What are the goals shaping the HPL–Indwell partnership?* Our conclusions about these goals, presented under the theme "A Little Baby Branch for Big Community Needs" are predominantly based on our media analysis, although we also compare our conclusions with findings from the interview analysis. The themes presented in subsequent sections were derived from the interviews and offer a response to the second research question: *How does the branch create opportunities for equitable and meaningful social encounters?* The description of the branch's goals provides a springboard for elaborating on the role of library services, the staff, COVID-19, and library partnerships in strengthening Parkdale's social infrastructure and thereby promoting the UN's sustainable development goals (SDGs). When quoting media, we cite the author and year. When quoting interviewees, we cite their organization and a code.

A Little Baby Branch for Big Community Needs

An overarching theme is that the Parkdale branch is intended to be a community resource for those who experience barriers to participating fully in community life. This theme is captured in an article naming McQuesten Lofts as a winner of an environmental sustainability design competition. This article sums up the buildings' goals:

> to address the city's rising housing affordability crisis, to be a step toward [Canadian indigenous] reconciliation, to contribute to the streetscape, and to provide a new public library branch for the neighborhood. (Rote, 2021)

The underlying goals shaping McQuesten Lofts and the Parkdale Branch thereby closely resemble the goals in the UN's 2030 Agenda for Sustainable Development, particularly Goal 9 – to "build resilient infrastructure, promote inclusive and sustainable industrialization and foster innovation" and Goal 11 – to "make cities and human settlements inclusive, safe, resilient and sustainable" (UN, 2015). The building's design and construction are intended to reduce energy consumption, promoting environmentally sustainable infrastructure. Its social and esthetic purposes are to foster neighborhood pride, belonging, and improved access to housing and community resources, such as a public library's information, technology, leisure, and social opportunities, promoting social inclusion and resilience.

Interviewees and media both emphasized common challenges that Indwell tenants and the Parkdale community experience when it comes to pursuing wellbeing and affordable and equitable access to community resources. While the documents portrayed the tenants' needs in a more sanitized manner, noting the distance to the nearest services or borrowing from Indwell's self-description to refer to tenants as "people seeking health, wellness, and belonging," the interviewees painted a more vivid account of tenant challenges. The interviewees drew attention to how many tenants are of low socioeconomic status, have low language and digital literacy, lack access to basic technology, are socially isolated, and/or lack good physical mobility. When reflecting on why McQuesten Lofts was chosen as the location for the Parkdale branch, an interviewee noted, "It is an area where people don't have a lot of opportunities" (HPL_I6). Likewise, the interviewees highlighted that many tenants experience mental health issues: "They are sometimes struggling with mental health or addiction or have experienced homelessness at some point in their not-so-distant past" (Indwell_I8). One interviewee proposed that the tenants' challenges are also reflected in the broader community: "We have lots of interactions with people who live in the apartment buildings [nearby], and a lot of the needs are very similar" (Indwell_I7). Highlighting these challenges sets the stage for grappling with how the branch's co-location creates social infrastructure.

Both the interviewees and media portray the branch and the Indwell–HPL partnership favorably. The media portray Indwell and HPL as impressive community organizations addressing social issues. For example, Indwell is described as "remarkable" and "respected and trusted" (Alter, 2021; Morse & Associates, n.d.). They are praised for building affordable and environmentally sustainable homes where once stood buildings that were "some of the most dilapidated and unsafe in the city" (Morse & Associates, n.d.). HPL is described as "innovative" and "a place for inspiration and growth" (INVIZIJ, n.d.-a; Morse & Associates, n.d.). Leveraging quotes from leaders in both organizations, the media frame the HPL–Indwell partnership as an apt approach to serving the community well.

Partnering for Social Infrastructure 235

For example, a Hamilton Spectator (2020) article quotes Indwell's Commercial Tenancies Coordinator: "Ensuring commercial tenants benefit the Indwell community and neighborhood is key for our charity. This partnership with Hamilton Public Library more than meets this goal." The media framed HPL's co-location in Indwell as a mutually beneficial partnership with community benefits.

On the ground, the staff similarly portrayed the branch favorably. For example, a library worker concluded the interview by emphasizing, "whoever came up with this idea to put in a little baby branch in this Indwell building was brilliant... Because I think it's such a life-changing thing for residents" (HPL_I3). Staff thus echoed the institutional sentiment within online media, highlighting the branch's capacity to meet community needs.

Equipped, Accessible, and Safe

Our analysis of the interviews highlighted the importance of the library's provision of material resources and information and communication technologies when it came to supporting the well-being of tenants. This emphasis on the library's services and resources is aligned again with the UN's 9th SDG, which encompasses a demand for increased "access to information and communication technology" and "universal and affordable access to the Internet." When asked about how the branch benefits tenants and how tenants use the library, common responses included printing, using the computers, accessing WiFi, and borrowing DVDs, CDs, and books. Interviewees drew attention to how the COVID-19 pandemic heightened the value of these services, especially for those who lacked sufficient access to technology.

In addition to supporting the UN's 9th goal, the library's material provisioning provides a foundation for it to serve as a social infrastructure. This idea is consistent with Layton and Latham (2021) investigation of a public park in the UK. Their research indicates that the park's regular upkeep allows for various types of social encounters, such as simple co-presence, where strangers share space, to civic engagement and friendship. Free access to books, movies, music, internet, printing, and digital devices draws people into a public space, where they can encounter others.

Both the interview and media analyses furthermore drew attention to the library's physical and geographic accessibility. The branch is designed with accessible features, such as accessible parking, washrooms, door openers, and ramps (HPL, n.d.-a). Library workers also indicated that they felt physically safe in the branch despite knowledge of neighborhood crime. After noting the crime and drug overdose challenges in the area, a library worker observed how they have regulars in the library "who think of the library as a home and take ownership of the library. There's a lot of eyes on the building all the time, so safety-wise, that's really great" (HPL_16). Physical accessibility and safety are prerequisites for ensuring spaces are welcoming (Latham & Layton, 2019).

All interviewees emphasized how the library's geographic location "smack dab in the middle" between two other HPL branches a few kilometers away, meant that individuals with limited physical mobility or those lacking the financial means for public transit could use the library (HPL_I6). An Indwell staff (I7) succinctly captured this theme: "Having something that is walkable and in an accessible location means the difference between using a service and not using a service." Removing physical and geographic barriers and drawing people in with services is essential to ensuring that they want to participate in and can benefit from the library's social spaces. The library's co-location may help in creating "resilient infrastructure" (see UN, 2015, Goal 9) and in making communities "inclusive, safe, resilient and sustainable" (see UN, 2015, Goal 11).

Friendly Faces and Friendly Spaces

In addition to material provisioning and physical accessibility, our interview analysis indicated that the library is socially accessible. Both library and Indwell workers appeared to play a role in making the branch a sociable space by removing social barriers that prevent individuals from using the library. Indwell workers noted that they supported tenants in mending their relationships with the library, as showcased in the following quote:

> It's the history that our tenants have and their relationship with libraries. It took a while for that relationship to start building and it's still building… Whenever there is a need, and we see, "the library can meet this need," we send the tenant over to the library at least to say hi and connect with the staff there and start building that relationship. (Indwell_I1)

When referring to the tenants' history, Indwell participants highlighted how tenants may have experienced anxiety while traveling to a library previously, while others may feel that they are unable to use the library due to a bad experience, late fines (HPL removed late fine policies in 2020), or because they are unsure of what the library offers and if they can afford it. Bringing awareness to the library's free resources appeared to be both an ongoing challenge and a joy associated with having the branch in the building.

Once tenants are in the library, HPL staff help make the branch socially accessible by facilitating "a sense of neighborliness in the area" (Indwell_I7). Staff seek to offer "a friendly face and a friendly space" (Indwell_I4), be "engaged and welcoming" (Indwell_ I7), "non-judgmental" (HPL_I2, I5), and treat members with "privacy, dignity, and respect" (HPL_I6). Reflecting on the branch's social environment, one interviewee noted, "It could have gone way different if we had staff members who were super transactional" rather than relational (HPL_I6). Another emphasized how they provide an "intangible connection" for members:

> They just need to come in and see a smile, even though it's under a mask and know that there are people here that aren't going to judge them, they're going to help them. (HPL_I5)

The staff's willingness to work relationally, non-judgmentally, and respectfully may help to mend the strained tenant–library relationship, and thereby aid tenants in accessing the library's social infrastructure.

The staff's capacity to foster social accessibility also appeared to be supported by the library's small size. Its small and quiet nature gives staff the time to build relationships so that members feel comfortable asking for help:

Partnering for Social Infrastructure 237

> It is small and not too busy, the staff are able to find that information for people and because we have built up these relationships with these tenants, they come in and they ask. (HPL_I6)

Another library worker, echoing this sentiment, explained "time isn't rushed here. We're just suspended in this safe, literary, knowledgeable space" (HPL_I5). The library workers emphasized how the library's free resources also supported social accessibility, making comments such as "I'm not selling anything, which is really nice, so you can just come in and say hi and go. You don't have to borrow anything" (HPL_I2) and "[the library] is giving folks the space to exist without capitalism looming over them" (HPL_I5). These relaxed vibes create a context ripe for staff to provide a socially accessible space, where community members can encounter others, converse, and seek entertainment, leisure, learning, technology, and help with day-to-day challenges.

Having the capacity to build relationships with members may also support library workers in being responsive to community needs and interests. Being responsive to a community is an element of sociable public spaces (Latham & Layton, 2019). The library workers' ability to respond to community needs and interests was clearly illustrated as the interviewees discussed a special Indigenous collection and a grassroots coloring program. An interviewee observed among tenants a "curiosity and need to learn more about Indigenous communities" (Indwell_I1), which was evident when the library first opened. Hearing requests that staff could not meet, the Parkdale manager worked to create a special Indigenous collection:

> We had a lot of people coming in and looking for information about residential schools, Indigenous experiences, Indigenous cookbooks. Because it's such a small collection, we didn't have a lot. We could order stuff in but that's not really good enough when someone wants to see themselves reflected in their own library collection.... Now we have this brand new Indigenous collection. (HPL_I6)

This collection exemplifies how library workers were able to slow down, listen to library users, and then actively respond to requests. Five participants also discussed a grassroots coloring group: "We have a group of ladies who love to come in and photocopy coloring sheets together" (HPL_I3). Another noted, "each week they have a new person who comes to get their coloring done" (HPL_I5). Staff began to respond by pre-printing coloring sheets and noted that in the future they plan to offer a formal coloring program. This programming and collection development, initiated by library users, showcases both library users' agency and how staff can help support it.

The notion that the staff plays a role in shaping the library's infrastructure is aligned with scholars, such as Simone (2004) and Amin (2008), who reason that infrastructure is dynamically shaped by the relationships between people and the infrastructure's material elements. While the library's physical and geographic accessibility, free services, and small size provide an opportunity for library workers to slow down, listen to, and chat with tenants, the library would still not be socially accessible or responsive to community needs if the library workers chose to serve tenants transactionally and if Indwell workers did not encourage tenants to mend their relationships with the library.

COVID-19's Impact

COVID-19 public health mandates, such as social distancing, impacted the library's social environment and the tenant's awareness of library services. Since its opening in July 2021, the library has not been able to offer in-person programming and its "Grand Opening" was significantly limited. Two participants noted that online programming, which is in adherence to public health mandates, is inaccessible to tenants who do not have access to the internet, a digital device, or lack the digital literacy to attend. This sentiment showcases the importance of addressing the UN's (2015) 9th SDG to increase access to information and communication technologies and the internet. With the increasing digitalization of basic services and community resources, increased access to digital literacy and technology is essential to building resilient, inclusive, and sustainable infrastructure.

Interviewees likewise suggested that online programming does not create the same levels of sociability as in-person programming. When asked about how the library could better serve tenants, all interviewees noted that they were eager to see HPL in-person programs, such as book and film clubs, language learning conversation circles, storytimes, and digital literacy training. Interviewees articulated how in-person programming facilitates positive social relationships because attendees encounter the same people regularly with whom they share a common interest. In a small way, COVID-19 restrictions may have supported the branch's ability to be a social infrastructure. Without programming commitments, staff indicated that they had more time to listen to library users, and thereby pay closer attention to community interests and needs.

Redistributing Social Infrastructure

This study suggests that simply providing access to library collections and spaces may not be enough to bolster social capital and community resilience, but rather staff capacity and thoughtful design and service provision are also needed to make the library's social infrastructure accessible. This idea mirrors Wyatt et al.'s (2018) conclusion that "an enhanced public culture will not flow automatically from the mere availability of new technologies" (p. 2936). In their research on Australian public libraries' role in the implementation of a national broadband network, they suggest public institutions are needed to make community resources accessible, especially to marginalized populations. They conceptualize libraries as "redistributive technology" that allows for a flow of resources and activities across various societal domains (p. 2944). One way this flow takes place is through partnerships (Wyatt et al., 2018), such as the one between Indwell and HPL.

This concept of public libraries as "redistributive technology" can be applied to the idea of libraries as part of a community's network of social infrastructure. Interviewees mused about how their organizations might share spaces, expertise, and resources to meet neighborhood needs. An Indwell worker (I7) noted, for example, that green spaces "are pretty lacking in the neighborhood," so it would be nice to see the library hosting community programs in McQuesten Lofts' courtyard. Partnering to increase access to Indwell's courtyard exemplifies how

Partnering for Social Infrastructure 239

library partnerships can help address the UN's (2015) 11th goal to provide "universal access to safe, inclusive and accessible, green and public spaces." All interviewees also discussed how HPL could offer programming in Indwell's spaces to overcome the limitations of having small square footage. While HPL workers highlighted some drawbacks to renting in an apartment building, they appreciated how their location "makes [them] feel very much a part of that [Indwell] community" (HPL_I2). The branch's co-location provides convenient opportunities for advancing both organizations' shared goal of supporting community well-being.

Furthermore, interviewees noted how other community organizations, such as museums, educational institutions, hospitals, and non-profits, partner with the library in ways that benefit Indwell tenants. Participants explained that social and healthcare workers book Parkdale's meeting room to meet with tenants in a convenient and private location. They also gave examples of how the library partners with various local organizations to increase the accessibility of information, training, leisure, and fitness. Here, we see the library as not only acting as social infrastructure but also redistributing the social capital of other social infrastructure organizations. Acting as, redistributing, and bringing together various types of social infrastructure via partnerships, the library may foster new modes of creating social capital and advancing community resilience to build more sustainable communities in the twenty-first century.

CONCLUSION

Our case study captures various ways in which the HPL–Indwell partnership might strengthen the neighborhood's social infrastructure. Providing well-maintained, diverse, and financially, physically, socially, and geographically accessible services, being responsive to the community, encouraging users' agency, and redistributing external community resources via partnerships, HPL's Parkdale branch appears to tick all the boxes when it comes to Latham and Layton (2019) description of strong social infrastructure. Many scholars have painted public libraries as vital social infrastructure organizations. Our research extends this idea by highlighting how the co-location of the library in affordable housing creates opportunities for partnerships with other social infrastructure organizations and thereby fosters new ways for marginalized individuals to tap into a community's social capital. The library's co-location may reduce barriers to services for community members who have experienced homelessness, poverty, addiction, mental health problems, and who are on the disadvantaged side of the digital divide. Lastly, our study draws attention to the important role of library workers in facilitating sociability.

In addition to painting public libraries as social infrastructure, LIS scholars have positioned public libraries as vehicles to advance the UN's 2030 Agenda for Sustainable Development (e.g., Mansour, 2020). Including goals such as "end poverty in all its forms everywhere," the UN's targets are ambitious (UN, 2015). Despite the agenda's loftiness, it provides an ideal for world leaders to rally around. By acting as social infrastructure and thereby supporting community resilience, public libraries help actualize the UN's goals locally. In our research, we saw the HPL–Indwell partnership, in particular, addressing the UN's (2015) 9th and 11th goals to "build resilient infrastructure, promote inclusive and sustainable industrialization and foster innovation" and to "make cities and human settlements inclusive, safe, resilient and sustainable." Public libraries that are strategically co-located in affordable housing, that are socially, physically, and geographically accessible, well-equipped with services and partnerships tailored to the community, and operated by staff who take a relational approach to their work, may help to advance a public library's commitment to promoting a sustainable future.

ONLINE MEDIA

Alter, L. (2021, January 11). How to build affordable social housing to passive house standard. *Treehugger*. https://www.treehugger.com/affordable-social-housing-passive-house-5094979

Courey, R., & Brouwer, A. (2021, June 29). Applause for Hamilton's Shelter Health Network. *Indwell*. https://indwell.ca/2021/06/29/applause-for-hamiltons-shelter-health-network/?utm_source=rss&utm_medium=rss&utm_campaign=applause-for-hamiltons-shelter-health-network

Hamilton Public Library (HPL). (n.d.-a). *Parkdale Branch*. https://www.hpl.ca/branches/parkdale-branch

Hamilton Public Library (HPL). (n.d.-b). *Parkdale Branch Hamilton Public Library | Red Book by HPL*. https://redbook.hpl.ca/node/32306

Indwell. (2021, June 9). *McQuesten Lofts: New homes bring new hope*. https://indwell.ca/2021/06/09/mcquesten-lofts-new-homes-bring-new-hope/

INVIZIJ Architects. (n.d.-a). *Hamilton Public Library – Parkdale Branch*. https://invizij.ca/project/hamilton-public-library-parkdale-branch/

INVIZIJ Architects. (n.d.-b). *McQuesten Lofts – Indwell*. https://indwell.ca/mcquesten-lofts

Kouniakis, A. (2021, July 14). New branch of Hamilton Public Library opens in East End. *InTheHammer*. https://www.insauga.com/new-branch-of-hamilton-public-library-opens-in-east-end/

Lorinc, J. (2021, April 9). Housing's bottom line: Can passive house approach save long-term costs? *The Globe and Mail*. https://www.theglobeandmail.com/real-estate/toronto/article-housings-bottom-line-can-passive-house-approach-save-long-term-costs/

Mann, K. (2020a, April 10). Library branch to be incorporated into east Hamilton affordable housing project – Hamilton. *Globalnews.ca*. https://globalnews.ca/news/6804474/library-branch-east-hamilton-affordable-housing-project/

Mann, K. (2020b, September 23). Indwell opens newest affordable housing community in Hamilton – Hamilton. *Globalnews.ca*. https://globalnews.ca/news/7352794/indwell-housing-hamilton/

Morse & Associates. (n.d.). *Featured project: Signs for hope for affordable housing: Creating community at McQuesten Lofts with Indwell*. Retrieved February 11, 2022, from https://www.morseassociates.ca/featured-project

Ontario Construction News. (2020, June 3). Record air tightness reached in larger-scale affordable housing projects. *Ontario Construction News*. https://ontarioconstructionnews.com/record-air-tightness-reached-in-larger-scale-affordable-housing-projects/

Passive House Institute US, Inc. (2021, February 17). *Certified Project Database: Indwell McQuesten Lofts and Hamilton Public Library – Parkdale Branch*. https://www.phius.org/projects/1594

Rennison, J. (2020, December 25). Tenants at Hamilton's McQuesten Lofts are home just in time for Christmas. *The Hamilton Spectator*. https://www.thespec.com/news/hamilton-region/2020/12/25/tenants-at-hamiltons-mcquesten-lofts-are-home-just-in-time-for-christmas.html

Rote, L. (2021, November 8). Meet the 2021 Passive Design Competition Winner. *Gb&d Magazine*. https://gbdmagazine.com/2021-passive-design-competition/

REFERENCES

Aldrich, D. P., & Meyer, M. A. (2015). Social capital and community resilience. *American Behavioral Scientist, 59*(2), 254–269. https://doi.org/10.1177/0002764214550299

Amin, A. (2008). Collective culture and urban public space. *City, 12*(1), 5–24. https://doi.org/10.1080/13604810801933495

Anderson, E. (2011). *The cosmopolitan canopy*. Norton.

Braun, V., & Clarke, V. (2006). Using thematic analysis in psychology. *Qualitative Research in Psychology, 3*(2), 77–101. https://doi.org/10.1191/1478088706qp063oa

Creswell, J., & Poth, C. (2016). *Qualitative inquiry and research design: Choosing among five approaches.* New York, NY: Sage Publications.

Derr, L. A. (2017). Public Libraries are safe (and neutral spaces)...when people aren't in them! *Transform Libraries, Transform Societies*. International Federation of Library Associations. http://ifla-test.eprints-hosting.org/id/eprint/2272/

Gerrard, J., & Farrugia, D. (2015). The 'lamentable sight' of homelessness and the society of the spectacle. *Urban Studies, 52*(12), 2219–2233. https://doi.org/10.1177/0042098014542135

Hodgetts, D., Stolte, O., Chamberlain, K., Radley, A., Nikora, L., Nabalarua, E., & Groot, S. (2008). A trip to the library: Homelessness and social inclusion. *Social & Cultural Geography, 9*(8), 933–953. https://doi.org/10.1080/14649360802441432

Horgan, M., Liinamaa, S., Dakin, A., Meligrana, S., & Xu, M. (2020). A shared everyday ethic of public sociability: Outdoor public ice rinks as spaces for encounter. *Urban Planning, 5*(4), 143–154. https://doi.org/10.17645/up.v5i4.3430

Indwell. (2022). *About us*. https://indwell.ca/about-us/

Klinenberg, E. (2018). *Palaces for the people: How social infrastructure can help fight inequality, polarization, and the decline of civic life*. Broadway Books.

Koontz, C. M. (2007). A history of location of US public libraries within community place and space: Evolving implications for the library's mission of equitable service. *Public Library Quarterly, 26*(1–2), 75–100. https://doi.org/10.1300/J118v26n01_05

Latham, A., & Layton, J. (2019). Social infrastructure and the public life of cities: Studying urban sociality and public spaces. *Geography Compass, 13*(7), 1–15. https://doi.org/10.1111/gec3.12444

Layton, J., & Latham, A. (2021). Social infrastructure and public life – notes on Finsbury Park, London. *Urban Geography, 0*(0), 1–22. https://doi.org/10.1080/02723638.2021.1934631

Liinamaa, S., Horgán, M., Dakin, A., Meligrana, S., & Xu, M. (2021). Everyday multiculturalism on ice: Observations from hockey-free outdoor urban public ice rinks. *Canadian Ethnic Studies, 53*(3), 261–275. https://doi.org/10.1353/ces.2021.0028

Mansour, E. (2020). Libraries as agents for development: The potential role of Egyptian rural public libraries towards the attainment of Sustainable Development Goals based on the UN 2030 Agenda. *Journal of Librarianship and Information Science, 52*(1), 121–136. https://doi.org/10.1177/0961000619872064

Mattern, S. (2014). Library as infrastructure. *Places Journal*. https://doi.org/10.22269/140609

McCormick, K. (2019, September 27). *A new chapter: Cities are tackling the housing crunch – by building above the library*. Lincoln Institute of Land Policy. https://www.lincolninst.edu/publications/articles/new-chapter

Nelson, J. (2022, October 19). Housing trust group, AM affordable housing break ground on $44M seniors housing project in Miami. *Business Online*. https://rebusinessonline.com/housing-trust-group-am-affordable-housing-break-ground-on-44m-seniors-housing-project-in-miami/

Palmer, M. (2022). Study of future public library trends & best practices. *Public Library Quarterly, 41*(1), 83–107. https://doi.org/10.1080/01616846.2020.1868224

Putnam, R. D. (2000). Bowling alone: America's declining social capital. In L. Crothers & C. Lockhart (Eds.), *Culture and politics: A reader* (pp. 223–234). Palgrave Macmillan US. https://doi.org/10.1007/978-1-349-62965-7_12

Radice, M. (2016). Unpacking intercultural conviviality in multiethnic commercial streets. *Journal of Intercultural Studies, 37*(5), 432–448. https://doi.org/10.1080/07256868.2016.1211624

Simone, A. M. (2004). People as infrastructure: Intersecting fragments in Johannesburg. *Public Culture, 16*(3), 407–429. https://www.muse.jhu.edu/article/173743

Staeheli, L., & Mitchell, D. (2007). *The people's property?: Power, politics, and the public*. Routledge. https://doi.org/10.4324/9780203936382

Trussell, D. E., & Mair, H. (2010). Seeking judgment free spaces: Poverty, leisure, and social inclusion. *Journal of Leisure Research, 42*(4), 513–533. https://doi.org/10.1080/00222216.2010.11950216

United Nations (UN). (2015). *Transforming our world: The 2030 Agenda for Sustainable Development.* https://sdgs.un.org/2030agenda

van Melik, R., & Merry, M. S. (2021). Retooling the public library as social infrastructure: A Dutch illustration. *Social & Cultural Geography, 0*(0), 1–20. https://doi.org/10.1080/14649365.2021.1965195

Vårheim, A. (2017). Public libraries, community resilience, and social capital. *Information Research, 22*(1), 1–19. https://hdl.handle.net/10037/12470

Wyatt, D., Mcquire, S., & Butt, D. (2018). Libraries as redistributive technology: From capacity to culture in Queensland's public library network. *New Media & Society, 20*(8), 2934–2953. https://doi.org/10.1177/1461444817738235

SECTION FIVE

LIBRARIES NURTURING POSITIVE PEACE

INTRODUCTION TO SECTION FIVE: SUSTAINABLE COMMUNITIES AND THE ROLE OF THE PUBLIC LIBRARY

Kaurri C. Williams-Cockfield and Bharat Mehra

FRAMING OF SECTION FIVE: ["LIBRARIES NURTURING POSITIVE PEACE"]

Section Five features case studies that provide examples of programs that promote peace on a local level [SDG 16] and focus on inclusion, diversity, equity, accountability, and justice for all across the community-at-large including both social and institutional application [SDG 16]. Promoting peace through the building of strong institutions ties directly into the premise of this book. Libraries promote peace within their communities because they are already interconnected with their service communities (Mehra & Robinson, 2009). The nature of public libraries and public library work establishes community networks and provides information and resources which, in turn, allows for the generation of new knowledge (Lankes, 2011, p. 15).

The chapters in this section operationalize significant elements of the public library – sustainable communities (PLSC) framework visualized in the introduction to the book. In Chapter 18 ["Libraries are Sustainability Leaders"], Rebekkah Smith Aldrich and Lisa Gangemi Kropp discuss a case study on the application of the Triple Bottom Line sustainability process to the planning and policy development for Lindenhurst Memorial Library in Lindenhurst, New York. Reviewer David Leonard, President; BPL, LIS Doctoral Candidate, Simmons University, writes:

How Public Libraries Build Sustainable Communities in the 21st Century
Advances in Librarianship, Volume 53, 245–247
Copyright © 2023 by Kaurri C. Williams-Cockfield and Bharat Mehra
Published under exclusive licence by Emerald Publishing Limited
ISSN: 0065-2830/doi:10.1108/S0065-283020230000053022

This chapter begins to formally recognize the obligations of librarians to adopt a philosophy of climate justice and values of sustainability in our work with communities and internally as cultures and organizations; using a key framework and a specific US case study.

In Chapter 19 ["Reflecting on Public Library–Social Work Collaboration: Current Approaches and Future Possibilities"], Rachel D. Williams and Lydia P. Ogden discuss the public library–social work collaboration and present a series of models for implementing this type of collaboration.

In Chapter 20 ["The Intersection of US Public Libraries and Public Health"], Suzanne Grossman discusses collaborations between public libraries and community health organizations to expand access to medical information.

In Chapter 21 ["Public Libraries' Contribution to Sustainable Dementia-Friendly Communities"], Timothy J. Dickey discusses the methodologies for providing library services to persons living with dementia.

In Chapter 22 ["With Literacy and Justice for All: Library Programs for Refugees and Newcomers"], Claire Dannenbaum reflects on her interviews with library staff in libraries across the United States, in the Netherlands, and in Germany where she gathered information on programs and services to refugees and newcomers. In this chapter, she breaks library programs and services into four categories: the library as sanctuary, the library as storehouse, the library as gateway, and the library as bridge.

STRATEGIC COLLECTIVE ACTIONS

The thematic threads flowing through the five chapters in this section highlight how different library case studies operationalize the following significant strategic collective actions:

- Apply the principles of sustainability across the spectrum of library services, resources, and programming;
- Demonstrate how libraries respond to individuals in crisis;
- Build effective library partnerships with mental health organizations;
- Develop programs and services, as well as provide access to resources, so people living with dementia can effectively use the library;
- Support newcomers, refugees and immigrants as they transition to a new place be it city, state, or country.

These five chapters present case studies that illustrate ways that public libraries build peace within a community. The programs discussed in these chapters illustrate how public libraries, as strong and stable institutions, are ideally suited to amplify and reinforce existing community resources.

KEY CONCEPTS AND TERMS

Economic Stewardship – Fiscal viability of a decision.
Environmental Stewardship – Caring for the Earth and its natural resources.

Introduction to Section Five 247

Social Equity – Ensuring that all members of a community are treated with respect, empathy, and dignity.

Sustainable Thinking – Refers to the alignment of a library's core values and resources – including staff time and energy, facilities, collections, and technology.

Trauma-Informed Institution – Recognizes the prevalence of trauma, and provides services that actively avoid re-traumatization and promotes a sense of safety for all members, including those providing services.

Triple Bottom Line – A decision-making rubric focused on the balance of environmental stewardship, social equity, and economic feasibility.

REFERENCES

Lankes, R. D. (2011). *The Atlas of New Librarianship.* MIT Press. https://davidlankes.org/new-librarianship/the-atlas-of-new-librarianship-online/#Download

Mehra, B., & Robinson, W. C. (2009, Winter). The community engagement model in library and information science education: A case study of a collection development and management course. *Journal of Education for Library and Information Science, 50*(1), 15–38.

RESOURCES AND RELEVANT ORGANIZATIONS

Alzheimer's Association, Chicago, IL, US. https://www.alz.org/

Dementia Friends, UK. https://www.dementiafriends.org.uk/

Dementia Friends, US. https://dementiafriendsusa.org/

Family Caregiver Alliance, San Francisco, CA, US. https://www.caregiver.org/

IFLA Guidelines for Library Service to Persons with Dementia. https://www.ifla.org/files/assets/hq/publications/professional-report/104.pdf

IFLA Sanctuary, Storehouse, Gateway, Bridge: Libraries' Role in Making Refugees Feel Welcome. https://www.ifla.org/files/assets/hq/topics/libraries-development/documents/world_refugee_day_article.pdf

Implementing a Trauma-Informed Approach, Public Libraries Online, US. https://publiclibrariesonline.org/2020/04/implementing-a-trauma-informed-approach/

Library Memory Project, Wisconsin, US. https://www.librarymemoryproject.org/

Medical Library Association, Chicago, IL, US. https://www.mlanet.org/

National Immigration Forum, Washington, D.C., US. https://immigrationforum.org/

Public Library Association, ALA, Chicago, IL, US. https://www.ala.org/pla/

Sustainability and Libraries: ALA and Sustainability, American Library Association, Chicago, IL, US. https://libguides.ala.org/SustainableLibraries

Sustainable Libraries Initiative, Bellport, NY, US. https://sustainablelibrariesinitiative.org/

Trauma-Informed Libraries, Capital District Library Council, Latham, NY, US. https://cdlc.libguides.com/trauma-informed_libraries/home

United Nations Intergovernmental Panel on Climate Change, Geneva, Switzerland. https://www.ipcc.ch/

World Health Organization, United Nations. https://www.who.int/

CHAPTER 18

LIBRARIES ARE SUSTAINABILITY LEADERS

Rebekkah Smith Aldrich and Lisa Gangemi Kropp

ABSTRACT

The library profession must embrace the idea that every job is a climate job, and confront the realities of the wider world through a lens of climate justice, as they prioritize relevant and responsive services and programs. The broad issue of sustainability has permeated the core of library services and is transforming the foundation upon which public libraries build their ideals.

By viewing every job as a climate job, libraries and library workers are true sustainability leaders. The triple bottom line (TBL) framework leads libraries into the realm of sustainable thinking, allowing what once felt overwhelming and unattainable to turn into something powerful and dynamic because of collective impact and the recognition that: local matters, working together matters, focusing on diversity matters, and helping all voices be heard matters. Libraries matter because we continue to work together toward meaningful change.

This chapter explores a unique library certification program centered on sustainability and the TBL framework that allows library workers from public, academic, and school libraries to shine a lens on climate justice and climate action work, through offering innovative programs, collections, and services that also use the United Nations (UN) Sustainable Development Goals (SDGs) as a guide toward making every job a climate job.

Keywords: Sustainability; triple bottom line; climate justice; climate action; public libraries; academic libraries; sustainable thinking; climate job; sustainable development goals; sustainable libraries certification program; sustainable libraries initiative

---

How Public Libraries Build Sustainable Communities in the 21st Century
Advances in Librarianship, Volume 53, 249–261
Copyright © 2023 by Rebekkah Smith Aldrich and Lisa Gangemi Kropp
Published under exclusive licence by Emerald Publishing Limited
ISSN: 0065-2830/doi:10.1108/S0065-283020230000053023

INTRODUCTION

Through a commitment to equity, access, and intellectual freedom, libraries have created and defended the knowledge commons that provides the necessary pipeline to open access, community connections, resource sharing and shared life experiences. Libraries create connections for their communities and continually iterate the curation of content in this framework based on the local, regional, national, and global trends impacting the provision of resources and services.

The broad issue of sustainability has been linked to public libraries since the work of the American Library Association (ALA) Task Force on the Environment (ALA, 1990) in the 1990s and grew broadly with the inception of the UN SDGs in 2014 (International Federation of Library Associations and Institutions (IFLA), 2014). Community sustainability aligns directly with the tenets of library service and is becoming a transformative initiative for public libraries around the world. The concept of sustainability, bolstered by the framework provided by the SDGs, allows libraries of all types to contribute to local community resilience in relation to global community resilience by weaving individual threads of their local service community into a cohesive cloth that strengthens the social fabric of all our communities.

In response to the demands of its membership, ALA named sustainability as a core value of the profession in recognition of the UN Intergovernmental Panel on Climate Change (IPCC) finding that the immediate consequences of climate change were far more dire than originally predicted (ALA, 2019). The calls for urgent climate action issued by scientists, policy makers, and advocates from around the world should be heeded by all. The library profession will need to embrace the idea that every job is a climate job and confront the realities of the wider world through a lens of climate justice as they prioritize relevant and responsive services and programs (ALA Council Committee on Sustainability, 2022, p. 4).

THEORETICAL FRAMEWORKS

Due to social and economic disruption, the impacts of climate change, and political separatism, our societies can be presented as, feel, or actually be, fragmented. This leads to distrust and destabilization of communities. As a library's leadership considers how best to position the library in a community to contribute to its resilience, it should focus on the aspirations of its community and find commonalities to bridge growing divides. To do this work authentically, librarians must look internally at our own institutions and ensure we are effective in meeting community needs.

On an international level, the UN SDGs are impacting policy and decision making on a much broader scale than in the United States. In the United States, a lack of attention due to political inaction at the federal level means that many Americans consider the word "development" in the SDGs as referring to "developing" countries. The Center for Sustainable Development at Brookings reports that the United States is not on track to fully achieve a single SDG (2022).

A growing number of library professionals in the United States are working to convey the urgency around climate action and to streamline the entry points for this work by simplifying complex concepts around sustainable development, climate action, and the economic shifts necessary to both mitigate and adapt to climate change (Aldrich, 2018, p. 90). The following are two key frameworks that have garnered traction in the US library community and are serving as the catalyst for work that looks more like the SDG-focused efforts in other countries:

- Sustainable Thinking (Aldrich, 2018)
- Triple Bottom Line (Elkington, 1997; Shaffer, 2018).

Sustainable Thinking

Sustainable Thinking is a concept that aligns decision making with sustainable, resilient, and regenerative actions to affect a necessary mindset shift to re-center organizational culture with a focus on helping communities thrive in the face of disruption. Sustainable Thinking, as applied to public libraries, refers to the alignment of a library's core values and resources – including staff time and energy, facilities, collections, and technology – with the local and global community's right to endure, bounce back from disruption, and thrive by bringing new and energetic life to fruition through choices made in all areas of library operations and outreach in the face of the breakdown of traditional approaches, policies, and doctrines that no longer serve, or in fact, never served, society in the modern world (Aldrich, 2018, pp. 41, 62).

Triple Bottom Line

Thinking sustainably is holistic, asking the leader to consider all aspects of almost every choice. From how we craft benefits and support for library workers to facility decisions and service, program, and outreach design, holism is complicated and can feel overwhelming. A simple framework to make this work more achievable is called the TBL that provides a definition of sustainability and was adopted by the ALA (2019) as a core value of the library profession in 2019. TBL asks businesses to think beyond the traditional bottom line of profits and to consider the environmental and social costs of decisions, since ignoring these factors will deplete natural resources and the workforce, thereby negatively impacting the traditional bottom line in the long term (Elkington, 1997; Shaffer, 2018). Libraries may not focus on profits, but we do have fiscal realities to confront, particularly as the economy is at the center of the causes of climate change. As we consider TBL as a decision-making rubric to help library leaders make better decisions, we are seeking to balance:

- Environmental Stewardship
- Social Equity
- Economic Feasibility

Environmental Stewardship is the care for the Earth and its natural resources, from seeking renewable sources of energy, to water conservation, to responsible use of natural resources (NOAA, 2022).

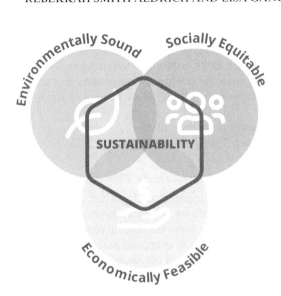

Photograph of TBL. Source: Sustainable Libraries Initiative.

Social Equity are the issues surrounding justice, equity, diversity, and inclusion, ensuring that all members of a community are treated with respect, empathy, and dignity (United Way of the National Capital Area, 2021).

Economic Feasibility refers to the fiscal viability of a decision. Is it affordable to the institution or community or, perhaps, is it something an institution or community cannot afford to ignore in the face of the other two elements of the TBL despite what may, at the outset, seem like a large investment (Aldrich, 2018, p. 65).

This call for every library, regardless of location, size, or type, to consider climate justice speaks to the critical ingredient of effective work on the topic of climate change: the focus on local initiatives. Grassroots discussions, understanding, and action are identified as mechanisms for addressing the four keys to success associated with *iterative risk management* as identified by the UN IPCC in 2014 (UN, 2014) and adapted by Aldrich (2018). These four key areas along with their definitions are:

- *Local Matters* refers to adaptations that strengthen communities because they are place and context-specific.
- *Working Together* refers to complementary actions that are planned and implemented across levels, from individuals to governments.
- *Focus on Diversity* recognizes that diverse interests, circumstances, social-cultural contexts, and expectations benefit the decision-making process.
- *Help All Be Heard* refers to the expanded capacity that occurs when increasing the voice and influence of low-income and vulnerable community groups and expanding their partnerships with local government.

Libraries are particularly well positioned to assist, if not lead, in all of these key areas. Libraries and library employees work in almost every town, school,

Libraries Are Sustainability Leaders 253

campus, hospital, prison, and corporation. Libraries support local units of society in scope and scale and pull groups of people together to work on common issues and build connections with other social justice focused groups in the community to achieve collective impact.

A PRACTICAL APPROACH: SUSTAINABLE LIBRARIES CERTIFICATION PROGRAM

Libraries have repeatedly proven that they are resilient entities, adapting and changing services as new technologies emerge, as the library as a third space in the community takes hold, and as library programs and services shift to incorporate equity, diversity, inclusion, and justice (EDIJ) work.

The notion of shifting our economic model to create healthy, information rich, safe spaces and simultaneously address the systemic social issues that leave segments of our populations more vulnerable in the face of climate change is ambitious. But that is exactly the reason why *libraries* need to focus on climate change. What other community organization has the platform to influence both organizational and community culture through such a mindset shift?

> We all need access to clean air, clean water, clean food and a safe place to call home. Climate change threatens all basic building blocks of life. (Council Committee on Sustainability, 2022, p. 3)

In 2015, the Sustainable Libraries Initiative (SLI) (n.d.) was formed by volunteer members of the New York Library Association, representing public, school, and academic libraries. The group convened to acknowledge that the impacts of climate change demanded a response from the library community. The initiative focused on moving away from "going green" checklists or once-a-year attention on the issue on Earth Day and began to consider how to shift mindset to address both:

- Climate Change Mitigation, the reduction of greenhouse gas emissions which are causing climate change; and
- Climate Change Adaptation, helping communities adapt and build their resilience in the face of the impacts of climate change such as food scarcity and severe weather.

The one thing all in the initiative agreed upon was that this, while overwhelming, was a true leadership opportunity for libraries, as the issues are connected to seemingly everything: the economy, politics, technology, and long-standing inequities in society. The group focused on how to make the topic understandable, approachable, and most importantly, actionable. The initiative is designed to be adaptive and scalable for libraries of different sizes and types. Resources include webinars and training, a "Road Map to Sustainability" designed to walk libraries through a series of prompts and real-life examples that show how incremental changes can build over time to effective change within a library and the community it serves, recommended reading, vendor lists, and more.

The centerpiece of the SLI, now a national program, is its award-winning Sustainable Library Certification Program (SLCP) (SLI, n.d.) that allows public libraries, academic libraries, and school librarians to work through a series of action items to achieve the designation of a sustainable library or, in the case of school libraries, librarian. The SLCP addresses work in the following categories for public, academic, and school libraries:

Public and academic libraries focus on the following categories:

- Organizational Commitment
- Energy
- Materials Management – Waste and Recycling
- Materials Management – Purchasing
- Transportation
- Land Use
- Water
- Collective Impact
- Social Cohesion
- Community Resilience
- Financial Sustainability
- Collections

School libraries focus on the following categories:

- Partnerships and Community Involvement
- Leading Beyond the Library
- Social Equity and Resiliency
- Standards and Curriculum
- Collections

The goal of the certification program is to help participants achieve a mindset shift by deliberately and intentionally working through the progression of categories to influence organizational culture. Each category has required and recommended action items, allowing libraries of different sizes to find areas within their individual buildings that are manageable to focus on with staff. There is no set timetable or deadline. Each library and its team, or each individual school librarian working through the categories, can proceed at a pace that is comfortable and allows for meaningful institutional change to occur. The categories are not just checklists of work to accomplish. They are built to allow foundational and lasting change to become embedded in the workflow, policies, and procedures of each institution. The following case study of the Lindenhurst Memorial Library, a public library located in Lindenhurst, NY, illustrates the certification program and its positive impacts on the mindset of the library's board and staff.

The Context: Lindenhurst Memorial Library Case Study

Lindenhurst Memorial Library serves 42,000 residents spread over a six-mile radius that runs down to the Great South Bay, a large body of water situated between Long Island, NY and Fire Island, NY and includes Lindenhurst Village and North Lindenhurst. The population served by the library is based on the boundaries of the Lindenhurst Union Free School District as stated in the Lindenhurst Memorial Library charter. On October 30, 2012, Superstorm Sandy came ashore on the south side of Lindenhurst flooding half of the village's streets and took two days or more to recede. Those in North Lindenhurst had no electricity for over a week due to wind and tree damage (Taylor, 2013). The library is physically located within the Village of Lindenhurst, and did not lose electricity during the storm. Library administration made the decision to keep the building open for longer hours to allow residents to charge devices, gather information, and have a warm place to go. However, what residents really needed was long-term access to Federal Emergency Management Agency (FEMA) support and other insurance agencies. The library made the decision to dedicate its one community room to become an official FEMA/State Disaster Recovery Center (Lohr, 2012). For the next nine months, a steady stream of residents came to the library seeking answers and for assistance filling out claim forms.

In the six years after Superstorm Sandy, the library had a change in library administration (new director and board members) and had a bond referendum for a $14.9 million building renovation and expansion project voted down by residents. What changed in the public's perception of the library? It had seemingly gone from an essential part of the safety net of the community to having a lack of trust equity during the six-year time period. It became clear that there was a disconnect between the library, the community, and the organizations it served. This is when the library director made the decision to enter the Sustainable Libraries Certification Program (L. Kropp, personal communication, June 20, 2022).

DISCUSSION OF THE CASE STUDY

The authors provide a brief discussion of key thematic threads that emerged in the application of the SLCP at the Lindenhurst Memorial Library.

The Public Library as a Strong Institution

The SLCP does not exclusively focus on environmental issues. It uses the TBL model and incorporates social equity and fiscal responsibility into its design. Those areas spoke to library administration overall because they saw the real-life impacts of all three areas through the role they played in the aftermath of Superstorm Sandy. They knew that their role needed to be centered on relevant and strongly responsive community service and on creating a gathering place that served everyone in the community. As SDG 16 states, we must promote peaceful and inclusive societies, providing justice for all while building effective, accountable, and inclusive institutions (UN, 2015). There was clear work to do if the library wanted to affect a mindset shift not only within the community, but also with staff and administration to show that sustainability work was necessary to build a stronger, more resilient library and community and to teach residents how they could respond to climate change and adaptation within the community (L. Kropp, personal communication, June 20, 2022).

Public libraries, like Lindenhurst, focused their work around the 12 categories for public libraries outlined in the SLCP to begin building the necessary mindset shift in staff, administration and the community. These 12 categories have a direct correlation with the UN SDGs and provided the library with an internationally focused starting point around which to expand programs and services.

Organizational Commitment

Starting with an organizational commitment meant talking with both administration and staff to gauge interest and to begin shaping what this work would look like. A staff survey administered in the initial first steps of the process helped set a starting line, surfacing personal beliefs, attitudes and perceptions of the areas staff felt the library was not addressing under the TBL umbrella. Staff opted in for either more information about the program, or to voluntarily join the library's sustainability team. This team was adapted to the needs and size of each participating library. There were 45 staff members at the start of the certification process at Lindenhurst, and 7 were active members of the sustainability team, including the Business Manager and Head Custodian, ensuring continuity across all departments and areas of the library.

Energy, Materials Management, Transportation, and Water

Sections on energy, materials management, transportation, and water allowed the team to gauge cost savings to the community made when the library board invested in new windows; HVAC (heating, ventilation, and air conditioning system), and a white roof to raise its reflectivity back in 2013. The library's energy consumption post infrastructure work showed more than a 30% savings in energy bills. The team took a look at recycling measures in the building and saw multiple areas for improvement. Conducting a waste audit as part of the certification showed that if the library could begin consistent recycling efforts, it would divert 35–40% of current waste going to the dumpster.

Through a unique partnership with the village, the library began recycling its cardboard, paper, and plastic by placing its recyclables for pick-up in front of the administration building. These first steps gave the library a positive starting point to share with the community, as we began working behind the scenes on strengthening community partnerships. Along the way, the board focused on creating a sustainability policy, reviewing financial areas to ensure a healthy fund balance for fiscal sustainability, and embedding sustainable language into staff job descriptions and other areas such as collection management and purchasing policies. The board voted to eliminate late fees, helping to remove barriers to materials that disproportionately affect lower income families and individuals. This work was the equivalent of the library "putting on its oxygen mask first" in order to have a strong base from which to serve the community.

Photograph of Library Garden. Source: Photo courtesy of Lindenhurst Memorial Library (https://www.lindenhurstlibrary.org).

Collective Impact, Social Cohesion, and Community Resilience

In order to focus on action items in the areas of collective impact, social cohesion, and community resilience, staff members joined local organizations such as the Kiwanis and Rotary clubs, the Chamber of Commerce, and other civic-based groups. They began further integrating the library into the community to help advance issues and projects that were community – not library – driven. The issue of food insecurity was present in the local community and became a larger need during the early COVID-19 pandemic. One example was the expansion of the library's community garden and a newly formed seed lending library. Local residents and members of both the Kiwanis and Key clubs donated time in the garden, weeding and helping to maintain the space. Over the last three growing seasons, the library has donated over 200 pounds of produce directly to community members and to local food pantries.

In 2022, Library Youth Services staff started a "Mutt Club" and planted vegetables in the garden that are pet friendly. The library also partnered with their state senator to be a drop off point for his pet food drive, collecting 136 pounds of pet food for the local shelter.

Additionally, the library created the dedicated staff position of "sustainability coordinator" during the certification process to further embed the notion that this was not a "one and done" checklist of action items. The board and staff committed to making the topic of creating a strong and resilient community a

Photograph of recycling center. *Source: Photo courtesy of Lindenhurst Memorial Library (https://www.lindenhurstlibrary.org)*

vital component to library best practices and services. One of the first things the sustainability coordinator accomplished was the creation of a Little Free Pantry within the library building, in addition to the food pantry drop off boxes. Now, the library was letting the public know that they didn't have to wait or stand in line at a food pantry to receive care. They could come into the building (open 58 hours a week) anytime it was open, to take or leave items on the shelves of the Little Free Pantry space, with dignity.

During 2020 and 2021, when library services were limited due to pandemic restrictions, community members still came to drop off food to the pantry bins, donating over 1,300 pounds of food and other essential items. These donations demonstrated the impact a small group can have on a larger audience, and it helped the library's sustainability team extend their efforts to introduce programming and services that would educate the community about climate adaptation and mitigation.

Expanded Service Capacity

Going through the SLCP provided the foundation needed for the library to demonstrate to the community ways in which they could collectively work together. The library hosted its first Repair Cafe to showcase repairing and repurposing materials and appliances instead of throwing them out. The Sustainability Coordinator applied for and received a *"Resilient Communities: Libraries Respond to Climate Change"* grant from ALA in 2020. This grant allowed the library to purchase materials for a sustainability collection as well as being designated as a Climate Resilience Hub through the organization Communities Responding to Extreme Weather (CREW) (n.d.). In 2021, a community wide emergency prepare-a-thon held in partnership with the Village of Lindenhurst, involved over 10 agencies and featured the library's sustainability coordinator working with the local Red Cross chapter to show residents what types of paperwork they should have easy access to in the event of an emergency, what to pack in an emergency bag for family and pets during hurricane season, etc. A partnership with the State University of NY at Stony Brook placed a social worker intern at the library to assist residents with social services requests and applications, connecting them to counseling services, homeless shelters, and other agencies. The library mentored the community on collective impact by participating in the Great Give Back – a day of service opportunities for library patrons across New York (About GGB – *The Great Give Back*, n.d.). In 2021, the Great Give Back saw 263 libraries participate in service events such as food drives, beach and river clean-ups, and coupon collections, partnering with over 80 local and national organizations. During these events in 2021, over 20,000 items were collected and donated, including food, toiletries, books, pet supplies, and coupons.

After SLCP Certification

After achieving the SLCP certification, the board began implementing a revised building renovation and expansion plan, which the community supported and passed by public referendum in October 2019. This community support allowed the library to fully utilize sustainable design in their renovation plans. The library received over $220,000 in grants to add a 73-KW solar panel array to the roof, two electric vehicle (EV) car charger stations, solar parking lot lights, and energy-efficient LED lighting to the building.

The library's participation in the SLCP positioned it as a strong collective impact partner in the community as this clearly demonstrated the "Five Conditions of Collective Success" (Kania & Kramer, 2011). On Earth Day in April 2022, the Suffolk County Executive held a press conference in the library's parking lot to announce a $12 million investment in EV charging infrastructure. He chose the library as the location for this event deliberately, citing their leadership on the topic of sustainability and community resilience, which was a **common agenda** for the county. The **shared measurement systems** utilized – reduction of greenhouse gas emissions and reduction of food insecurity – was a metric county officials, area businesses, and service organizations had identified as well, aligning the library with the larger effort. The library's strong emphasis on partnerships to avoid redundancies and to build on the work of others resulted in **mutually reinforcing activities** that strengthened the community overall. The library's administration deliberately built a system of **continuous communication** with leaders in the community, becoming embedded in the collective impact work of the community and establishing itself as a trusted partner. This was evidenced by the turnout at the 2022 Earth Day event with several key municipal leaders noting the library as part of their network on the issue of reducing greenhouse gas emissions. The library director, their new Sustainability Coordinator, and the library's governance board all demonstrated what creating a micro-**backbone support organization** looks like. They did not leave this effort by chance or osmosis. A dedicated staff person and directives from the board to the director to focus on connecting with others in the community doing this work allowed the library to be part of this collective impact effort.

CONCLUSION

This case study shows what the creators of the SLI (n.d.) recognized: that the process of going through the certification program created systemic change within the library and exemplified the best practices of collective impact in the field, while also encouraging libraries to become collective impact co-creators in their communities. By adopting the triple bottom line framework for decision-making and cross-referencing activities with the SDGs, library leaders in the SLCP share a common agenda, allowing them to create the individual set of building blocks needed in their own community, to shape the mindset shift toward making the world a better place. Libraries are well suited to promote peaceful and inclusive societies for sustainable development, and the SLCP helps library leaders provide effective, accountable, and inclusive institutions at all levels. The TBL framework leads libraries into the realm of sustainable thinking, allowing what once felt overwhelming and unattainable to turn into something powerful and dynamic because of collective impact and the recognition that: local matters, working together matters, focusing on diversity matters, and helping all voices be heard matters. Libraries matter because we continue to work together toward meaningful change.

REFERENCES

ALA Council Committee on Sustainability. (2022). *Sustainability in libraries: A call to action.* Sustainability Briefing. American Library Association. Retrieved January 3, 2023 from https://www.ala.org/aboutala/sites/ala.org.aboutala/files/content/SustainabilityInLibraries_Briefing_Final_April2022.pdf

Aldrich, R. S. (2018). *Sustainable thinking: Ensuring your library's future in an uncertain world.* ALA Editions, an Imprint of the American Library Association.

Aldrich, R. S., Antonelli, M., Dallas, S., Ho, A., Lesneski, T., Tanner, R., Woodruff, M., & Zabriskie, C. (2018). *ALA Special Task Force on Sustainability.* American Library Association. https://olos.ala.org/sustainrt/tag/ala-special-task-force-on-sustainability/

American Library Association (ALA). (1990). Resolution on the Environment. https://www.ala.org/aboutala/sites/ala.org.aboutala/files/content/governance/policymanual/updatedpolicymanual/ocrpdfofprm/50-12environmental.pdf

American Library Association (ALA). (2019). *Resolution for the adoption of sustainability as a core value of librarianship.* https://bit.ly/3nBEX87

Communities Responding To Extreme Weather (CREW). (n.d.). https://www.climatecrew.org/

Council Committee on Sustainability. (2022). *Sustainability in libraries: A call to action.* American Library Association. https://www.ala.org/aboutala/sites/ala.org.aboutala/files/content/SustainabilityInLibraries_Briefing_Final_April2022.pdf

Elkington, J. (1997). *Cannibals with forks: The triple bottom line of 21st century business.* New Society.

International Federation of Library Associations and Institutions (IFLA). (2014). *Lyon Declaration on Access to Information and Development.* The Lyon Declaration. Retrieved January 3, 2023, from https://www.lyondeclaration.org/

IPCC. (2014). *Climate Change 2014: Synthesis Report. Contribution of Working Groups I, II and III to the Fifth Assessment Report of the Intergovernmental Panel on Climate Change* [Core Writing Team, R. K. Pachauri and L. A. Meyer (Eds.)]. IPCC.

Kania, J., & Kramer, M. (2011). Collective impact (SSIR). *Stanford Social Innovation Review.* Retrieved September 21, 2022, from https://ssir.org/articles/entry/collective_impact

Lohr, B. C. (2012, November 7). Lindy Library Is Official FEMA Disaster Recovery Center. *Patch.* https://patch.com/new-york/lindenhurst/lindy-library-is-official-fema-disaster-recovery-center

National Oceanic and Atmospheric Administration (NOAA). (2022). *Stewardship definitions: Educating people in environmental stewardship practices.* U.S. Department of Commerce. https://www.

noaa.gov/office-education/noaa-education-council/ monitoring-resources/common-measure-definitions/stewardship-definitions

OECD. (2017). *What people know and think about the sustainable development goals.* OECD Development Communication Network (DevCom). https://www.oecd.org/development/pgd/International_Survey_Data_DevCom_June%202017.pdf

SDG. (2022). https://www.brookings.edu/wp-content/uploads/2022/03/2022_Brookings_State-of-SDGs-in-the-US.pdf

Shaffer, G. L. (2018). *Creating the sustainable public library: The triple bottom line approach.* Libraries Unlimited.

Sustainable Libraries Initiative (SLI). (n.d.). *Sustainable Libraries Certification Program.* Sustainable Libraries Initiative. Retrieved September 22, 2022, from https://sustainablelibrariesinitiative.org/ about-us/program-faq

Taylor, A. (2013, October 25). Hurricane Sandy, Before, After, One Year Later. *The Atlantic.* https://www.theatlantic.com/photo/2013/10/hurricane-sandy-before-and-after-one-year-later/100616/

The Great Give Back. (n.d.). About GGB. https://thegreatgiveback.org/index.php/about-tggb/

United Nations (UN). (2014). *AR5 Climate Change 2014: Impacts, adaptation, and vulnerability report.* https://www.ipcc.ch/report/ar5/wg2/

United Nations (UN). (2015). *Transforming our world: The 2030 Agenda for Sustainable Development.* United Nations Department of Economic and Social Affairs. Retrieved January 4, 2023 from https://sdgs.un.org/2030agenda

United Way of the National Capital Area. (2021, August 27). *What is social equity? Definition & examples.* United Way. https://unitedwaynca.org/blog/what-is-social-equity/

CHAPTER 19

REFLECTING ON PUBLIC LIBRARY–SOCIAL WORK COLLABORATION: CURRENT APPROACHES AND FUTURE POSSIBILITIES

Rachel D. Williams and Lydia P. Ogden

ABSTRACT

This reflective chapter examines recent trends in social work–public library partnerships. The chapter begins by framing interprofessional collaboration between social work and public libraries as a vehicle for the collective impact that can create lasting and sustainable change in communities. Next in the chapter is an overview of the current state of public libraries' capacity to support individuals in crisis through community partnerships. Next is a description on how interprofessional collaboration can support public libraries in general and the importance of collaboration with social work more specifically. A presentation of the existing models of public library–social work partnerships and their impact on the role of public libraries in their communities follows, with a discussion of the services provided by public libraries, and how partnerships might change the nature of social work practice. Finally, the chapter concludes with a discussion of the barriers and challenges to these partnerships with an eye toward the future of such partnerships and developing their capacity to

How Public Libraries Build Sustainable Communities in the 21st Century
Advances in Librarianship, Volume 53, 263–271
Copyright © 2023 by Rachel D. Williams and Lydia P. Ogden
Published under exclusive licence by Emerald Publishing Limited
ISSN: 0065-2830/doi:10.1108/S0065-283020230000053024

enhance the health and wellbeing of their patrons, and the safety and resilience of their cities and communities.

Keywords: Public libraries; social work; interprofessional collaboration; social work–public library partnerships; health and wellbeing; sustainable communities; strong institutions

INTRODUCTION: THE SOCIAL WORK–PUBLIC LIBRARY PARTNERSHIP

The shared commitment to equitable provision of services and resources to their communities and a commitment to supporting human rights are values that align the fields of public librarianship and social work. Public libraries offer safe and climate-controlled shelter, multimedia resources, programming, and a dynamic array of services, all without a direct cost to their patrons. It is no wonder that a person might turn to public libraries during a crisis. Indeed, in the United States, members of the public have done so increasingly in the last two decades, seeking safety and assistance in libraries during mental health crises, crises related to substance use, and crises related to housing and mental health treatment in response to changing mental health policies and deinstitutionalization processes, the opioid epidemic, and affordable housing shortages (Feuerstein-Simon et al., 2022; Pressley, 2017; Real & Bogel, 2019). While housing, mental health, and substance use challenges are not the typical domains of public libraries, they are central to social work practice. Thus, public libraries can, and recently have, benefitted from partnerships with social workers. These partnerships support the knowledge and skill development of library staff so that they can continue to effectively provide services to all patrons, and particularly those experiencing crises.

Interprofessional collaborations between social workers and public libraries can also be framed as a vehicle for collective impact. Collective impact is defined as "the commitment of a group of important actors from different sectors to a common agenda for solving a specific social problem" (Kania & Kramer, 2011). Collective impact comprises five different facets, including a common agenda, shared measurement systems, mutually reinforcing activities, continuous communication, and backbone support organizations. Interestingly, social work–public library partnerships already embrace two facets of collective impact initiatives, including a focus on a common agenda and participation in mutually reinforcing activities. The commitment to these two facets of collective impact initiatives is particularly valuable for public libraries and their ability to address an array of social problems within communities. The collective impact approach moves beyond collaboration and relies on a framework that includes continuous support via external organizations and years of communications work that results in shared understandings and measurement approaches. While social work–public library partnerships reflect some aspects of collective impact initiatives, they are still growing.

To demonstrate the potential of public library–social work partnerships, in this chapter, we began by providing an overview of the current state of public libraries' capacity to support individuals in crisis through community partnerships, describing how interprofessional collaboration can help in general, and the importance of collaboration with social work more specifically. We also pointed to collective impact as a framework by which social work–public library partnerships can make a lasting and sustainable impact in communities. In the next section, we present the existing models of public library–social work partnerships and their impact on the role of public libraries in their communities, the services provided by public libraries, and how these partnerships might change the nature of social work practice as well. Finally, we discuss the barriers and challenges to these partnerships with an eye toward the future of such partnerships and developing their capacity to enhance the health and wellbeing of their patrons, and the safety and resilience of their cities and communities.

PROMISING MODELS OF PUBLIC LIBRARY AND SOCIAL WORK PARTNERSHIPS

Public library staff increasingly work with patrons who are dealing with complex and difficult life concerns. Being able to address those concerns requires appropriate knowledge, skills, capacity, and time, all of which can be barriers for library staff who want to help. As a recent NPR piece explained, patrons experience increasingly complex challenges that are often beyond the scope of what library workers are trained to handle (Benson, 2022). This is where social workers come in. Social workers in libraries build relationships with staff, patrons, and community partners, and connect patrons with resources and support. Partnerships between social workers and public libraries started in 2009 at the San Francisco Public Library, and the number and kinds of partnership models continue to develop. There are several existing models of public library–social work partnerships, each with their own strengths and limitations.

Full-Time Staff Model

The full-time staff model has full-time social workers on staff within a single library. Application of this model means that there is always someone with special training available to work with patrons in crisis. That person provides resources and referrals to other social service agencies and resources and serves as a highly specialized reference person of sorts. For example, Richland Library in South Carolina has a robust team of social workers and has offered social work services for several years (Richland Library, 2022). While this approach can be successful, the primary barrier with this model, as with others that include social workers, is adequate and continual funding for the social worker's salary. There are also issues related to role diffusion (what is the social worker's job and what is the librarian's job), and perhaps a sense of professional boundaries. Do social workers belong in libraries? While social workers are accustomed to serving roles in host institutions (i.e., institutions that are not inherently social work institutions, such as schools, police departments, courts, and hospitals) and frequently serve on interdisciplinary teams as a result, library–social work collaborations are relatively new as of 2009 and are not as commonplace.

Part-Time Staff Model

Partnership models that rely on part-time social work staff offer the same strengths and barriers as full-time on-staff social workers and require less funding. Due to their part-time nature, part-time social workers might not be onsite when a crisis emerges. Therefore, they have a limited presence in the library and a limited capacity to address the needs of people in crisis. Similarly, some public libraries have partnered with social service agencies that send social workers to libraries on a rotating schedule or on an as-needed basis, which again can provide important services within libraries but would not provide a reliable presence in case of an acute crisis. When interdisciplinary mobile crisis teams are available in a community to help an individual in acute psychiatric distress, the problems associated with the part-time nature of the social workers in these cases are diminished. This leaves a gap in services for clients who are experiencing other types of crises or who may be experiencing psychiatric symptoms that do not require mobile crisis or other emergency services but are challenging to manage for library staff without specific training.

Internships

Social workers receive a significant portion of their professional training through intensive internships. Hiring multiple interns can address the problems of intermittent scheduling, since having two or more could ensure regular coverage. Funding issues are also addressed through the internship model since the internships are typically either unpaid or reimbursed through federal work-study and other external funding sources. However, social work interns need supervision from qualified social workers, which likely would have to be found outside the library system. Ideally, public libraries would be able to host social work interns in addition to hiring social workers who can provide a consistent presence and support. Furthermore, interns typically stay only nine months, leading to high rates of intern staffing turnover in a system that may rely on knowledge of community resources and community partnerships, such as is gained over time. Wahler et al. (2022) outline best practices for public libraries considering partnerships that involve hiring social work student field placements.

The Trauma-Informed Library Transformation (TILT) project, developed by the University of Georgia School of Social Work and the Athens Clarke-County Library, relies heavily on interns who staff resource tables, perform community assessments, evaluate initiatives, link patrons to area resources, and ensure library services are provided using a trauma-informed lens (Eades, 2019). The project also included a social work needs assessment of the community and established an after-school peer-mentoring program for teen girls from local high schools. This project represents a specific public university-based school of social work partnership with a public library that models how to successfully staff a library with interns. While there is turnover of individual interns, commitment from a single university and a constant fieldwork advisor addresses the issue of intern turnover while retaining the cost-effectiveness of the model for libraries.

Trauma-Informed Library Service (TILT)

It is useful to consider briefly what is meant by the term "trauma" in the TILT model and elsewhere and what it means for services provided by any institution to be trauma-informed. According to the Substance Abuse and Mental Health Services of the US (SAMHSA),

> Individual trauma results from an event, series of events, or set of circumstances that is experienced by an individual as physically or emotionally harmful or life threatening and that has lasting adverse effects on the individual's functioning and mental, physical, social, emotional, or spiritual well-being. (SAMHSA, 2014, p. 7)

SAMHSA defines trauma-informed services as services that provide individuals with a sense of safety and security, that establish trustworthiness of and between service providers, and that use collaboration and mutuality in decision-making and delivery of services, avoiding authoritative approaches. Furthermore, where possible, peer support and/or peer-delivered services are facilitated, enhancing the experience of both trustworthiness and mutuality for many. This model of trauma-informed practice ensures stakeholders are empowered and that their voices and choices are valued. Historical and present-day experiences of oppression are acknowledged, along with cultural and gender-based differences that can contribute to one's experience in receiving services. All told, a trauma-informed institution recognizes the prevalence of trauma and provides services that actively avoid re-traumatization. TILT promotes a sense of safety for all members, including those providing services. This means that TILT approaches are designed in support of not just patrons, but library staff as well.

When considering the role of crisis intervention in public libraries, it is therefore important to consider the experiences of both patrons and library staff. Whether social workers are present in a library or not, it is useful for all employees to be versed in some level of crisis management training, including how to identify a patron in crisis, how to interact, and when to reach out for help from other professionals, whether those are on-staff social workers or social work interns, mobile crisis workers, or other emergency services. It then follows that library staff would also benefit from institutional practices that support their wellbeing using trauma-informed principles.

Staff Training Model

The need for trauma-informed library service connects to the final model of social work and public library partnership. In this model, social workers, who are routinely trained in crisis intervention, design and implement training for lay-persons, including library staff, to effectively engage in trauma-informed crisis intervention work. This model has inherent advantages. No social worker needs to be onsite at the library at any time, except when part of a mobile crisis team or other urgent response intervention. It is cost-effective since it does not require adding expensive salary lines to a library employment roster. If offered at multiple, convenient times, such training can be done with minimal disruption to daily operations at a library. Furthermore, issues of role confusion between librarians and social workers are avoided. Although not all librarians see it as part of their role to help clients experiencing psychosocial crises, they do want to be able to help and do the right thing – to act skillfully (Williams & Ogden, 2021). Those efforts to help and do the right thing can lead to role diffusion and even a sense of burnout. Despite these drawbacks, this model is the most efficient way for libraries to improve their trauma-informed crisis intervention services to patrons. Additional support – and again, training – is provided to enhance library staff wellbeing, especially in communities where working with patrons in crisis is more commonplace.

THE VALUE OF THE COLLECTIVE IMPACT FRAMEWORK

As described above, current approaches to social work–public library partnerships outlined are successful, but also present potential barriers. Major barriers include funding, the emotional toll on staff, professional capacity, and roles/boundaries. Looking at the perceptions of library social workers, Giesler (2021) similarly identified role confusion as a barrier and further noted isolation and differing philosophies as additional challenges. When developing social work–public library partnerships, adopting a collective impact framework can be helpful. A collective impact framework can be defined as "the commitment of a group of important actors from different sectors to a common agenda for solving a specific social problem at scale" (University of Kansas, 2022). Weaving equity throughout, collective impact initiatives rely on five conditions, including a common agenda, shared measurement, mutually reinforcing activities across stakeholders, continual communication through building relationships and trust, and backbone support. These conditions contribute to a framework in which not just immediate, short-term needs are met. With collective impact, long-term social change can occur – change that is not reliant on already having a specific solution and processes identified is possible. Additionally, in collective impact initiatives, it is important to have funding resources that support "collective processes, measurement reporting systems, and community leadership that enable cross-sector coalitions to arise and thrive" (Kania & Kramer, 2011). Aligning funding goals to the long-term goals of a collective impact initiative positively reduces the emotional toll and expands the professional capacity to support these kinds of partnerships by giving stakeholders the agency and support to develop long-term, sustainable processes. For public library–social work partnerships, a collective impact framework can mean the difference between an isolated, short-term solution and a long-term change within not just the library, but the broader community as well. Collective impact approaches introduce opportunities to build social work–public library partnerships into sustainable ones that may also include additional stakeholder organizations such as senior centers, public health departments, schools, municipal departments, local businesses, and other community anchors and advocates.

Building and leveraging social work–public library partnerships within communities has influenced the perception of public libraries and impacted the nature of public library work. Developments in public library services and the adaptive use of library spaces go beyond the overlap of tasks between library workers and social workers. First, in pointing to library services, Winberry and Potnis (2021) examine the perception of social innovation in public libraries, identifying several areas, including lifelong learning; emergency response; civic engagement; economic development; and diversity and inclusion. Supporting social innovation and critical needs of community members in libraries has encouraged social work–public library partnerships. Public libraries are viewed as essential organizations and as community anchor institutions (Taglang, 2015). Second, as openly accessible spaces, public libraries offer shelter, services, and support for all community members, and particularly those in crisis. From providing community resource fairs to mobile technology labs to emphasizing inclusive rather than punitive policies and practices, public libraries provide a wide range of support for their communities. As a result, a notable amount of work performed by public library staff relies on community engagement and providing support for people in crisis. These collaborative efforts are central to being able to meet the needs of patrons in crisis in a sustainable way.

LIBRARIES AS STRONG INSTITUTIONS

The public library–social work collaborations described above support the United Nations Development Programme Sustainable Development Goal 3 to ensure healthy lives and promote well-being for all, and at all ages (United Nations Development Programme, 2022). These collaborations help ensure the health and wellbeing of all community members are meaningfully addressed, either directly or indirectly, through the many dynamic resources provided at libraries. These dynamic resources might include, for example, wellness initiatives like yoga, cooking classes, workforce training and resources, and community partnerships with social work and public health. Additionally, public library–social work collaborations support the United Nations Development Programme Sustainable Development Goal 16 by reinforcing the role of the public library as an effective, accountable, and inclusive institution that promotes inclusion and justice for all community members (United Nations Development Programme, 2022). Social work–public library partnerships are part of the larger picture of developing sustainable cities and communities, as outlined in the United Nations Development Programme Sustainable Development Goal 11 through the provision of a safe and equitable place for all, and the ability to serve as a resilient backbone of their communities (United Nations Development Programme, 2022). Public libraries are important for community identity, development, and connecting people and ideas, which, in turn, support the development of sustainable communities (American Library Association, 2022).

CONCLUSION

Introducing a collective impact lens to existing models of social work–public library partnerships allows us to develop a vision for sustainable, long-term actions using processes designed to address complex community needs. However, these approaches traditionally focus on isolated impact for one library in one segment of a community. A collective impact approach invites the possibility of cross-sector, broader communities of practice designed to address difficult problems in a way that scales local context into broader knowledge sharing. The result of this approach is supported, sustainable action that has far-reaching implications for public library practice. A vision for the future of public library–social work partnerships is one that is well-funded, allows collaboration to "arise and thrive," and acknowledges the impact of trauma on library staff, social workers, and community members, particularly patrons experiencing crises. This future focuses on the health and wellbeing of all and allows the public library to be one among many stakeholders focused on common agendas that support the safety, resilience, and sustainability of communities.

REFERENCES

American Library Association. (2022). Impact on Community Development. Libraries Matter. https://www.ala.org/tools/research/librariesmatter/impact-community-development

Benson, D. (2022). *Why your local library might be hiring a social worker*. Shots: Health news from NPR. https://www.npr.org/sections/health-shots/2022/01/03/1063985757/why-your-local-library-might-be-hiring-a-social-worker

Eades, R. B. (2019). Implementing a trauma-informed approach. *Public Libraries*, 58(5), 58–63. https://publiclibrariesonline.org/2020/04/implementing-a-trauma-informed-approach/

Feuerstein-Simon, R., Lowenstein, M., Dupuis, R., Dolan, A., Marti, X. L., Harvey, A., & Ali, H. (2022). Substance use and overdose in public libraries: Results from a five-state survey in the US. *Journal of Community Health*, 47(2), 344. https://doi.org/10.1007/s10900-021-01048-2

Giesler, M. (2021). Perceptions of the public library social worker: Challenges and opportunities. *The Library Quarterly*, 91(4), 402–419. https://doi.org/10.1086/715915

Kania, J., & Kramer, M. (2011). Collective impact. *Stanford Social Innovation Review*. https://ssir.org/articles/entry/collective_impact#

Pressley, T. (2017). Public libraries, serious mental illness, and homelessness: A survey of public librarians. *Public Library Quarterly*, 36(1), 61–76. https://doi.org/10.1080/01616846.2017.1275772

Real, B., & Bogel, G. (2019). Public libraries and the opioid crisis, part 2: Community-centered responses. *Public Library Quarterly*, 38(3), 270–289. https://doi.org/10.1080/01616846.2019.1635326

Richland Library. (2022). Meet with a social worker. https://www.richlandlibrary.com/services/meet-social-worker

SAMHSA. (2014). SAMHSA's Concept of Trauma and Guidance for a Trauma-Informed Approach. https://ncsacw.acf.hhs.gov/userfiles/files/SAMHSA_Trauma.pdf.

Soska, T. M., & Navarro, A. (2020). Social workers and public libraries: A commentary on an emerging interprofessional collaboration. *Advances in Social Work*, 20(2), 409–423. https://doi.org/10.18060/23690

Taglang, K. (2015, April 17). Literacy and Access Roles Help Libraries Remain Vital Community Anchors. Benton Institute: 40 Years of broadband and society. https://www.benton.org/blog/literacy-and-access-roles-help-libraries-remain-vital-community-anchors

United Nations Development Programme. (2022a). What are the sustainable development goals? https://www.undp.org/sustainable-development-goals

United Nations Development Programme. (2022b). Goal 3: Good health and well-being. https://www.undp.org/sustainable-development-goals#good-health.

United Nations Development Programme. (2022c). Goal 11: Sustainable cities and communities. https://www.undp.org/sustainable-development-goals#sustainable-cities-and-communities

United Nations Development Programme. (2022d). Goal 16: Peace, justice, and strong institutions. https://www.undp.org/sustainable-development-goals#peace-justice-and-strong-institutions

University of Kansas. (2022). University of Kansas Community Toolbox: Chapter 2, Section 5. Collective Impact. https://ctb.ku.edu/en/table-of-contents/overview/models-for-community-health-and-development/collective-impact/main

Wahler, E. A., Ressler, J. D., Johnson, S. C., Rortvedt, C., Saecker, T., Helling, J., Williams, M. A., & Hoover, D. (2022). Public library-based social work field placements: Guidance for public libraries planning to become a social work practicum site. *Public Library Quarterly*. https://doi.org/10.1080/01616846.2022.2044264

Williams, R. D., & Ogden, L. P. (2021). What knowledge and attitudes inform public librarians' interactions with library patrons in crisis? *Journal of Librarianship and Information Science*, *53*(1), 62–74. https://doi.org/10.1177%2F0961000620917720

Winberry, J., & Potnis, D. (2021). Social innovations in public libraries: Types and challenges. *The Library Quarterly*, *91*(3), 337–365. https://doi.org/10.1086/714315

CHAPTER 20

THE INTERSECTION OF US PUBLIC LIBRARIES AND PUBLIC HEALTH

Suzanne Grossman

ABSTRACT

While public libraries are well-established as a place to borrow books and use reference materials, they are less recognized for the services and programs they offer to their local communities. These programs and services often directly or indirectly impact the health of patrons and the larger community.

While some public libraries offer programs that address patron health in collaboration with other health professionals, such as those at local universities, public health departments, and other health-related organizations, these collaborations are often informal, offered for an indefinite period of time, and rely on finite funding. While public health professionals and organizations are often overlooked in public library collaborations, they are a natural fit for collaboration.

As public libraries serve the needs of vital and often vulnerable members of our communities, it is important to build sustainable community partnerships when offering programs and services that impact patron health. This will not only identify organizations committed to improving the health of these populations and those that provide reliable resources; it will also streamline information and provide consistent information to identify safe and reliable resources on social media, the internet, and in the community.

This chapter serves as a reflective narrative which explores how public libraries and community organizations can collaborate, identifies anticipated challenges, and describes considerations and strategies for addressing these challenges. The ultimate goal is to identify how libraries can expand the depth and breadth

---

How Public Libraries Build Sustainable Communities in the 21st Century
Advances in Librarianship, Volume 53, 273–282
Copyright © 2023 by Suzanne Grossman
Published under exclusive licence by Emerald Publishing Limited
ISSN: 0065-2830/doi:10.1108/S0065-283020230000053025

of both library services and public health organizations to sustainably improve the health of the local community.

Keywords: Public health; public libraries; sustainable partnerships; community organizations; health literacy; healthy communities

HOW US PUBLIC LIBRARIES ADDRESS HEALTH

Public libraries in the United States (US) are well-established as a place to borrow books and use reference materials. However, they are less recognized for the services and programs they offer to their local communities which often address the health-related needs of their patrons. For example, some libraries hire social workers to connect patrons with mental health services (Benson, 2022). There are also many examples of how public libraries have partnered with local universities to promote health through exercise classes, access to information, and reading help for school children (Lenstra, 2019). The types of collaborations between public libraries and community partners to promote health are seemingly limitless. As a community hub, public libraries address patrons' health, both directly (e.g., offering health advice) and indirectly (e.g., addressing the social determinants of health [SDOH]).

One way in which public library programs directly address patron health is by building health literacy (Public Library Association (PLA), 2019). Healthy People 2030 distinguishes between organizational and personal health literacy. Organizational health literacy is defined as, "the degree to which organizations equitably enable individuals to find, understand, and use information and services to inform health-related decisions and actions for themselves and others" (Office of Disease Prevention and Health Promotion, n.d.-a). Therefore, public libraries, by definition, support and promote organizational health literacy of their patrons. Personal health literacy focuses on how individuals find, understand, and use information (Office of Disease Prevention and Health Promotion, n.d.-a). Public libraries support personal health literacy of their patrons by directing them to information that is reliable and easy to understand. Libraries have been found to help a variety of populations develop health literacy, including older adults, underserved populations, and the general public (Barr-Walker, 2016; Centers for Disease Control & Prevention, 2022).

While helping patrons develop health literacy, it is important for librarians to consider the readability of consumer health information to which patrons have access, including circulating and digital materials related to health. Some libraries have health lending libraries with blood pressure cuffs, food scales, and other health-related materials for patrons to check out and monitor their health at home (Dunnington, 2017). Libraries also collaborate with community partners to provide services directly related to health. For example, the Brooklyn Public Library has partnered with Visiting Nurse Service of New York to provide weekly blood pressure screenings and the Virginia Department of Health has supplied free COVID-19 testing kits to be distributed at 38 state library branches and systems (Brooklyn

Public Library, 2022; Virginia Department of Health, n.d.). These resources help patrons to learn and make decisions about their own health, including navigating diagnoses, seeking out treatment, and understanding complex medical systems (American Library Association, 2022).

More commonly, library programs and services indirectly impact health, as they relate to the SDOH (Morgan et al., 2018). SDOH contribute to health outcomes and are related to characteristics of the social and physical environment (Office of Disease Prevention and Health Promotion, n.d.-b). Philbin et al. (2019) identified 10 SDOH that public libraries address through their programs and services: health care access, addiction, stress, food, early life, the social gradient, social exclusion, work and employment, disaster response, and social support. Other scholars have identified additional determinants of health that public libraries address including education and literacy, mental health, finances, legal aid, and housing (Morgan et al., 2018; Philbin et al., 2019; Whiteman et al., 2018). Some examples of common public library programs indirectly related to health include storytimes for young children and parents/ caregivers; English language and culture classes to help newcomers to the US learn the language, navigate complicated systems, and meet people; as well as a place for school children to do homework afterschool and get assistance with their homework. Many public libraries also provide career services, such as assistance searching for jobs, preparing a resume and job application, and interview preparation (Holcomb et al., 2019). Helping patrons to secure employment enables patrons to earn a stable income to afford housing, food, and other necessities, which ultimately improves their health and well-being. The myriad ways in which public libraries address SDOH are important as they help patrons to build and develop skills, navigate systems to improve patrons' quality of life.

FRAMEWORK FOR SUSTAINABLE PARTNERSHIPS

Public libraries often have similar goals to public health programs as they promote the health of populations and communities, as well as health education initiatives, which help individuals develop skills to improve health literacy and own health (World Health Organization, 1998). Existing collaborations between public libraries and public health organizations are often temporary. Therefore, looking at a sustainable model for partnership can help to formalize these collaborations to benefit patrons, library staff, and public health organizations in reaching the shared goal of building healthy communities.

It is important to acknowledge how, on a micro-level, public libraries address sustainable development goal (SDG) 16. The United Nations launched SDGs in 2015 as "a universal call to action to end poverty, protect the planet, and ensure that by 2030 all people enjoy peace and prosperity" (United Nations Development Programme, 2022). SDG 16, in particular, focuses on "peace, justice, and strong institutions" (United Nations Development Programme, n.d.). This means that SDGs cannot be met without organizations that support the health and well-being of communities and constituents (United Nations Development

Programme, n.d.). Library partnerships with other community health organizations that promote a similar mission and goals related to accessing health-related information can address SDG 16. These partnerships build stronger institutions through shared decision making and outcomes as they prioritize health and well-being within their communities (United Nations, n.d.).

This chapter explores how US public libraries and community organizations collaborate, identifies anticipated challenges in these collaborations, and describes considerations and strategies for addressing these challenges. The goal is to identify how collaborations among public libraries and public health organizations expand the scope and depth programs to sustainably improve the health of local communities.

PUBLIC LIBRARIES AND PUBLIC HEALTH: POTENTIAL FOR COLLABORATION

Public libraries provide access to information and follow their mission as a community space that welcomes all people. They provide educational and social opportunities for all patrons (American Library Association, n.d.). They bring people together and promote social and community connections through a range of programs and services (Klinenberg, 2018). These programs include classes (e.g., cooking, English as a second language), job preparation (e.g., resume writing and searching for jobs), and community engagement (e.g., health fairs). Often, these programs are offered through collaborations with community organizations and partners. The format of these collaborations depends on many factors including funding, identifying the most pressing community health needs, the size and bandwidth of both the library and health organization, and the time that can be dedicated to such a collaboration. These collaborations are important as they provide help and support for patrons as well as library staff.

There are many examples of collaborations between public libraries and health-serving organizations across a range of health-related topics. The following two case studies provide examples of successful library and public health partnerships.

In response to the opioid epidemic, the Philadelphia Free Library, Philadelphia Department of Public Health, and the University of Pennsylvania collaborated to offer overdose reversal training. A total of 29 hour-long trainings were held in 10 public library branches across the city and open to all community members. This training was found to significantly increase participants' confidence in responding to an overdose and intent to carry and administer naloxone when needed (Lowenstein et al., 2021).

While this is an important program that clearly addressed the needs of the library community, which was greatly impacted by the opioid epidemic, this is an example of how public library and public health collaborations are often informal, offered for a finite period of time, and rely on continued funding. However, building a partnership that incorporates the five conditions of collective impact (Kania & Kramer, 2011) would address these limitations by building sustainable programs. The five conditions of collective impact are: (1) *common agenda*, or that organizations have a mutual understanding of the problem and steps to solving the problem; (2) *shared measurement systems*, using consistent data collection and measurement methods; (3) *mutually reinforcing activities*, or coordinating multiple stakeholders; (4) *continuous communication*, longstanding and ongoing partnerships to build trust among community stakeholders, and (5) *backbone support organizations* with staff dedicated to the particular collaboration (Kania & Kramer, 2011). Therefore, following a collective impact framework would require that public libraries and health-serving organizations create a shared, sustainable vision so that these collaborative programs become part of all stakeholders involved, rather than a temporary collaboration or a singular event that takes place in the library (Kania & Kramer, 2011). Through this formalized process, institutional support including sustainable funding, designated staff, and program evaluation, would also be needed (Kania & Kramer, 2011).

There are emerging examples of collective impact initiatives between public libraries and health-serving organizations. One example is a collaboration between the Chicago Public Library and the Chicago Housing Authority to address a shortage of affordable housing. In 2019, the city opened three publicly subsidized housing locations with public library branches in each building (Kimmelman, 2019). This project aimed to not only increase availability and affordability of housing, but also to serve as a community hub through access to onsite public libraries. The physical library space in each of these housing locations includes access to books, magazines, technology, and other information resources, meeting spaces, and includes additional seating so that children have a place to study after school. Access to these services in low-income communities is important as it provides a hub for people to spend time and build community, as well as a place for community members to access resources, complete homework, or access other necessary information. As of 2019, the city planned to include skill-development workshops, such as resume writing, interview skills, and other job preparation skills in collaboration with other organizations in the community (Chicago Public Library, 2019). This public housing–public library partnership provides a centralized resource and common space for community members to learn and interact with each other.

By formalizing the roles of the library and the housing authority in this collaboration, each partner has a specific role and area of expertise. The buildings were designed so that the library space met the needs of the collaborating partners. While this level of partnership may not be possible in all collaborations, alternative versions could include libraries renting or providing space within library facilities for local health or social service partners, which would expand access for community members to these services. It is important to consider how public library–public health partnerships can frame their collaborations to meet the conditions of collective impact and SDG 16.

ANTICIPATED CHALLENGES

Public library patrons often have queries about health information (Shubik-Richards & Dowdall, 2012; Whiteman et al., 2018; Wood et al., 2000), although the quality of information provided varies from library to library and librarian to librarian (Rubenstein, 2015). Rubenstein (2015) found that the health information librarians provided depended on several factors, including confidence, anxiety, and comfort providing health-related information, as well as professional training.

Therefore, public librarians' own health literacy can impact their ability to provide health-related information, as well as concerns that the information they provide will serve as medical advice (Rubenstein, 2015). Librarian confidence related to the provision of health information is often rooted in their own health literacy and their ability to identify reliable sources of health information and understand the information to answer patrons' health related questions (Yi & You, 2015). As a result, public librarians often have difficulty responding to patron questions related to direct health information. This can be exacerbated if, for example, there are existing health-related collaborations in the library that end, as patrons may expect the same level of health information from the librarians as they did from the health-related partner. Public librarians have reported feeling comfortable when addressing inquiries indirectly related to health, such as education and literacy (Morgan et al., 2018; Whiteman et al., 2018). However, another challenge is that library spaces are often communal and not private, so patrons have reported confidentiality concerns when discussing personal information with librarians (Yi & You, 2015). Patrons and librarians continue to report obstacles accessing and providing health information.

These challenges became particularly evident as the COVID-19 pandemic forced many public libraries to become central figures in their communities to stop the spread of the virus. Many public libraries now serve as COVID-19 testing and vaccination sites, telehealth hubs, and sites where community members can take home free rapid tests (Weil, 2022; Virginia Department of Health, n.d.). The pandemic allowed public libraries to fill the role of a trusted health information source.

LIBRARIAN TRAINING AND HEALTH INFORMATION

Training public librarians to provide health information has shown to increase librarian confidence and preparedness in responding to these inquiries (Morgan et al., 2018; Radick, 2015; Rubenstein, 2015; Wood et al., 2000). The role of health information in Library and Information Science (LIS) programs has increasingly become a topic of conversation, and studies have shown that LIS programs do not adequately prepare students to address health-related patron inquiries (Detlefsen, 2012). To address this, the Medical Library Association has developed a health information professional (HIP) training as a part of the LIS curriculum for "information professionals...who have specialized knowledge in quality health information resources" (Medical Library Association, 2022a). However, how well this training prepares LIS students to work as librarians with specialized knowledge of health information is still emerging (Ma et al., 2018).

There are also programs for existing staff, such as the Medical Library Association's Consumer Health Information Specialization (Medical Library Association, 2022b) which focuses on preparing public librarians to address queries directly related to health, participation may create a burden for the employee given the time and cost of participating in the training. Additionally, this training requires that librarians keep up with the demand of health-related patron inquiries (Friedheim, 2017; Weil, 2022). Therefore, by developing sustainable partnerships with health-serving community partners, librarians can point the patron to both information and services that directly address their health-related inquiry.

A branch of the Free Library of Philadelphia, the South Philadelphia Health and Literacy Center, which opened in 2016, seeks to do just that. This building includes a free library branch as well as a primary care office for the Children's Hospital of Philadelphia, a city health center, and a recreation center (Children's Hospital of Philadelphia, 2017). In addition to a lending library, the library helps patrons with health-related inquiries before or after doctors' appointments, often in the building. Librarians can also direct patrons to the doctors' offices in the building if they have a question that librarians do not feel comfortable answering.

CONSIDERATIONS AND STRATEGIES

This chapter is focused on public health–public library collaborations specific to the United States; however, there are many examples of these collaborations in other countries and looking to these models and examples may help the United States in identifying ways to develop sustainable collaborations. Libraries in Scandinavian countries, for example, have developed ongoing outreach to welcome immigrant populations. Specifically, libraries in Norway have served as a meeting place to help immigrants' social and political integration in a new culture (Audunson et al., 2011; Johnston & Audunson, 2019). Additionally, Canada and the UK provide a glimpse into how community-led public libraries can address budget cuts and build sustainable partnerships when meeting the needs of the community (Pateman & Williment, 2013).

While there are many opportunities for collaboration, public libraries are an often-overlooked area for community outreach and collaboration in the field of public health. As public libraries serve the needs of vital and often vulnerable community members, it is important to build sustainable community partnerships when offering programs and services that impact patron health. By working together to build sustainable programs, public libraries and health-serving organizations can efficiently and effectively collaborate to reach their shared goals of improving community health ultimately benefiting library patrons as they will receive consistent health-related messaging from community partners, know where to go for information, and be confident in the information they receive. Building partnerships that focus on collective impact and SDG 16 can help formalize these collaborations, provide sustainable funding and staffing, and promote the shared goal of improving the health and well-being of the individuals and communities that the library and health-related organization serve.

ACKNOWLEDGMENT

The author would like to thank Dr Ann C. Klassen, Dr Denise Agosto, Rabbi Nancy Epstein, Dr Mark Winston, Dr Ana Martinez-Donate, Lisa Jane Erwin, Dr Carolyn Cannuscio, and the Healthy Library Initiative.

REFERENCES

American Library Association. (2022, June 27). *Health Information in Libraries.* Resource Guides, American Library Association. https://libguides.ala.org/health-information

American Library Association. (n.d.). *Libraries Matter: Impact Research.* http://www.ala.org/tools/research/librariesmatter/

Audunson, R., Essmat, S., & Aabø, S. (2011). Public libraries: A meeting place for immigrant women? *Library & Information Science Research, 33*(3), 220–227. https://doi.org/10.1016/j.lisr.2011.01.003

Barr-Walker, J. (2016). Health literacy and libraries: A literature review. *Reference Services Review, 44*(2), 19–205.

Benson, D. (2022, January 3). Why your local library might be hiring a social worker. *NPR.* https://www.npr.org/sections/health-shots/2022/01/03/1063985757/why-your-local-library-might-be-hiring-a-social-worker

Brooklyn Public Library. (2022, May 9). Blood pressure screening. *Brooklyn Public Library: Events & Classes.* https://www.bklynlibrary.org/calendar/blood-pressure-screening-kings-bay-library-20220509

Centers for Disease Control and Prevention. (2022, January 19). *Health Literacy: Libraries.* https://www.cdc.gov/healthliteracy/education-support/libraries.html

Chicago Public Library. (2019, January). *Mayor Emanuel, Chicago Public Library and Chicago Housing Authority Open Innovative Library Projects.* https://www.chipublib.org/news/mayor-emanuel-chicago-public-library-and-chicago-housing-authority-open-innovative-library-projects/

Children's Hospital of Philadelphia. (2017, December 29). South Philadelphia health and literacy center: Special synergy. *Community Impact Report.* https://www.chop.edu/news/south-philadelphia-health-and-literacy-center-special-synergy

Detlefsen, E. G. (2012). Teaching about teaching and instruction on instruction: A challenge for health sciences library education. *Journal of the Medical Library Association, 100*(4), 244–250. https://doi.org/10.3163/1536-5050.100.4.005

Dunnington, S. (2017, October 16). South Philly Library patrons can now check out health equipment. Billy Penn at WHYY. https://billypenn.com/2017/10/16/south-philly-library-patrons-can-now-check-out-health-equipment/

Friedheim, N. (2017, February 9). Libraries struggle with a new role: Social services center. *Honolulu Civil Beat.* https://www.civilbeat.org/2017/02/libraries-struggle-with-a-new-role-social-services-center/

Holcomb, S., Dunford, A., & Idowu, F. (2019, September). *Public libraries: A community's connection for career services.* John J. Heldrich Center for Workforce Development, Rutgers University Edward J. Bloustein School of Planning and Public Policy. https://files.eric.ed.gov/fulltext/ED601682.pdf

Johnston, J., & Audunson, R. (2019). Supporting immigrants' political integration through discussion and debate in public libraries. *Journal of Librarianship and Information Science, 51*(1), 228–242. https://doi.org/10.1177/0961000617709056

Kania, J., & Kramer, M. (2011). Collective impact. *Stanford Social Innovation Review, 9*(1), 36–41. https://doi.org/10.48558/5900-KN19

Kimmelman, M. (2019, May 15). Chicago finds a way to improve public housing: Libraries. *The New York Times.* https://www.nytimes.com/2019/05/15/arts/design/chicago-public-housing.html

Klinenberg, E. (2018). *Palaces for the people: How social infrastructure can help fight inequality, polarization, and the decline of civic life.* Crown.

Lenstra, N. (2019). Exercise your resources: Public libraries partner with academic institutions for health programming. *American Libraries*, *50*(5). https://link.gale.com/apps/doc/A587260987/BIC?u=viva_jmu&sid=bookmark-BIC&xid=47a2ccd7

Lowenstein, M., Feuerstein-Simon, R., Dupuis, R., Herens, A., Hom, J., Sharma, M., Sheni, R., Encarnacion, L., Flaherty, C., Cuellar, M., & Cannuscio, C. (2021). Overdose awareness and reversal trainings at Philadelphia public libraries. *American Journal of Health Promotion*, *35*(2), 250–254. https://doi.org/10.1177/0890117120937909

Ma, J., Stahl, L., & Knotts, E. (2018). Emerging roles of health information professionals for library and information science curriculum development: A scoping review. *Journal of the Medical Library Association*, *106*(4), 432–444. https://doi.org/10.5195/jmla.2018.354

Medical Library Association. (2022a). Explore a career in health sciences information. *Medical Library Association*. https://www.mlanet.org/page/explore-this-career

Medical Library Association. (2022b). Professional development: Consumer health information specialization. *Medical Library Association*. https://www.mlanet.org/page/chis

Morgan, A. U., D'Alonzo, B. A., Dupuis, R., Whiteman, E. D., Kallem, S., McClintock, A., Fein, J. A., Klusaritz, H., & Cannuscio, C. C. (2018). Public library staff as community health partners: Training program design and evaluation. *Health Promotion Practice*, *19*(3), 361–368. https://doi.org/10.1177/1524839917735304

Office of Disease Prevention and Health Promotion. (n.d.-a). *Healthy literacy in Healthy People 2030*. U.S. Department of Health and Human Services, Office of the Assistant Secretary for Health, Office of the Secretary, U.S. Department of Health and Human Services. https://health.gov/healthypeople/priority-areas/health-literacy-healthy-people-2030

Office of Disease Prevention and Health Promotion. (n.d.-b). *Social determinants of health*. U.S. Department of Health and Human Services, Office of the Assistant Secretary for Health, Office of the Secretary, U.S. Department of Health and Human Services. https://health.gov/healthy-people/priority-areas/social-determinants-health

Pateman, J., & Williment, K. (2013). *Developing community-led public libraries*. Routledge. https://doi.org/10.4324/9781315576817

Philbin, M. M., Parker, C. M., Flaherty, M. G., & Hirsch, J. S. (2019). Public libraries: A community-level resource to advance population health. *Journal of Community Health*, *44*(1), 192–199. https://doi.org/10.1007/s10900-018-0547-4

Public Library Association (PLA). (2019). *Health literacy, programming, and consumer health information*. http://www.ala.org/pla/initiatives/healthliteracy

Radick, L. (2015). Improving health literacy, one public library at a time. *American Libraries Magazine*, *November/December 2015*, 48–53.

Rubenstein, E. L. (2015). Health information and health literacy: Public library practices, challenges, and opportunities. *Public Library Quarterly*, *35*(1), 49–71. https://doi.org/10.1080/01616846.2016.1163974

Shubik-Richards, C., & Dowdall, E. (2012). *The library in the city: Changing demands and a challenging future*. The Pew Charitable Trusts Philadelphia Research Initiative. https://www.pewtrusts.org/-/media/legacy/uploadedfiles/wwwpewtrustsorg/reports/philadelphia_research_initiative/philadelphialibrarycitypdf.pdf

United Nations. (n.d.). *Goal 16: Promote just, peaceful and inclusive societies*. United Nations: Sustainable Development Goals. https://www.un.org/sustainabledevelopment/peace-justice/#:~:text=Goal%2016%3A%20Promote%20just%2C%20peaceful%20and%20inclusive%20societies&text=Conflict%2C%20insecurity%2C%20weak%20institutions%20and,great%20threat%20to%20sustainable%20development

United Nations Development Programme. (2022). *The SDGs in action*. United Nations Development Programme. https://www.undp.org/sustainable-development-goals

United Nations Development Programme. (n.d.). *Goal 16: Peace, justice, and strong institutions*. United Nations Development Programme. https://www.undp.org/sustainable-development-goals#peace-justice-and-strong-institutions

Virginia Department of Health. (n.d.). *Supporting testing access through community collaboration*. Virginia Department of Health. https://www.vdh.virginia.gov/coronavirus/protect-yourself/covid-19-testing/stacc/

Weil, J. Z. (2022, January 18). The public library is the latest place to pick up a coronavirus test. Librarians are overwhelmed. *The Washington Post*. https://www.washingtonpost.com/dc-md-va/2022/01/18/librarians-coronavirus-tests-workers/

Whiteman, E. D., Dupuis, R., Morgan, A. U., D'Alonzo, B., Epstein, C., Klusaritz, H., & Cannuscio, C. C. (2018). Public libraries as partners for health. *Preventing Chronic Disease*, *15*(64), 170392. http://doi.org/10.5888/pcd15.170392

Wood, F. B., Lyon, B., Schell, M. B., Kitendaugh, P., Cid, V. H., & Siegel, E. R. (2000). Public library consumer health information pilot project: Results of a National Library of Medicine evaluation. *Bulletin of the Medical Library Association*, *88*(4), 314–322.

World Health Organization. (1998). *Health promotion glossary*. https://apps.who.int/adolescent/second-decade/section/section_9/level9_15.php

Yi, Y. J., & You, S. (2015). Understanding the librarian/user gap in perception of health information services: A phenomenographic approach. *Journal of Librarianship and Information Science*, *47*(4), 356–367. https://doi.org/10.1177/0961000614532861

CHAPTER 21

PUBLIC LIBRARIES' CONTRIBUTION TO SUSTAINABLE DEMENTIA-FRIENDLY COMMUNITIES

Timothy J. Dickey

ABSTRACT

Persons living with dementia (PLWD) constitute a global epidemic of more than 50 million people around the world, and tens of millions more serve as their caregivers. Public libraries must learn to assist, support, and sustain those with dementia in their communities. The good news is that some of the most powerful non-pharmacological interventions for PLWD – healthy lifestyle choices, lifelong learning for mental stimulation, and the stimulation and support of social networks – all are embedded in public libraries' core mission. Thus, library services for the underserved population of PLWD and their caregivers can make a huge collective impact toward sustainable communities, social justice, and strong institutions.

Libraries can provide this help through dementia-friendly customer service and through programming that both supports individuals and develops and strengthens social relationships. Libraries can further promote good health and well-being, both through information resources and with targeted older adult programming. We can simultaneously contribute to social justice, mitigating the stigma and the deleterious effects of dementia which can be worse within minority communities. The positive impact of library dementia services can

---

How Public Libraries Build Sustainable Communities in the 21st Century
Advances in Librarianship, Volume 53, 283–292
Copyright © 2023 by Timothy J. Dickey
Published under exclusive licence by Emerald Publishing Limited
ISSN: 0065-2830/doi:10.1108/S0065-283020230000053026

even be magnified through collective impact when different institutions within a community work together toward dementia-friendly standards.

This reflective chapter details the operation of library services for PLWD and their caregivers, providing concrete examples of dementia-friendly customer service, collection development, information and reference services, and a wide variety of older adult programming. Together, these library dementia services can create a powerful and positive impact through lifelong learning, mental stimulation, and social connections.

Keywords: Older adults; older adult programming; public libraries; library dementia services; dementia-friendly customer service; persons living with dementia (PLWD); lifelong learning; social relationships

INTRODUCTION

Persons living with dementia (PLWD) constitute a global epidemic, and public libraries are already serving this growing population in our communities. This reflective chapter defines and explores library services for PLWD and their caregivers; it also provides concrete examples of dementia-friendly customer service, collection development, information and reference services, and a wide variety of older adult programming. Together, these library dementia services support powerful and positive impacts on individuals through lifelong learning, mental stimulation, and social connections, and they contribute to sustainable communities even as the population ages.

PUBLIC LIBRARIES AND DEMENTIA SERVICES

Some 55 million people around the world live with Alzheimer's Disease and related dementias; the "estimated total global societal cost of dementia" exceeds $1.3 trillion per year (World Health Organization, 2019). In America, there are an estimated 6.5 million PLWD in 2022, and tens of millions more providing unpaid caregiving support to them (Alzheimer's Association of the United States, 2022). Dementia also menaces minority communities with a "silent epidemic" of more insidious impact:

> Even when racially and ethnically diverse older adults do receive a diagnosis, they are more likely to be diagnosed at a later stage and receive a less comprehensive diagnostic evaluation than the ethnic majority group, making them more vulnerable to adverse outcomes. (Alzheimer's Disease International, 2021, p. 233)

Thus, library services for PLWD are also a pressing issue of social justice. The COVID-19 pandemic has only deepened the repercussions on older adults waiting for diagnoses, or those living at risk in care facilities (ADI, 2021, p. 249).

In response to this epidemic, public libraries are learning to assist, support, and sustain PLWD in their communities. Some great news lays the foundation for library dementia services: some of the most powerful non-pharmacological interventions for dementia – healthy lifestyle choices, lifelong learning for mental stimulation, and the stimulation and support of social networks (ADI, 2018) – are already embedded in public libraries' core mission. Healthy living and mental and social stimulation not only comprise a good prescription for sustaining brain health in the face of cognitive decline, but these same practices can also in many cases be shown clinically to *delay or even prevent* cognitive decline as adults age (ADI, 2018, p. 23; de Waal et al., 2013; Gibbs, 2021).

Sustainable Development of Communities

Library services for the underserved population of PLWD and their caregivers thus make a huge collective impact on the broader society, as categorized in the *United Nations Sustainable Development Goals* (2015). Specifically, library dementia services contribute to UN SDG #3 "Good health and well-being," as a specific aspect of ensuring health and well-being for people as they age and face potential challenges of cognitive decline. By becoming themselves more inclusive toward PLWD, public libraries further serve the interests of social and institutional justice (Goal #16). And finally, public libraries as core institutions within their communities cooperate with other institutions in creating cities and communities that are more dementia-friendly, and thus are more "inclusive, safe, resilient and sustainable" (Goal #11).

Public libraries accomplish all of these goals through the application of social capital (Wojcichowska & Topolska, 2021): directing *resources* from the library – library programs, dementia-friendly services, and collection development – toward serving the dementia community and effecting broader social change. Library dementia services help both the underserved and often stigmatized (ADI, 2012) older adults with dementia, and their caregivers, effectively to function within the larger community. Libraries provide this help both through dementia-friendly customer service, and through programming that both supports individuals, and develops and strengthens social relationships. Libraries further promote good health and well-being through information resources and with targeted older adult programming. Public libraries thus also simultaneously contribute to social justice, mitigating the stigma and the deleterious effects of dementia, which can be worse within minority communities.

Case Studies in Collective Community Impact

"Collective impact" magnifies the positive impact of library dementia services (Kania & Kramer, 2011), when different institutions within a community work together toward cooperation and dementia-friendly standards. Libraries, on the one hand, might be embedded in a process across multiple sectors of a community, following the collaborative model of the organization Dementia-Friendly America (2022). In this model, a city such as Tempe, AZ, adopts collaborative and sector-specific recommendations in multiple community sectors (banks, local government, healthcare, faith communities, businesses, and libraries), to create a local ecosystem where PLWD are more able to thrive and maintain their daily living (City of Tempe, AZ, 2022).

Such collaborative efforts, across sectors including libraries, may even extend throughout a state. The Wisconsin Alzheimer's Institute (University of Wisconsin-Madison, 2022), for instance, empowers institutions in many sectors to share resources and resources and innovative ideas for dementia care. One project specific to the public library sector supports dementia-programming partnerships among 21 public libraries across Wisconsin; information about their activities, resources, partners, and email updates are available to other interested libraries, and freely across the web (Library Memory Project, 2022).

Alternatively, public libraries within a community may choose first to empower themselves with dementia-friendly training and inclusive practices, and then serve as a community backbone, sharing their vision with local leaders in other sectors. The Akron-Summit County (OH) Public Library provides a recent example. This public library system first embarked on a project of dementia-friendly practices: training all library staff as certified Dementia Friends (Dementia Friends USA, 2022), creating circulating Memory Kits to engage PLWD and their caregivers, and maintaining a new Resource page on the library website. The library staff then turned around and shared the dementia-friendly commitment and impact in workshops given for local civic and governmental leaders (Akron-Summit County Public Library, 2022).

SERVING USERS LIVING WITH DEMENTIA

Whether serving as a backbone of community action, or working within multi-sector collaborations to meet a common agenda, public libraries have a great deal to offer PLWD and caregivers in their communities. Several core areas of traditional public library service specifically support good brain health, provide social justice, and sustain PLWD through the central non-pharmacological interventions of healthy lifestyles, mental stimulation, and social stimulation (Dickey, 2020). Staff at all public libraries with older adults in their service population can learn:

- Dementia-friendly communication and customer service;
- Collection development to support dementia-inclusive information services, literacy, and lifelong learning; and
- Appropriate older-adult programming.

Customer Service and Communication with PLWD

The first library service area that materially advances our society toward greater dementia-inclusive practice is customer service and communication. Staff in a library public service department must be trained in awareness and dementia-inclusive practices, and the training should exist in continuous communication with other organizations. Though the progress of dementia symptoms is *highly* individualized, some general guidelines exist for use in libraries (see, for instance, the brief tips in IFLA, 2007, as well as Family Caregiver Alliance, 2022; Dickey, 2020;

Gillick, 2020; Miller, 2015). Some of the most common recommendations for communication with PLWD include the following:

- Make eye contact, and speak to the person instead of about them.
- Get the person's attention before speaking, and avoid distractions.
- Speak clearly and slowly.
- Pay attention to body language, both theirs and your own.
- Use simple language.
- Repetitions and consistent phrasing help to avoid confusion.
- Be a creative listener to show understanding, tolerance, and respect.
- Use simple yes or no questions, and allow extra time for responses.
- Include every-day and comfortable topics in your conversation, such as the weather, familiar objects or subjects.
- Be calm and supportive, and above all, be positive!

Many of these tips directly respond to the basic challenges from cognitive decline in short-term memory, situational focus, and vocabulary, with potential behavioral issues, and lead to more positive relationships with users, while avoiding stigmatization.

Once again, libraries' impact is magnified either through collective impact in shared community efforts or library leadership within the community, and it often depends on partnerships and training. Brief but comprehensive staff training can be obtained through Dementia Friends USA (2022). Communication and customer service training for all frontline library staff is relatively easy to obtain (Bridges Library System, 2021; Akron-Summit County Public Library, 2022) and feeds immediately back into the community's health, well-being, and social justice.

LIBRARY COLLECTION DEVELOPMENT FOR PLWD

The physical collections in many public libraries further contain a cornucopia of materials appropriate for PLWD, as well as for caregivers (and for the education of library staff). Alzheimer's disease and several other forms of dementia do affect the creation of short-term memory and thus commonly degrade a person's ability to follow a long narrative plot. But importantly – and contrary to common wisdom – reading ability *does not disappear* for many PLWD (Bourgeois, 2001; Claridge & Rimkeit, 2018). This research finding is important for public librarians with older adults in their service area: dementia does not make reading programs and literacy moot. On the contrary, librarians already embrace the possibility of dementia-friendly reading programs (Rimkeit & Claridge, 2017). In addition, parts of our current library holdings, when re-purposed, leverage the power of "shared reading" between PLWD and caregivers or library staff (Billington, 2013; Latchem & Greenhalgh, 2014).

This means that libraries' collection development ideally encompasses support for PLWD and their caregivers, with the library thus serving as a dementia-inclusive leader in the community. The IFLA *Guidelines for Library Service to*

Persons with Dementia (2007) proposes a number of appropriate types of library materials:

- Illustrated books, with choices from both the adult and juvenile collections;
- Books for reading aloud;
- Media materials, audio books, music, and kits of sensory and memory-evoking materials; and
- Informational books for caregivers and staff.

Materials Selection

Librarians in this dementia-friendly practice select books with interesting adult topics, large fonts, smaller blocks of text, and evocative illustrations, for reading by, and with PLWD. At the same time, we must avoid any stigma associated with picture books: juvenile non-fiction, or "two-lap books" specifically designed for shared reading often make the best choices. Guides and reading lists are available, such as one by the Alzheimer's Association & the Green-field Library (2019; see also Dickey, 2020). Keeping older adults actively participating in reading for as long as possible allows us to reap benefits in slowing the progress of dementia, and perhaps even preventing some cases of cognitive decline (Lee et al., 2018; Wilson et al., 2021).

In addition, libraries should stock and maintain the most current information in print and online to meet the various information and reference needs of older adults and the caregivers for those experiencing cognitive decline. The information needs encompass diet and brain-healthy living (for prevention), as well as titles on medicine, neurology, caregiver issues, consumer finance, long-term care, and end-of-life support. A variety of memoirs (there even exist first-person memoirs by PLWD) and fiction for all ages that treats PLWD honestly and sensitively rounds out the pertinent collection. As with customer service and communication training, these collection development choices strengthen libraries as community resource hubs to support the information needs of PLWD and caregivers alike.

LIBRARY PROGRAMS FOR PLWD

Finally, there exists a wide variety of library programming options for older adults that offer specific therapeutic benefits for those either living with, or trying to stave off, cognitive decline. Libraries' positive impact on healthy and sustainable communities through participation in dementia services in fact reaches its peak in our adult programming choices. In addition to supporting literacy therapy through reading programs and shared reading with caregivers, many public libraries already are offering two popular instances of dementia-friendly programming: Memory Cafés and the Tales and Travel program. Both programs offer regular mental and social stimulation to older adults and their caregivers, both are easily adopted as an extension of regular library adult programming, and both allow the library to position itself as a leader (or collective-impact collaborator) within the broader community.

Memory Cafés and Tales and Travel

Memory Cafés involve a regular monthly gathering of PLWD (or persons with Mild Cognitive Impairment) and their caregivers, providing both mental and social stimulation and some respite for the care partner (Dementia Society of America, 2022). An hour-long Café meeting usually contains an activity or a discussion topic, designed to stimulate reminiscences and engagement in conversation. The benefits for those living with dementia and Mild Cognitive Impairment (MCI) that library staff have documented for the program include: reducing social isolation, providing enjoyable social interaction, letting the library be an entry point into helpful resources, and basic access to information (Lokvig, 2016). Similarly, the program known as Tales and Travel centers the focus for a monthly social gathering on shared reading and activities that specifically imagine travel to distant countries or provinces. The librarian facilitator leads those with early-stage dementia or MCI and their caregivers in shared reading of folk-tales or poetry, and exploration of maps and images and recipes, all to stimulate social and mental reminiscences around travel (Tales & Travel Memory Programs, 2022). Even during the pandemic, libraries remained active by offering both Memory Cafés and Times and Travel programs in virtual or hybrid environments. Again, the regular mental and social stimulation provide powerful benefits to the neurological and emotional health of the participating older adults.

Art and Music Therapies

The research into art therapies for dementia is not yet comprehensive, but it seems clear that *any kind of creative engagement* (music, dance, poetry, storytelling, painting, drama) strengthens mental "resilience," builds awareness of control over life, and can even counter depression and behavioral issues (NeuroArts Blueprint. With the Aspen Institute and Johns Hopkins University, 2022; McFadden & Basting, 2010). Art therapies can also forge connections to one's culture, and to individual memories as a kind of "life story and reminiscence work." So any kind of creative expression in library programs can boost neuroplasticity and mental resilience, as well as supporting creative cultural connections, and arts programming thus taps more deeply into the potential for community impact.

Music is known as the most powerful memory-preserving art form, as musical memories travel multiple neural pathways and persist longer than other types of information (Clift et al., 2018; King et al., 2019). Capitalizing on the cognitive and behavioral benefits of music therapies, some libraries thus offer sing-along programs or even host dementia choirs to provide musical (and social) stimulation for PLWD. Libraries also partner with organizations using music therapies such as Music and Memory (2022); this program provides PLWD with personalized playlists of music important to their own past (on donated iPods or phones), to reach deeper musical memories, and to stimulate better cognition.

Similar arts programs engage PLWD through other arts media, including a visual-arts program from New York's Museum of Modern Art (2022). The Museum's "Meet Me" provides specialized dementia-friendly events for PLWD and their caregivers, sparking conversations and reminiscence therapies around visual art;

MOMA partners with other museums and cultural heritage institutions to bring the program to other local communities. The Alzheimer's Poetry Project (APP, 2022) facilitates creative engagement with poetry for PLWD, in events that blend shared writing of poetry, and spirited group performances; APP also works with libraries as hosts or program partners. Even drama has its place in the spectrum of dementia-friendly arts programming, with TimeSlips (2022), a complete program of playwriting and shared dramatic production activity among volunteers and PLWD. In all of these examples, public libraries can embrace a leadership position, either within a community-wide multi-sector approach to PLWD, or as a leading institution, sharing the vision of offering regular mental and social stimulation associated with these programs.

CONCLUSION

In sum, library services for PLWD and their caregivers are already empowering sustainable communities as individuals' age. Pertinent library dementia services include dementia-friendly customer service, collection development, information services, and a variety of older-adult programming, including powerful arts-based programs. Together, public library dementia services can create a strong and positive collective impact through lifelong learning, mental stimulation, and social connections. Libraries can either act on their own as a community leader and backbone in developing dementia services, or collaborate with other sectors for maximum collective impact; thus, we are serving PLWD both as individual institutions and as partners with other libraries and with other community stakeholders. Libraries are exercising a leadership role not only in inclusion, justice, and support for neurodiverse persons, but also in strengthening community resilience. In this way libraries can be, in the words of one librarian pioneer in the field, sustainably "part of the dementia care team" (Riedner, 2015) as strong institutions at the heart of our communities.

REFERENCES

Akron-Summit County Public Library. (2022). *Dementia-inclusive library*. https://www.akronlibrary. org/about/accessibility/dementia-inclusive

Alzheimer's Association and the Green-field Library. (2019). *Reading material for persons living with dementia*. Alzheimer's Association. https://www.alz.org/media/documents/reading-material-for-plwd-rl-2019.pdf

Alzheimer's Association of the United States. (2022). *2022 Alzheimer's Disease facts and figures. With special report: More than normal aging: Understanding mild cognitive impairment*. https://www.alz.org/media/documents/alzheimers-facts-and-figures.pdf

Alzheimer's Disease International. (2012). *World Alzheimer report 2012: Overcoming the stigma of dementia*. https://www.alzint.org/u/WorldAlzheimerReport2012.pdf

Alzheimer's Disease International. (2018). *World Alzheimer report 2018: The state of the art in dementia research: New frontiers*. https://www.alzint.org/resource/world-alzheimer-report-2018

Alzheimer's Disease International. (2021). *World Alzheimer report 2021: Journey through the diagnosis of dementia*. https://www.alzint.org/resource/world-alzheimer-report-2021

Alzheimer's Poetry Project. (2022). *Sparking creativity with poetry*. http://www.alzpoetry.com

Billington, J. (2013). A literature-based intervention for older people living with dementia. *Perspectives in Public Health*, *133*(3), 165–173.

Bourgeois, M. (2001). Is reading preserved in dementia? *The ASHA Leader*. https://doi.org/10.1044/leader.FTR2.06092001.5

Bridges Library System. (2021). *Library Memory Project*. https://bridgeslibrarysystem.org/memory-project

City of Tempe, AZ. (2022). *Dementia-friendly Tempe*. https://www.tempe.gov/government/human-services/family-community-support/senior-services/dementia-friendly-tempe

Claridge, G., & Rimkeit, S. (2018). Can she still read? How some people living with dementia responded to the reading experience. *Extensive Reading World Congress*, *4*, 266–275.

Clift, S., Gilbert, R., & Vella-Burrows, T. (2018). Health and well-being benefits of singing for older people. In N. Sunderland, N. Lewandowski, D. Bendrups, & B. L. Bartleet (Eds.), *Music, health and wellbeing* (pp. 97–120). Palgrave Macmillan.

de Waal, H., Lyketsos, C., Ames, D., & O'Brien, J. (2013). *Designing and delivering dementia services*. Wiley Blackwell.

Dementia Friends USA. (2022). *Dementia Friends USA*. https://dementiafriendsusa.org

Dementia Society of America. (2022). *Memory Café Directory*. https://www.memorycafedirectory.com

Dementia-Friendly America. (2022). *What is Dementia-Friendly America?* https://www.dfamerica.org/what-is-dfa

Dickey, T. J. (2020). *Library dementia services: How to meet the needs of the Alzheimer's community*. Emerald.

Family Caregiver Alliance. (2022). *The family caregiver alliance*. https://www.caregiver.org

Gibbs, D. (2021). *A tattoo on my brain: A neurologist's personal battle against Alzheimer's Disease*. Cambridge University Press.

Gillick, M. (2020). *The caregiver's encyclopedia*. Johns Hopkins.

International Federation of Library Associations (IFLA). (2007). *Guidelines for library services to persons with dementia*. The ILFA. https://www.ifla.org/wp-content/uploads/2019/05/assets/hq/publications/professional-report/104.pdf

Kania, J., & Kramer, M. (2011, Winter). Collective impact. *Stanford Social Innovation Review*, *9*(1). https://doi.org/10.48558/5900-kn19

King, J. B., Jones, K. G., Goldberg, E., Rollins, M., MacNamee, C, Moffit, C., Naidu, S. R., Ferguson, M. A., Garcia-Leavitt, E., Amaro, J., Breitenbach, K. R., Watson, J. M., Gurgel, R. K., Anderson, J. S., Foster, N. L. (2019). Increased functional connectivity after listening to favored music in adults with Alzheimer dementia. *Journal of Prevention of Alzheimer's Disease*, *6*(1), 56–62.

Latchem, J., & Greenhalgh, J. (2014). The role of reading on the health and well-being of people with neurological conditions: A systematic review. *Aging & Mental Health*, *18*(6), 731–744. https://doi.org/10.1080/13607863.2013.875125

Lee, A., Richards, M., Chan, W., Chiu, H., Lee, R., & Lam, L. (2018). Association of daily intellectual activities with lower risk of incident dementia among older Chinese adults. *JAMA Psychiatry*, *75*(7), 697–703.

Library Memory Project. (2022). *Welcome to the Library Memory Project*. https://www.librarymemoryproject.org

Lokvig, J. (2016). *The Alzheimer's or Memory Café: How to start and succeed with your own café*. Endless Circle Press

McFadden, S., & Basting, A. (2010). Healthy aging persons and their brains: Promoting resilience through creative engagement. *Clinics in Geriatric Medicine*, *26*(1), 149–161.

Miller, S. (2015). *Communicating across dementia: A how-to book*. Robinson.

Museum of Modern Art. (2022). The MOMA Alzheimer's Project: Making art accessible to persons with dementia. https://www.moma.org/visit/accessibility/meetme

Music & Memory. (2022). Music & Memory: Help spread the music and give life to someone you love. https://musicandmemory.org

NeuroArts Blueprint. With the Aspen Institute and Johns Hopkins University. (2022). NeuroArts Blueprint: Advancing the science of arts, health, and wellbeing. https://neuroartsblueprint.org

Riedner, M. B. (2015). Librarians' role as part of the care team for Alzheimer's patients. *Journal of Consumer Health on the Internet*, *19*(2), 143–147.

Rimkeit, S., & Claridge, G. (2017). Literary Alzheimer's: A qualitative feasibility study of dementia-friendly book groups. *New Zealand Library & Information Management Journal, 56*(2), 14–22.

Tales and Travel Memory Programs. (2022). *Tales and Travel.* http://talesandtravelmemories.com

TimeSlips. (2022). TimeSlips: Bringing meaning and purpose into the lives of elders through creative engagement. https://www.timeslips.org

United Nations Department of Economic and Social Affairs. (2015). *Sustainable Development Goals.* https://sdgs.un.org/goals

University of Wisconsin-Madison. Wisconsin Alzheimer's Institute. (2022). *Wisconsin Dementia Resource Network.* https://wai.wisc.edu/wdrn

Wilson, R., Wang, T., Yu, L., Grodstein, F., Bennett, D., & Boyle, P. (2021). Cognitive activity and onset age of incident Alzheimer Disease dementia. *Neurology, 97,* e922–e929.

Wojcichowska, M., & Topolska, K. (2021). Social and cultural capital in public libraries and its impact on the organization of new forms of services and implementation of social projects. *Journal of Library Administration, 61*(6), 627–643.

World Health Organization. (2019, September). *Dementia fact sheet.* https://www.who.int/news-room/fact-sheets/detail/dementia

CHAPTER 22

WITH LITERACY AND JUSTICE FOR ALL: LIBRARY PROGRAMS FOR REFUGEES AND NEWCOMERS

Claire Dannenbaum

ABSTRACT

According to the UN High Commission on Refugees, over 82 million people are currently displaced globally and of those nearly 25 million are refugees. Every community in the United States – urban, suburban, and rural – is shaped by newcomers seeking safety, opportunity, and self-improvement. Libraries are often the place that feels most welcoming to refugees and newcomers, making them well positioned to offer relevant and impactful programs and services to these communities. Using the International Federation of Library Associations' (IFLA) conceptual rubric of sanctuary, storehouse, gateway, and bridge, my research explores a variety of programs and services deployed by libraries to address the needs of refugee and newcomer populations. Based on fieldwork in the United States, the Netherlands, and Germany, this chapter describes how libraries impact refugees and newcomers in decisive and meaningful ways. From informal gatherings to national government collaborations of digital content, libraries provide an array of compassionate, effective, scalable interventions for newcomers. Such interventions also positively impact the non-displaced communities in which they operate, fostering deeper connections between newcomers and their communities. Library services to refugees and newcomers provide a broad collective impact in the global crisis of displacement and belonging.

Keywords: Library programs; refugees; newcomers; community outreach; engagement; literacy

---

How Public Libraries Build Sustainable Communities in the 21st Century
Advances in Librarianship, Volume 53, 293–304
Copyright © 2023 by Claire Dannenbaum
Published under exclusive licence by Emerald Publishing Limited
ISSN: 0065-2830/doi:10.1108/S0065-283020230000053027

Nothing is harder on the soul/than the smell of dreams/while they are evaporating.

Mahmoud Darwish

THE SOCIAL CONTEXT OF IMMIGRATION

Across the globe, human migration is a huge crisis and, along with climate change, one of the gravest challenges of the twenty-first century. The UN High Commission for Refugees estimates there are currently 84 million forcibly displaced human beings on the planet (United Nations High Commission on Refugees, 2022). Millions of people have fled their homes due to war, political persecution, and direct or indirect impacts of climate change such as drought, flooding, and economic collapse. Millions of people have no access to basic rights such as citizenship, paid employment, freedom of movement, or education. An estimated 25 million people are refugees seeking asylum in another country, and half that number are under the age of 18.

Of the 84 million forcibly displaced individuals, some have refugee status, many are without any official status, and many are awaiting asylum. It is important to underscore that an individual's status is subject to expert interpretation. It may even be unknown to them. The determination of eligibility for refugee or asylum status in the United States is an especially fraught process requiring lengthy periods of waiting and uncertainty, personal exposure, financial costs, and, often, expert legal representation (United States Citizenship Immigration Services, 2022).

Currently, nearly 700,000 asylum decisions are awaiting approval in the United States. In 2018, only 54,000 cases were approved according to the National Immigration Forum Fact Sheet (National Immigration Forum, 2018). Under President Trump, Congress reduced the cap and eliminated candidates from the top-three source countries of displacement at that time (Syria, Afghanistan, and South Sudan). President Biden's Citizenship Act of 2021 will begin to correct the unresponsive policies of previous administrations, but getting comprehensive legislation passed in the divisive climate of our current Congress will be hard going.

It is in the context of the shamefully inadequate immigration policy in my own country that I sought to explore how libraries support social justice through literacy with new citizens, refugees, and asylum seekers. My project involved interviewing library staff in three countries: the United States, the Netherlands, and Germany; each with its own definitions of legal status and political climate. Each of these countries presents a particular context for the individual seeking refuge; and yet many challenges for newcomers are shared. For this reason, I use the term "newcomer" as an umbrella term for individuals who are new citizens, refugees, asylum seekers, or have an unknown status.

For eight weeks in April and May 2019, I visited multiple libraries and interviewed library staff about their programs for newcomers. My inquiry focused on libraries as providers of service in the context of trauma, political marginalization, and displacement experienced by newcomers. I sought to understand how programs are shaped by cultural specificity, government support, public perception, and the local communities in which these libraries function.

I visited libraries in the United States, the Netherlands, and Germany, and interviewed library staff at nine institutions: Midland branch of Multnomah County Library (MCL), Portland, OR, and Brooklyn Public Library Central, New York, NY; Openbare Bibliotheek Amsterdam (or OBA), and Centrale Bibliotheek Den Haag in the Netherlands; Stadtbibliothek Köln, and the Kalk branch library, Köln; Freie Universität Bibliothek; the Asylothek (now called Bibliothek der Heimaten); and Zentral-und Landesbibliothek Berlin, all in Germany.

THE ACTIVIST HISTORY OF US LIBRARIES

I want to underscore the rich history of libraries in responding to social crises. American public libraries have long offered a variety of services to refugees and asylum seekers, services that are grounded in the Enlightenment values on which many American public libraries were founded. These values include the intellectual freedom to pursue ideas without censorship, access to information in the support of democracy, and the betterment of individuals through literacy and knowledge. As an American librarian, this history offered a foundation for thinking about library programs in the United States and comparison to other countries.

As such, libraries are institutions that are instrumental in supporting responsive and inclusive participation within communities as described by United Nations Sustainable Development Goals #16 (United Nations Sustainable Development Goals, 2022). By providing access to information, and the practical means of interpreting information through literacy and community building, libraries implicitly protect fundamental freedoms that undergird democratic values. Newcomers share many of these values and provide possibilities for the expansion of more inclusive communities and institutions.

The work of belonging to a community – of having a voice and agency in that community – requires literacy, and this is true for newcomers as well as the communities that receive them. Indeed, for American citizens, libraries as institutions are singular in demonstrating a level of social capital unlike any other, and hundreds of American public libraries participate in programs that support newcomers.

In some ways, libraries have been performing literacy triage since the establishment of the first public libraries almost 200 years ago, whether delivering books to remote locations, providing books and literacy programs in Black communities in the age of Jim Crow, and bookmobile service to migrant work camps (Brady & Abbott, 2015). The promotion of literacy and access to information for all are codified in the American Library Association's own code of ethics which explicitly advocates for and upholds democratic values vis-à-vis principles of intellectual freedom, equitable access, and affirming "the inherent dignity and rights of every person" (American Library Association, 2021). Recent examples of literacy triage include numerous library services for the unhoused/homeless, multilingual storytimes for children in many public libraries, outreach to communities in poverty, and for families navigating the carceral system.

INFORMATION POVERTY

Many library programs for newcomers are fueled by similar concepts of social justice. Activities designed for newcomers are strategic interventions addressing the multitude of challenges experienced by newcomers directly. I have found the concept of "information poverty" developed by Dr Elfreda Chatman to be applicable in this context (Chatman, 1999). Dr Chatman was a librarian and sociologist who did extensive research in the 1980s and 1990s within two marginalized communities: women prisoners and impoverished, rural communities in the American South. Her research explored how people living in conditions of precarity (such as incarceration or remote rural poverty) are disadvantaged by the complexities of formal information systems.

Individuals and communities experiencing information poverty struggle to understand what information is, how it works, and how it can improve their condition(s). Often, this results in distrust with information from outside the trusted network. For example, in rural communities' distrust of government agencies, lack of access to broadband, and economic and social isolation can result in information poverty. Similarly, incarcerated people are mired in complex legal and carceral knowledge systems resulting in extreme forms of information poverty (Federal Bureau of Prisons, 2022).

According to Chatman, the designation of who is "inside" and who is "outside" is a social construction based on accepted sources of knowledge, and is fundamental to the concept of information poverty. As librarian Natalia Bowdoin (2021) describes in her work with refugees from the Central African Republic (CAR) living in Georgia, USA, many refugees remain challenged by profound cultural shifts required to adapt to childrearing, notions of discipline, housing, and understanding the law. In some instances, cultural differences compound these newcomers' ability to integrate into local communities, thus experiencing information poverty.

Chatman's concept of information poverty does not assume or equate to low intelligence. Many newcomers are highly educated individuals with advanced degrees, professional expertise or otherwise skilled, and who may also be proficient in multiple languages. Chatman's concept centers on the *inability to understand the information systems outside one's own support networks*, resulting in self-limiting behaviors. We also see evidence of information poverty in the concept of insider/outsider knowledge that parallels political discourse in the US today. The branding of individuals with high levels of education as "elites" creates us/them rhetoric that discounts learned knowledge as not relevant to the common (presumed to be "uneducated") worldview.

Information poverty intersects with the experience of many displaced people. Lack of language skills, emotional trauma, cultural difference, and byzantine social services systems all function as impediments to newcomer integration. The privatization of education in the United States is especially impactful for newcomers who are also economically marginalized. Through the development of thoughtful community programs, public libraries are becoming increasingly adept at addressing social needs.

THE INTERNATIONAL FEDERATION OF LIBRARY ASSOCIATIONS

To shape my understanding of the programs I visited, I borrowed a rubric of metaphors from the IFLA, an international organization that advocates for the recognition and promotion of libraries and library users globally. In June 2018, IFLA published a statement titled "Libraries' Role in Making Refugees Feel Welcome," calling on libraries to create programs for refugees and newcomers using the spatial metaphors of *sanctuary, storehouse, gateway*, and *bridge* (International Federation of Library Associations, 2018).

The IFLA rubric is remarkable in its description of services using *affective* metaphors rather than prescriptive programs. Common library programs such as those that target literacy, social connection, and multicultural exchange are not explicitly named. The IFLA statement instead centers the meaning of said programs on the *user's experience* of library programs rather than specific literacy program outcomes.

As it happened, the metaphors of sanctuary, storehouse, gateway, and bridge proved to be an extremely evocative framing device for my itinerary. The metaphors functionally ascribe the needs of individuals who are experiencing extreme levels of precarity and uncertainty. The metaphors also created latitude for me as a researcher to interpret programs based on a range of fieldwork inputs: interviews with staff, observations of library spaces, interactions with library users, and promotional materials developed by the library itself.

As human beings, we need sanctuary. We aggregate our understanding of the world into knowledge, and we need gateways and bridges to link ourselves to others. Refugees and newcomers relocate with a broad range of educational, economic, and social experience. They navigate multiple ways of relating to new circumstances, develop a sense of belonging, and define community for themselves.

Library programs embody these metaphors fully. The following are selected examples of programs serving newcomers in the libraries I visited.

THE LIBRARY AS SANCTUARY

What makes a library a sanctuary? Sanctuaries are places of safety and refuge and libraries offer sanctuary to users. Every library employee that I interviewed in all three countries noted a shared belief that newcomers experience significant grief and uncertainty, financial stress, and trauma. The Asylothek in west Berlin (now called Bibliothek der Heimaten) is a volunteer-run library housed in a resettlement residence (Asylothek, 2022). Approximately 30 people live in a cluster of residences in a leafy, suburban neighborhood with the Asylothek in a community space. Originally housed in the Templehof Refugee Intake Center – a vast former Nazi-era airport hangar turned refugee housing – the Asylothek provides a quiet space to read, study, and learn with collections of fiction, nonfiction, and learning in multiple languages. It is homey and low-key, and offers a reading circle, computer access, and informal German language tutoring. According to the United Nations High Commission on Refugees (2022), Germany took in over one million refugee newcomers in 2015/2016, the largest number of any European country, and exponentially more than the USA.

The cozy, informal character of the Asylothek is a deliberate antidote to the impersonal nature of state bureaucracy. While Germany has a comparatively sophisticated intake system for refugees and asylum seekers, the sheer number of people using this system results in many impersonal interactions. Public libraries in Berlin provide rich content and formal literacy programs, and the Asylothek functions as a neighborhood "home base" for refugee residents to learn new skills and increase integration (Asylothek, personal communication, 2019). The Asylothek attracts many volunteers – some of whom live in the neighborhood – who assist residents with programs such as dessert and movie screenings, job searches, and facilitated discussions. Similar volunteer-run libraries have been created in multiple locations in Germany, in small towns, in suburbs, and in urban areas. In general, these programs promote personal well-being, build supportive networks for children and adults, and improve social integration within the local community.

Residents in group houses often lack privacy and quiet, so the Asylothek also functions as a place for solitude in stressful conditions. A beautifully illustrated book about English roses became a touchstone for a Syrian woman living in Berlin. After her home and garden were completely destroyed by bombing, she found that gardening books offered her solace and helped her cope with deep emotional loss (Asylothek, personal communication, 2019).

The Openbare Bibliotheek Amsterdam (or OBA) offers sanctuary in another way. While many libraries provide safe space for all genders and sexual orientations, refugees who identify as LGBTQ will find a number of features to encourage an explicit sense of belonging at this library. During my visit, an exhibit of photographs and personal narratives featuring LGBTQ refugees was on display. Situated nearby, a bookcase painted bright pink highlighted resources of importance to LGBTQ people from the library's collection. These pink bookcases are on wheels so they can be easily moved and provide focal points within collections, exhibits, or contexts. Low cost, mobile, and flexible, the pink bookcases also function as signifiers of relevance, belonging, and safe space for the LGBTQ community within the library setting.

THE LIBRARY AS STOREHOUSE

A storehouse primarily contains the inventory of value and utility. At MCL Midland branch, a multilingual collection serves library users in six languages of significance in the greater Portland community: English, Chinese, Spanish, Russian, Vietnamese, and Somali. Midland branch collects fiction, non-fiction, magazines, and film/video in these world languages, which is then circulated across the Multnomah system (Multnomah County Library, 2022). The program "We Speak Your Language," centralizes the work of multilingual library staff who coordinate the library's programs, collections, and outreach throughout Portland. Midland branch serves as a hub-and-spoke radiating in multiple directions and to multiple communities (Multnomah, personal communication, 2019).

With Literacy and Justice for All 299

Citizenship classes, ESL conversation circles, computer skills classes, storytimes for toddlers, and activities for elders (among other offerings) are coordinated by a diverse library staff. This group is also responsible for the planning and coordination of activities with other local social service organizations both on-site and through "pop-up" activities at health clinics, schools, and neighborhood events (Multnomah, personal communication, 2019).

Another example of the library as a storehouse is the EU digital project to collect personal narratives of newcomers at the Stadtbibliothek in Cologne. Over a three-year period, the EU supported libraries in four countries to record and collect an archive of personal stories by newcomers. The result is *A Million Stories, Refugee Lives*, a digital repository of stories, drawings, videos, and interviews created by refugees now living in Germany, Greece, Sweden, and Denmark (A Million Stories, Refugee Lives, 2019). This complex project offered newcomers an opportunity to be creative, to be expressive, and to be heard as individuals, sharing their lived experience.

The Stadtbibliothek Cologne was one of the participants in this ambitious archival effort. This undertaking required considerable coordination of videographers, interviewers, transcribers, and translators – many of whom were volunteers. It also required willing participants to share very personal stories, including tragic or traumatic experiences, the loss of family and friends, displacement, and also small successes (Stadtbibliothek, personal communication, 2019). As an archive, *A Million Stories* creates both a historical record of a specific period of human migration and stands witness to the conditions and realities of displacement, and how our collective human experience is shaped by war and disaster.

THE LIBRARY AS GATEWAY

The gilded entrance to Brooklyn Public Library Central is massive and almost mythical. Walking through the majestic grand portal can feel overwhelming and functions viscerally as a threshold. Within a few feet of the door, one can discern a symphony of world languages: Spanish, English, Arabic, Turkish, French, Haitian Creole, and Yiddish, and multiple flavors of English. Brooklyn Public Library (BPL) is a comprehensive system of 59 branch libraries across the borough; a sister to the New York Public Library and the Queens Public Library systems. Phenomenally, according to the BPL website, there is a public library branch within 0.5 miles of *every single resident* in Brooklyn. Over 120,000 individuals participate annually in programs specifically designed for newcomers at BPL, including citizenship classes, English language learning, children's story times, job training, book clubs, and interview practice (Brooklyn Public Library, 2022).

Library staff coordinates and liaises with other organizations to provide programming for residents (Brooklyn Public Library, personal communication, 2019). Workshops on opening a food cart, career and business development, and training for nannies are popular, and the results of these programs are truly inspiring. For example, a group of Bangladeshi women developed a successful baby-sitting cooperative that was born and nurtured by Brooklyn Public's support for small business planning (Brooklyn Public Library, personal communication, 2019).

BPL serves these newcomers' aspirations by designing tools and resources appropriately scaled for personal development. From entry-level English language learning to basic accounting to navigating city code, BPL programs offer extensive and comprehensive opportunities for newcomers. Scalable and no- or low-cost, these programs function as social and educational pathways for self-improvement, economic empowerment, and personal success in the newcomer's community.

The BPL is also a gateway in a more literal sense: both the Immigrant Justice Corps and the Immigration Advocacy Network provide consultations at the BPL Central branch. Advocacy organizations meet with thousands of asylum seekers every year to assist with paperwork, advise clients, and, in some instances, represent their cases in a courtroom. While the fear of Immigration & Customs Enforcement (ICE) (and government agencies generally) is widespread in immigrant communities, the library maintains its identity as a safe space (BPL, personal communication, 2019). And finally, the library café, Emma's Torch, is a culinary training program for newcomers. A library visitor can order chai tea, Tibetan momos, and read a magazine in the library lobby while your baby chews on a board book. If we ever achieve peace among nations, I am convinced that it will transpire in a public library!

THE LIBRARY AS BRIDGE

Creating connections between newcomers and local government is another paradigm for library programming. Libraries in both the Netherlands and Germany benefit from and collaborate with government agencies that oversee immigrant and refugee resettlement and integration. Within a week of the first massive exodus from Syria in 2015, many Cologne residents contacted the library seeking ways to volunteer. Now over 120 volunteers at the Statdbibliothek in Cologne are providing support for newcomers by connecting them with no-cost German language learning, assistance with job searching, and professional coaching at a space called the Sprachraum (or Conversation Space).

Sprachraum volunteers are trained and overseen by the library staff, but functions independently of the library with its own hours, and its own identity (Statdbibliothek, personal communication, 2019). For example, a group of Kurdish newcomers have created an extensive support system through the Sprachraum, and informal lectures and concerts are held there. According to the Library's outreach director, Sarah Dudek, "the beginning was always putting out fires. Now volunteers understand that the process of integration is slow, even slower for some – and maybe even a lifetime." The library has arranged for experts to coach volunteers about issues of cultural sensitivity/difference, trauma awareness, and the effects of post-traumatic stress disorder (PTSD) such as anxiety and sadness from the effects of war, life in refugee camps, and loss of family. Over time, volunteer training became more structured, and also more effective. Dudek believes that offering asylum seekers and volunteers opportunities for sustained interaction and learning creates more grounded outcomes. Many clients have actually become volunteers themselves which helps to affirm agency in the larger community.

With Literacy and Justice for All 301

Another example of the library as bridge is Taalhuis (or Language House), a Dutch language learning initiative in the Netherlands providing multiple opportunities at locations in libraries and in the community. Each Dutch library develops programs best suited for its locale. Language learning initiatives at Bibliotheek Den Haag include books for babies delivered to homes, conversation groups, "easy reader" collections for language learners, and a variety of classes to support citizenship examinations (Bibliotheek Den Haag, 2022).

This rich array of programs supports newcomers from birth through senior years; programs are completely free and open to anyone to begin or resume at any time. Interestingly, Taalhuis supports literacy for both newcomers and Dutch citizens who have low literacy levels. This illustrates how library services developed with newcomers in mind can (and often do) benefit a wider community of users. Dutch primary school is based on a common curriculum that incorporates themes delivered throughout the school year across the country: democracy, poetry and language, nature and biology, and Dutch history, etc. The Dutch Ministry of Education has also developed materials for newcomer language learning for adults that intentionally follow these themes. By integrating language learning materials with the national common curriculum, children and their parents are able to learn topics and vocabulary in support of each other, enabling newcomer parents to take a more active role in their children's learning and experience of school.

Reka Dekkan-Makai, the librarian overseeing the program at Den Haag's central library at the time of my visit shared many stories of success. One particular story of a Turkish grandmother was especially resonant for me. Though she had lived in the Netherlands for almost two decades, a strict marriage had kept this particular woman extremely isolated from Dutch society. When her husband divorced her and remarried, she embarked on learning Dutch at her grandchildren's neighborhood elementary school. Now this grandmother regularly meets with friends to practice Dutch, reads books in Turkish and Dutch from the library's collection, and has discovered an entirely new level of freedom in her early 60s. The library was a bridge into Dutch society that had previously not been available to her due to social constraints, lack of language skills, and gendered barriers (Bibliotheek Den Haag, personal communication, 2019).

CONCLUSION

This research prompted me to reflect on my own experience as an insider and outsider in different communities, and to reflect on assumptions I have made about newcomers in my own community and workplace. It has also enabled me to consider how information poverty is present in each of us to some degree. Each of us – as human beings of a particular place, time, and ability – is both an insider to specific bodies of knowledge and an outsider to others based on our social status, culture, gender, beliefs, etc.

Newcomers bring these same complicated selves to their new communities of residence. Newcomers bring knowledge, skills, and understandings of the world that are both necessary and relevant to every society in which they land. UN SDG

16 underscores the requirement of addressing the needs of displaced people, and of creating opportunities for social integration and community cohesion. The purpose of developing library services for refugees and newcomers is not simply to teach a person how to pass a test or get a job, though those outcomes are important. Libraries are mission-driven to help people reach potential *as they themselves define it*.

On the train trip between Cologne and Berlin, I happened to sit next to a young man, a refugee newcomer from Allepo, Syria. Abdullah A. was friendly and open to conversation, and his English language proficiency enabled us to chat for the duration. Abdullah told me about his preparations for an entrance exam to study nursing. He was studying hard but deeply afraid of failure. He was new to the German language and still finding footing in German society but, in less than two years, Abdullah was embarking on the education necessary to begin a new chapter in life. We chatted about my research project, exchanged contact info, and hugged good-bye at the German train station.

Several weeks later, upon my return to the United States, I happened to watch a film called *Human Flow* by Ai Weiwei (Ai, 2017). Ai's film is a personal and visual reflection on the scale of human displacement across the globe. And then suddenly, there was Abdullah on the screen, engaging with the filmmaker in a mock "exchange" of identity, including exchanging their passports and domiciles: Abdallah's tent in a refugee camp for Ai's posh apartment in Berlin (where he has resided since exiled from China). It was a poignant interlude in the film that under-scored how arbitrary and random our individual luck and stability might be.

Between the time of Ai's filming in 2016 and my train ride in April 2019, Abdullah had found sanctuary, was learning a new language, and was embarking on a journey of personal and professional development. He is a young adult with many of the same fears, hopes, and aspirations as we have reading this article: earning a living, finding friendship and love, and dreaming of a future in which he is a participant and not a victim. Already, through his display of courage, stamina, and resilience, he is an asset to Germany.

Whether or not Abdallah ever set foot in a library is irrelevant to my thesis that library services to newcomers are critical work we do for a sustainable human future. And yet, his story is a case in point why library services to newcomers are so vital to all our well-being. His success is vital to our well-being, just as every library users' potential is vital to social progress.

My research indicates clearly that the work libraries do is necessary for supporting newcomers as they seek to better their lives. Library programs and resources can be foundational to newcomer success by improving opportunities for social stability, skill-building, language development, and personal expression. The range of programs in the small set of libraries I visited, the care with which library staff approach problems, and personal expressions of care were truly remarkable. The metaphors of sanctuary, storehouse, gateway, and bridge offer a model for framing the needs of newcomers and mitigating displacement. Being conscious of and intentional about the many ways that library services and resources impact newcomer communities is an important step in creating mean-ingful, effective, and compassionate programs and services.

With Literacy and Justice for All 303

FURTHER READING

A Million Stories, Refugee Lives. (2019). http://refugeelives.eu/

Ai, W. (2017). *Human Flow*. Participant Media and Amazon Studios. Directed by Ai Weiwei.

American Library Association. (2021). Professional ethics. https://www.ala.org/tools/ethics

Asylothek. (2022). Bibliothek der heimaten. https://asylothekberlin.wordpress.com/bibliothek-der-heimaten-2/

Bibliotheek Den Haag. (2022). Nederlands leren. https://www.bibliotheekdenhaag.nl/leren.html

Bowdoin, N. T. (2021). *Intersections of information behavior, trauma, and the affective domain for resettled refugees from the Central African Republic* [Paper presentation]. Association of College and Research Libraries. April 13–16, 2021.

Bowdoin, N. T., Hagar, C., Monsees, J., Kaur, T., Middlebrooks, T., Miles-Edmonson, L., White, A., Vang, T., Olaka, M. W., Yier, C. A., & Chu, C. M. (2017). Academic libraries serving refugees and asylum seekers: Approaches for support. *College & Research Libraries News, 78*(6), 298–338.

Brady, H., & Abbott, F. (2015). A history of US public libraries. Digital Public Library of America. https://dp.la/exhibitions/history-us-public-libraries

Brooklyn Public Library. (2022). Immigrants. https://www.bklynlibrary.org/learn/immigrants

Chatman, E. A. (1999). A theory of life in the round. *Journal of the American Society for Information Science, 50*(3), 207–217.

De La Peña McCook, K. (2007). Librarians as advocates for the human rights of immigrants. *Progressive Librarian, 29*(Summer), 51–54.

Dowling, M. (2017). Project Welcome: Libraries planning for resettlement and integration of refugees. *American Libraries, 48*(Supplement), 24–26.

Federal Bureau of Prisons. (2022). Custody and Care: Education. https://www.bop.gov/inmates/custody_and_care/education.jsp

Finnell, J. (2009). The bookmobile: Defining the information poor. *MSU Philosophy Club (blog). March 7,* 2009. http://msuphilosophyclub.blogspot.com/2009/03/bookmobile-defining-information-poor.html

Hoffert, B. (2008). Immigrant nation. *Library Journal, 133*(14), 34–36.

International Federation of Library Associations. (2015). Responding! Public libraries and refugees. https://www.ifla.org/publications/node/9921

International Federation of Library Associations. (2018). Sanctuary, storehouse, gateway, bridge: Libraries and refugees – a briefing. https://www.ifla.org/publications/sanctuary-storehouse-gateway-bridge-libraries-and-refugees-a-briefing/

Koerber, J. (2016). Celebration & integration. *Library Journal, 141*(10), 48–51.

Kong, L. (2013). Failing to read well: The role of public libraries in adult literacy, immigrant community building, and free access to learning. *Public Libraries Online, 52*(1). https://publiclibrariesonline.org/2013/03/failing-to-read-well-the-role-of-public-libraries-in-adult-literacy-immigrant-community-building-and-free-access-to-learning/

Lloyd, A., Lipu, S., & Kennan, M. A. (2010). On Becoming Citizens: Examining social inclusion from an information perspective. *Australian Academic & Research Libraries, 41*(1), 42–53.

McDermott, I. E. (2016). How public libraries can help Syrian refugees. *Online Searcher, 40*(2), 35–37.

Multnomah County Library. (2022). Featured languages. https://multcolib.bibliocommons.com/explore/featured_lists/languages

Murray, S. (2009). *The library: An illustrated history*. Skyhorse Publications.

National Immigration Forum. (n.d.). Fact Sheet: US Asylum Process. https://immigrationforum.org/article/fact-sheet-u-s-asylum-process/

National Immigration Forum. (2020). "Fact Sheet: US Refugee Resettlement." https://immigrationforum.org/article/fact-sheet-u-s-refugee-resettlement/

Pender, W., & Garcia, J. Jr. (2013). With literacy for all. *Public Libraries, 52*(1), 8–10.

Shen, L. (2013). Out of information poverty: Library services for urban marginalized immigrants. *Urban Library Journal, 19*(1), 1–12.

Thompson, K. M. (2007). Furthering understanding of information literacy through the social study of information poverty. *Canadian Journal of Information & Library Sciences, 31*(1), 87–115.

TRAC Immigration. (2021). A mounting asylum backlog and growing wait times. https://trac.syr.edu/immigration/reports/672/

United Nations High Commission on Refugees. (2019). Figures at a glance: statistical yearbook. https://www.unhcr.org/en-us/figures-at-a-glance.html

United Nations High Commission on Refugees. (2022). Germany. https://www.unhcr.org/en-us/germany.html

United Nations Sustainable Development Goals. (2022). Goal 16. https://sdgs.un.org/goals/goal16

United States Citizenship and Immigration Services. (2022). Explore My Options. https://www.uscis.gov/forms/explore-my-options

United States Citizenship and Immigration Services and the Institute of Museum and Library Services. (2010). Library services for immigrants: A report on current practices. https://eric.ed.gov/?id=ED508138

INDEX

Academic libraries, 59, 253
Accountability, 79
Action-oriented frameworks, 15
Active Mediation, 89
  funding for, 140
Activist history of US libraries, 295
Adult & Youth Social Justice
    Partnership, 78–79
Affordable housing, 230
African American woman, 51
  Agder County, 143
Agenda for Sustainable Development
    (2030), 2, 139, 154, 173
Aging in place, 154
Aging with public libraries, 154–155
Agriculture, 70
Akron-Summit County Public
    Library, 286
ALA Special Task Force on
    Sustainability, 75
ALU LIKE, Inc., 39, 44, 47
ALU LIKE/The Native Hawaiian
    Library, 39, 46
Alzheimer's Poetry Project (APP), 290
American librarianship, 40–41
American Library Association (ALA),
    28, 107, 166, 176, 178, 206,
    250, 295
  ALA-accredited LIS Program, 40
  Council, 75
American Medical Association, 220
American public libraries, 295
Anglo-centric American model of
    librarianship, 40
Anglo-centric LIS framework, 39, 41
Anglo-centric public library system
    (HSPLS), 42
Anti-Black racism, 92–93
  in Canada, 93–94
Anti-racism
  anti-black racism in Canada, 93–94

community partnerships, 97–98
learning outcomes and
    opportunities, 98–99
library sector responses to anti-
    black racism, 94–95
nonprofit, 78
partnerships with higher education,
    97
partnerships with public
    libraries, 96
recreating program, 100
role of community center in
    addressing anti-black
    racism, 95–96
United Nations Sustainable
    Development Goals,
    99–100
*Anti-Racism in Library and
    Information Science*, 97
Art therapies, 289–290
Asosiasi Perpustakaan Perguruan
    Tinggi Katolik, 59
Aspen Institute Forum for
    Community Solutions, 1
Asset Management Working
    Group of the United
    Nations Environment
    Programme's Finance
    Initiative, The, 74
Association for Information Science and
    Technology (ASIS&T), 5
Association for Information Science
    and Technology conference
    (2020), 5
Association for Information
    Science and Technology
    conference advisory
    committee (2019), 7
Asylothek in West Berlin, 297–298
Asylum seekers, 294–295, 298, 300
Athens Clarke-County Library, 266

INDEX

Backbone support organizations, 2, 277
Backpack library, 146
Baltimore County, 23
    Public Library, 206
Baltimore-based MVLS, 24
Baramsup Library
    about BPL, 186–188
    case study methodology, 188
    findings, 188–191
    with global communities, 192–193
Baramsup Nature School program, 194
Baramsup Picturebook Library
    (BPL), 186–188, 193
Batik painting technique, 64
Beyond Identities Community
    Center, 108
Bias-fraught services, 98
Bibliothek der Heimaten (see
    Asylothek in West Berlin)
Bill & Melinda Gates Foundation,
    61, 67
Black Chamber of Commerce, 98
Black children and youth, 94
Black communities, 92, 94, 96–100, 295
    black community-based
    organizations, 100
Black Community Centre, 95–97
Black Community Public Library, 87,
    89, 92–93, 95–97, 99–101,
    223–224
Black experiences in Canada, 92
Black Lives Matter movement, 92
Black renaissance, 95
Black young people, 93
Black Youth Action Plan (BYAP), 97
Black-centered programs, 98
Black-led programs, 98
Black-led services, 92
Black–centered collections, 92
Black–centered services, 92
Blount County, 222
Blount County Public Library, The
    (BCPL), 222
Blount County Recovery Court Life
    Skills Curriculum, 222–223

Board members, 95
Book culture, 168
Book Year, 145
Bridge, library as, 300–301
Brooklyn Public Library (BPL), 274,
    299–300
Bukit Panjang Public Library, The,
    211

Call to Action, The, 226
Canada
    anti-black racism in, 93–94
    Anti-Racism Strategy, 94
    Black Community Public Library,
    92
    Information Highway Advisory
    Council, 204
Canadian public libraries, 101
Capitalist economic systems, 181
Caplan Foundation, 126
Caregivers, 130–131
Center for Racial and Ethnic Equity
    in Health and Society
    (CREEHS), 209
Centers for Disease Control and
    Prevention (CDC), 208
Centers for Disease Control's National
    Center for Health and
    Statistics, 220
Central African Republic (CAR), 296
Certification process, 81
Chamber of Commerce, 257
Chicago Housing Authority, 277
Chicago Public Library, 277
Children
    ecological sensitivity, empowering,
    190–191
    education, 126, 128–129
    environmental science education
    literature, 191
    exercise, 146–147
Citizenship, 294
Citizenship Act of 2021, 294
Civic commons, 166
Civic-based groups, 257
Civil Legal Justice project, 21

Index

Clean energy, 7
Cleveland Public Library, 20, 108
Climate action, 250
   library collaborative, 167–168
   planning model for libraries and
      community organizations,
      168–173
   V4C committee partnerships, 167
Climate and Equity Pledge, 82
Climate change, 166, 168, 294
Climate change issues, 7
Climate job, 250
Climate justice, 250
Climate Preparedness, 172
Climate Resilience Hub, CREW as, 169
Climate Resilient Development, 166
Coca-Cola Foundation Indonesia,
   62–63
Code Red for Humanity, 171
Coded contents, 188
Collaboration, 166, 168, 172, 221, 230
Collaborative Group, 169
Collective action
   in local communities, 206–207
   public libraries as collective
      action and development
      incubators, 207–211
Collective community impact, case
   studies in, 285–286
Collective community of praxis, 44
Collective impact, 3, 32–33, 257–258,
   264, 285
   value of collective impact
      framework, 268–269
Collective Impact Forum, The (2016),
   1
Collective praxis, 47
   data and analysis, 44–50
   designing, 43–44
   envisioning, 50
   geography of LIS practitioner
      inquiry, 50–52
   from LINQ to Hui 'Ekolu, 39–40
   literature review, 42–43
   local culture as praxis, 40–42
   research questions, 42

   synthesizing public libraries in
      Hawai'i, 39
Collective processes, 268
Colonized approach, 38
Colorado, 180
Commercial spaces, working family
      and community engagement
      in, 210–211
Common agenda, 259, 276–277
Communities Responding to
      Extreme Weather (CREW),
      137, 258
   as Climate Resilience Hub, 169
Community Based Participatory
      Research and Community
      Engagement Studio models,
      210
Community organizations, 276
   planning model for, 168–173
Community partnerships, 97–98
   in access to justice work, 21–22
Community/communities, 221
   asset mapping, 78
   center role in addressing anti-black
      racism, 95–96
   changes from small library, 188
   coalitions and expertise,
      224–225
   community-based citizens
      committee, 166
   community-based educational
      spaces, 38
   community-based research, 98
   community-engaged learning
      partnership, 99
   community-engaged library, 19
   community-led and directed
      approach, 99
   community–led partnerships,
      93
   consultation process, 96
   data, 225
   development, 32
   engagement, 59, 210–211
   events, 188
   health, 92

knowledge creation via graphic medicine library programs, 209–210
leadership, 268
limitations of existing frameworks for supporting library work as community work, 28–29
local and regional communities, 190–191
meeting, 120
outreach, 204–205, 279
partners, 223
of practice, 14
of praxis, 15
programs, 97
resilience, 257–258
rural, local communities, 188
selection, 95
skills, 71
sustainability, 250
Congress of Black Women of Canada, 98
Connected Learning (CL), 208
Conservation commissions, 183
Construction process, 77
Consultation process, 96
Continuous communication, 172, 259, 277
Cooperation, 138
County municipality, 144
Court staff, 21
COVID-19, 187
Gunungkidul public library activities during, 66–71
health measures, 66
pandemic, 29, 31–34, 60, 66, 71, 170, 207, 220
Crisis intervention in public libraries, 267
Cultural knowledge, 51
Cultural literacy, 77
Cultural practices, 176
Culture, 178
Customer service and communication with PLWD, 286–287
Cyber Clinics in Rural Areas, 24

Data gathering process, 5
Data science, 205
Debrief/wrap up, 129
Dementia services, 284–286
serving users living with dementia, 286–287
Dementia-friendly customer service, 284
Denver Public Library, 221
Department of Library and Information Science, 66
Design for Freedom movement, 77
first pilot project, 77
Design for Freedom's first pilot project, 77
Development funding, 139–140
Development incubators, public libraries as collective action and, 207–211
Digital library services, 146
Digital transformation, 205
of business and commerce, 205
Diversity, 6
Diversity audits, 78
Diversity Plans for Academic Libraries, 79
Doughnut economics, 76, 177, 183
Drought, 294

Early literacy strategies, 128
Eastern Seaboard of the United States, 51
Ecological sensitivity, 191
Economic and manufacturing systems, 178
Economic collapse, 294
Economic development, libraries promoting, 199–200
Economic feasibility, 252
Economic growth, 19
Economic issue, 7, 76
Economic paradigms, 177
Education, 173, 294
Educational organizations, 223
Effective change management, 76
Effective partnership, 108

Index 309

Eidskog Library, 146
Electric vehicle (EV), 259
Employees, 107
Energy, 256
Environmental, social, and
governance (ESG), 15, 74
coordinator role, 79–80
framework, 78
institutional transformation, 76–77
library action items, 80
measuring impact, 80–82
New Canaan library, 77–79
practices, 74–75
principles, 76
strategy, 80
sustainability and libraries, 75–76
Environmental education, 82
Environmental health, 177
Environmental programming, 77
Environmental stewardship, 251
Equitable institution, 77
Equity, 250
public libraries, 213
Equity, Diversity, and Inclusion
Committee (EDI
Committee), 78–79
Equity, diversity, inclusion, and justice
(EDIJ), 253
Europe, Middle East, and Africa
(EMEA), 19
European Union, 61
Evidence-based evaluation, 80
Evidence–based path, 81
Experience, 114
of youths lives, 115
Expungement, 22

Facilitators, 131
Family dynamics, 210
Family engagement, 126
in library-supported learning via
radio, 208–209
programming, 126
Family Literacy model, 126
Federal Emergency Management
Agency (FEMA), 255

Financial resources, public libraries
secure, 212
Fixit Clinic, 179–180, 183
Flooding, 294
Focus on Diversity, 252
Focus on Library Staff Care, 226
Folsom Public Library, 18
Food technology, 70
Forum for Youth Investment, 1
Forum Perpustakaan Perguruan
Tinggi Indonesia, 59
Forum Perpustakaan Perguruan
Tinggi Muhammadiyah dan
Aisyiyah, 59
Forum Perpustakaan Perguruan
Tinggi Negeri, 59
Freedom movement, 77, 294
Froland Library, 143, 145
FSG, 1
Full-time staff model, 265–266
Funding
for active mediation, 140
assignment of, 151–152

Gardu Pintar, 68
Gateway, library as, 299–300
Gender neutral language, 107
Gender-diverse programming, 108
Geography of LIS practitioner
inquiry, 50
limitations of inquiry-based
practitioner research, 52
researcher identity and limitations,
51
Gerontologists, 154
Global communities, 186, 188,
192–193
Global Health Crisis, 220–221
Global models, 15
Global population aging, 155
Gloppen Library, 146
Go on trips, 140
Google for Libraries Build Business,
206
Government of Ontario, The, 93
Governments, 204

Grace Farms Foundation, 77
Grantmakers for Effective
Organizations, 1
Graphic communication, 209
Graphic design, 71
Graphic medicine library programs,
community knowledge
creation via, 209–210
Group trust, 110
Gunungkidul, 63–64
social inclusion activities in
Gunungkidul County,
64–66
Gunungkidul Public Library, 64–65,
67
activities during COVID-19
Pandemic, 66–71
Gunungkidul Regency, 60, 68
Library, 64
Public Library, 60

Hamilton Public Library (HPL),
230–231
Hawai'i, 41
County, 41
Hawai'i-based Hui 'Ekolu project,
51
Hawai'i-based LIS groups, 42
synthesizing public libraries in,
39–40
Hawaiian librarians, 51
Hawaiian public library system, 42
Health and wellbeing, 265
Health disparities, 209
Health information, 278–279
Health information professional
(HIP), 278
Health literacy, 274
Health-related community coalitions,
225
Healthy communities, 275
Healthy eating and active living
(HEAL), 32
Heating, ventilation, and air
conditioning system (HVAC
system), 256

Hedmark County Library, 142
Help All Be Heard, 252
Higher education, partnerships with,
97
Homeless youth population, 109
Homelessness, 114, 117, 231
Honolulu County, 41
Horten Library, 145
HPCA, 204
HSPLS libraries, 39, 44, 47
Hui' Ekolu, 45
community, 43
envisioning collective praxis model,
50
impacts of Hui' Ekolu collective
praxis, 44
from LINQ to, 39–40
model, 50
professional development model,
51
reflective memos, 48–50
slack communications, 45–47
Hula dancer, 45
Human migration, 294

Immigrant Justice Corps, 300
Immigration & Customs Enforcement
(ICE), 300
Immigration, social context of,
294–295
Immigration Advocacy Network, 300
Incarceration, 117
Incheon city government, 187
Inclusion, 245
Inclusive approach, 92
Inclusive institution, 77
Indiana Business Research Center, 205
Indika Rural Public Library, 67
Indivisible Massachusetts Coalition,
166
Indonesia, 58, 61, 66
library social inclusion in, 61–62
Indonesian Coca-Cola Foundation, 61
Indonesian population, 58
Indwell–HPL partnership, 230
Inequalities, 7

Index 311

Infectious diseases, 6
Information and Communication
     Technology (ICT), 28, 39
Information poverty, 296
Information professionals, history of,
     4–7
Information services (IS), 5
Information sharing, 250
Information technology (IT), 204
Infrastructure, 66
Inhabited islands' county system, 41
Innovation, 199
Innovative technology, 108
Inquiry-based practitioner research,
     limitations of, 52
Institute of Museum and Library
     Services (IMLS), 14, 40,
     119, 208, 221
Institutional ESG approach, 74
Institutional transformation, 76–77
Intellectual freedom, 250
Intelligent Island strategy, 204
Interactive program, 179
Intergenerational programming, 157
Intergovernmental Panel on Climate
     Change (IPCC), 166, 176
International Federation of Library
     Association (IFLA), 5, 28,
     62, 64–65, 139, 250, 297
     Public Libraries Section, 157
Internationally recognized
     sustainability goals, 7
Internet of Things (IoT), 205
Internships, 266–267
Interprofessional collaborations, 264
Intersectionality, 115
     of socio-cultural knowledge, 50
Interview skills, 277
Iterative process, 154
Iterative risk management, 252

Japan's Info-communications, 204
Jaringan Perpustakaan Perguruan
     Tinggi Kristen, 59
Job preparation skills, 277
Job satisfaction, 30

Justice, libraries and access to,
     21–25
Justice Gap Report, 21

Kalamazoo, 225
Kalamazoo County Opioid Coalition,
     225
Kalamazoo Public Library, 224
Kansas City Public Library's
     partnership, 22
Kate Raworth's Doughnut Economics,
     76
Kaua'i County, 41
Kemadang rural library, 67
Kindness by Design, 110
Kiwanis and Rotary clubs, 257
Know your community, 116
Knowledge economy, 204–206
     role of libraries in knowledge
          economy and sustainable
          development, 205–206
Knowledge infrastructure, 214
Knowledge management, 205
Knowledge Online, 45–47
Knowledge-based economy, 214
Korean Decimal Classification
     (KDC), 189
Korean traditional process, 191

Land acknowledgment, 78
Laos, building school libraries for
     children in, 192–193
Laptops, 181
Law librarians, 21
Leadership challenges, public
     libraries will face program
     sustainability and, 213
Learning, 126
Learning outcomes, 98–99
Legal Aid, 21–22
Legal Aid Clinic, 15
Legal Aid on wheels, 23–24
Legal assistance
     libraries and access to justice,
          21–25
     libraries and SDGs, 19

312 INDEX

strongest impact on quality
education, 20–21
Legal community, 21
Let's Learn Together Outside (LLTO),
126, 129
advice for future program
implementation, 134
children's education, 128–129
debrief/wrap up, 129
evidence of LLTO program success,
133
implementation training, 129–130
open-ended questions, 131
PACT Time®, 129
parent time, 127–128
participating libraries, 131–133
practical application, 129
response to implementation
training, 130
responses from implementing
libraries, 133–134
responses to LLTO, 133
storytelling, 130–131
structure of program, 127
understanding importance of
meaningful conversation,
131
LGB TGEQ+ books, 120
LGB TGEQ+ youth, 117
LGB TGEQ+ youth homelessness,
118
LGBTQ, 298
LGBTQIA+ community, 106–108,
110
LGBTQIA+ employees, 107
LGBTQIA+ equity, 107
LGBTQIA+ library services, 109
LGBTQIA+ materials, 107
Librarian convention (1876), 40
Librarians, 168, 177
training, 278–279
Librarians Inquiry Forum, The
(LINQ), 39
to Hui 'Ekolu, 39–40
Libraries Advocating for Social
Justice, 87–88

Library & Information Science (LIS),
34, 94, 278
geography of LIS practitioner
inquiry, 50–52
inquiry scholars and practitioners,
52
programs, 38
scholars, 95
theory, 47
Library programs, 23, 293
activist history of US libraries, 295
facilitators, 127
IFLA, 297
information poverty, 296
library as bridge, 300–301
library as gateway, 299–300
library as sanctuary, 297–298
library as storehouse, 298–299
for PLWD, 288–290
social context of immigration,
294–295
Library social inclusion, 15, 61, 65, 67
in Indonesia, 61–62
program, 61
Library work
limitations of existing frameworks
for supporting library
work as community work,
28–29
in relation to sustainable
communities, 29–30
Library/libraries, 18–25, 58, 74–76,
110, 115, 121, 166, 176, 178,
181, 183, 206, 225–226, 250,
253
and access to justice, 21
action, 119–120
action items, 80
activities, 139
classification systems, 189
collaborative, 167–168
collection development for PLWD,
287–288
community, 276
community coalitions and
expertise, 224–225

Index 313

community partnerships crucial
in access to justice work,
21–22
concept, 142
cyber clinics in rural areas, 24
dementia services, 284–285
education, 157
encouragement, 145
family and youth engagement in
library-supported learning
via radio, 208–209
history of, 4–7
intersectionality/overlap, 115
in knowledge economy and
sustainable development,
205–206
leadership, 212
legal aid on wheels, 23–24
libraries offer training and space,
222–223
libraries taking action, 119–120
library and legal aid, 22
library-specific technology, 96
literature review, 114
methodological insights, 114
mobilizing climate change, 163–164
model, 178
national and global health crisis,
220–221
nurturing positive peace, 245–246
partnerships, 221–222
planning model for, 168–173
programming, 157
promoting economic development,
199–200
science researchers, 212
SDGs represented in library legal
aid programming, 24–25
sector responses to anti-black
racism, 94–95
services for PLWD, 284
staff, 115, 226
statistics and overlapping factors,
116–119
stigma and stereotype, 114–115
story, 120–121

success along way, 224
systems, 157
workers, 31–32, 34, 115
youth homelessness, 116
Life Skills Curriculum program, 222
Lifelong learning, 284–286
Lindenhurst Memorial Library Case
Study, 254–255
Linear-degenerative economic
systems, 177, 183
Literacy, 294
Literacy strategies, 126, 128
Literacy triage, 295
Literary trail destinations, 144–145
Literature trails, 142
Living Cities, 1
Local communities, 188, 190–191
sustainable development and
collective action in, 206–207
Local culture as Praxis, 40–42
Local health department, 223
Local higher education institutions, 92
Local intersectionalities, learning,
48–50
Local Matters, 252
Local organizations, 98, 183
London Black community, 96, 98
*Lyon Declaration on Access
to Information and
Development*, 5

Makerspaces, 183
Malaysia's Multimedia Super
Corridor 2020 plan, 204
Marginalization, 93
Maryland Legal Aid (MLA), 22–23
Maryland Volunteer Lawyers Service
(MVLS), 24
Massachusetts, 176, 181
Massachusetts Library System, 171
Materials, 127, 129–130
management, 256
Maui County, 41
McKinney-Vento Act, 116
McQuesten Lofts, 230
Meaningful conversation, 131

314   INDEX

Measurement reporting systems, 268
Measurement systems, 177
Mediation methods, 145
Medical device, 180
Medical Library Association's
     Consumer Health
     Information Specialization,
     278–279
Meet Me, 289
Memory Cafés and Tales and Travel
     program, 289
Mental health, 147
Micro-backbone support
     organization, 259
Million Stories, Refugee Lives, A, 299
Mini-Library, 145
Minister of Culture, The, 143
Ministry of Education, 188
Momentum, 109–110
Muhammadiyah, 59
Multicultural Programming Advisory
     Committee, 78–79
Multidisciplinary approach, 177
Multi-level approach, 121
Multnomah County Library (MCL),
     295
Municipal public library, 96
Music therapies, 289–290
Mutt Club, 257
Mutually reinforcing activities, 259, 277

Nā Hawai'i 'Imi Loa (NHIL), 43–44
Narrative inquiry, 114
National Book Year (2019), 138, 140,
     143
     literature trail, 143
National Center for Families Learning
     (NCFL), 88, 126–127, 129
National efforts, 204
National Health Crisis, 220–221
National Information Infrastructure
     (NII), 204
National Leadership Grant, 221
National Library, 63, 139
     funding for active mediation, 145
     organizations, 75

National Library Board of Singapore,
     67
National Library of Norway, 138
National Library of Republic of
     Indonesia, The, 59–60,
     62–63
National Library Policy, 139
National Runaway Safeline (NRS),
     119
National Science Foundation, 204
National Strategy for Libraries, 147
National Strategy for Libraries 2020–
     2023, *The*, 138–139, 141
Native Hawaiian Library, 39–40
Natural disaster, 18
Nature, 187, 190–191
Nature-based activities, 130
New Canaan library, 77–79
New Canaan's Indigenous people, 78
New-Norwegian trail library, 141–142
Newcomers, 294
Ngawu Rural Public Library, 67
Nomination process, 95
Non-government organizations, 192
Non-profit Hawaiian social services
     organization, 39
Non-profit organizations, 231
Nordland County Library, The, 143
North American context, 38
North American LIS graduate
     programs, 38
North Norwegian and literary trail
     destinations, Troms reads,
     144
Norway National Library, 88

OCLC Global Council (2020),
     5, 7, 19
OCLC Public Libraries Respond to
     Opioid Crisis research, 224
Older adults, 284–285
     engagement, 154–155
     programming, 284–286
Online marketing, 71
Ontario Government, 97
Open-air libraries, 138–140

Index 315

in Froland, Agder County, 145
Openbare Bibliotheek Amsterdam
(OBA), 295, 298
Opioid crisis, 222
Opioid epidemic, 220
Opioid strategy, 220
Opioid-related programming, 226
Oral language skills, 128
Organizational change, 77
management, 74
Organizational commitment, 256
Organizational governance, 77
Organizational health literacy, 274
Outdoor life and health aspects, 140
Overlap, 115

Paid employment, 294
Palaces for the People (Klinenberg),
231
Parent and Child Together Time®)
(PACT Time®), 89,
126–127, 129
Parent Education, 126
Parent time, 126–128
sessions, 130
Parenting adults, 127
Parkdale Landing, 230
Part-time leadership, 79
Participants, 1
Partner organizations, 99
Partnerships, 25, 108–109, 221–222
Part-time staff model, 266
Patrons, 274–275
Peer navigators, 225
Pellissippi State Community College,
223
People, Planet, Profit (triple bottom
line), 75
Perception of social innovation, 269
PerpuSeru, 59, 63–64
achievement of, 62–63
in Gunungkidul Public Library, 66
program, 59, 61–62
Perpustakaan Balai Pintar, 68
Perpustakaan Berbasis Inklusi
Sosial, 61

Persistent Family Engagement
concept, 134
Persons living with dementia (PLWD),
284
customer service and
communication with,
286–287
library collection development for,
287–288
library programs for, 288–290
library services for, 284
materials selection, 288
Phenomenological qualitative
methods, 118
Philadelphia Department of Public
Health, 276
Philadelphia Free Library, 276
Phones, 181
Physical library building, 66
Picture books, 187, 189–190
PIMCO analysis, 75
Pioneer Valley Library Collaborative
(PVLC), 163
Planning model for libraries and
community organizations,
168–173
Plants, 191
Plethora of research, 51
Point Source Youth, 119, 121
PolicyLink, 1
Population aging, 154
Positive momentum, 82
Pottsboro Area Library, 208
Powerful countries, 177
Pratt Library, The, 22
Praxis concept, 42
Preliminary model, 28
Primary program activity, 44
Private schools, 59
Private–public-small libraries, 186
Product-oriented approach, 38
Professional development, 42
Profit, 75
Program, intent of, 179
Program development, 92
Program structure, 179

316 INDEX

Program sustainability and leadership challenges, public libraries will face, 213
Programming, 168–169, 190
context, 129, 133–134
Project organization, 210
Project outcome, 81
Public authorities, 140
Public consultation process, 96
Public health, 139, 141, 276–277
Public Health Initiative, 221
Public Health Partners, 156
Public librarians, 39, 278
collective praxis for, 51
Public libraries
align with sustainable development goals, 155–157
Public libraries, 2, 7, 20, 28, 30, 38, 58–60, 66, 106, 108–110, 131, 154, 156–157, 168, 176, 178, 205, 220, 250, 264, 276–277, 284
aging with, 154–155
as collective action and development incubators, 207
communicate urgent need for change, 212–213
and dementia services, 284–286
engagement, 154
face program sustainability and leadership challenges, 213
lessons learned from public library incubators in United States and Singapore, 211
partnerships with, 96
programs, 155
respond to opioid crisis with communities project, 220
role of, 13–15
role of libraries in knowledge economy and sustainable development, 205–206
RUR, 208–209
scholars, 207
secure financial resources, 212

serve as influential champions for sustainable development, 212
serve equity, 213
services, 42
serving users living with dementia, 286–287
shopping mall libraries, 210–211
as social infrastructure, 231–232
as strong institution, 255–256
sustainable communities and role of, 87–89, 163–164, 199–200
sustainable development and collective action in local communities, 206–207
synthesizing public libraries in Hawai'i, 39–40
in United States, 274
WHLL, 209–210
workers, 28–30, 33
Public Libraries Act, 142
Public Libraries Build Sustainable Communities in the 21st Century, 1
Public Library Association (PLA), 81, 221, 274
Public Library of Gunungkidul, The, 60, 66–67, 71
Public library pride
employees, 107
kindness by design, 110
momentum, 109–110
partnership, 108–109
responsive policies, 107–108
youth, 108–109
Public library social inclusion
achievement of PerpuSeru, 62–63
Gunungkidul, 63–64
Gunungkidul, public library, and rural libraries, 64
Gunungkidul public library activities during COVID-19 pandemic, 66–71
library social inclusion in Indonesia, 61–62
library social inclusion program, 61

Index
317

social inclusion activities in
Gunungkidul county, 64–66
Public library–community
partnerships, 15
Public library–sustainable
communities (PLSC), 8, 13,
87, 163, 199, 245
Publishing companies, 192
Purba Pustaka Rural Public Library, 67

Quality education, 25, 110
impact on, 20
Quality of life, 138, 141

Radio, family and youth engagement
in library-supported
learning via, 208–209
Rainbow Round Table, The, 107
Raise Up Radio (RUR), 212–213
Raworth's economic theory, 177
Recovery Court program, 222, 224
Recovery Institute of Southwest
Michigan, 224
Recycling committees, 183
Redistributive technology, 238
Reference and User Services
Association (RUSA),
157–158
Reference Services Section (RSS), 157
Reflection process, 157
Reflective memos, 45, 48–50
Refugees, 294
Regency Public Library of
Gunungkidul, 64
Regional communities, 190–191
Religious organizations, 59
Repair events, 177, 182
case study, 179
implementation, 180
intent of program, 179
outcomes, 180–182
program structure, 179
steps for holding repair event,
182–183
sustainable communities and repair
events, 176–179

Research studies, 29
understanding library work in
relation to sustainable
communities, 29–30
Residents, 138
Responsive policies, 107–108
Resume writing, 277
Retention strategies, 134
Review process, 4
Right-to-repair databases, 183
Right–to–repair movement, 183
Rigid economic systems, 178
RIO+20 Conference, 4
Røros Library, 146
Rural communities, 188
Rural libraries, 64, 186, 212
Rural library workers, 31
Rural public library, 67
workers, 31
Rural Women's Health Project, 209
Rural-serving libraries, 208

Sanctuary, library as, 297–298
School libraries, 59
for children in Laos, building,
192–193
Schools, 183
Science, Technology, Engineering, and
Medicine (STEM), 92
Sengkang Public Library, 211
Service capacity, expanded, 258–259
Shared measurement systems, 109,
172, 259, 277
Shopping mall libraries, 210–211
Sidoharjo Rural Public Library, 67
Singapore
Intelligent Island strategy,
204, 210
lessons learned from public library
incubators in, 211–213
shopping mall libraries case, 204
Skill-development workshops, 277
Slack communications, 45–47
Slack participant communications, 45
Small-and medium-size businesses,
206

Small-scale collection management
    system, 97
Social capital, 18
Social change, 206
Social cohesion, 257–258
Social connectedness, 29, 31
Social crises, 295
Social determinants of health
    (SDOH), 274–275
Social equity, 252
Social exclusion, 61
Social health, 177
Social inclusion activities, 67–68
    in Gunungkidul County, 64–66
Social infrastructure
    COVID-19's impact, 238
    equipped, accessible, and safe,
        235–236
    friendly faces and friendly spaces,
        236–237
    little baby branch for big
        community needs, 233–235
    methods, 232–233
    public libraries as, 231–232
    redistributing, 238–239
    results, 233–239
Social infrastructure, 4, 178
Social justice, 75, 78, 82
Social justice issues, 7
Social relationships, 285
Social resilience, 178
Social responsibility, 74, 178
Social support, 92
Social work, 264
Social workers, 265–266
Social work–public library
    partnerships, 264–265
    libraries as strong institutions,
        269–270
    promising models, 265–268
    value of collective impact
        framework, 268–269
Social-inclusion-based libraries, 61
South Korea's IT839 strategy, 204
South Korea's Ministry of Foreign
    Affairs, 193

South Philadelphia Health and
    Literacy Center, 279
Special Report (1876), 40
Sprachraum, 300
Springfield MA's Allen Bird Club, 172
Stadtbibliothek Cologne, 299
Staff development, 15
Staff training model, 267–268
STEM, 96
Stereotype, 114–115
Stigma, 114–115, 231
Stordal Municipality, 142
Storehouse, library as, 298–299
Storytelling, 52
Strategic collective actions, 14–15,
    88–89, 164, 200, 246
Strategic planning, 6
Strong institutions, 269–270
Substance Abuse and Mental
    Health Services of the US
    (SAMHSA), 267
Sumber Ilmu Rural Public Library, 67
Superstorm Sandy, 255
Sustainability, 28, 75–76, 166, 168, 250
    background, 139
    benefits, 147–149
    book is off, 145
    children's exercise, 146–147
    about development funding,
        139–140
    about funding for active mediation,
        140
    goals, 139
    library in nature, 141
    library on go, 142–143
    literary trail destinations in Troms
        County, 145
    literary trails in world heritage, 146
    local history hikes in Froland,
        physical and digital trails,
        143–
    Measures for Active Mediation
        Supported by National
        Library, 145–146
    mini-library, 145
    National Book Year 2019, 140

Index 319

National Book Year 2019, 143–144
national library policy, 139
new-Norwegian trail library,
141–142
outdoor life and health aspects, 140
presentation of projects and
activities, 141
reading trip, 146
SLCP, 253–255
theoretical frameworks, 250–253
Troms reads North Norwegian and
literary trail destinations,
144
words at Tyrielden, 146
Sustainability Committee, 77, 79
Sustainability coordinator, 257
Sustainability goals, 139, 147
Sustainable community/communities,
245–247, 269
development, 32
library work in relation to, 29–30
and repair events, 176–179
and role of public library, 13–15,
87–89, 163–164, 199–200
Sustainable development
and collective action in local
communities, 206–207
of communities, 285
public libraries serve as influential
champions for, 212
role of libraries in knowledge
economy and, 205–206
Sustainable economic development,
206
Sustainable economic growth, 199
Sustainable Libraries Certification
Program (SLCP), 253–255
after SLCP certification, 259
Sustainable Libraries Initiative (SLI),
81, 253
Sustainable partnerships, 279
framework for, 275–276
Sustainable Thinking, 75, 251
Systemic process, 74

Taalhuis, 301

Tamarack Institute, 1
Templehof Refugee Intake Center, 297
Texas and Tuscaloosa Public Library
in Alabama, 208
Theoretical intervention, 28
TinyCat (library-specific technology),
96
Training programs, 60
Transformative Leaders series, 6
Transitional-age youth (TAY), 117
Transportation, 256
Trauma-Informed Library
Transformation project
(TILT project), 266–267
Triangulation of meaning concept, 47
Triple Bottom Line (TBL), 15, 75,
251–253
Tyrielden, words at, 146

UHM LIS Program, 40, 43–44
United Nations (UN), 13, 139, 166,
206
Action Briefs, 5
General Assembly Open Working
Group, 5
Office on Drugs and Crime, 220
Statistics Division, 9
sustainability goals, 28
Toolkit on Synthetic Drugs, 220
United Nations 2030 Agenda for
Sustainable Development
(UN 2030 Agenda for
Sustainable Development),
230
United Nations Sustainable
Development Goals
(SDGs), 19–25, 28, 30,
99–100, 113, 138, 154, 173,
206, 250
history of, 4–7
in library legal aid programming,
24–25
public libraries align with, 155–157
SDG 16, 275
United States (US), 28, 204, 220, 274
activist history of US libraries, 295

anticipated challenges, 277–278
considerations and strategies, 279
educators, 208
framework for sustainable
partnerships, 275–276
health, 274–275
lessons learned from public library
incubators in, 211–213
librarian training and health
information, 278–279
and public health, 276–277
United States' High-Performance
Computer Act (HPCA),
204
United Way Worldwide, 1
University of Georgia School of
Social Work, 266
University of Pennsylvania, 276

V4C committee partnerships, 167
V4C members, 168
Virginia Department of Health, 274
Visiting Nurse Service of New York,
274
Visualizing Place-Based Knowledge,
47–48
Voices of Youth Advocates, 107–108
Voices Rising Together (VRT), 166
Volunteer groups, 192

Waste management, 78
Water, 256
We Speak Your Language program, 298
Web-based services, 205

Wellfleet, 181
recycling committee members, 180
Wellfleet Library, 180
Wellfleet Public Library, 179, 181
Wellfleet Public Library Fixit Clinic,
180
Wellfleet Public Library on Cape Cod,
176
What Health Looks Like (WHLL),
209–210
library leaders, 212
projects, 212–213
Wheelchair, 180
Wicomico Public Libraries (WPL), 24
Winter Forest Library, 192
Wisconsin Alzheimer's Institute
(2022), 286
Wisdom community, 98
Wood, 191
Working families, 207, 211, 214
and community engagement in
commercial spaces, 210–211
Working Together, 252
World Heritage, 146
Wrap Up, 129

Xayaboury province, 192

Yogyakarta Special Region, 63
Youth, 108–109
of color, 117
engagement in library-supported
learning via radio, 208–209
homelessness, 116

Printed and bound by CPI Group (UK) Ltd, Croydon, CR0 4YY

23/05/2024

14505907-0005